PORTLAND
BEST PLACES

PORTLAND BEST PLACES

The most discriminating guide to
Portland's restaurants, lodgings, shopping,
nightlife, arts, sights, and outings

Kim Carlson

SASQUATCH BOOKS
SEATTLE

Printed in the United States
Distributed in the United States by Sasquatch Books
Distributed in Canada by Raincoast Books Ltd.

Fourth edition.

00 99 98   6 5 4 3 2 1

ISSN: 1095-9742
ISBN: 1-57061-123-8

Associate Editor: Carrie Floyd
Cover illustration: Fred Ingram
Interior design: Lynne Faulk
Composition: Kate Basart
Interior illustrations: Jerry Nelson
Maps: David Berger
Cover design: Karen Schober

Special Sales
Best Places® guidebooks are available at special discounts on bulk purchases
for corporate, club, or organization sales promotions, premiums, and gifts. Special editions, including personalized covers, excerpts of existing guides, and corporate imprints, can be created in large quantities for specific needs. For more
information, contact your local bookseller or Special Sales, Best Places Guidebooks, 615 Second Avenue, Suite 260, Seattle, Washington 98104, (800)775-0817.

Best Places®. Reach for it first.

SASQUATCH BOOKS
615 Second Avenue, Suite 260
Seattle, WA 98104
(206)467-4300
books@sasquatchbooks.com
www.sasquatchbooks.com

CONTENTS

Acknowledgments

During the creation of this edition of *Portland Best Places,* I had dozens of conversations with friends and acquaintances about their favorite spots in and around town. Thanks to everyone who gave me an opinion; I never tire of hearing them.

Kudos, too, go to all the writers who contributed to the book: Alicia Ahn, Caryn Brooks, Gail Dana, Jan Halliday, James McQuillen, Lori Root, Terry Ross, and David Sarasohn. Without their expertise and diligence, the book could not have been done. Praise to Jarrett Greco, who fact-checked many chapters, and to Chloe Busch and Zanni Schauffler who also helped with that task; to Andrea Pepitone, who did double duty as a writer and fact checker; to Kris Fulsaas, for copy-editing the manuscript, and to Sherri Schultz, for proofreading it. Associate Editor Carrie Floyd made invaluable contributions of time and humor, and Sasquatch editors Meghan Heffernan and Kate Rogers gave patient and cheerful guidance; I thank them all.

Finally, a big hurrah to Stephanie Irving, formerly of Sasquatch Books and current editor of our parent book *Northwest Best Places.* Stephanie was the editor of the first edition of *Portland Best Places,* back in 1990, and her fingerprints are still all over the book.

—Kim Carlson
Editor

Introduction

Portland is such a likable city that visitors often leave singing its praises. They go home, talk it up at a few cocktail parties, begin to lose sleep—and the next thing you know they're stuffing all their worldly goods into a U-Haul and moving within a block of a McMenamin's pub or a Coffee People, within walking distance to Powell's.

But although the city's population continues to swell, Portland manages to maintain that elusive charm so desirable to citizens everywhere: quality of life. There's no question that Portland has its share of the woes common to every city in America at the end of the twentieth century. But despite any problems, the City of Roses has managed to hold onto its soul. Except for its weather—which even web-footed locals complain about once in awhile—Portland has enough enticements to win over even the most cynical urban critics. There's the thriving downtown core, built up around the intriguing brick-covered and art-filled Pioneer Courthouse Square. An evolving and varied arts scene embraces the visual, literary, and performing arts. The ever-increasing number of urban parks and greenspaces—including Forest Park, the largest city park in the nation—create quiet respites within Portland proper. Plenty of recreational opportunities are within a two-hour drive, too, including hiking at the Oregon Coast, board sailing in the Columbia Gorge, and skiing on Mount Hood. And Portland's excellent mass transit system includes the Metropolitan Area Express (MAX), a light-rail system that runs from Hillsboro to Gresham.

And then there's the food.

In the last decade, Portland has experienced a food renaissance of sorts. Talented chefs—both up-and-comers from the area and newcomers from other parts of the world—are embracing the ingredients of the region: fresh fish, berries, apples, pears, and nuts. There's a great amalgam of styles, ingredients, and inspiration happening, and we've also seen many cuisines represented for the first time in the city—or for the first time with excellent results. (For instance, just when we thought we knew Thai food, along came Lemongrass and Typhoon. And Spanish cooking, like that served at La Catalana or Tapeo, has a newfound legion of fans in the city.) One result of this culinary bounty is that our expectations have increased—many Portland diners will settle for nothing less than fabulous food. And it's our good fortune that we no longer have to.

Come to Portland, or, if you're already here, get busy. We've provided itineraries in this edition to make the going easy, but you might find that charting your own way is the most fun of all. Take the kids to OMSI, trip through the Pearl District on First Thursday, stroll through the Rose Garden. And when you've worked up an appetite, seek out one of the city's better places to eat. We've given you our 200 top picks—50 more than in the last edition—plenty of new spots as well as old favorites. Is yours here?

—Kim Carlson

ABOUT BEST PLACES® GUIDEBOOKS

Best Places® guidebooks, which have been published continuously since 1975, represent one of the most respected regional travel series in the country. Each guide is written completely independently: no advertisers, no sponsors, no favors. Our reviewers know their territory, work incognito, and seek out the very best a region has to offer. Because we accept no free meals, accommodations, or other complimentary services, we are able to provide tough, candid reports about places that have rested too long on their laurels and to delight in new places that deserve recognition. We describe the true strengths, foibles, and unique characteristics of each establishment listed.

Portland Best Places is written by and for locals, and is therefore coveted by travelers. It's written for people who live here and who enjoy exploring the city's bounty and its out-of-the-way places of high character and individualism. It is these very characteristics that make *Portland Best Places* ideal for tourists, too. The best places in and around the city are the ones that denizens favor: independently owned establishments of good value, touched with local history, run by lively individuals, and graced with natural beauty. With this latest edition of *Portland Best Places*, travelers will find the information they need: where to go and when, what to order, which rooms to request (and which to avoid), where the best music, art, and shopping is, and how to find the the city's hidden wonders.

We're so sure you'll be satisfied with our guide, we guarantee it.

Note: Readers are advised that places listed in previous editions may have closed or changed management, or may no longer be recommended by this series. The reviews in this edition are based on information available at press time and are subject to change. The editors welcome information conveyed by users of this book, A report form is provided at the end of the book, and feedback is also welcome via email: books@sasquatchbooks.com.

HOW TO USE THIS BOOK

This book is divided into ten chapters covering a wide range of establishments, destinations, and activities in Portland. All evaluations are based on numerous reports from local and traveling inspectors. Best Places® reporters do not identify themselves when they review an establishment, and they accept no free meals, accommodations, or any other services. Final judgments are made by the editors. Every place featured in this book is recommended.

Stars Restaurants and lodgings are rated on a scale of zero to four stars (with half stars in between), based on uniqueness, loyalty of local clientele, performance measured against the establishment's goals, excellence of cooking, cleanliness, value, and professionalism of service. Reviews are listed alphabetically. All places in the book are recommended, even those with no stars.

★★★★	The very best in the region
★★★	Distinguished; many outstanding features
★★	Excellent; some wonderful qualities
★	A good place
(no stars)	Worth knowing about, if nearby
[*unrated*]	New or undergoing major changes

&. Appears after listings with wheelchair-accessible facilities.

Price range Prices for lodgings are based on high-season rates (off-season, rate changes vary but can be significantly less). Call ahead to verify, as all prices are subject to change.

$$$	Expensive (more than $80 for dinner for two, including tip; more than $100 for one night's lodgings for two)
$$	Moderate (between expensive and inexpensive)
$	Inexpensive (less than $30 for dinner for two, including tip; less than $70 for one night's lodgings for two)

Map Indicators The letter-and-number code listed after each phone number refers to coordinates on the fold-out maps included in this book. Single letters (as in F7) refer to the downtown Portland map; double letters (FF7) refer to the Greater Portland map on the flip side. If an establishment does not have this code listed, its location falls beyond the boundaries of these maps.

Addresses All listings are in Portland unless otherwise specified. If an establishment has two Portland-area locations, we list both addresses; if there are more than two, we list the original, downtown, or recommended branch, followed by the words "other branches."

Phone Numbers All area codes are 503 except where indicated. Telephone numbers beginning with 503 in this book are long-distance from Portland.

Email and Web Site Addresses With the understanding that more people are using email and the World Wide Web to access information and to plan trips, Best Places® has added email and Web site addresses of establishments, where available. Please note that the World Wide Web is a fluid and evolving medium, and that web pages are often "under construction," or, as with all time-sensitive information, may no longer be valid.

Checks and Credit Cards Most establishments that accept checks also require a major credit card for identification. Credit cards are abbreviated in this book as follows: American Express (AE); Diners Club (DC); Discover (DIS); MasterCard (MC); Visa (V).

[KIDS] and [FREE] We have provided kids and free labels throughout the book to indicate attractions and events that are especially suited to children or free of charge.

Indexes All restaurants, lodgings, theaters, museums and galleries, shops, parks and gardens, and major attractions are listed alphabetically at the back of the book. Restaurants are also indexed by star-rating, type, and location at the beginning of the Restaurants chapter, and nightspots are indexed by type and location at the beginning of the Nightlife chapter.

Reader Reports At the end of the book is a report form. We receive hundreds of reports from readers suggesting new places or agreeing or disagreeing with our assessments. They greatly help in our evaluations. We encourage you to respond.

Money-Back Guarantee Please see page 351.

RESTAURANTS

Restaurant Index

★
Abou Karim
Albertina's
Anne Hughes Kitchen
  Table Cafe
Aztec Willie & Joey Rose
  Taqueria
Big Dan's West Coast
  Bento
The Brazen Bean
Buster's Smokehouse
  Texas-Style Bar-Be-Que
Cafe Sol
Caffe Fresco
Casablanca
Caswell
Chen's Dynasty
Cocina del Sol
Cornelius Pass Roadhouse
  and Brewery
Cozze
Czaba's Barbecue and
  Catering, Inc.
Doris' Cafe
El Burrito Loco
El Palenque
Escape From New York
  Pizza
Fat City Cafe

Fellini
Foothill Broiler
Formosa Harbor
Garbonzo's
Giant Drive-In
Grand Central Bakery and
  Cafe
Gustav's German Pub and
  Grill
Gypsy
Hidden House
Hokkaido
Hot Lips Pizza
Ixtapa
Kitchen Venus
Kornblatt's
La Cruda
Little Wing Cafe
Marinepolis
Mediterranean Grill
Misohapi
Nature's Marketplace
Nicholas
O'Connor's
Old Wives' Tales
Perry's on Fremont
Plainfield's Mayur
Riccardo's Ristorante
Rich's
Rustica

Taqueria Chavez
Tara Thai II
Thai Little Home
Thai Touch
Tiger Bar
Vista Springs Cafe
Widmer's Gasthaus
Wild Heron Cafe
Wu's Open Kitchen

No Stars
Big Bear Bagels
Cucina! Cucina!
Dan and Louis' Oyster Bar
Dante's Ristorante
Fa Fa Gourmet
The Golden Loaf Bakery
  and Deli
Good Dog/Bad Dog
Jamie's
Main Street Restaurant
New York Richie's
Old Spaghetti Factory
Pharmacy Fountain
Pumpernickles
Tad's Chicken 'n'
  Dumplings

[unrated]
Avalon

FOOD AND OTHER FEATURES

American
American Palate
Atwater's
Beaches Restaurant & Bar
Besaw's
Black Rabbit Restaurant
  and Bar
Bread and Ink Cafe
Caswell
Esplanade at RiverPlace
  (RiverPlace Hotel)
Gypsy
Hall Street Grill
Harborside
The Heathman Restaurant
  and Bar
Hidden House
Huber's
Kitchen Venus
London Grill (The Benson
  Hotel)
Montage, Le Bistro
O'Connor's

Perry's on Fremont
Pharmacy Fountain
Rich's
Sammy's Restaurant and
  Bar
Sheldon's Cafe at the Grant
  House
Three Square Grill
Zell's: An American Cafe

Bakeries, Plus
Big Bear Bagels
Grand Central Bakery and
  Cafe
Il Fornaio

Barbecue
Buster's Smokehouse
  Texas-Style Bar-Be-Que
Campbell's Barbecue
Czaba's Barbecue and
  Catering, Inc.
Doris' Cafe
Tennessee Red's

Bento
Big Dan's West Coast
  Bento
Misohapi
Murata

Bistros
Besaw's
Bread and Ink Cafe
Cafe du Berry
Caprial's Bistro and Wine
Montage, Le Bistro
Rich's
Trio
Wild Abandon

Breakfasts, Stellar
Besaw's
Bijou Cafe
B. Moloch/The Heathman
  Bakery and Pub
Bread and Ink Cafe
Cafe du Berry
Caffe Fresco

4

Fat City Cafe
Foothill Broiler
The Heathman Restaurant
and Bar
Kornblatt's
Marco's Cafe and Espresso
Bar
The Original Pancake
House
Red Electric Cafe
Shakers
Wild Heron Cafe
Zell's: An American Cafe

Brewpubs

Alameda Brewhouse
B. Moloch/The Heathman
Bakery and Pub
Cornelius Pass Roadhouse
and Brewery
Harborside
Hawthorne St. Ale House
Portland Brewing Co.'s
Brewhouse Taproom
and Grill
Widmer's Gasthaus

Brunch

B. Moloch/The Heathman
Bakery and Pub
Brasserie Montmartre
Bread and Ink Cafe
Compass Cafe
Esplanade at RiverPlace
(RiverPlace Hotel)
Fiddleheads
Gypsy
Hands On Cafe
Il Fornaio
Indigine
Jo Bar and Rotisserie
Kitchen Venus
London Grill (The Benson
Hotel)
Main Street Restaurant
Mediterranean Grill
Papa Haydn
Pavillion Bar and Grill
Red Star Tavern and Roast
House
Rich's
Ron Paul Catering and
Charcuterie
Sammy's Restaurant and
Bar
Sweetwater's Jam House
Three Square Grill
Wild Abandon
Wildwood

Burgers

Beaches Restaurant & Bar
Besaw's
Bijou Cafe
Bread and Ink Cafe
Cornelius Pass Roadhouse
and Brewery
Fat City Cafe
Foothill Broiler
Giant Drive-In
Jamie's
Jo Bar and Rotisserie
L'Auberge
Marco's Cafe and Espresso
Bar
O'Connor's
Perry's on Fremont
The Ringside
Shakers
Zell's: An American Cafe

Caribbean

Bima
Salvador Molly's Sun Spot
Cafe
Sweetwater's Jam House

Children, Good For

Alexis
Aztec Willie & Joey Rose
Taqueria
Buster's Smokehouse
Texas-Style Bar-Be-Que
Chez Jose/Chez Jose East
Cocina del Sol
Cucina! Cucina!
Dan and Louis' Oyster Bar
Fat City Cafe
Foothill Broiler
Formosa Harbor
Giant Drive-In
Higgins
Jamie's
Kornblatt's
Marco's Cafe and Espresso
Bar
Marinepolis
Old Spaghetti Factory
Old Wives' Tales
The Original Pancake
House
Perry's on Fremont
Pizzicato
Salvador Molly's Sun Spot
Cafe
Tad's Chicken 'n'
Dumplings
Vista Springs Cafe

Wild Heron Cafe
Wu's Open Kitchen
Zell's: An American Cafe

Chinese

Chen's Dynasty
Fa Fa Gourmet
Fong Chong
Formosa Harbor
Hunan
Wu's Open Kitchen

Coffee and More

*(See also Coffee and
Desserts in the Nightlife
chapter)*
Andrew's Restaurant and
Catering
Anne Hughes Kitchen
Table Cafe
The Brazen Bean
Caffe Fresco
Il Fornaio
Main Street Restaurant
Marco's Cafe and Espresso
Bar
Pumpernickles
Square Peg

Continental

Andrew's Restaurant and
Catering
Atwater's
Esplanade at RiverPlace
(RiverPlace Hotel)
L'Auberge
Red Hills Provincial Dining
Roland's
Waterzooies Northwest
Winterborne

Delicatessen/Gourmet
Take-out

*(See also Markets and
Delicatessens in the
Shopping chapter)*
The Golden Loaf Bakery
and Deli
Grand Central Bakery and
Cafe
Il Fornaio
Kitchen Venus
Kornblatt's
Nature's Marketplace
New York Richie's
Pumpernickles
Ron Paul Catering and
Charcuterie

Desserts, Heavenly
(See also Coffee and Desserts in the Nightlife chapter)
The Brazen Bean
Bread and Ink Cafe
Grand Central Bakery and Cafe
The Heathman Restaurant and Bar
Higgins
L'Auberge
Marco's Cafe and Espresso Bar
Papa Haydn
Wildwood
Zefiro

Dim Sum
Fong Chong

Ethiopian
Jarra's Ethiopian Restaurant

French
Cafe des Amis
Cafe du Berry
Couvron
The Heathman Restaurant and Bar
L'Auberge
Toulouse

German
Gustav's German Pub and Grill
Widmer's Gasthaus

Greek
Alexis
Berbati
Nicholas

Hawaiian
Noho's Hawaiian Cafe

Indian
Bombay Cricket Club Restaurant
India House
Indigine
Plainfield's Mayur
Swagat

Inventive Ethnic
Avalon
Bima
Fellini
Fiddleheads

Indigine
Mediterranean Grill
Salvador Molly's Sun Spot Cafe
Saucebox
Sweetwater's Jam House
Tiger Bar
Zefiro

Italian
(See also Pizza)
Assaggio
Basta's
Bugatti's Ristorante
Caffe Mingo
Cozze
Cucina! Cucina!
Dante's Ristorante
DaVinci
Delfina's
Genoa
Gino's Restaurant and Bar
Il Fornaio
Il Piatto
La Macchia
La Prima Trattoria
Old Spaghetti Factory
Paparrazzi Pastaficio
Pazzo Ristorante
Riccardo's Ristorante
Rustica
3 Doors Down

Japanese
Big Dan's West Coast Bento
Bush Garden
Hiro
Hokkaido
Ikenohana
Koji Osaka-Ya
Marinepolis
Misohapi
Murata
Obi
Umenoki

Jewish/Kosher
Kornblatt's

Juice Bars
Nature's Marketplace
Wild Heron Cafe

Korean
New Seoul Garden

Late Night/Lounge
Brasserie Montmartre
Fellini

Garbonzo's
Gypsy
Montage, Le Bistro

Lunch, No Dinner
Albertina's
Andrew's Restaurant and Catering
Big Bear Bagels
Big Dan's West Coast Bento
Bijou Cafe
Briggs & Crampton's Table for Two
Caffe Fresco
Fat City Cafe
Little Wing Cafe
Pharmacy Fountain
Pumpernickles
Shakers
Zell's: An American Cafe

Middle Eastern
Abou Karim
Al-Amir
Garbonzo's
The Golden Loaf Bakery and Deli
Nicholas

Milk Shakes
Bijou Cafe
Fat City Cafe
Foothill Broiler
Giant Drive-In
Jamie's
Perry's on Fremont
Pharmacy Fountain
Vista Springs Cafe

Moroccan
Casablanca
Marrakesh

Northwest Cuisine
Andrew's Restaurant and Catering
B. Moloch/The Heathman Bakery and Pub
Caprial's Bistro and Wine
Compass Cafe
Esplanade at RiverPlace (RiverPlace Hotel)
Fiddleheads
Hands On Cafe
The Heathman Restaurant and Bar
Higgins
Indigine

L'Auberge
Marco's Cafe and Espresso
  Bar
Paley's Place
Pavillion Bar and Grill at
  Greenwood Inn
Ron Paul Catering and
  Charcuterie
Sheldon's Cafe at the Grant
  House
Tina's
Tribeca
Wild Abandon
Wildwood
Zefiro

Onion Rings

Alameda Brewhouse
Portland Brewing Co.'s
  Brewhouse Taproom
  and Grill
The Ringside
Ruth's Chris Steak House
Salvador Molly's Sun Spot
  Cafe
Wildwood

Outdoor Dining

Albertina's
American Palate
Aztec Willie & Joey Rose
  Taqueria
Basta's
Beaches Restaurant & Bar
Black Rabbit Restaurant
  and Bar
B. Moloch/The Heathman
  Bakery and Pub
Bugatti's Ristorante
Cafe Sol
Caffe Fresco
Chez Jose East
Compass Cafe
Cornelius Pass Roadhouse
  and Brewery
Fellini
Hall Street Grill
Hands On Cafe
Harborside
Indigine
La Macchia
L'Auberge
Misohapi
O'Connor's
Papa Haydn
Perry's on Fremont
Portland Brewing Co.'s
  Brewhouse Taproom
  and Grill

Riccardo's Ristorante
Ron Paul Catering and
  Charcuterie
Salvador Molly's Sun Spot
  Cafe
Sammy's Restaurant and
  Bar
Tapeo
Thai Villa
Toulouse
Trio
Typhoon!
Waterzoies Northwest

Pizza

B. Moloch/The Heathman
  Bakery and Pub
Cucina! Cucina!
Dante's Ristorante
DaVinci
Delfina's
Escape From New York
  Pizza
Gypsy
Harborside
Hawthorne St. Ale House
Hot Lips Pizza
La Macchia
La Prima Trattoria
Nature's Marketplace
New York Richie's
Pazzo Ristorante
Pizzicato
Vista Springs Cafe

Sausages

B. Moloch/The Heathman
  Bakery and Pub
Campbell's Barbecue
Good Dog/Bad Dog
Portland Brewing Co.'s
  Brewhouse Taproom
  and Grill
Ron Paul Catering and
  Charcuterie
Widmer's Gasthaus

Seafood

Couch Street Fish House
Dan and Louis' Oyster Bar
Hall Street Grill
Harborside
Higgins
Jake's Famous Crawfish
Lemongrass
McCormick & Schmick's
  Seafood Restaurant
McCormick's Fish House
  and Bar

Opus Too
Typhoon!
Waterzoies Northwest
Winterborne

Soup/Salad/Sandwich

Anne Hughes Kitchen
  Table Cafe
Big Bear Bagels
Bijou Cafe
Caffe Fresco
Fat City Cafe
Grand Central Bakery and
  Cafe
Hands On Cafe
Hidden House
Jake's Grill
Little Wing Cafe
Main Street Restaurant
Marco's Cafe and Espresso
  Bar
Nature's Marketplace
New York Richie's
Pharmacy Fountain
Pumpernickles
Red Electric Cafe
Shakers
Sheldon's Cafe at the Grant
  House
Square Peg

Southeast Asian

Avalon
Bangkok Kitchen
Cocina del Sol
Lamthong
Lemongrass
Pho Hung
Pho Van
Saigon Kitchen
Saucebox
Tara Thai II
Thai Little Home
Thai Orchid
Thai Restaurant
Thai Touch
Thai Villa
Thanh Thao
Tiger Bar
Typhoon!
Yen Ha

Southern/Soul Food

(see also Barbecue)
Delta Cafe
Doris' Cafe
Montage, Le Bistro

South of the Border
Aztec Willie & Joey Rose
   Taqueria
BJ's Brazilian Restaurant
Chez Grill
Chez Jose/Chez Jose East
Cocina del Sol
El Burrito Loco
El Palenque
Esparza's Tex-Mex Cafe
Ixtapa
La Cruda
Salvador Molly's Sun Spot
   Cafe
Taqueria Chavez

Spanish
Cafe Sol
Fernando's Hideaway
La Catalana
Tapeo

Steak
Jake's Grill
The Ringside
Ruth's Chris Steak House
Sayler's

Sushi
Bush Garden
Hiro
Hokkaido
Ikenohana
Koji Osaka-Ya
Marinepolis
Murata
Obi
Umenoki

View
Atwater's
Beaches Restaurant & Bar

Esplanade at RiverPlace
   (RiverPlace Hotel)
Harborside

Wine Bar
Assaggio

Wood-Fired Oven
(See also Barbecue)
Beaches Restaurant & Bar
B. Moloch/The Heathman
   Bakery and Pub
Hawthorne St. Ale House
Jo Bar and Rotisserie
La Prima Trattoria
New York Richie's
Pazzo Ristorante
Red Star Tavern and Roast
   House
Toulouse
Wildwood

LOCATION

Alameda
Alameda Brewhouse
Perry's on Fremont
Trio
Winterborne

Beaverton
Chen's Dynasty
Hall Street Grill
Ikenohana
Lamthong
Marinepolis
McCormick's Fish House
   and Bar
New Seoul Garden
Pavillion Bar and Grill at
   Greenwood Inn
Sayler's
Swagat

Belmont
Bangkok Kitchen
Genoa
Sweetwater's Jam House
Wild Abandon

Burlingame
Chez Jose
The Original Pancake
   House

Chinatown
Fong Chong

Downtown
Abou Karim

Al-Amir
Alexis
Atwater's
Berbati
Bijou Cafe
B. Moloch/The Heathman
   Bakery and Pub
Brasserie Montmartre
Bush Garden
Cafe Sol
Couch Street Fish House
Couvron
Dan and Louis' Oyster Bar
Esplanade at RiverPlace
   (RiverPlace Hotel)
Fernando's Hideaway
Formosa Harbor
Good Dog/Bad Dog
Harborside
The Heathman Restaurant
   and Bar
Higgins
Hot Lips Pizza
Huber's
Hunan
India House
Jake's Famous Crawfish
Jake's Grill
Kornblatt's
Lamthong
London Grill (The Benson
   Hotel)
McCormick & Schmick's
   Seafood Restaurant

Murata
O'Connor's
Pazzo Ristorante
Red Star Tavern and Roast
   House
Ron Paul Catering and
   Charcuterie
Saucebox
Toulouse

Dundee
Red Hills Provincial Dining
Tina's

East Side, Close In
Anne Hughes Kitchen
   Table Cafe
Caswell
Cozze
Il Piatto
Indigine
La Catalana
La Cruda
Lemongrass
Montage, Le Bistro
Nicholas
Noho's Hawaiian Cafe
Old Wives' Tales
Saigon Kitchen
Tennessee Red's
Thai Touch
Zell's: An American Cafe

Gladstone
Thai Restaurant

Gresham
Buster's Smokehouse
  Texas-Style Bar-Be-Que
Main Street Restaurant
Roland's

Hawthorne
Big Bear Bagels
Bombay Cricket Club
  Restaurant
Bread and Ink Cafe
Casablanca
Chez Grill
Compass Cafe
Garbonzo's
The Golden Loaf Bakery
  and Deli
Hawthorne St. Ale House
Jarra's
Thanh Thao
3 Doors Down

Hillsboro
Cornelius Pass Roadhouse
  and Brewery

Hillsdale
Garbonzo's
Pizzicato
Red Electric Cafe
Salvador Molly's Sun Spot
  Cafe
Three Square Grill

Lake Oswego
Giant Drive-In
Hiro
Riccardo's Ristorante
Thai Villa
Wild Heron Cafe
Wu's Open Kitchen

Laurelhurst
Esparza's Tex-Mex Cafe

Lloyd Center/Irvington
Albertina's
Aztec Willie & Joey Rose
  Taqueria
Chez Jose East
Cucina! Cucina!
Grand Central Bakery and
  Cafe
Kitchen Venus
Paparrazzi Pastaficio
Ron Paul Catering and
  Charcuterie
Rustica

Milwaukie
Buster's Smokehouse
  Texas-Style Bar-Be-Que
DaVinci
Mediterranean Grill
Thai Restaurant

Multnomah
Fat City Cafe
Marco's Cafe and Espresso
  Bar
O'Connor's

Newberg
Ixtapa

Northeast
*(See also Alameda;
East Side, Close In; Lloyd
Center/Irvington; Rose City)*
Doris' Cafe
Gustav's German Pub and
  Grill
Pumpernickles
Sayler's

North Portland
Czaba's Barbecue and
  Catering, Inc.
El Burrito Loco
Widmer's Gasthaus

Northwest
*(See also Chinatown;
Old Town/Skidmore;
Pearl District)*
American Palate
Basta's
Besaw's
Big Dan's West Coast
  Bento
The Brazen Bean
Briggs and Crampton's
  Table for Two
Cafe des Amis
Caffe Fresco
Caffe Mingo
Delfina's
Escape From New York
  Pizza
Foothill Broiler
Garbonzo's
Gypsy
Il Fornaio
Jamie's
Jo Bar and Rotisserie
Kornblatt's
La Macchia
L'Auberge

Marrakesh
Misohapi
Paley's Place
Papa Haydn
Pharmacy Fountain
Pizzicato
Plainfield's Mayur
Portland Brewing Co.'s
  Brewhouse Taproom
  and Grill
The Ringside
Sammy's Restaurant and
  Bar
Swagat
Tapeo
Thai Orchid
Tribeca
Typhoon!
Umenoki
Waterzoies Northwest
Wildwood
Zefiro

Old Town/Skidmore
Alexis
Berbati
Bijou Cafe
Couch Street Fish House
Dan and Louis' Oyster Bar
Fong Chong
McCormick & Schmick's
  Seafood Restaurant
Obi
Opus Too
Ruth's Chris Steak House

Pearl District
Bima
Fellini
Little Wing Cafe
Shakers
Square Peg
Tiger Bar

Portland Heights
Pizzicato
Vista Springs Cafe

Raleigh Hills
Hot Lips Pizza
La Prima Trattoria

RiverPlace
Harborside
Esplanade at RiverPlace
  (RiverPlace Hotel)

Rose City
Hokkaido
Yen Ha

Sellwood
Assaggio
El Palenque
Gino's Restaurant and Bar

SE Powell
Campbell's Barbecue
Pho Hung

Southeast
*(See also East Side, Close
In; Gladstone; Hawthorne;
Laurelhurst; Sellwood;
SE Powell; Westmoreland)*
Pho Van
Taqueria Chavez

SW Macadam Avenue/ Johns Landing
Avalon
Cafe du Berry
Koji Osaka-Ya
Old Spaghetti Factory
Ron Paul Catering and
Charcuterie

Tigard
Buster's Smokehouse
Texas-Style Bar-Be-Que
Cucina! Cucina!
Tara Thai II
Wu's Open Kitchen

Troutdale
Black Rabbit Restaurant
and Bar
Tad's Chicken 'n'
Dumplings

Tualatin
Cocina del Sol
Rich's

West Linn
Bugatti's Ristorante
Thai Orchid

West Slope
Hands On Cafe

Westmoreland
BJ's Brazilian Restaurant

Caprial's Bistro and Wine
Fiddleheads
Papa Haydn

Woodstock
Delta Cafe

Vancouver, Washington, and Vicinity
Andrew's Restaurant and
Catering
Beaches Restaurant & Bar
Dante's Ristorante
Fa Fa Gourmet
Hidden House
Nature's Marketplace
New York Richie's
Sheldon's Cafe at the Grant
House
Thai Little Home

Restaurants

TOP 200 RESTAURANTS

Abou Karim ★ Relaxed, moderately priced, and roomy, Portland's long-established downtown Middle Eastern restaurant has a broad, loyal following—despite some stiff competition around town. Abou Karim is an inviting place to put away some pita—and offers a wide range of kabobs, grilled chicken and lamb dishes, and a particularly addictive baba ghanouj. Maybe the best way to dine here is to gather three friends for a Mezza: a quartet of kabobs supported by baba ghanouj, hummus, tabbouleh, falafel, grape leaves, and a range of other Middle Eastern soul food. A starter for four; a dinner for two. ■ *221 SW Pine St; 223-5058; map:I5; $$; beer and wine; AE, DC, MC, V; checks OK; lunch Mon–Fri, dinner Mon–Sat.* &

Alameda Brewhouse ★½ While the last decade has brought lots of good beer to Portland via brewpubs, few of these pubs have given us a reason to get excited about the food. All of that has changed, however, as we approach the millennium. Now you can order filet mignon with your pint of ale in a setting more restaurantlike than publike. Located in the heart of the Beaumont neighborhood, the Alameda Brewhouse typifies the upscale brewpub. Inside this lofty warehouse replete with harvest icons, people crowd into wood booths to share huge kick-ass plates of nachos or an order of salmon cakes. The menu ranges from Reuben sandwiches and pizza to shrimp fettuccine and a tasty rendition of fish and chips. The beer, brewed in the back, is also available in a 2-quart carryout, and—oh yeah—*it's* good, too. ■ *4765 NE Fremont; 460-9025; map:FF4; $$; full bar; MC, V; checks OK; lunch, dinner every day.*

Al-Amir ★★ The elaborately crenellated Bishop's House Building has hosted many restaurants in its time; this elegant, skillful Lebanese outpost has now outlasted them all. Starring here are the smoky, intense baba ghanouj and the creamy hummus, but the kitchen's reach is extensive. The shish kabob, lamb vibrant with spices and juices, highlights a menu that reaches to *kharouf muammar,* a huge pile of moist, faintly sweet lamb chunks, and *dujaj musahab,* a charcoal-grilled chicken breast in lemon and olive oil. Don't depart without trying the stuffed grape leaves. A little Lebanese beer makes the light through the stained-glass windows shine even more brightly. ■ *223 SW Stark St; 274-0010; map:I4; $$; full bar; AE, DC, DIS, MC, V; local checks only; lunch Mon–Fri, dinner every day.* &

Albertina's ★ This place should be honored for good karma alone. Except for the head chef and kitchen manager, all help in the former orphanage is volunteer, and revenues are used to support the Albertina Kerr Center for the Treatment of Physically and Emotionally Disturbed Children. The inexpensive three-course lunch also happens to be quite good: the menu, which changes weekly and is surprisingly inventive, offers dishes like Florentine Ham Roulade, Oriental Chicken in Spinach Nest, or Cappuccino Sundae. You'll need a reservation (two seatings daily). Next door in the Economy Jar you'll find heirloom jewelry and china sets to pass down through your own family. ■ *424 NE 22nd Ave; 231-0216; map:FF5; $; beer and wine; MC, V; checks OK; lunch Mon–Fri.* &

Alexis ★★ Most restaurants offer a meal—Alexis is a party. The welcome here is warmer than the flaming *saganaki* (Greek cheese ignited with ouzo). From the first course of chewy squid to the last of seriously sweet baklava, the food is authentic and memorable. Plump grape-leaf packets are available meatless or with lamb, and the little pillows of filo and feta known as *tiropitas* are worth the 15-minute wait. In fact, regulars often order these and other appetizers and call it dinner. Baskets of warm house bread come with the meal—and if you like what you taste, take heart: Alexis sells it by the loaf. The Alexis Bakourous family and their loyal staff attentively patrol the premises, and on weekends they're joined by Aurelia, the region's hottest Middle Eastern dancer. ■ *215 W Burnside; 224-8577; map:J5; $$; full bar; AE, DC, MC, V; local checks only; lunch Mon–Fri, dinner every day.* &

American Palate ★★ The food at this Northwest hideaway is as direct as its name: creative American cuisine solidly prepared. Pan-seared monkfish here actually shows why the fish is called "poor man's lobster"; it's sweet and tender and holds its texture. Grilled pork tenderloin with an apple-scallion fritter treats a delicate meat equally respectfully. Desserts change, but a chocolate mousse cake chases cocoa through an exploration of tones and textures, and cinnamon bread pudding can bolster your patriotism.

The service and the cozy dining room are equally direct—which doesn't keep them from being comfortable and successful, either. ■ *1937 NW 23rd Pl; 223-6994; map:GG7; $$; full bar; AE, DIS, MC, V; local checks only; lunch Mon–Fri, dinner Mon–Sat.* &

Andrew's Restaurant and Catering ★★ Some come for the almond biscotti and good coffee. Others like the outdoor seating that lends this little cafe in Vancouver something of a European air, although there is a decidedly Northwest flavor to the menu and a small-time feel to the cafe. Lunch is refreshingly unpretentious: polenta with pesto or marinara sauce; smoked salmon pasta or spinach lasagne; a focaccia sandwich; an array of fresh, imaginative salads (from roasted eggplant to an Asian noodle variation). Best of all, nothing here exceeds $7.50. ■ *611 W 11th St, Vancouver, WA; (360)693-3252; map:BB6; $; no alcohol; MC, V; checks OK; breakfast, lunch Mon–Fri.* &

Anne Hughes Kitchen Table Cafe ★ Some know Anne Hughes from her coffee room at Powell's Books; others know her from the poster promoting art that she posed for sans clothes a few years back. And then there are those who made her acquaintance here at this cozy soup kitchen in southeast Portland. There are three soups a day—maybe Hungarian vegetable, chicken Thai coconut, and split pea—served with French bread, focaccia, or corn bread. Also, for lunch (and dinner, too) there are a couple of different sandwich choices, and Greek and caesar salad, as well as a daily special. Breakfast here means a simple muffin and cappuccino, and in between the usual mealtimes the cafe stays open, making it a good afternoon place to stop in for a cup of coffee and slice of homemade marionberry pie. ■ *400 SE 12th; 230-6977; map:GG5; $; beer and wine; no credit cards; checks OK; breakfast, lunch, dinner Mon–Fri.*

▼

Top 200 Restaurants

▲

Assaggio ★★½ This is the place for carbo-loading. For $10 a person, Assaggio will serve you three courses of pasta—maybe a spicy spaghetti alla puttanesca, followed by a carbonara and perhaps some penne dense with woodsy wild mushrooms and leeks. Or you can skip their picks and explore the 20 pasta choices by yourself—it's hard to go wrong. Take a deep breath and start out with three different kinds of polenta with three different toppings—notably, smoky grilled artichokes with Parmesan shavings. Try to fit in another combination of bruschettas—maybe wild mushrooms on one, Tuscan bean salad on the other.

Next door, a wine bar offers barrelfuls of Italian wines by the glass, as well as in 3-ounce tastes. The barolos are braced with tiny Italianate tapas, crostinis, or mouthfuls of salads. The rooms where all this happens are as carefully decorated as the pasta. And those who take up long-distance running or rowing (anything to give you an excuse) won't feel guilty coming back. ■ *7742 SE 13th Ave; 232-6151; map:JJ5; $$; beer and wine; MC, V; no checks; dinner Tues–Sat.* &

Atwater's ★★★ Taking over Portland's showcase restaurant— 30 floors up and looking Mount Hood in the eye—Bay Area chef Joe Nouhan has kept the emphasis on local ingredients and fitted them into a spirited continental-inspired menu. It switches seasonally, and each month Nouhan offers a lively regional four-course prix-fixe dinner, which might be inspired by cuisines hailing from Paris or Morocco or the American South. The menus cover a lot of ground, but Nouhan has the range to follow them, from a deep bouillabaisse to juicy, pungent herb-crusted lamb. The Northwest's fruits burst through Deborah Putnam's American-themed desserts; peach shortcake is a terrific argument for summer, and pecan sweet potato tart seems like a natural for fall. Because Nouhan's arrival is relatively recent, his range of possibilities is as wide as the view; cooking classes and wine dinners are becoming more prevalent. More informal but equally artful options—lobster club sandwiches, prosciutto-wrapped peaches, and a $65 ounce of beluga caviar—are available in the glossy bar, with live jazz on weekends. Either menu offers access to the literally voluminous wine list—the contents of which are housed in the huge, etched-glass wine cellar in the middle of the dining room. ■ *111 SW 5th Ave; 275-3600; map:J4; $$$; full bar; AE, DC, DIS, MC, V; no checks; dinner every day.* &

Avalon [*unrated*] Since its splashy, flashy opening in 1994, Avalon, with its dramatic, angular design and dazzling riverside location, has been rising like the Willamette in winter. We liked what happened at Avalon in 1997 and were about to assign it a three-star rating, but in early 1998, at press time, we learned that a new chef, Roy Breiman, had come up from the Napa Valley to revamp the kitchen. Chef Breiman takes his inspiration from Europe and the Far East (he studied cooking in the south of France and spent time in Hong Kong and Thailand), and the result is a menu of blended cuisines, described as "French with an Asian infusion." Menu items include Vietnamese "Pot au Feu" (beef tenderloin served in a consommé with carrots, potatoes, basil, red chiles, and lime) and a spicy beef, lobster, and black truffle salad. We look forward to trying the "new" Avalon and giving it a fresh star rating in the next edition. By that time a luxury hotel will probably sit right next door (plans are under review). Up in the high-tech, postmodern bar, one of Portland's more animated places to be seen, there's live jazz, cigars, and 25 different wines by the glass. ■ *4630 SW Macadam Ave; 227-4630; map:JJ6; $$; full bar; AE, DC, MC, V; checks OK; lunch Mon–Fri, dinner every day.* &

Aztec Willie & Joey Rose Taqueria ★ [KIDS] In one corner of this cavernous room, with its flying-saucer tables and high turquoise ceiling, is an attractive bar that serves up frosty margaritas by the pitcher; in the opposite corner is an inviting glass-walled playroom for the little ones. It's an unusual mix, but it works to attract parents in search of mealtime distraction for both themselves and their children. Like its sister taquerias, **Santa Fe** (831 NW 23rd Ave, 220-0406) and **Mayas** (1000 SW Morrison St, 226-1946), this one herds its diners down a cafeteria line offering burritos, tacos, and enchiladas—a half-dozen kinds each. The menu's strength lies in the number of items available, including a vividly flavored chile verde taco and a chicken mole enchilada. The chiles rellenos are also worth a try. No credit cards are accepted, but there is an ATM on the premises. ■ *1501 NE Broadway; 280-8900; map:FF5; $; full bar; no credit cards; no checks; lunch, dinner every day.*

Bangkok Kitchen ★★ Portland's Thai restaurant market may have drawn some newer, more elaborate contenders, but crowds still stream here for the unadorned basics of Southeast Asian cooking: hot-and-sour soups, curries, salads of fresh shrimp and lime, and noodles. The funky, informal atmosphere—with waiters in jeans and T-shirts and a no-frills decor—has attracted a faithful following of neighborhood locals and cross-river pilgrims who come for the family feeling and the famous whole crisp sea bass in chile sauce. Kids are more than welcome—the staff members wear their sense of humor like name tags. ■ *2534 SE Belmont St; 236-7349; map:GG4; $; beer and wine; no credit cards; checks OK; lunch Tues–Fri, dinner Tues–Sat.* &

Basta's ★★ As you come through the entryway, Basta's may appear to be a different restaurant from the place you've learned to love: the appetizer case has been replaced by an aquarium, and the menu seems more ambitious, with additional beef and veal dishes among the pastas. However, Basta's continues doing what it has done well since its opening: serving well-priced and mostly reliable Italian fare in a Tuscan-fun atmosphere (a former fast-food hangout nicely modified into an art-filled trattoria). Although the diners on the patio might be casually attired, there's a well-dressed caesar salad on the menu, and deftly pan-fried oysters. The emphasis is on pasta, about a dozen shrewd entrees with flavoring from wild mushrooms to duck. But there are some choices for carnivores, and the kitchen has a way with lamb— especially the slow-cooked lamb shank in an herby tomato-pancetta sauce. Breads are irresistible. ■ *410 NW 21st Ave; 274-1572; map:GG7; $$; full bar; MC, V; checks OK; lunch Mon–Fri, dinner every day.* &

Beaches Restaurant & Bar ★★ Perched above the Columbia River, with an open view and a contemporary interior, this young spot has become a favorite of Vancouver residents. Its easygoing casualness pleases suits and shorts and kids alike, who all come for the simple menu of wood-oven specialties, whole-meal salads, pastas, steamed mussels, and half-pound burgers. It offers a few comfort-food signatures such as the popular Jack Daniel's flamin' wings, seafood cioppino, and hot berry cobbler. The swinging

▼

Top 200
Restaurants

▲

bar fills up seven nights a week, and there's a growing, reasonably priced wine list. ▪ *1919 SE Columbia River Dr, Vancouver, WA; (360)699-1592; map:BB5; $$; beer and wine; AE, DC, MC, V; checks OK; lunch, dinner every day.*

Berbati ★★ There have been a lot of changes to this once-intimate Greek restaurant that now shares quarters with Berbati's Pan— one of the city's best venues for live music. But, fortunately, a lot has stayed the same, too. Named for a village in Greece, Berbati is the kind of welcoming place you'll want to drop into frequently. Order a table full of appetizers, and expect to be satisfied. The chicken souvlaki is served alongside a wedge of buttery, mustard-kissed potato. The *tiropita*—a hot, cheese-filled pastry—is so smooth it cries out for a glass of pine-scented retsina. You can still order a plate of some of Portland's best calamari, but now the squid competes on the menu with almost-as-good pan-fried oysters. And you can still find delicious roasted chicken and dolmathes to write home to Greece about, but now there's penne pasta too. You'll still see many of the same friendly faces, find the same comfortable dining area, and be able to order a shot of ouzo from the same intimate bar. ▪ *19 SW 2nd Ave; 226-2122; map:J6; berbati@teleport.com; www.teleport.com/~berbati/; $$; full bar; MC, V; local checks only; dinner Tues–Sat.* &

Besaw's ★★ In the best tradition of the quintessential neighborhood cafe, Besaw's serves three square meals a day in a bright, high-ceilinged dining room that beckons the neighbors—as well as others from well beyond the reaches of Nob Hill—back for repeat performances. The place has been here since the turn of the century, and it's aged beautifully; everything seems polished, from the mirror above the bar to the gracious service to the dinner menu that changes nightly. The half-dozen dinner specials include something for just about everyone: meat, pasta, and seafood, prepared with a nod to the season (maybe garlicky roasted chicken or Columbia River sturgeon with roasted red pepper aioli). For a hearty breakfast try the Farmer's Hash, with chunks of peppers and potatoes, or the French toast. Lunch might be a classic hamburger and a glass of Hefeweizen. ▪ *2301 NW Savier St; 228-2619; map:GG7; $; full bar; MC, V; checks OK; breakfast, lunch Tues–Sun, dinner Tues–Sat.* &

Big Bear Bagels What makes this little bagel shop unique (besides all the stuffed bears) is the huge variety of cream cheese spreads: lox with herbs, cucumber-dill, honey-walnut, pineapple, basil-tomato, salsa, spinach . . . you get the picture. Add to that list hummus, nut spreads, and turkey salad, and you'll never be at a loss for bagel toppers. Big Bear bakes up 16 different kinds of bagels, including an amazing four-seed version. ▪ *1852 SE Hawthorne Blvd; 238-7647; map:GG5; $; no alcohol; no credit cards; local checks only; breakfast, lunch every day.*

Big Dan's West Coast Bento ★ Bento has become a growth industry in Portland, but Big Dan's is still a big favorite; the line stretches out to the street. The core here is yakitori bentos, Japanese box lunches. Open only for lunch, this enterprise offers skewers of barbecued beef, chicken, lamb, or shrimp served on brown or white rice, sauced with a simultaneously sweet and spicy yakitori concoction. Of the side dishes, try the humbao, a steamed bun filled with barbecued pork. Don't ask for Diet Coke; beverages here are as authentic as the sauce: tropical fruit drinks and iced coffee. ▪ *2346 NW Westover Rd; 227-1779; map:FF7; $; no alcohol; no credit cards; local checks only; lunch Mon–Fri.*

Bijou Cafe ★½ The constantly changing lunch menu may produce items such as a summer fruit and nut salad, or steamed fish with red curry sauce and basmati rice. The specials mingle with the standards, including red snapper hash and Japanese noodle salad, and lunches are popular enough that you can get crowded out of the tables and up to one of the counters. But the real crush still happens mornings, especially weekend mornings, when the lines stretch out the door for grilled cinnamon bread, terrific scrambled eggs, and sometimes three kinds of pancakes. The Bijou, with its gleaming mirrors and almost-as-gleaming hardwood floors, long ago attained breakfast-landmark status in Portland, and the remodeling of neither the restaurant nor the entire surrounding neighborhood has changed its position. Tofu and granola still pop up in various places on the menu, but they're now joined by microbrews and local wines. And since the breakfast menu is served all day, you can pick just the right vintage to go with a blueberry pancake. ▪ *132 SW 3rd Ave; 222-3187; map:J5; $$; beer and wine; no credit cards; local checks only; breakfast, lunch every day.* &

Bima ★½ The question, really, is whether the food is the point here at all. Sure, fans of the vaguely Caribbean menu speak well of the elaborate tacos; and the grilled fish dishes and lunchtime skewers—from porcini mushrooms to squid—can be lively and inviting. The oozy tres leche cake is refreshing, too. But the star here is the scene, architecturally and socially. Once you pass through its nondescript industrial-area door, Bima has one of Portland's most dramatic spaces: concrete warehouse walls towering up to a layered bare-wood ceiling, the room splashed with color and asymmetrical furniture. Nights, the bar is lit up by a Pearl District art crowd—and sometimes they even eat something. ▪ *1338 NW Hoyt; 241-3465; map:L1; bima5@aol.com; $$; full bar; AE, MC, V; no checks; lunch, dinner Mon–Sat.* &

BJ's Brazilian Restaurant ★★ Portland's only Brazilian restaurant is a boisterously colored place of blues and yellows and purples, with a huge mural of Rio de Janeiro sweeping across one wall. But its most dramatic element is its version of *feijoada*, Brazil's national dish, a deep stew of black beans, pork, and sausage. Chicken dishes, including one baked in dark beer and red palm oil, are also admirable, as are the small, deep-fried meat pies called *pastels*. Everything comes with rice, a grain dish called *farofa*, and a mixture of chopped cilantro and red pepper that should be spooned on everything in sight. A dark Brazilian beer called Xingu is served up in huge bottles, or you can try the potent *cacha*, a sugarcane liquor. ■ *7019 SE Milwaukie Ave; 236-9629; map:JJ5; $$; full bar; MC, V; checks OK; lunch Mon–Fri, dinner Mon–Sat. &*

Black Rabbit Restaurant and Bar ★★ One thing that strikes a guest immediately at Edgefield, the estate home of Black Rabbit Restaurant and a smattering of smaller, less formal eateries and watering holes, is that everyone seems to be having a good time. Even the people who work here are smiling. One reason may be that there's something for everyone to like on these 25 acres. That's true of Black Rabbit Restaurant, too: not only is there the large, pleasant dining room, with its white-clothed tables and booths along the perimeter, but there's also a bar serving light meals and, outside, a New Orleans–style courtyard that is Edgefield's most elegant and romantic spot for supping on a summer evening. What the menu lacks in surprises, it makes up for in successes. A grilled salmon fillet is served with saffron aioli and wild rice. Grilled pork chops encrusted with herbs and served with roasted potatoes in a garlicky butter are an even better choice, as are the sautéed prawns spiked with poblano chiles and lime juice. When the food matches the Columbia Gorge-ous setting, when the wind carries to your nose the scent of herbs from the nearby estate gardens or the smell of hops from the on-site brewery, and when there's a bed-and-breakfast room right upstairs reserved in your name, Edgefield's Black Rabbit is a great place to spend a Saturday evening. ■ *2126 SW Halsey, Troutdale; 492-3086; $$$; full bar; AE, DIS, MC, V; local checks only; dinner every day. &*

B. Moloch/The Heathman Bakery and Pub ★★ After going through more formats than Windows 95, the Heathman's casual cousin across the South Park Blocks has found a keeper—for a while, at least. This time it's more formal and more hearty, as Mark Bernetich takes over the menu. B. Moloch is still a brewpub, but now it's also a place with sweeps of tiles, rich wood, and table service. All this is set off by walls of windows, high ceilings hung with artful banners, and Second Empire caricatures. The food is more meaty and less delicate, with smoked pork chops, smoked sausages, and hanger steaks. There are still salads, pastas, and serious sandwiches, such as smoked lamb on focaccia and a Reuben with house-cured pastrami. B. Moloch continues to serve one of the city's better breakfasts, with such dishes as an open-faced smoked salmon and crème fraîche

▼

Top 200 Restaurants

▲

omelet. And the place always provides some of Portland's best people-watching—inside and outside. Things here might seem stable now, but rumor has it that David Machado, who came to Heathman Management from Pazzo Ristorante in 1997, has plans for future changes. ■ *901 SW Salmon St; 227-5700; map:G2; $$; full bar; AE, DC, MC, V; checks OK; lunch, dinner every day, brunch Sat–Sun.* &

Bombay Cricket Club Restaurant ★½ Where else can you watch cricket, sip mango margaritas, and feast on succulent tandoori chicken? This lively little restaurant on Hawthorne serves familiar Indian food—curries, vindaloo, tandoori, biryani—and a small selection of Middle Eastern dishes, while the TV on the bar broadcasts recorded cricket matches. If cricket is not your thing, never mind; once the meal begins you'll find yourself focused on the intriguing flavors before you: samosas dipped into a tangy tamarind chutney, chewy naan stuffed with onions and spices, and garlicky-hot fish vindaloo. The only disappointment is that the condiments that usually accompany an Indian meal—mango chutney, yogurt raita, and dal—have to be ordered separately here. ■ *1925 SE Hawthorne Blvd; 231-0740; map:GG5; $$; full bar; AE, MC, V; checks OK; dinner every day.*

Brasserie Montmartre ★★ There are several places to eat in Portland after midnight, but there's only one real restaurant at that hour. Until 2am weekdays and 3am on weekends, the Brasserie offers everything from veal with mushrooms to eggs Benedict to beluga caviar. The major ingredient, however, may be the scene—Doc Martens and suits, nightly local jazz, an occasional strolling magician, and dancing—all happening behind a glass and wood exterior as flashy as the black-and-white-checked floor. But the food deserves notice, too. It's surprising how consistent it is, whatever the hour—and it's always a good time for the sweetly succulent crab cakes or the roast lamb sandwich on focaccia. Dining at more traditional times, you might notice the petrale sole in a caper-butter sauce—and the framed crayoned illustrations on the walls. The flashy remodeling of the outside is about to produce some redrawing of the menu—which could happen at all hours. ■ *626 SW Park Ave; 224-5552; map:H2; $$; full bar; AE, DC, DIS, MC, V; checks OK; lunch, dinner every day, brunch Sat–Sun.* &

Top 200 Restaurants

The Brazen Bean ★ Before a fire destroyed the offbeat Bean in 1997, Generation X went there to smoke cigars and to sample the wide, creative range of beverages that can go with them—from Armagnac to chai to Scotch older than some of the customers. The "menu" also featured other legal smokables and a few entrees, together with some enthralling desserts, including a messy but delectable chocolate fondue. The new Bean will feature a regional antipasto bar (pâtés, cheeses, and cured meats—no entrees), seasonal outdoor seating, and late-night hours. We loved the original place, set in a lovely Victorian mansion just around the corner from Zefiro, and we hope the redone version (scheduled to open spring '98; same location) is just as charming. ■ *2075 NW Glisan St; 294-0636; map:GG7; $; full bar; AE, MC, V; no checks; dinner Mon–Sat.*

Bread and Ink Cafe ★★½ At this lofty, well-lit bistro in the heart of the Hawthorne neighborhood, there have been changes in both the ownership and the kitchen, leaving some things warmly recognizable and some a bit more ambitious than we've come to expect. Longtime fans will still find impressive baked desserts (including a poppyseed cake that will ensnare people who didn't think they liked poppyseed cake), rugged black bean chili, a Sunday-warming three-course Yiddish brunch, and a serious hamburger, with homemade condiments that do it justice. Dinner now seems to aim a bit higher, with roast steelhead and duck cooked two ways; the results are more solid than soaring. But Bread and Ink, with its wall drawings and huge windows onto Hawthorne, still draws its loyal crowd—along with a few more adventurous diners. ■ *3610 SE Hawthorne Blvd; 239-4756; map:GG5; $$; beer and wine; AE, DIS, MC, V; checks OK; breakfast, lunch Mon–Sat, dinner every day, brunch Sun.* &

Briggs and Crampton's Table for Two ★★★ It's been years now since the meal that defines "intimate"—one table, one seating, one lunch—burst onto the pages of the *Wall Street Journal* and *People* magazine. And still, at 8:30am sharp on the first business day of the quarter, people leap for their phones to try to snag a reservation in the following three months. For $75, not counting wine or tip, a couple gets a four-course lunch designed to order: the week before, you send over a list of what you like, what you can't stand, and what makes you break out. Then you show up, and encounter something like halibut steaks with a red pepper salsa or roasted rack of lamb in a saffron-tomato demiglace, and an orange mascarpone torte. And you linger; people have been known to make lunch last until dinner. The intricate presentation of each course dazzles, as do the pretty china and the intimate setting. ■ *1902 NW 24th Ave; 223-8690; map:FF6; $$$; beer and wine; MC, V; checks OK; lunch Tues–Fri (by appointment only).*

Bugatti's Ristorante ★★½ Lydia Bugatti and John Cress's endearing Italian restaurant in West Linn features fine Italian wines, seasonal foods, and a menu that changes every few weeks. Anytime, keep watch for rigatoni carbonara and spaghetti frutti di mare. There's a nice olive oil spiked with garlic for bread-dipping, but save room for dazzling desserts such as the cloudlike tiramisu. The well-dressed yet simple dining room is quite large, but reservations are a good idea; it's a popular place. ■ *18740 Willamette Dr, West Linn; 636-9555; map:NN5; $$; beer and wine; MC, V; local checks only; dinner Tues–Sun.* &

Bush Garden ★★ There's an extensive Japanese menu here, with several unexpected offerings such as scallop batayaki and different views of tofu—along with the widest choice of tatami rooms in Portland. But the most interesting options come through the sushi bar, where you can expertly rattle off words like "uni," "ama ebi," and "toro"; point and look hopeful; or just ask the chef to surprise you. Chefs here turn out versions of sushi and sashimi not found elsewhere—Alaskan roll with surimi and smoked salmon, fiery spicy tuna maki, pungent pickled plums. They also like to show off; ask for a translation of the day's specials. Or just leave it to the chef's inspiration, and end up with something like a deliciously crunchy, sweet soft-shell spider crab roll. ▪ *900 SW Morrison St; 226-7181; map:H3; $$; full bar; AE, DC, MC, V; no checks; lunch Mon–Fri, dinner every day.* &

Buster's Smokehouse Texas-Style Bar-Be-Que ★ Take a deep whiff. The wood-smoke ovens leave their mark on both the meat and the atmosphere. Brisket, links, chicken, beef, and pork ribs all pass through the cooker and come out estimably smoky and juicy. The barbecue sauces have a sweet brown-sugar base and come in three temps; have a beer with the hottest. Accompaniments are simple: fries, slaw, beans, and stuffed jalapeño peppers—for devils only. There's an equal emphasis on barbecue essentials at the original Milwaukie location as well as at the Gresham branch (667-4811). The Buster's in Tigard features a mesquite broiler, for those of faint disposition. ▪ *17883 SE McLoughlin Blvd, Milwaukie; 652-1076; map:II5; $; beer and wine; DIS, MC, V; checks OK; lunch, dinner every day.* & ▪ *11419 SW Pacific Hwy, Tigard; 452-8384; map:KK8; $; full bar; DIS, MC, V; checks OK; lunch, dinner every day.* &

Cafe des Amis ★★★ Dennis Baker knows exactly what he's doing, and a generation of diners know exactly what they want him to do. Baker's specialties have become landmarks: delicate, briny Dungeness crab cakes; rich, intense soups ranging from cream of mussel to carrot with a hint of lemongrass and wasabe; a buttery, 2-inch-thick fillet of beef in a port and garlic sauce; cobblers and fruit tarts that look as if they've just been glazed in a Boulevard St. Germain pâtisserie. Of course, you might just skip the entree and make a light, satisfying meal of soup and salad and some pâté. But before you do, at least consider the moist salmon, or the duck in blackberry sauce. For true bistro status, this cozy, intimate cafe tucked onto a northwest Portland residential street would need only outdoor tables—and a climate change that not even Baker could cook up. ▪ *1987 NW Kearney St; 295-6487; map:GG7; $$; full bar; AE, MC, V; checks OK; dinner Mon–Sat.* &

Cafe du Berry ★★ Although the light industry of lower Macadam Avenue is rapidly giving way to upscale markets and housing complexes, longtime resident Cafe du Berry still seems an anomaly. It's a comfy little quasi-French restaurant (with warm baguettes, perfect crèmes caramels, and well-prepared entrees) that shares a building with a furniture-stripping shop. But don't worry about fumes in your food: the atmosphere is bright, welcoming, and just a bit European. Here you can pick up coq au vin to go or, if you fancy the company, sit down in cozy surroundings for a plate of salmon, peppered steak, or veal sweetbreads accompanied by a bottle of wine from a small but carefully chosen cellar. Upscalish prices are the only sign of pretension, but in compensation, portions are larger than the French would countenance. The trademark French toast is a breakfast staple for morning commuters and even worth a trip for more northerly residents. Lunch might be soup, sandwich, or a plate of linguine alfredo. ▪ *6439 SW Macadam Ave; 244-5551; map:II6; $$$; beer and wine; AE, MC, V; checks OK; breakfast, lunch every day, dinner Wed–Sat (reservations only).*

Cafe Sol ★ In the former home of beloved Panini—bygone sweetheart of the downtown lunch crowd—Cafe Sol shines on its own merit. Sit out for streetside tapas or take it inside for conviviality in the close quarters of this Spanish restaurant that swarms with regulars. Your meal starts with bread and a garlic-tomato-basil-olive oil spread that nicely whets your appetite for the savories to follow, including a tapas of octopus and potato stew or a hearty and delicious made-to-order paella. Gazpacho is a cream-like purée of roasted tomatoes, peppers, and garlic, served with slivers of cucumber; spinach pie is a wedge of luscious filo crust in which the green filling is enlivened with olives and anchovies. Incidentally, Cafe Sol is a great place to dine solo; most evenings there's flamenco dancing on the small wooden stage or at least a guitarist to entertain you—and it's one of the easiest places in town to strike up a conversation with those at the next table. Reservations in the evening are a good idea. ▪ *620 SW 9th Ave; 243-2181; map:H2; $$; beer and wine; DIS, MC, V; local checks only; lunch, dinner Tues–Sat.*

Caffe Fresco ★ The breakfast potatoes, graced with seasonal vegetables and provolone, are about the only thing that's complicated at this neighborhood spot—hence their name, "Complicated Potatoes." Everything else is refreshingly straightforward—especially the home-baked goods, which include a variety of scones, muffins, and coffee cakes (it's not uncommon to see eight different kinds of Bundt cake in the case). There's a 10-grain hot cereal laced with chopped hazelnuts and lots of brown sugar, and crisp waffles. Lunch features a soup of the day, a delicious house salad tossed with raspberry vinaigrette, and innovative—in a good way—sandwiches served on crusty Grand Central bread: smoked turkey with homemade salsa, vegan muffaletta with eggplant caponata, or chèvre and pesto with sun-dried tomatoes. Hard by the granola-graced Food Front Co-op, Caffe Fresco has a natural, neighborly feel to it, but its quality can draw habitués of glitzier eateries. ■ *2387 NW Thurman St; 243-3247; map:FF6; $; no alcohol; no credit cards; local checks only; breakfast, lunch every day.* &

Caffe Mingo ★★ This resolutely casual new trattoria—on a stretch of NW 21st Avenue that's become to restaurants what NW 23rd is to shopping—rejects both reservations and high prices. Instead, it maintains a solid, inviting version of Italian cafe cuisine, from vivid shrimp *spiedini* to pillowy gnocchi to a headliner of Northwest mushrooms roasted in parchment. The menu is limited but handled well, and a wide sampling won't get you a hefty bill. As you work slowly through your lemon tart, relax and enjoy the moment—and just ignore all those people clustered on the street waiting for your table. ■ *807 NW 21st Ave; 226-4646; map:GG7; $$; beer and wine; AE, DC, MC, V; local checks; dinner Mon–Sat.* &

Campbell's Barbecue ★★ People who come into this little house along Powell Boulevard and inhale deeply get more of a barbecue hit than some places provide in a rack of ribs. The dining area is quaint, the servers cheerful and efficient, and side dishes—especially the potato salad and the corn bread—are inviting. But what packs the place is an exuberant vision of barbecue. Pork ribs are messy and satisfying, slathered with the smoky brown-sugar sauce, but there are plenty of other options: smoked turkey, chicken, beef, or sausages. A space is available for parties, though some people claim any meal here is a party, and the party's never over until they've run out of peach cobbler. ■ *8701 SE Powell Blvd; 777-9795; map:HH3; $; no alcohol; AE, DIS, MC, V; no checks; lunch, dinner Tues–Sat.* &

Caprial's Bistro and Wine ★★½ As hot regional chef Caprial Pence has been raising her own profile, with a weekly Oregon Public Broadcasting cooking show and more cookbooks, so has her neighborhood bistro continued to attract fans; the place has taken Caprial's famous name and acquired an additional chef, Mark Dowers. The result has been no loss of imagination and a bit more consistency, and a packed dining room for lunches and dinners (an expansion in 1998 should spread things out a bit). Vivid flavors shoot around the storefront, from Hot as Hell Chicken at lunch (grilled chicken with chile sauce over pungent peanut-sauced pasta) to dinner entrees such as steelhead with lemongrass aioli. There are also creative sandwiches and salads, and an intense array of desserts: a chocolate turtle cake can make you forget that the name originally belonged to a candy. The menus shift around but never stray too far from the Northwest; dishes just get here in a different way. The walls are lined with a sizable retail wine supply; a $2 corkage fee gets any bottle from the shelf to your table. ▪ *7015 SE Milwaukie Ave; 236-6457; map:JJ5; $$; beer and wine; MC, V; checks OK; lunch Tues–Sat, dinner Wed–Sat.*

Casablanca ★ Among Portland's many new restaurants, this Moroccan hot spot spellbinds diners with elaborate atmosphere and decoration, and food that provides its own richness. Dinner begins with enticing appetizers, such as filo pastries enfolding seafood or chicken. Entrees run to couscous, kabobs, and tagines (intense Moroccan stews). Baklava is as rich, sweet, and flaky as you'd expect from a place that specializes in filo. And if, in this crazy world, the problems of two little people "don't amount to a hill of beans," at least it's worth finding out what Casablanca does with beans, notably lentils and garbanzos. ▪ *2221 SE Hawthorne Blvd; 233-4400; map:HH5; $$; beer and wine; AE, MC, V; local checks; lunch Mon–Fri, dinner every day.* &

Caswell ★ Depending on the night, Caswell feels like a nice restaurant that just happens to have a bar, or a great bar that just happens to serve food that goes well with cocktails and beer. The best things on the menu are the smaller plates: bruschetta with goat cheese and sweet red peppers, grilled polenta with fresh mozzarella and marinara, cold tuna with olives and capers on bread. Pizza, pasta, and a handful of entrees such as gumbo and chicken curry round out the menu, and everything is reasonably priced (nothing runs over $9 on the food menu, and the average bottle of wine costs $16). Its location off the beaten path has kept Caswell a cherished secret among southeast Portlanders, but word is slowly getting out. ▪ *533 SE Grand Ave; 232-6512; map:GG6; $; full bar; AE, MC, V; checks OK; lunch Mon–Fri, dinner Mon–Sat.*

Chen's Dynasty ★ A new location in Beaverton gives Chen's a fresh face, but nothing else has changed much here. The menu is huge, with excursions into each region of China, and there are steamed, boiled, and vegetarian dishes—cholesterol concern strikes everywhere. But it shouldn't dissuade you from the Heavenly Sliced Duck, the chicken with pine nuts, or the four-jewel scallops. Leave time for eating here: you may need longer than you think to pay attention to the lengthy menu, but you'll also want to pay attention to the food. The roomy new restaurant is handily located for Nike and high-tech employees. It features an ocean-size selection of seafood entrees and a brisk take-out business. Surprisingly, there's yet another Chen's set to open in Beaverton in 1998. ▪ *15915 NW Schendel Ave, Beaverton; 533-9888; $$; full bar; AE, MC, V; checks OK; lunch, dinner every day.* &

Chez Grill ★★ As the Hawthorne Renaissance spread west and east, it clearly needed a place for a good margarita. It's now found one, and it also has a reasonably priced, unreasonably creative

▼

Top 200 Restaurants

▲

take on Mexican food. Grilled-fish tacos might come stuffed with
chinook salmon, jack cheese, wild greens, and pico de gallo,
while the standard quesadilla is infused with braised lamb and
caramelized onions, or barbecued pork. Even the Southern
Hemisphere gets a Southwestern twist when New Zealand lamb
shanks are braised with chipotle peppers. The list goes on, bol-
stered by the night's inspirations, and you can think about it
while scooping guacamole—thick, with large, soft hunks of ripe
avocado—onto fresh tortillas. Especially when warm breezes
blow in through open picture windows, Chez Grill is a strikingly
pleasant place to hang out—even before your first margarita.
■ *2229 SE Hawthorne Blvd; 239-4002; map:HH5; $$; full bar;
MC, V; local checks only; lunch Mon–Sat, dinner every day.* &

Chez Jose ■ Chez Jose East ★½ [KIDS] The larger, flashier north-
east outpost has a bar and a menu that's a bit bigger, but most
dishes appear in both places—to general satisfaction. Chicken
breast with a spicy peanut sauce, grilled shrimp with a chipotle
honey dip, and mole tamales span both sides of the Willamette, in
addition to the specials on each blackboard. Sometimes a bowl of
the rich black bean soup with a dollop of sour cream is all you
need. The original Chez, with its iguana kitsch, faux marble pil-
lars, and Lewis and Clark College hangers-on, is still highly pop-
ular, although its look is beginning to seem stuck in the '80s.
Chez Jose East, on trendy NE Broadway, has a lot more seating, a
booming bar, and garden tables when it's not raining. There's a
kids' menu, too. ■ *8502 SW Terwilliger Blvd; 244-0007; map:JJ6;
$; full bar; MC, V; local checks only; lunch Mon–Sat, dinner every
day.* & ■ *2200 NE Broadway; 280-9888; map:FF5; $; full bar;
MC, V; local checks only; lunch Mon–Sat, dinner every day.* &

Cocina del Sol ★ [KIDS] In some ways, Cocina del Sol stands as
alone as a tropical island; there's probably not another place for
miles around where you can start your meal with chips and salsa,
move on to sizzling lemongrass beef strips eaten in a tortilla, and
finish it all with flourless, Kahlua-laced chocolate cake. But the
Tualatinos who flock to this happy, busy suburban hot spot don't
seem to mind the incongruities one bit. A table on the screened
porch upstairs helps you pretend you really have drifted off to a
sunshiny place far from Portland—where a Black Forest drink
concoction feels right at home with a panang curry and moist
fish tacos. The children's menu—complete with buttered rice as
an entree—will make even the youngest *compañero* feel wel-
come. ■ *18770 SW Boones Ferry Rd, Tualatin; 691-2731;
map:NN9; $$; full bar; AE, MC, V; checks OK; lunch Tues–Sat,
dinner Tues–Sun.* &

Compass Cafe ★★ Weekend brunch on Hawthorne Boulevard
hasn't been the same since the Tabor Hill Cafe changed hands
a few years ago. Fortunately, we can point you in the same general

direction but a few blocks east, to the Compass Cafe, which has established itself as an excellent alternative. Everything is thoughtfully prepared here, from the old favorites—plump spinach-mozzarella omelets, featherlight pancakes—to the extraordinary—French toast stuffed with a delicate apricot-currant cream cheese and sprinkled with strawberries and sliced almonds, a combination so flavorful you might forgo syrup. The breakfast burrito is a black bean and vegetable omelet folded into a flour tortilla, served alongside a beautiful oven-roasted potato-and-caramelized-yam combination and melt-in-your-mouth sweet corn pudding. The Compass hops at night, too, with a dressy, global menu that combines monthly specials such as Peruvian Causa (sort of a shepherd's pie of rock shrimp, salt cod, and chard between layers of potato—extraordinary) with more standard menu items—pasta, meats and fish, and vegetarian options. The garden area out back, complete with fountain, attractive plantings, and a sizable number of tables, is another reason to head in this direction. ■ *4741 SE Hawthorne Blvd; 231-4840; map:HH4; $$; beer and wine; DIS, MC, V; checks OK; dinner Tues–Sat, brunch Sat–Sun.* &

Cornelius Pass Roadhouse and Brewery ★ Residents of the burgeoning suburbs along Highway 26 west of Portland appreciate this longtime McMenamin Brothers institution for its proximity to home, but others come from miles around for its true charm: housed in an 1866 clapboard farmhouse, the place is just *warm.* You can eat reliable pub burgers and sip great brew in one of four softly lit rooms or, on balmy afternoons and languid evenings, head out to the balcony or to a picnic table on the lawn. Just what every brewpub should be: utterly inviting. ■ *Just south of Hwy 26, on Cornelius Pass Rd, Hillsboro; 640-6174; $; beer and wine; AE, MC, V; checks OK; lunch, dinner every day.*

Couch Street Fish House ★½ Little has changed here in the last decade, which might be the reason that folks out for a special dinner tend to reserve spots at the newer, sleeker, more youthful restaurants in town. That said, there are Couch Street devotees who appreciate seeing their name on a board at the entrance ("Happy Anniversary, Mr. and Mrs. Your-Name-Here") and enjoy the lavish table settings and choreographed service (complete with silver domes simultaneously whisked from the entrees). They expect, and receive, menu items such as charbroiled prawns served with a peach mustard, perfectly grilled salmon, moist crab cakes, and Maine lobster. The dessert list is extensive, and the house's specialty, chocolate-dipped strawberries injected with Grand Marnier, is a toothsome treat. The low-lit, brick-walled interior is almost clubby, and the Old Town location is finally fashionable. ■ *105 NW 3rd Ave; 223-6173; map:K6; $$$; full bar; AE, DC, MC, V; checks OK; dinner Mon–Sat.* &

▼

Top 200 Restaurants

▲

Couvron ★★★ This tiny, elaborate restaurant is named after hostess Maura Demes's French hometown, but it could also be called the *Oklahoma* restaurant—each dish is as high as an elephant's eye. Chef Tony Demes, adding another dimension to presentation, stacks up his dishes into napoleons or small hillocks, and sends stalks or sprays of herbs towering up from them. It takes a lot of cooking skill to match this architecture, and Demes appears to be up to the challenge: roasting monkfish or rabbit, or constructing condominiums of beef and garlic potatoes, or scallops and herb ravioli. Desserts include soufflés, tarte Tatin, and chocolate arrangements with all the complexity of a microchip. You can also waive all decisions by going for the six-course tasting menu for $45, but even with the regular menu, you won't have any problem filling up your evening. And now Couvron offers lunch, which can fill up your afternoon with roasted duck confit, saffron risotto with wild mushrooms, or bouillabaisse. The dining rooms may feel a bit small and crowded, but the location is striking—Couvron is directly on the new Westside light-rail line. It deserves its own station. ■ *1126 SW 18th Ave; 225-1844; map:GG6; $$$; beer and wine; AE, MC, V; local checks OK; dinner Tues–Sat.*

Cozze ★ This friendly neighborhood Italian place has made a reputation with weekly renditions of the feast from the movie *Big Night*. Mondays—by reservation only—each course of the meal is faithfully re-created, leading up to a sizable roast suckling pig and ending in a conga line. Other nights are less lively, but the mood is just as warm. The menu runs to a pile of pastas—the lobster and potato raviolis are of particular interest—and some meat dishes, including a particularly juicy pork chop (not directly related to the roast suckling pig). Cozze's own tomato-based "ooh-la-la" sauce tends to appear frequently, and you shouldn't miss the eggplant tapenade. ■ *1205 SE Morrison; 232-3275; map:HH5; $$; beer and wine; AE, DIS, MC, V; local checks only; lunch Mon–Fri, dinner Tues–Sun.* &

Top 200
Restaurants

Cucina! Cucina! [KIDS] Portland has two outposts of this Seattle restaurant chain, where the level of enthusiasm runs almost as high as the level of noise. The place buzzes with hungry suburbanites (at the Tigard location) and Blazers fans (at the Rose Quarter spot), who come for the dozen or so pizza and pasta options and the generous selection of breads (including a winning foccacia), antipasti, and desserts. Everything is busy, busy, busy—from the decor to the menu to the kitchen. The food is just above average, but it's a bright, cheerful spot and kids love it (toddlers can get busy right away with gobs of dough to shape their own creations). Accordion music on the sound system, bicycles hanging from the ceiling, Italian language broadcasts in the rest rooms, and wildly painted everything give the place a fun, if now formulaic, atmosphere. ■ *10205 SW Washington Square Rd, Tigard; 968-2000; map:LL9; $$; full bar; AE, DIS, MC, V; checks OK; lunch, dinner every day.* Ġ ■ *1 Center Ct, Rose Quarter; 238-9800; map:N8; $$; full bar; AE, DIS, MC, V; checks OK; lunch, dinner every day.* Ġ

Czaba's Barbecue and Catering, Inc. ★ When you see the giant black oil drums smoking out front, it's not too hard to guess what the menu is likely to be. It may not be classic barbecue—classic barbecue sauce doesn't have apricot and citrus elements—but it works, and people pile in here for pork and beef ribs, hot links, chicken, and catfish in adjustable degrees of heat. Michael "Czaba" Brown, who somehow found barbecue inspiration while growing up in Portland, also puts effort and imagination into side dishes, such as Southern succotash, cabbage salad, and vivid garlic toast. ■ *5907 N Lombard St; 240-0615; map:EE7; $; beer and wine; DIS, MC, V; checks OK; lunch, dinner Tues–Sat.*

Dan and Louis' Oyster Bar [KIDS] The Wachsmuth family has held their restaurant together through thick and thin for almost a century. Tourists who visited Portland before the advent of the automobile came to this Old Town establishment for seafood—and tourists are still coming. Among the place's charms are its value ($8.50 for the classic oyster fry, served alongside a hunk of sourdough and a haystack of iceberg lettuce sprinkled with tiny pink shrimp), and its pie and coffee (the marionberry is wonderful). Among its problems are efficient but unexciting preparations. The decor is family-friendly, with lots to look at, from plates on the walls to maritime bric-a-brac everywhere. You might encounter a setback or two—undercooked french fries, service that's friendly enough but absent for longer than you might wish—but you might also come to appreciate the predictability and charm of the place. Lots of regulars do. ■ *208 SW Ankeny St; 227-5906; map:J6; $; beer and wine; AE, DC, DIS, MC, V; local checks only; lunch, dinner every day.*

▼

Top 200 Restaurants

▲

Dante's Ristorante From the outside, you might not even notice this hunkered-down gray building, but inside, the gregarious Caltagirone family serves up good-value Italian specialties such as spaghetti all'Amatriciana (with a light garlic-pancetta sauce), prawns Mediterranean, and predictable but generous full-meal-deal raviolis, manicottis, and cannellonis. Pizzas are popular with kids, and the revamped interior brings a touch of the trattoria to this small but growing town north of Vancouver, Washington. Desserts include a locally loved tiramisu. The food is hearty; the wine list is by the glass. ■ *111 E Main St, Battle Ground, WA; (360)687-4373; $; beer and wine; MC, V; checks OK; dinner Mon–Sat.*

DaVinci ★★ This place is a major secret that the residents of Milwaukie obviously want to keep to themselves. Patrick Conner brings his San Francisco cooking experience to bear on a sub-

stantial Italian menu with multiple veal dishes, cioppino, specialties from the various regions of Italy, and pizza to go—and he
manages it all with prices that don't shock the suburban market.
Elegance and suave service are not the hallmark here, but solid,
skillful Italian cuisine (check out the scaloppine with mushrooms
or artichoke hearts) brings in local crowds and some well-informed
Westsiders. Admittedly, the outside doesn't look like a place that
orders its own abalone flown up from San Francisco, but don't be
dissuaded; Conner can connect Milan and Milwaukie. ▪ *12615
SE McLoughlin Blvd, Milwaukie; 659-3547; map:LL5; $$; full
bar; AE, MC, V; local checks; dinner Tues–Sun.* ⅋

Delfina's ★★ On a restaurant row that's become a fast track,
longtimer Delfina's has kept its traditional popularity while
reaching for some more ambitious menu efforts. What was a pop-
ular pizza-and-pasta place has followed the trend toward greater
Italian authenticity. Its menu is now smaller and oft-changing, and
the results are pleasing. The offerings extend to Dungeness crab
and pasta in a lemon cream sauce, seafood stew, rack of lamb,
and specials such as two-mushroom risotto with truffle oil. Mean-
while, the pastas are a lot more interesting than they once were.
Delfina's is building its own popular ambience with low lighting,
fresh-baked rustic breads that require manual disassembly, and
Italian language lessons broadcast in the restaurant. ▪ *2112 NW
Kearney St; 221-1195; map:GG7; $$; full bar; AE, DC, MC, V; no
checks; dinner every day.* ⅋

▼

▲

Delta Cafe ★★ Just up the boulevard from Reed College is this
hip hangout, decorated with ropes of beads hanging in the windows and Klimt reproductions on the walls, offering steaming
plates of Southern cooking on the Formica-topped tables. The
menu is pure Elvis, with some Cajun/Creole influence as well:
fried chicken, blackened catfish, jambalaya, pork ribs, collard
greens, "mash potatoes," corn bread, succotash, and apple-
cheddar pie for dessert. No grits, but if it's comfort food you're
after, there's a substantial portion of mac 'n' cheese for $3.50,
including the hot biscuit alongside. If your thirst matches your
appetite, wash it all down with a Jack Daniel's-spiked lemonade—
and you'll still find it difficult to spend $15 for dinner. ▪ *4607 SE
Woodstock Blvd; 771-3101; map:II4; $; full bar; no credit cards;
checks OK; lunch Sat–Sun, dinner every day.*

Doris' Cafe ★ Just because the first sign of the restaurant is the
barbecue smoker outside doesn't mean you should overlook the
rest of the menu here. Doris' is a full-scale soul food restaurant
from its oxtails to its fried fish and greens—and the fried chicken
wings here could put Buffalo out of business. Doris' has become
a meeting place in inner northeast Portland, and other establishments including a jazz-and-coffee bar next door, seem to be
emerging around it. This cool, attractive space with wood floors

and high ceilings is also one of the few places where Portlanders of all races regularly mingle, and a pile of rib tips is the perfect accompaniment for the socializing. The smoky barbecue comes in a sauce more sweet than angry; the fried chicken is lovely, fresh, and gently complex; and lunchtime means a run on the fried fish. Desserts vary, but the buttery pound cake and the mousselike sweet potato pie should not be missed. ▪ *325 NE Russell; 287-9249; map:EE5; $; full bar; AE, MC, V; local checks only; lunch, dinner every day.* &

El Burrito Loco ★ This place is not for the faint of heart or the mildly hungry. The namesake creation is a fresh, floury tortilla bursting around a chile relleno, strips of tender beef, and refried beans. It's the kind of crazy concoction that you occasionally *just gotta have right now*, and you might not find it anywhere else. Tacos, with chunks of pork, cilantro, tomatoes, and onion, are less filling, but they're so good and such a bargain that you will probably stuff yourself on a couple anyway. Take-out is big business here (you're invited to call ahead), although there are a few tables and some spare copies of Latino or University of Portland newspapers to read if you stay in. *Hasta luego*—we know you'll be back. ▪ *1942 N Portland Blvd (and branches); 735-9505; map:EE6; $; no alcohol; no credit cards; no checks; lunch, dinner every day.*

El Palenque ★ The crisp-shirted, bow-tied waiters lend an air of affable formality to this Sellwood Mexican and Salvadoran restaurant, but at heart it's a chips-and-salsa kind of place—warm, crisp chips and not-quite-scorching house salsa—truly addictive fare. The Mexican choices are *bueno*, but try the Salvadoran sampler for a real treat: plump pork and *loroco papusas*—two corn tortillas stuffed with pork or loroco (an aromatic flower) and cheese, served with cabbage and hot sauce—plus tamales, fried bananas and cream, black beans, rice—well, it's a substantial meal. Occasionally there's live guitar; sometimes the televisions are on. Almost always there is a brisk take-out business going on— another option when the addiction becomes unbearable. ▪ *8324 SE 17th Ave; 231-5140; map:II5; $; beer and wine; MC, V; checks OK; lunch, dinner every day.* &

Escape From New York Pizza ★ On NW 23rd Avenue, amidst the espresso shops, the hopelessly haute houseware shops, and the multitude of restaurants that serve anything your heart desires, sits this dependable storefront that serves one thing and one thing only: the classic Gotham pie—thin crust, spicy tomato sauce, and a massive cheese layer. EFNYP is not fussy. There are but a few choices of toppings available on pizzas by the huge, floppy slice—cheese, pepperoni, and a daily special such as olive and mushroom. There's a laid-back postcard-and-graffiti-style ambience that has so far admirably resisted gentrification. The servers are nice enough, but not effusive. Enough said. ▪ *622 NW*

23rd Ave; 227-5423; map:FF6; $; beer and wine; no credit cards;
local checks only; lunch, dinner every day. ⅃

Esparza's Tex-Mex Cafe ★★★ This rollicking down-home hangout is no longer just the best Tex-Mex restaurant in Portland—with loads of atmosphere, from the King on the jukebox to the marionettes dancing over the bar to nifty posters for Gene Autry Westerns in the back room. It's now, according to the neon sign on the bar, also the "Esparza's Tequila Shrine," with a wide array of curiously shaped bottles. This way, you can decide just which tequila goes with the Cowboy Tacos, filled with thick slabs of smoked sirloin, barbecue sauce, guacamole, and pico de gallo, or the Uvalde, a smoked lamb enchilada, or some *nopalitos*—the best cactus appetizer around. The menu and specials have a reach as wide as Texas—from red snapper to smoked pork loin (stuffed with spiced buffalo and ostrich) to tacos made from calves' brains. It's all hand-smoked and hand-designed by Joe Esparza, who perches at the bar, keeping as watchful an eye on the food as he does on the proceedings. ▪ *2725 SE Ankeny St; 234-7909; map:GG5; $$; full bar; AE, DC, MC, V; no checks; lunch, dinner Tues–Sat.*

Esplanade at RiverPlace (RiverPlace Hotel) ★★ Esplanade is a visually stunning place with picture windows that front the RiverPlace marina. Executive chef John Zenger has carefully designed a menu that might be described as Northwest nouvelle with continental input. The menu sings of Black Angus beef with four-peppercorn sauce and fire-roasted shallots, or pan-roasted sturgeon with huckleberry honey and mustard butter; and if execution sometimes seems wobbly, ingredients are always strong. Lunchers can light into a Northwest salmon club sandwich or fish and chips in microbrew batter. The deeply rich (and equally expensive) lobster bisque has endured, and elaborate salads run to choices such as grilled Bombay chicken with mango chutney dressing, or tea-smoked sturgeon with frisée. The admirable and scenic sit-down brunch, with a fantasy of a bread basket, is an excellent reason to gather at the river. ▪ *1510 SW Harbor Way; 295-6166; map:D5; $$$; full bar; AE, DC, MC, V; checks OK; breakfast, dinner every day, lunch Mon–Fri, brunch Sun.* ⅃

Fa Fa Gourmet It's in the 'burbs on the edge of a shopping center, but the Chia family makes this sprawling restaurant as authentically Chinese as you'll find in Vancouver. Chef/owner Tseng Chia has a skilled hand with spices and prepares both Sichuan and Hunan dishes. The menu is also popular with Japanese customers, and for good reason: a seaweed salad is on the menu, as are Drunk Chicken, five-spice duck, Bird's Nest Deluxe, crisp prawns in red chile sauce, and more routine family-style dinners. ▪ *11712 NE Fourth Plain Rd, Vancouver, WA; (360)260-1378; map:AA4; $$; full bar; MC, V; checks OK; lunch, dinner every day.*

Fat City Cafe ★ [KIDS] One look at the generous scoop of butter sitting atop the enormous pancakes and you know this place could never be called Skinny City. One taste and you probably won't care. Nothing is subtle, but that's fine with the regulars, who fill up this storefront in Multnomah just as they've been doing for years. Apparently it's fine, too, with the legions of newcomers who keep rolling into the village. The ham comes in slabs, the omelets could feed a family of four, the gooey cinnamon rolls are housemade, and the coffee is, well, hot. Lunchtime means the basics, and the old-time soda counter offers milk shakes worthy of it—when the machine's in order. ■ *7820 SW Capitol Hwy; 245-5457; map:II7; $; no alcohol; no credit cards; checks OK; breakfast, lunch every day.*

Fellini ★ Next door to Satyricon—famous for its long tenure as Portland's alterna-music headquarters—sits this way-hip lunch, dinner, and late-night eatery, where the food is better than you might expect from a place with so much attitude. There are menu items from around the world—Greece, Mexico, Thailand, Italy—and everything is quite good; not fussy, but good. Portions are substantial. You might start with an appetizer of hummus, tzatziki, olives, roasted peppers, and warm pita—and not want to go any further. But if you do, try the Bangkok Ho, a mound of crunchy vegetables in peanut sauce on brown rice, or the Zapatistas, a fire-roasted enchilada plump with vegetables, cheddar cheese, and chile sauce. Gyros and burgers round out the global offerings. This food is good for you, even if the secondhand smoke is not, and the black-light paintings, outdoor tables on sketchy NW Sixth Avenue, and black-Spandex-clad waiters who manage to convey nonstop boredom are so hip it hurts. ■ *121 NW 6th Ave; 243-2120; map:K4; $; full bar; MC, V; checks OK; lunch Mon–Fri, dinner every day.*

▼

Top 200
Restaurants

▲

Fernando's Hideaway ★½ There's a black-tie ambience and a spacious feel to this bi-level, downtown Spanish restaurant and bar, two factors that separate it from the city's other, more intimate tapas places (that's not to say you *have* to dress to eat here—it's still Portland, after all). The menu tangos, from the tapas menu with its plump prawns sautéed in chile oil and tender slivers of marinated octopus—a meal in itself when ordered from the bar—to the more ambitious dinners served back in the dining room, including a made-to-order paella on Sunday evenings. Finish with *helado limon*, a scoop of creamy lemon ice cream served in a frosty lemon, for dessert. Handily, there are about a dozen Spanish wines by the glass, along with an extensive list of wines by the bottle. ■ *824 SW 1st Ave; 248-4709; map:K4; $$; beer and wine; AE, MC, V; checks OK; dinner every day.* ⅁

Fiddleheads ★★★ Fernando Divina's vision of Western regional cuisine runs deep—back to a memory that there was regional cuisine before anybody called it the West. That can mean

Shoshone corn dumplings or Zuni-style succotash and fry bread, but it also means a dazzlingly skilled hand with all kinds of local fare, from a vibrant chowder of Dungeness, steelhead, and crawfish to a huckleberry sorbet that seems just off the mountain. Divina's vision—he calls it Cuisine of the Americas—reaches to masa-fried oyster tacos and posole, and he offers special, inspiring five-course vegetarian dinners. Located in Portland's laid-back (but rapidly gentrifying) Westmoreland neighborhood, Fiddleheads may be the most exciting of Portland's newer restaurants, set in a compact but elegant space adorned with Northwest Indian art. And just so you don't have to ask, *tatonka* means buffalo—braised with woodland mushrooms, mild chiles, and wild boar bacon. ■ *6716 SE Milwaukie Ave; 233-1547; map:II5; $$$; full bar; AE, DIS, MC, V; no checks; lunch Mon–Fri, dinner every day, brunch Sat–Sun.* &

Fong Chong ★★ Just because Fong Chong has been Portland's brightest dim sum place for a long time, don't think the offerings are just the same old chicken feet. Along with vibrant humbao buns and addictive sticky rice in a lotus leaf, you might find something surprising, such as shallot dumplings. This is where Portland's dim sum devotees put the cart before each course. The much larger House of Louie, under the same ownership, is across the street. But whether it's because of the Chinese grocery next door, or because the place is crowded and loud, or because watching the carts maneuver through the tables is like watching the Super Mario Brothers, we like Fong Chong better. It's fun, inexpensive, and impressively tasty. At night, Fong Chong is transformed into a quiet Cantonese eatery, with average preparations and a few surprises. ■ *301 NW 4th Ave; 220-0235; map:K5; $; full bar; MC, V; checks OK; lunch, dinner every day.* &

▼

Top 200
Restaurants

▲

Foothill Broiler ★ [KIDS] Come in at noon and you'll find yourself waiting in line—possibly longer than you might have expected—with socialites, construction workers, and realtors talking deals. This is a step-up-from-a-cafeteria kind of place, where you can have a hamburger and a cupcake—or a bowl of spaghetti and a malted milk shake. Burger patties come in three sizes, with good french fries or baked beans alongside. The cooks will even grill a tuna sandwich if that's the way you like it. The cafeteria line takes you past stalwarts like Jell-O with fruit and cottage cheese en route to some fine layer cakes, cheesecakes, and pies. Tile work, framed prints, and unexpected skylights in the back raise the interior from merely cafeterian to stylish. ■ *33 NW 23rd Pl; 223-0287; map:FF6; $; no alcohol; no credit cards; local checks only; breakfast, lunch Mon–Sat, dinner Mon–Fri.* &

Formosa Harbor ★ At lunch, this skillful, reasonably priced Chinese restaurant downtown is jammed; at dinner, finding a table is no problem. But at both meals, the flavors are vivid and clean—from

General Tso's Chicken to brimming bowls of soup or noodles. Try to make it here when asparagus is in season: Formosa Harbor stir-fries it quickly with a choice of meats, and produces something that tastes like spring on a chopstick. Lunch specials are highly satisfying, from twice-cooked pork to shrimp with cashews. Weekend nights, there is activity around the enormous two-story bar, but the more interesting events are happening in the kitchen. ■ *915 SW 2nd Ave; 228-4144; map:G4; $; full bar; AE, DIS, MC, V; no checks; lunch Mon–Fri, dinner Mon–Sat.* ఉ

Garbonzo's ★ The three falafel bars that make up this small chain dot the city—one on Hawthorne Boulevard, one on NW 21st Avenue, and one in Hillsdale—and each provides its respective neighborhood with a late-night spot to eat: Garbonzo's is open until 1:30am on weekdays and until 3am on weekends. The food is good—and, what's more, it's good for you. Chicken and kafta kabob, both served in pita bread, are stars on the menu, which is not particularly extensive—but not expensive, either. There are several salads to choose from, and a chicken soup that the kids will love. Can't sleep? Stop in for a midnight snack of hummus, baba ghanouj, and all the trimmings alongside the lamb kabob. Beats counting sheep any day. ■ *6341 SW Capitol Hwy (and branches); 293-7335; map:JJ6; $; beer and wine; AE, DIS, MC, V; no checks; lunch, dinner every day.* ఉ

Genoa ★★★★ For 25 years, the elaborate, minuetlike seven-course meals at Genoa have provided Portland with special interludes of elegance and artistry—and they seem to be getting even better. Cathy Whims, the current chef and co-owner, has been enlivening the kitchen with newer Italian inspirations, but without losing the distinctive Genoa grace notes.

The pasta course can still stop you in your tracks. Like the rest of the menu, it changes constantly, and might be ravioli di zucca, thin sheets enfolding squash, sweet potato, and biscotti crumbs. Preceded by an antipasto that could include marinated goat cheese and exquisite crostini, the pasta course is followed by the set entree of the evening, perhaps Muscovy duck with honey and grapes, something deft with fish, or a successful effort to make a steak more interesting—and Italian. That just gets you to a powerhouse dessert tray with a double-digit range of choices, from homemade pear ice cream with caramel to a creation that mixes fruit and chocolate into a result as intricate as a palazzo.

The remarkable part is that the extravagant meal and the three hours still pass leaving one seduced rather than overwhelmed. The famously dark dining room has lightened a bit, and the full experience is now balanced with a shorter option, offered on weekdays and early and late on weekends. Not every course will be spectacular, but a couple certainly will be, and the rest will be very good. Knowledgeable staff carefully describe the food and know the wine list. ■ *2832 SE Belmont St; 238-1464;* *map:GG5; $$$; beer, wine, and aperitifs; AE, DC, MC, V; checks OK; dinner Mon–Sat.* ♿

Giant Drive-In ★ [KIDS] The Giant Filler burger at this 900-square-foot drive-in resembles a natural wonder—the Grand Canyon with cheese. There are some 30 specialty burgers topped with the likes of soy sauce and pineapple, but the Filler is the one diagrammed on the company T-shirt: two burgers, ham, bacon, egg, cheese, and the kitchen sink. If you're less ambitious, order the Skinny, served with crisp fries and a real ice cream milk shake: it's like dying and waking up in 1955. And if the thick, addictive shake isn't enough of a dessert, try the homemade pecan pie. ■ *15840 SW Boones Ferry Rd, Lake Oswego; 636-0255; map:LL7; $; no alcohol; no credit cards; checks OK; lunch, dinner every day.*

Gino's Restaurant and Bar ★½ What was formerly the Leipzig Tavern—a smoky, dark watering hole created for those more interested in drinking than eating—has been transformed into the delightful Gino's. This is not the *au courant* Italian restaurant of the '90s—hip on authenticity, regionalism, or a different kind of pasta every day of the year—but good old-fashioned Italian-American cooking. Red-checkered tablecloths make a perfect backdrop for the fragrant (read "lots of garlic") and hearty food: steamed clams, caesar salad, wonderful garlic bread, and pasta—generous portions along the traditional meat-and-tomato theme, as well as linguine vongole and a ravioli daily special. The wine list alone, which features notable producers and remarkable prices (nothing over $15), is worth the trip across town. ■ *8057 SE 13th Ave; 233-4613; map:KK5; $–$$; full bar; MC, V; checks OK; lunch Tues–Sat, dinner Tues–Sun.*

▼

Top 200 Restaurants

▲

The Golden Loaf Bakery and Deli This small deli on Hawthorne offers delicious Middle Eastern fare in a humble setting. The hummus, baba ghanouj, and tabbouleh are addictive—especially when scooped up with Golden Loaf's own fresh-baked pita bread—and the prices are better than reasonable. Try the exotic *manaiish,* a pliable, round, flat bread rolled with tart spices and sesame seeds, accompanied by a bottle of pomegranate juice. ■ *1334 SE Hawthorne Blvd; 231-9758; map:GG5; $; no alcohol; no credit cards; checks OK; lunch, early dinner every day.*

Good Dog/Bad Dog A downtown hot dog stand with a pedigree, Good Dog/Bad Dog offers a dozen different sausages laden with fried onions in crusty baked rolls. It may be a challenge to your digestion, but your tongue won't be complaining as you work your way through Oregon Smokies, British bangers, garlic sausages, and specials such as Louisiana tasso sausages. They're made in-house, and are flavorful—if not always fiery. ■ *708 SW Alder St; 222-3410; map:H3; $; no alcohol; MC, V; checks OK; lunch, early dinner every day.*

Grand Central Bakery and Cafe ★

Everyone knows that the secret to making a good sandwich is good bread. Operating on that premise, Grand Central makes some of the best sandwiches in town: Black Forest ham and Swiss on sour rye, roasted chicken and cranberry chutney on Como, hummus and tomato on yeasted corn. Tables and countertop seating, as well as wine by the glass and an expanded menu, have successfully changed this spot's image from bakery to cafe. In addition to all the yummy breads and pastries, Grand Central sells marvelous cakes—chocolate, lemon, and carrot—by the slice or to take home whole. ■ *1444 NE Weidler; 288-1614; map:GG6; $; beer and wine; AE, DIS, MC, V; checks OK; breakfast, lunch, dinner every day.*

Gustav's German Pub and Grill ★

Many Portlanders grew up going to the Rheinlander on Sandy Boulevard, but as adults we're more likely to visit Gustav's German Pub and Grill when the craving for schnitzel and braised cabbage hits. The most recent addition to Horst Mager's fleet of restaurants, Gustav's lacks the German kitsch of its *vater*-restaurant, possessing a level of sophistication common to the city's upscale brewpubs. The food is undeniably hearty—Swiss cheese fondue, grilled bratwurst, rotisserie chicken, mashed potatoes—and truly satisfying on a cold and rainy Portland night. Wash it all down with a glass of Pilsner Urquel or Spaten Munich (just a couple of the many excellent beers on tap). Those who can't bear not to go to the Rheinlander should check out Gustav's Bier Stube, right next door. ■ *Gustav's German Pub and Grill: 12605 SE 97th; 653-1391; map:FF2; $$; full bar; AE, MC, V; no checks; lunch, dinner every day.* ■ *Gustav's Bier Stube: 5035 NE Sandy Blvd; 288-5503; map:FF4; $$; full bar; AE, MC, V; no checks; lunch, dinner every day.*

Gypsy ★

Everything happens late at this Northwest hot spot—often, late enough to annoy the neighbors. But the atmosphere in this uniquely decorated restaurant—which looks something like a 1950s vision of the 21st century—is lively and pulsing. In keeping with the vintage of the decor, the food tends toward comfort fare: meat loaf, large servings of macaroni, pizzas, and some livelier pastas. There are also more unusual items, such as Bermuda triangles—crisp tricornered chicken dumplings—but the emphasis here is more scene than cuisine. As a late-night place to see and be fed, the Gypsy draws a crowd. ■ *625 NW 21st Ave; 796-1859; map:GG7; $$; full bar; AE, MC, V; no checks; lunch, dinner every day, brunch Sat–Sun.* &

Hall Street Grill ★★

The owners of this longtime Beaverton restaurant have been riding the wave of seafood success in the 'burbs long enough; now they want a piece of the action in Portland, too. Their latest venture—the Pearl District's ¡Oba!, Portuguese for "great"—is too new to judge yet, but Hall Street regulars can rest assured that their restaurant isn't changing:

there are still fresh salads, made with a vast array of garden greens; plump crab cakes that satisfy equally well as a starter or as dinner; and steak-cut salmon served with roasted vegetables which just might make anyone forget that such a thing as beef exists (burning under the grill are local vineyard cuttings, giving salmon and seafood specials an inviting, tangy undertone). The rock salt–roasted prime rib is a permanent menu fixture—a favorite that has been known to sell out quickly—and the grilled steaks are terrific. A superb burnt cream with a hard sugar crust leads the strong list of desserts; berry cobbler, in season, is also a strong finish. ■ *3775 SW Hall Blvd, Beaverton; 641-6161; map:HH9; $$; full bar; AE, DC, MC, V; checks OK; lunch Mon–Fri, dinner every day.* &

Hands On Cafe ★★ If only every institute of higher learning had a cafeteria like this one. The campus of the Oregon College of Art and Craft may seem an unlikely place to sit down to dazzling baked goods—from scones to solid breads to stunning, ever-changing desserts—but the ovens here are as artful as the kilns next door. Low-key lunch and early dinner menus stress salads, soups, and stews, but this is not standard salad-bar fare: fresh tuna and pasta salad with capers, a cabbage roll stuffed with ground veal, white bean pâté on focaccia. At the popular Sunday brunch, the inspiration ranges from the Pacific Northwest to New Orleans to Peru. Pumpkin bread and bowls of strawberries sprinkled with candied ginger will keep you busy while you wait (and you might have to wait a bit longer than you'd like) for the main course to arrive. ■ *8245 NW Barnes Rd; 297-1480; map:GG9; $; no alcohol; no credit cards; checks OK; lunch, dinner Mon–Fri, brunch Sun.*

Harborside ★★ On a warm Portland afternoon—and there really are such things—Harborside may have the best location in the city. At one end of the RiverPlace promenade, it looks out on the Willamette and a marina full of gleaming boats. The restaurant is sizable, with terraced levels giving each table a view, but it seems to put almost as many tables out on the promenade. On any Portland evening, the Pilsner Room brewpub next door—run by Hood River's Full Sail Ale folks—gets almost as full. The substantial menu reflects many influences of the other McCormick & Schmick's outposts, but is a little more casual. Location and corporate ties make seafood a strong presence, but it might surface in different styles, such as seafood pot-stickers or Northwest salmon cakes. Harborside seafood stew shows both respect and spice, and fresh fish can be treated in striking ways. People who get enough maritime impact from the view might dip into blackened chicken fettuccine or a bronzed pork sandwich—and there are lots of designer pizzas. ■ *0309 SW Montgomery St (in River-Place); 220-1865; map:C5; $$, full bar; AE, DIS, MC, V; checks OK; lunch, dinner every day.*

Hawthorne St. Ale House ★½ Take away the boisterous element and what you have here is a fine place to eat. Spawned by Bridgeport Brewing Company, the pub takes beer as its theme, although that's easy to forget, given the upscale—especially for Hawthorne—menu and tony interior. The pizzas, baked in a wood-fired oven, are terrific, especially the one with pancetta and tomato. There's also a variety of knife-and-fork sandwiches and, to top it all off, a marbled fudge brownie served warm with vanilla ice cream. ■ *3632 SE Hawthorne Blvd; 233-6540; map:GG5; $; beer and wine; MC, V; checks OK; lunch, dinner every day.*

The Heathman Restaurant and Bar ★★★★ There's only one place in Portland—and perhaps not a lot of places anywhere—in which you could start with a napoleon of grilled apple and St. Andre cheese and move on to roast suckling pig. Philippe Boulot, who's been at the Heathman helm since the early 1990s, collaborates with his wife, Susan, native Portlander and pâtissier—and both have brilliantly left their marks. (Entrees and appetizers come and go, driven by the seasons and Philippe's inspirations, but Susan's warm chocolate gourmandise cake endures—joined, in season, by fresh berry napoleons.) Boulot doesn't exactly merge classic French cuisine with Pacific Northwest trends; rather, he expands the classics to absorb local ingredients, producing, maybe, a pasta tossed with Pacific prawns and buttery nuggets of foie gras or a stunning salmon in a pesto crust with a shard of crisp salmon skin planted on top. Or he might treat the salmon to a Thai barbecue. Boulot has been creating new wine events for the Heathman and diving deep into local produce—surfacing with fiddlehead ferns, organic baby greens and radishes, and a tart dried-cherry jus for roasted pheasant. The king salmon hash prevails at breakfast, and lunch inspires its own creations, including rich soups, pungent salads, and heartening stews. Evenings bring jazz, and brandy from upstairs and downstairs bars. ■ *1001 SW Broadway; 241-4100; map:G2; www.holog.com/heathman; $$$; full bar; AE, DC, MC, V; checks OK; breakfast, lunch, dinner every day.* &

Hidden House ★ Across the Columbia River in Vancouver, the Hidden family made their money with a brick factory in the late 19th century. Their handsome brick home was opened as a restaurant by Susan Courtney in 1976, and she has succeeded in turning it into a reliable—if old-fashioned—place for an intimate dinner or a comforting lunch. The "complete dinner" menu offers about a dozen standards (Swiss almond chicken, garlic-roasted tenderloin, roast pork tenderloin with peach salsa). A "beggar's banquet" of soup, salad, and homemade poppyseed or pumpkin bread is a midday favorite, as is the "BBFGT," a bacon, basil, and fried green tomato sandwich. There's a fairly inclusive Northwest wine list. A satellite spot, the **Paradise Cafe**, is open for breakfast and lunch next door (1304 Main St, (360)696-1612). ■ *100 W*

13th St, Vancouver, WA; (360) 696-2847; map:BB6; $$–$$$; beer
and wine; AE, DIS, MC, V; checks OK; lunch Mon–Fri, dinner
Tues–Sun.

Higgins ★★★ When chef Greg Higgins first headed a few blocks south from the Heathman Hotel, where he'd been a pioneer of Pacific Northwest cuisine, to his own place on Broadway, his dishes seemed at times to have a few extraneous ingredients thrown in without thought. But Higgins—the chef and the restaurant—has become increasingly sure-handed and consistent. That means a deeply, deftly seasonal Northwest menu, strong on local meats, poultry, and especially seafood—perhaps a saffron bourride of regional shellfish, or a delicate special of grilled Columbia sturgeon in a fish stock laced with anchovy. (This restaurant has a particular allure for people who like their fish cooked gently.) Spectacular presentation endures, especially in desserts, which might be a roasted pear in filo or a chocolate-almond-apricot tart. Thinner wallets will appreciate Higgins's bar next door, which serves bistro fare after 2pm every day—and opens for cigars after 10pm. This may be the only fine restaurant in the city that goes out of its way to welcome young children. ■ *1239 SW Broadway; 222-9070; map:F2; $$$; full bar; AE, DC, MC, V; checks OK; lunch Mon–Fri, dinner every day.* &

▼

▲

Hiro ★★ This unexpected little sushi bar in a Lake Oswego shopping center is marked by two things: Trail Blazer memorabilia—it's a hangout for team members, many of whom live in the suburb—and exquisite, impressive sushi. Behind the bar, Hiro himself assembles elaborate rolls and sushi pieces using ingredients of remarkable freshness and sometimes unusual identity: monkfish liver? The nightly specials board contains marine offerings uncommon in the region, such as a particularly rich variety of yellowtail, and there's usually toro, the fatter slices of tuna belly. When he's not sculpting small gems for the bar, Hiro is often assembling vast arrays of sushi to go. Everyone seems to know everybody here—even if no Blazers show up. ■ *6334 SW Meadows Rd, Lake Oswego; 684-7521; map:MM8; $$; beer and sake; AE, MC, V; no checks; lunch Mon–Fri, dinner Mon–Sat.*

Hokkaido ★ When you walk into this sizable Japanese restaurant, head right for the sushi bar that curls around the rear; it has the most interesting food here, and sitting at it will give you the best view of the evening's specials. (It will also speed up the service, sometimes a useful assistance.) Aim for the soft-shell crab Spider Roll, scallops in a creamy sauce, and the crunchy *ama ebi* shrimp. If you need hot reinforcement afterward, there's a remarkably reasonably priced *yosenabe*, a crowded and vivid seafood stew. Or you can always just return to the sushi specials. ■ *6744 NE Sandy Blvd; 288-3731; map:FF3; $$; beer and wine; MC, V; no checks; lunch, dinner Tues–Sun.*

Hot Lips Pizza ★ You'll have plenty of choices for toppings at this longtime favorite pizzeria: sun-dried tomatoes, Montrachet, Oregon blue cheese, fresh garlic, herbs soaked in olive oil, myriad sausages, and how about good old pepperoni? Patrons can choose from about 40 toppings in designing pies with lots of cheese and just enough housemade sauce, on a soft and chewy hand-thrown crust. Hot Lips does enough business in by-the-slice sales that it can usually offer a selection of four or five varieties. Besides the downtown location near PSU, there's a suburban branch in Raleigh Hills (4825 SW 76th Ave, 297-8424). ▪ *1909 SW 6th Ave; 224-0311; map:C1; $; beer and wine; MC, V; local checks only; lunch, dinner every day.*

Huber's ★½ One of the very oldest of Portland's watering holes, Huber's celebrated its 118th year—and uncounted numbers of turkeys served—in 1997 by doubling its size and breaking out toward the sidewalk with more dark wood tables and a showplace kitchen. It's also expanded its menu, but the core here is still turkey, in every form imaginable; this menu has more turkey recipes than a post-Thanksgiving weekend. If you're nervous about turkey salad or enchiladas, choose the standard version served with solid stuffing and creamy gravy. Evenings, the emphasis switches to Spanish coffee—with brandy, liqueur, and rum, mixed and set afire at your table. During these hours, the crowd gets even thicker than the gravy. ▪ *441 SW 3rd Ave; 228-5686; map:H4; $$; full bar; AE, DC, MC, V; checks OK; lunch, dinner Mon–Sat.* ⅃

Hunan ★½ If all the portions of chicken in tangy sauce served here were laid out in a row—which would be a great waste—they might rival the Great Fowl of China. The specialties here have been on the menu from the beginning, and there must be a reason for that. After nearly two decades, Hunan still produces some of Portland's most consistently good Chinese cooking, and at a more reasonable cost than many of the city's Peking palaces. Favorites such as Lake T'ung T'ing Shrimp, dumplings in hot oil, and beef with orange flavor grace the menu. And the restaurant's versions of the spicy standards—General Tso's chicken, twice-cooked pork, dry-sautéed string beans—are pungent and massively popular. ▪ *515 SW Broadway; 224-8063; map:I3; $$; full bar; MC, V; no checks; lunch Mon–Sat, dinner every day.*

Ikenohana ★★ The suburban strip-mall storefront opens into a modest space (with a tiny sushi bar in one corner) where Japanese paper screens and lanterns give a private and charming feel, and even when things are busy it's not noisy. The menu allows a wide range of options, from sushi and sashimi to tempura, katsu dishes, teriyaki, and noodles. You can't go wrong here: the sashimi is elegantly presented and very fresh and firm. A plentiful plate of sushi includes wonderful mackerel and eel.

Even the simple yakisoba noodles are spicy and cooked just right. If you look like you don't know how to mix the wasabe sauce for the sushi, the waitress will show you. ■ *14308 SW Allen Blvd, Beaverton; 646-1267; map:II9; $; beer and wine; MC, V; no checks; lunch Mon–Fri, dinner every day.* &

Il Fornaio ★★ Il Fornaio is, inescapably, a California chain. But once you forgive it that, you'll notice that the skill of the staff using its grills and ovens is undeniable, as demonstrated by everything from the wide range of crusty breads to the substantial menu of pastas and entrees. Lobster ravioli is lovely and briny, and if "chicken under a hot brick" sounds like fowl abuse, it somehow produces something meaty and pungent. The room is huge and at dinnertime is often filled with both diners and aromas; the aromas are rich, but one of the attractions here is that diners don't have to be. Morning is a mellower time, when small groups linger over cappuccino and whatever the bakers have just brought from the ovens (there are fresh pastries every morning). The menu goes on an annual tour of Italy; any given month features cuisine—from the breads to the wines—of a given region, from Sicily to the Veneto. ■ *115 NW 22nd Ave; 248-9400; map:GG6; www.ilfornaio.com; $$; full bar; AE, MC, V; local checks only; lunch, dinner every day, brunch Sat–Sun.* &

▼

Il Piatto ★★½ Since it opened in 1994, sweet Il Piatto has developed an almost cultlike following, in part because of its warm and reassuring atmosphere—the dining room is bathed in candlelight and furnished with well-worn treasures from Grandma's attic. The power of the menu is in the pasta, with almost a dozen options (the simplest are often the best). Steamed mussels in a broth of saffron and white wine and Torta al Formaggio de Capra (layered potatoes and herbed goat cheese) are a good start for a meal of appetizers, while a huge portion of aggressive liver-pâté crostini can not only fill you up but stand up to whatever reasonably priced wine you pick. The pork saltimbocca shows both liveliness and tenderness, while a cinnamon gelato makes an outrageous finale. ■ *2348 SE Ankeny St; 236-4997; map:GG5; $$; beer and wine; MC, V; checks OK; lunch Tues–Fri, dinner every day.* &

India House ★½ With stiff competition to keep it honest, India House has maintained its place near the top of the list of local Indian eateries. This pleasant restaurant serves the full range of Indian food with a consistency that has attracted a solid, happy constituency of downtown diners. Dishes from north and south India, including tandoori-roasted specials, make weekend dinner a crowded, festive affair, and the daily lunch buffet has caught on, too. Bring a group to adequately sample the generous menu. ■ *1038 SW Morrison St; 274-1017; map:H2; $$; beer and wine; AE, DIS, MC, V; no checks; lunch Mon–Sat, dinner every day.*

Indigine ★★½ Chef/owner Millie Howe's restaurant has followed its pattern for years now, and it's got the fans to keep it flying. Weekdays, Northwest ingredients are blended with Eastern spices and other inspirations, producing crisp-skinned pesto roast chicken or thick crab cakes at hearteningly reasonable prices. Saturdays are reserved for the blowout East Indian feast, an extravaganza that might start with something like tandoori chicken wings and apricot chutney, followed by a fresh seafood salad, and then lead into a searing shrimp-and-sausage vindaloo or chicken with saffron butter. Not everything bursts with fire and flavor, but the handcrafted items on the crowded dessert tray—from pecan pie to saffron-laced yogurt to *boccone dolce*—send diners away purring. When the weather allows, dinner on the back deck is delightful. ■ *3725 SE Division St; 238-1470; map:HH4; $$; beer and wine; MC, V; checks OK; dinner Tues–Sat, brunch Sun.* &

Ixtapa ★ After the long string of fast-food places along Highway 99W, this little restaurant right in Newberg is a refreshing change. You'll be given a hearty welcome as you're ushered into the narrow, colorful, and lively space. The service really hustles: you won't get much time to peruse the long menu. You may like your Mexican food a little spicier than this, but we think you will appreciate the freshness and lightness of the dishes. Grilled chicken is excellent, and the beans—the real test of a Mexican restaurant—are just right. ■ *307 E 1st St, Newberg; 538-5956; $; full bar; MC, V; checks OK; lunch, dinner every day.* &

▼

Top 200 Restaurants

▲

Jake's Famous Crawfish ★★ In a restaurant that's more than 100 years old, you should take some time to read the menu. That's a particularly good idea here, because the menu goes on for a while—from the fresh list of 30 to 40 items, to daily inspirations, to the long list of Jake's standards. It's a restaurant strong on tradition, from the polished wooden fixtures to the waiters' white jackets, but the menu runs to constant experimentation—you might find spearfish and prawn brochettes with habanero barbecue sauce, or stuffed prawns with Jamaican spices. More familiarly, there are bouillabaisse, Maine lobster, various terrific smoked seafood choices, and, at least at the right time of year, crawfish. The combination of old tradition and new ideas applied to very fresh seafood could keep Jake's going for another century. Those without reservations might wait an hour, knowing their patience will be rewarded with some of the better seafood in the city and some of the best service anywhere. Jake's was an early fan of Oregon wines, and it has also assembled a powerful dessert tray—starting with the trademark truffle cake and three-berry cobbler and ending (where you should) with the huckleberry crème brûlée. ■ *401 SW 12th Ave; 226-1419; map:I2; $$; full bar; AE, DC, MC, V; checks OK; lunch Mon–Fri, dinner every day.* &

Jake's Grill ★ ½ Sure, this is a McCormick & Schmick's place, so there is some fresh seafood. But it's also the three-meal-a-day Governor Hotel dining room, and a steak house feels right at home in this grandly restored building. Choose from eight kinds of juicy steak and fist-thick double lamb chops. The range is wide, with a comfort-food section of meat loaf and macaroni (almost too pedestrian) and more interesting sandwiches and salads, such as blackened rockfish and spinach, Dungeness crab roll, and a smoked salmon clubhouse. Appetizers and desserts are familiar from the other M&S outposts, along with the high-ceilinged, turn-of-the-century saloon decor. The styles shift during the day: lunch is casual, while the mood at dinner is more flashy. You really should dress for that huge wood-and-glass bar—and the lamb chops. ■ *611 SW 10th St; 241-2100; map:I2; $$$; full bar; AE, DC, MC, V; checks OK; breakfast, lunch, dinner every day.* ら

Jamie's [KIDS] If the family's on the prowl for a decent one-third-pound burger (or twice that size, if you request it), a real milk shake served with a pouf of whipped cream on top, and a little distraction in the form of '50s tunes on the jukebox, this may be your spot. A minichain, with restaurants in Eugene, Salem, Beaverton, and Portland, Jamie's succeeds because of its quality; the food is 10 times better than what you'll get at a fast-food chain restaurant. The menu is extensive (there are 17 choices each of burgers and sandwiches), and the ice cream in that Black Cow is the real thing. While we adults might wish that the atmosphere were a little warmer—with a little less goofy nostalgia—kids adore it. ■ *838 NW 23rd Ave (and branches); 248-6784; map:GG7; $; beer only; MC, V; local checks only; breakfast, lunch, dinner every day.*

Jarra's Ethiopian Restaurant ★★ Several Ethiopian restaurants have appeared in Portland over the years, but Jarra's is still the place to go for an explosive, sweat-inducing Abyssinian stew. This is the restaurant to teach you what's wat: made with chicken, lamb, or beef, the wat (stews) are deep red, oily, and packed with peppery after-kicks. Full dinners come with assorted stewed meats and vegetables, all permeated with vibrant spices and mounded on injera—the spongy Ethiopian bread that doubles as plate and fork. Tucked into the bottom of an old Portland home, this is the neighborhood's unequaled heat champ. ■ *1435 SE Hawthorne Blvd; 230-8990; map:HH5; $; full bar; MC, V; checks OK; dinner Tues–Sat.* ら

Jo Bar and Rotisserie ★★ The broiler brother of next-door Papa Haydn has emerged as a big player in the NW 23rd restaurant stakes; loyal customers have made this young restaurant a busy place. Two huge wood-burning ovens blaze along the back wall, roasting succulent chicken, duck, pork loin, and leg of lamb. Burgers and breads also go through the fire. Salads, such as smoked salmon and caviar on wild greens, are inventive and inviting. Service and desserts can be uneven, but the restaurant bloodlines here are terrific. And any place that makes Paul Thomas cabernet-merlot its house wine must know what it's doing. ■ *715 NW 23rd Ave; 222-0048; map:GG7; $$; full bar; AE, MC, V; checks OK; lunch Mon–Sat, dinner every day, brunch Sun.* ら

Kitchen Venus ★ A decidedly down-to-earth take-out place, with a handful of sit-yourself-down-and-have-a-piece-of-pie tables, Kitchen Venus resembles Aunt Bea's kitchen (if only *she* had played Grateful Dead on the RCA): there's a vintage 1950s fridge stocked with plenty of cold drinks, lots of chewy cookies for Opie to stuff in his pockets, and always something good to eat. Owner Samantha Le Vine has garnered a loyal following of harried diners in search of a quick meal that resembles Mom's cooking. The glass case exhibits the daily offerings—meat loaf, lasagne, enchiladas, postmodern polenta, macaroni and cheese, and so on—all available for take-out or eating in. There are also sandwiches and, for dessert, devil's food cake, Rice Krispies treats, and the mysterious moon pies. ■ *1932 NE Broadway; 288-3333; map:FF5; $; no alcohol; MC, V; checks OK; lunch, early dinner Mon–Sat, brunch Sun.*

Koji Osaka-Ya ★★ Sushi bars are everywhere, but this operation is clearly one of the best full-service Japanese restaurants around—especially since it's multiplied by four. From the original place in southwest Portland—with sumo wrestling broadcasts—to the tiny, always jammed place downtown, to the newer suburban outposts in Wilsonville and Beaverton, Koji offers a wide Japanese menu. Besides the basic teriyakis, there are a bunch of slurpy Japanese noodle soups (hold to the pork-bone broth), multiple *donburis* in elaborate arrangements atop oversize rice bowls, and pungent appetizers of vividly flavored bits of meat or tofu. The sushi bar is wide-ranging—try the salmon box sushi—and check out the day's specials; the chef may be doing something inspiring with ramen. If there have to be chain restaurants, Koji may have the strongest links. ■ *7007 SW Macadam (and branches); 293-1066; map:JJ6; $$; full bar; AE, MC, V; no checks; lunch, dinner every day.*

Kornblatt's ★ Kornblatt's may have added a fancy downtown branch in an architecturally striking building, but the core menu here is still chewy, determined bagels; pungent corned beef; and forceful chopped liver. The bagels come in mind-bending varieties—blueberry cinnamon?—but the super onion warms to the excellent smoked fish, just as the cold cuts are bolstered by a pickle bowl on the table. Cabbage borscht, blintzes, and kugel are inspiring, and there is even a shot at a pot roast, with latkes. If you have a choice, stay with the original branch on NW 23rd. ■ *628 NW 23rd Ave; 242-0055; map:GG7; $; beer and wine; MC, V; checks OK; breakfast, lunch, dinner every day.* ■ *1000 SW Broadway; 242-2435; map:I3; $; beer and wine; MC, V; checks OK; breakfast, lunch, dinner every day.* ら

▼
Top 200 Restaurants
▲

La Catalana ★★ This was one of the first Spanish-food restaurants to blaze trails to Portland a few years ago; now there are several more. La Catalana has held its own, though, mainly because the food in this sweet, relaxed place bursts with flavor, color, and intrigue. A half-dozen entrees share the menu with a strong list of tapas; paella is a specialty, but you might also try the grilled salmon fillet served with a minty salsa. Among the tapas are beautifully roasted *padron* peppers that are just spicy enough to heighten the flavors in a mild salad of tomato and *mahon* (Spanish goat cheese). Razor clams are lightly floured and fried in butter and olive oil with a burst of lemon—and a little magic. Servers here seem to know when you want to be left alone—or when they might ply you with samples from the kitchen. Lemon ice cream is luscious served in a hollowed-out lemon. La Catalana expanded a while back, making reservations less crucial; but if you prefer an intimate setting, call ahead and ask to be seated in the original dining room. ■ *2825 SE Stark St; 232-0948; map:GG5; $$; beer and wine; MC, V; local checks only; dinner every day.* &

La Cruda ★ It means "the hangover" in Spanish, but don't wait for the "morning after" to come in: La Cruda's a smart place to *start* the evening. Tacos, tortilla soup, burritos, enchiladas (including a spicy rock shrimp version that has quite a following), and quesadillas make up the menu; but the choices for fillings are numerous—try the pork—and tortillas come in four varieties (flour, roasted tomato, spinach, and chipotle pepper). The salsa bar mixes things up further: there are red and green salsas, and always something fruity, such as pineapple or melon. The place has a comfy quality—furnishings seem genuinely retro—and a lot of reasons to come back: great margaritas, a scintillating jalapeño-pumpkin ice cream, fresh chips. And if you do have a hangover, they make a fresh-tasting plate of breakfast tacos and a mean Bloody Mary. ■ *2500 SE Clinton St; 233-0745; map:HH5; $; full bar; MC, V; checks OK; breakfast Sat–Sun, lunch, dinner every day.* &

La Macchia ★½ Only two blocks away—yet worlds apart—from the California Pizza Kitchen's Oregon branch, La Macchia belongs only to Portland. Authentic Italian-style pizzas—sparsely adorned thin-crust wonders—are served in this unfussy and colorful eatery. It's the little things—panini sandwiches, cappuccinos in antique china cups, Italian Renaissance icons, unpretentious service, and the smell of fresh basil—that make La Macchia so charming. When weather permits, the outdoor patio is a great place to while away the afternoon with a glass of wine or to sit and listen to live tunes in the evening. ■ *2340 NW Westover; 226-8082; map:GG7; $; full bar; AE, MC, V; checks OK; lunch Tues–Sun, dinner every day.*

Lamthong ★ ½ Two restaurants with Broadway addresses, one in Beaverton and one in Portland, serve up equally delicious Thai cooking in interesting surroundings. Winning young waiters are straight out of *The King and I* in long white linen jackets, red velvet breeches, and white stockings, and they bring forth wonderful dishes. Crisp noodles, spicy beef—served hot and curled into a lettuce leaf resembling Hiroshige's wave—and flawless beef curry, the specialty of the house, laced with threads of fresh coconut, are among the offerings. Phad Thai provides a lovely blend of textures and flavors: lime, mint, cilantro, peanuts, noodles. The Portland location sports the classier dining room; both spots share the same menu. ■ *213 SW Broadway; 223-4214; map:I4; $$; beer and wine; AE, MC, V; no checks; lunch Mon–Fri, dinner Mon–Sat.* ■ *12406 SW Broadway, Beaverton; 646-3350; map:HH9; $$; beer and wine; AE, MC, V; no checks; lunch Mon–Fri, dinner every day.* &

La Prima Trattoria ★ ½ New chef Ken Gordon arrived in 1997 to redesign La Prima Trattoria's menu and bring it more down-to-(Italian)earth—even though this shopping-center restaurant had gotten off to a promising start only the year before. The huge wood-burning oven is at the center of attention, churning out chicken, trout, pizzas, and calamari, along with nightly specials such as a mixed grill. The menu runs trattoria-true to pastas, with a dozen offerings, including macaroni with four cheeses and lasagna with three. The kitchen makes its own sausage—found on pizzas and pastas—and you can get a sizable antipasto while you're thinking about it all. Despite the picture-window view of a parking lot, La Prima is comfortable and warm, an ornament to its suburban neighborhood, and quite possibly the best trattoria within 100 yards of a Fred Meyer anywhere. ■ *4775 SW 77th Ave; 297-0360; map:II9; www.citysearch.com\pdx\laprima; $$; beer and wine; AE, MC, V; checks OK; lunch Mon–Fri, dinner every day.* &

L'Auberge ★★★ This warm, three-level, dual-personality establishment has long been among Portland's more notable restaurants, with a cuisine that might best be called Northwest continental. In recent years it has wandered a bit, but new chef Michael Parmentier is bringing the menu back to its roots. The L'Auberge chicken, veal, and spinach pâté is a perennial favorite, along with the elegant desserts, led by the legendary poached lemon cheesecake. These days, dinner choices may also include smoked mushroom ravioli in a tomato-watercress coulis, Dungeness crab and crayfish cakes, or a vanilla-roasted poussin with a polenta terrine. At $39, the four-course prix-fixe dinner may dip into several themes.

Up a few steps from the relaxed, restrained elegance of the dining room, the bar is a softly lit den of upscale hipness with a well-stoked hearth in winter and, in all seasons, a witty, personable staff. Instead of the onion soup, the muscular bar menu, and the desserts, you could just get some cheese and brandy and a

▼

Top 200 Restaurants

▲

view of the fire—or, in summer, a deck that is all the outdoor
activity some Portlanders need. ▪ *2601 NW Vaughn St; 223-3302; map:FF7; $$$; full bar; AE, DC, DIS, MC, V; local checks only; dinner every day (Sun, dinner in bar only).* & *restaurant only*

Lemongrass ★★★ Just as Srichan Miller rose from a northeast Portland storefront into the larger Bangkok Kitchen, her daughter Shelley Siripatrapa has moved from the same storefront, where she opened Lemongrass in 1993, into an elegant old Portland Victorian, where she dispenses dazzling curries and seafood. The menu is limited, but the focus is powerful. Tastes here are bright and sharp, sweet and hot and tangy, from emerald pools of green curry to snap-your-eyes-open shrimp with garlic and basil. Even fried rice, a cliché in other places, here pulses with chile paste. There's a choice of heat intensity, but getting much past mild takes you into a place of pain. There are no reservations, and nothing is cooked ahead of time; you'll wait for a table, and then wait again at your table. But after you do, you'll come back and wait again. ▪ *1705 NE Couch St; 231-5780; map:GG6; $$; beer and wine; no credit cards; checks OK; lunch Mon–Tues and Thurs–Fri, dinner Thurs–Tues.*

Little Wing Cafe ★ Given this alleyway cafe's popularity with the Pearl District's lunch crowd, come noon it's hard to find a spot at one of the Formica tables. Standard lunch items (soup, salad, sandwiches) are gussied up with interesting and fresh ingredients, and all the sandwiches are served on Grand Central bread. Daily specials exhibit the kitchen's creativity; you might find a portobello mushroom burger or lemongrass chicken. While Little Wing is open from early morning until early evening, lunch is served only from 11am to 3pm; the rest of the time you can rest your gallery-going feet and eat a cookie. ▪ *529 NW 13th Ave; 228-3101; map:K1; $; no alcohol; MC, V; checks OK; lunch Mon–Sat.*

▼

**Top 200
Restaurants**

▲

London Grill (The Benson Hotel) ★★ In the hearts of many Portlanders, but power lunchers in particular, the London Grill occupies a permanent position. While Trader Vic's, its fellow Benson restaurant, has been replaced by a middling California Italian-food chain eatery, the London Grill remains steady. The tableside cooking carts still glide across the room, the ingredients are still of highest quality, the flambé flames still reach for the ceiling, and the strains of the harpist still wash over the deep, comfortable armchairs at each table. (Comfortable is good; you may be waiting awhile.) Waiters, practiced in the art of tableside service, produce endearing versions of steak Diane and crêpes Suzette, and the crab cakes are thick with crabmeat. But in many cases, both innovation and flavoring seem to be restrained (okay, subtle menu changes reflect an interest in heart-healthy cuisine). The longest wine list in town is especially strong on French bottlings. ▪ *309 SW Broadway; 295-4110; map:I3; $$$; full bar; AE, DC, MC, V; checks OK; breakfast, lunch, dinner every day, brunch Sun.* &

Main Street Restaurant Three meals a day are served in this cheery place—which in its lifetime has matured from a grocery to a deli to a restaurant. And though the food will never bring throngs of Portlanders over to Gresham, a wayward soul could wander in and not be disappointed. The Main Street Restaurant is a little hard to find unless you know your way around this east Portland suburb (next door is a housewares shop brimming with luxurious goods), but persevere: it makes a good stop on the way to Mount Hood or out to the gorge. The breakfast items don't always live up to the mouth-watering descriptions on the menu— with the exception of the delicious potatoes—but the espresso drinks will cheer you in a hurry. Lunches and dinners run the gamut from caesar salad to Sichuan noodles to a chicken fajita, with daily specials posted on a blackboard. ■ *120 N Main St, Gresham; 661-7877; $$; beer and wine; AE, MC, V; checks OK; breakfast, lunch Mon–Sat, dinner Wed–Sat, brunch Sun.*

Marco's Cafe and Espresso Bar ★★ [KIDS] In the stroller's paradise of antique-rich Multnomah, Marco's has near-landmark status. Hang out in the sunny dining rooms, with their high ceilings and intriguing prints on the walls; there's a rack of reading material by the front door. It's lovely anytime—some prefer breakfast, with the French toast stuffed with apples and cinnamon and drenched with apple-flavored syrup, while others vote for the variety of organic burgers at lunch. Then there are southwest Portlanders who prefer to wait for evenings, when Marco's turns into an imaginative dinner operation, and the nightly changing entrees can run to halibut with caramelized leeks and Chicken Roma. The desserts are Marco's own, and solid. Children fit right in. ■ *7910 SW 35th Ave; 245-0199; map:II7; $-$$; beer and wine; AE, DIS, MC, V; local checks only; breakfast, lunch every day, dinner Mon–Sat.* &

Marinepolis ★ [KIDS] Teaching your kids about sushi can be like teaching them about caviar; for your wallet's sake, you almost hope they don't like it. But in this branch of a Japanese chain (which somehow landed in a Beaverton shopping mall), the instruction can be relatively painless and even entertaining. Decent, inexpensive sushi circles the dining area on a conveyor belt, you pick off what you want, and when you're finished the waitress counts the plates. Kids are enthralled, the fish is fine, and even if there's a certain assembly-line feel to it, the kitchen does take requests. And you don't even have to teach your kids to say *maguro*—just have them point. ■ *4021 SW 117th Ave (Canyonplace Shopping Center), Beaverton; 520-0257; $; beer and wine; MC, V; no checks; lunch, dinner every day.* &

Marrakesh ★½ Step into Marrakesh and take a magic carpet ride to a place where low lights reveal tapestried walls, and yards of fabric are draped tentlike from the ceiling. The appeal at this exotic restaurant is in the atmosphere and drama of the evening;

▼

Top 200 Restaurants

▲

unfortunately, the food falls short of fabulous, but you'll probably be so occupied with the scene that you won't notice. At one of the knee-high dining tables, get comfortable on a cushion: you're here for five courses. The meal begins with the customary finger-washing ceremony and ends with the sprinkling of orange water over your hands. In between, you eat without the benefit of utensils (unless you order something like couscous, in which case you might wangle a fork). The first course is a cumin-and-coriander lentil soup, and next comes an eggplant salad. The sweetened *bastela royale* (chicken pie) paves the way for your entree—maybe lamb with eggplant or braised hare in a rich cumin and paprika sauce. The easiest way to sample the fare is to go with three friends and order the Royale Feast. ▪ *1201 NW 21st Ave; 248-9442; map:FF7; $$; beer and wine; MC, V; no checks; dinner every day.*

McCormick & Schmick's Seafood Restaurant ★★★ With an array of vast new McCormick & Schmick's seafood palaces extending from Los Angeles to Washington, D.C., the original M&S maintains its excitement and liveliness, along with a kitchen that skillfully handles its extensive fresh list. The fresh dragnet reaches from Alaska to Florida to Chile, and the fish it brings to share can end up in roasted garlic vinaigrette, a tandoori glaze, or a fresh raspberry beurre rouge. Still headlining, however, is grilled alder-smoked salmon, and that smoky aroma announces the restaurant a block away. The place is frequently jammed and offers a lively bar scene, complete with a pianist and an extraordinary selection of single-malt Scotches. Call early for reservations for the monthly Cigar Nights, which could smoke a salmon right in the dining room. ▪ *235 SW 1st Ave; 224-7522; map:H5; $$; full bar; AE, DC, DIS, MC, V; checks OK; lunch Mon–Fri, dinner every day.*

▼
Top 200 Restaurants
▲

McCormick's Fish House and Bar ★★ Chef Jon Wirtis has maintained this suburban outpost of the M&S empire as a solid seafood house, with only a few nonmaritime options. With the same fresh list—and the same knowing, professional service—as the other links in the chain, McCormick's Fish House produces solid, skillful food that sometimes surprises. The mood and the feeling are more casual than those at downtown locations, but don't take that as a sign that you can confidently walk in without a reservation on weekends, on Thursday nights, or for Sunday brunch. ▪ *9945 SW Beaverton-Hillsdale Hwy, Beaverton; 643-1322; map:II8; $$; full bar; AE, DC, MC, V; checks OK; lunch Mon–Sat, dinner every day.* &

Mediterranean Grill ★ Joe Wisher spent years traveling the Mediterranean and returned to open a restaurant in the Portland suburb of Milwaukie. The results? A tangy orange-cured salmon fillet or a chickpea pancake in a veal-stock sauce; or you might get as far from the Mediterranean as pork Normande. With any luck, the baked apple with caramel and mascarpone will be available at the finish. And despite the proximity of the 7-Eleven just down the hill, this is a very comfortable restaurant—the atmosphere of a seaside villa is enhanced by the stucco walls and an extensive display of Mediterranean artwork. Apparently, Wisher didn't pick up just recipes. ▪ *2818 SE Park Ave, Milwaukie; 654-7039; map:LL5; $$; beer and wine; AE, MC, V; local checks only; lunch Wed–Fri, dinner Wed–Sun, brunch Sun.* &

Misohapi ★ If you can get beyond the bizarre lighting fixtures (which look something like worms emerging from colanders) Misohapi might surprise you. This is especially so if you're craving comfort noodle dishes—charcoal chicken with vermicelli (a winner), phad Thai (nice too), or flavor-rich yakisoba with skewered teriyaki chicken. Or go with one of the less starchy Thai or Vietnamese entrees: ginger beef, black bean garlic pork, or a self-proclaimed Thai-style General Tso's Chicken (we were convinced). Misohapi does a brisk bento take-out business; on nice days you can take your meal outside to a table on NW 23rd, and make passersby envious. ▪ *1123 NW 23rd Ave; 796-2012; map:GG7; $; full bar; DIS, MC, V; local checks only; lunch, dinner Mon–Sat.* &

Montage, Le Bistro ★★½ Portland's definitively hip late-night hangout is now open for lunch; you won't get the 2am energy, but you'll get the same unexpectedly good Southern/Cajun cuisine. (When Montage says "spicy," it's not kidding.) If you join the later group, you may have to wait for a spot at the long tables for such Cajun specialties as Spicy Mac (glorified macaroni with Cajun gravy, jalapeños, tomatoes, and Parmesan), blackened snapper, or jambalaya topped with crab, rabbit sausage, or alligator meat. Dinners are both ambitious and unique—from spicy frogs' legs to alligator pâté to green eggs and Spam. Round out your meal with a slice of pecan pie. The loud hum of conversation and music is punctuated with waiters' shouts to the open kitchen announcing an order of an oyster shooter single. Lots of wines are offered by the glass, and are promptly refilled with a nod in the right direction. The topnotch waiters manage to look as if they're having as good a time as most of the guests. ▪ *301 SE Morrison St; 234-1324; map:G9; $; beer, wine, and selected liquor; no credit cards; checks OK; lunch Mon–Fri, dinner every day.* &

Murata ★★★ At Murata's tiny sushi bar, the specials are listed in Japanese, with a "translation" underneath: Japanese names spelled out in English. Compromise is limited at a restaurant that often seems directly aimed at visiting Japanese businessmen; it's perhaps the only restaurant in Portland that closes on weekends because its core clientele is on the Delta nonstop back to Tokyo. But Murata is the best Japanese restaurant in the city. Once the specials have been translated, they're often worth the culinary gamble—crisp grilled sardines, mackerel necks, layers of deep purple tuna. If there's kasu cod, by all means order it, and if you've got some friends along, try one of the *nabe*—huge bowls of stewlike soups, thick with seafood. Those with time, money, and nerve should order (in advance) an elaborate Japanese multi-course Japanese banquet, *kaiseki*, which starts at $35 per person and runs as high as your wallet allows. Murata has recently branched out with its own bento parlor. ▪ *200 SW Market; 227-0080; map:D3; murata@teleport.com; $$; beer and wine; AE, DC, MC, V; no checks; lunch, dinner Mon–Fri.*

Nature's Marketplace ★ Nature's, Portland's long-favorite natural food store, arrived in Vancouver a year or so ago, updating the food scene in southwest Washington with its wide selection of organic produce and hormone-free meat, cooking classes, and hip, ready-to-cook foods. Too, the grocer's restaurant is good enough to grab some headlines. Take out or eat your food here in the bright and ecologically correct Cafe Court. You'll find ethnic dips, casseroles, salads, pizzas, a baked potato bar, marinated meats, European breads, rich desserts, and even breakfast. ▪ *8024 E Mill Plain Blvd, Vancouver, WA; (360)695-8878; map:BB4; $; beer and wine; DIS, MC, V; checks OK; open every day.*

New Seoul Garden ★★ This sprawling restaurant-nightclub on the busy Beaverton-Hillsdale Highway is both a symbol of Portland's rising Korean community and a fine place to eat. The livelier action—and the flashier dressing—may be in the nightclub in the back, but in the extensive dining room up front, beaming servers spread out splendid food from one of the area's widest Korean menus. At the opening of your meal, the table is covered with small bowls of *namul*—Korean salads—from kimchi to tiny dried fish, all of sharp, vivid flavor. The waiter then produces platters of raw, marinated beef, chicken, or pork and turns on the grill in the middle of the table, and you're on your own. The result is generally dazzling, but if hot tables make you nervous, there are also some Japanese dishes and huge bowls of Korean soups (generally charged with red pepper, and often hotter than the grill). The food is consistently vibrant and explosive—the only question is how, after a meal of it, one could possibly do karaoke. ▪ *10860 SW Beaverton-Hillsdale Hwy, Beaverton; 526-8800; map:II9; $$, full bar; AE, DIS, MC, V; no checks; lunch Mon–Fri, dinner every day.*

New York Richie's You'll get East Coast lip here (owner Richie Brose doubles as Hercules at Hollywood's Universal Studios) as well as the "elbow-dripper" (Philly cheese-steak sandwich) in this eat-in/take-out joint with an attitude. Richie's specializes in wood-oven pizzas, hot pastrami sandwiches, Italian subs, imported hot dogs, fresh chili, pastas and sauces, and cheesecake. ▪ *8086 E Mill Plain Blvd, Vancouver, WA; (360)696-4001; map:BB4; $; beer and wine; no credit cards; checks OK; lunch, dinner Mon–Sat.* &

Nicholas ★ It would be easy to drive by this place and never wonder what's behind the almost nondescript storefront. If you do this, however, you're missing out on one of the great food finds of Portland. People in the know gather in this small, simple restaurant to feast on delicious Middle Eastern and Greek food— at unbelievably low prices. Try anything here—from creamy, garlicky tzatziki to unusual and enticing Mediterranean pizza, made exotic by the toppings or spices added. The falafel is arguably the best in town. ■ *318 SE Grand Ave; 235-5123; map:GG5; $; no alcohol; no credit cards; checks OK; lunch, dinner Mon–Sat.*

Noho's Hawaiian Cafe ★½ This is a place to put away some serious food. Korean-cut short ribs, marinated in honey, garlic, and sesame seed sauce, are sublime; Phil's ono chicken is marinated in a ginger sauce and cooked until the chicken is as tender as tuna. Matter of fact, ahi is available too, as is pork—sometimes as a special. Dinners are available in three sizes that translate— in our minds, at least—to medium, large, or mega portions, and come with rice and a macaroni or green salad. There's also a yakisoba noodle plate with four choices of sauce. Noho's (formerly Local Boyz) is usually packed; if you can't get a table to put that food away on the premises, you might consider ordering it to go. ■ *2525 SE Clinton St; 233-5301; map:HH5; $–$$; no alcohol; AE, MC, V; checks OK; lunch, dinner every day.*

▼

Top 200
Restaurants

▲

Obi ★½ There is a standard Japanese menu here, but to order from it would be to miss the point. Obi is about sushi, a point clearly made by its signature T-shirt, showing owner Masahide Arima holding a large fish and a knife. At Obi, he combines these two elements strikingly, slicing and sculpting Tiger Eyes (salmon in a circle of squid), Crazy Rolls, and Rock 'n' Rolls. Each is creative and vividly fresh, and the menu goes on, regularly thickened with his new inspirations, as Arima spins tuna, salmon, flying fish eggs, avocado, and seaweed into unexpected new arrangements. Obi is a comfortable oasis in the midst of Old Town, but sushi like this—and even the T-shirts—would be welcome anywhere. ■ *101 NW 2nd Ave; 226-3826; map:J6; $$; full bar; AE, DIS, MC, V; no checks; lunch Mon–Fri, dinner Mon–Sat.*

O'Connor's ★ This Multnomah Village restaurant, with a real bar and friendly waiters, is a magnet for young southwest Portlanders on dates, families out for something special, and oldtimers who know a good thing when they see it. These loyal patrons come one week to imbibe margaritas and eat roasted vegetable quesadillas on the deck out back (which looks over busy Multnomah Boulevard), and then come back the next for the traditional beef (or turkey) burgers washed down with a microbrew. Part of the menu is a lengthy specials list, on which the entrees climb to the $15 level, but it's not difficult to eat for much less here (and still eat well). Desserts, such as the surprisingly light and luscious raspberry chocolate cheesecake, are made on the premises. There's a downtown location in the Yamhill Marketplace. ■ *7850 SW Capitol Hwy; 244-1690; map:JJ7; $$; full bar; AE, DIS, MC, V; checks OK; breakfast, lunch, dinner every day.* ■ *826 SW 2nd Ave; 227-3883; map:G5; $$; full bar; AE, DIS, MC, V; checks OK; breakfast, lunch Mon–Sat.*

Old Spaghetti Factory [KIDS] In an immense building on the west bank of the Willamette sits the international headquarters for this chain of more than two dozen restaurants which began in Portland. It's *the* place to join 35 of your closest friends for a spaghetti dinner—just don't set your expectations for the food too high. Dinners include an iceberg lettuce salad (which is about as good as it could be), chewy sourdough bread, and spumoni ice cream. You might try the Manager's Favorite spaghetti (any two sauces), with marinara on one half and browned butter and mizithra cheese on the other. An amazing assemblage of antiques—and a restored trolley car—provide lots of distraction throughout the several dining areas, and it's worth going upstairs to step on the magnificent old brass scale. Reservations are not accepted, and there's often a wait, but you can stroll along the river or hang out upstairs in the bar; when your table is ready, your name will be blasted over the sound system. ■ *0715 SW Bancroft St (and branches); 222-5375; map:II6; $; full bar; DIS, MC, V; checks OK; lunch, dinner every day.* ♿

Old Wives' Tales ★ [KIDS] Like most people, we come here with the kids. What with the playroom and the turkey franks, it's a healthful alternative to the ball pit and burgers at McDonald's. But don't avoid the place—even if you don't like the idea of being seated, say, next to a table of eight at which half the chairs are high chairs. When Holly Hart opened the restaurant in the early '80s it doubled as a feminist gathering place, with a back room where men and women met for heated discussions, and an indestructible playroom for the younger set. Now, although the playroom is still an important part of the ambience, the back room has long since become the "quiet room." The food and mood are the same as they ever were—and although intriguingly adult things are done to seafood, the motif continues to be whole-wheat correctness. There are Hungarian mushroom soup (something like a meatless stroganoff), vegetarian enchiladas, and carrot cashew burgers, plus hot pastrami sandwiches or chicken-topped caesars for the unconverted. The children's menu meets parental approval—but kids will like it too. ■ *1300 E Burnside; 238-0470; map:GG5; $; beer and wine; AE, DIS, MC, V; checks OK; breakfast, lunch, dinner every day.*

Opus Too ★★ Fortunately, the cooks at the mesquite-fed grill are as deft with the fish as they are with the great hunks of red meat that are still available. And while the fish tends to appear in austere simplicity, the béarnaise and beurre rouge sauces prevail, along with Cajun and barbecue possibilities, daily specials, and a range of lunchtime sandwiches. The decor is urban cool—tile floor, dark-wood booths, and a long swivel-chair bar overlooking the open kitchen and grills. A terrific sourdough bread is part of the deal, as is the live jazz that floats in from Jazz de Opus next door. A respectable wine list, fine desserts, and piles of fettuccine. ■ *33 NW 2nd Ave; 222-6077; map:J6; $$; full bar; AE, DC, DIS, MC, V; no checks; lunch Mon–Sat, dinner every day.* &

The Original Pancake House ★★ Lots of things may change in Portland, but the people waiting patiently outside this landmark restaurant seem to have been there since 1955. This place hums from the time it opens at 7am practically until it closes in midafternoon. The sourdough flapjacks—from wine-spiked cherry to wheat germ to a behemoth apple pancake with a sticky cinnamon glaze—are made from scratch. A good bet is the egg-rich Dutch baby, which arrives looking like a huge, sunken birthday cake, dusted with powdered sugar and served with fresh lemon. Omelets big enough for two (made from a half-dozen eggs) arrive with a short stack. The service is cheerful and efficient; after all, there are people waiting for your table. ■ *8600 SW Barbur Blvd; 246-9007; map:HH6; $; no alcohol; no credit cards; checks OK; breakfast, lunch Wed–Sun.*

Paley's Place ★★★ Success—meaning swift recognition as one of Portland's top-level restaurants coupled with extensive national media attention—hasn't gone to this place's head: it's gone to its bar. By expanding into a glossy polished bar area next door, Paley's Place has almost doubled its size, as well as its meal-times—it now serves lunch as well as dinner. The food here is best described as exquisite, with Northwestern freshness married to an artistic sensibility that Vitaly and Kimberly Paley brought from the dance and art world—as well as the kitchens—of New York. At dinner, that can mean Thai curry-crusted halibut with basmati rice, marinated fennel, and sweet corn basil broth, or roast saddle of venison with bacon, warm potato hazelnut salad, and rhubarb glaze. Lunchtime might bring a fresh tuna club sandwich with lemon pepper aioli, or duck confit with local plums. Menus change with the harvests, but a lemon buttermilk tart, with a blueberry sauce and an artful meltingness, should always be in season. And with more seating, Paley's may now more frequently offer something it has often been unable to provide: an available table. ■ *1204 NW 21st Ave; 243-2403; map:GG7; www. citysearch.com/pdx/paleysplace; $$$; full bar; AE, MC, V; local checks only; lunch Tues–Fri, dinner Tues–Sat.*

Papa Haydn ★★★ In both locations—northwest and southeast Portland—the dessert list is literally musical: it trills from

Autumn Meringue (layers of chocolate mousse and meringue festooned with chocolate slabs) to *boccone dolce* (a mountain of whipped cream, chocolate, meringue, and fresh berries) to Georgia peanut butter mousse torte to white chocolate mousse charlotte. At the northwest branch, the rest of the menu runs to pastas and pâtés, with a few elaborate choices such as smoked chicken or seasoned prime rib. The place has come a long way since the days when it served up lunchy items so people wouldn't feel guilty about just eating dessert. The southeast location (on Milwaukie Avenue) is more low-key, but both have lines stretching out the door. ■ *701 NW 23rd Ave; 228-7317; map:GG7; $$; full bar; AE, MC, V; local checks only; lunch, dinner Mon–Sat, brunch Sun.* ■ *5829 SE Milwaukie Ave; 232-9440; map:II5; $$; beer and wine; AE, MC, V; local checks only; lunch, dinner Tues–Sat, brunch Sun.* &

Paparrazzi Pastaficio ★½ Pasta places are as common these days as SpaghettiOs were in the '60s, but Paparrazzi's sweet potato-Parmesan ravioli with caramelized onion sauce is like nothing Chef Boyardee could ever have dreamed up. In all, there are some 20 pasta dishes to eat in or take out (a popular choice for nearby Irvington families), such as gnocchi topped with marinara or wide noodles flecked with radicchio and pancetta. There are a few thin-crust pizzas to choose from as starters, but if you're deciding between those and dessert, hold out for the divine, silky tiramisu (dessert offerings also include the locally rare cannoli). Besides the food itself, value is one of this restaurant's strengths: most pasta dishes come with soup or salad, bread, and ice cream for under $15. (We usually spend $2.50 more and substitute the tiramisu for our dessert.) The bi-level interior is decorated with the work of the namesake photographers, but has grown increasingly warm over time. ■ *2015 NE Broadway; 281-7701; map:FF5; $$; beer and wine; MC, V; local checks only; dinner Tues–Sun.*

▼

**Top 200
Restaurants**

▲

Pavillion Bar and Grill at Greenwood Inn ★★ Not so long ago, this was a somnolent hotel dining room just off Highway 217, specializing in roast beef and older diners. Then chef Kevin Kennedy came in and, with the aid of the folks who managed the Heathman downtown, upgraded the menu with Muscovy duck, fresh sturgeon, and considerable skill. Dinners are now elaborate and pulsate with Kennedy's homegrown herbs, and the moon coming in through the skylight illuminates the smoke-roasted Ellensburg rack of lamb. Sundays, the noontime sun gets an even better view, beaming onto endless brunch tables laden with fresh seafood, waffles made to order, Kennedy's pungent pâtés, and enough desserts to get you through to Monday—if not Thursday. ■ *10700 SW Allen Blvd, Beaverton; 626-4550; map:JJ9; $$$; full bar; AE, DIS, MC, V; local checks only; breakfast, lunch, dinner every day, brunch Sun.* &

Pazzo Ristorante ★★★ The wood-grill aroma reaches out into the entryway, and the shrewd diner will follow it inside. At Pazzo, one of Portland's most beloved restaurants, the dazzling menu ranges from thick veal chops to daily fish specials, which might involve an ethereal sea bass. Pasta offerings may include the trademark smoked salmon ravioli in lemon-asparagus cream and a skillfully executed risotto with woodsy wild mushrooms. Pazzo's dining options are a brick dining room perfumed by the grill, a bar festooned with hanging garlic, or one of several glass-enclosed private rooms. (There's also Pazzoria, a pizza, panini, and pastry hangout next door.) On Friday and Saturday nights, there's reserved seating in the romantic downstairs wine cellar. Knowledgeable and engaging servers recite the day's specials in reverent detail. Listen closely to the entire description; the kitchen lavishes particular care on side dishes, and your entree decision may depend on whether the accompaniment is silken garlic mashed potatoes, a forceful risotto, an enlivened bed of spinach, or an aggressive Tuscan bread salad. We hope the departure in late 1997 of executive chef and guiding light David Machado, who has moved over to the Heathman enterprises, won't be felt in the dining room. ■ *627 SW Washington St (in the Vintage Plaza Hotel); 228-1515; map:I3; info@pazzo.com; www. pazzo.com; $$$; full bar; AE, MC, V; no checks; breakfast, lunch, dinner every day.* &

Perry's on Fremont ★ [KIDS] The pies—the first thing you see on entering—are huge, and hugely popular; this place moves a lot of marionberry. Then there are great tic-tac-toe brownies and huge slabs of cake. Perry's draws lots of kids (and their parents) with its cheeseburgers and milk shakes; it's virtually the Alameda neighborhood's family center. On the entree and pasta list is a chicken pot pie that's everything chicken pot pie is supposed to be. ■ *2401 NE Fremont St; 287-3655; map:FF5; $; beer and wine; AE, DC, DIS, MC, V; checks OK; lunch, dinner Tues–Sat.*

Pharmacy Fountain You're not only walking into an inviting breakfast and lunch place; you're walking into 1955. This old soda fountain inside the Town Pharmacy is what nostalgia should be but hardly ever is: the waitresses smile, the omelets fluff, the meat in the turkey sandwiches is hand-carved from actual turkeys, and the cookies are inspiring. Almost every swiveling bar stool in the long, narrow eatery is occupied by folks who know the waitresses by name and who order eggs and hashbrowns for breakfast, enjoy half a grilled meat loaf sandwich and a cup of tomato soup for lunch, or maybe just share a late-afternoon milk shake. Don't even think of asking for an espresso. ■ *2334 W Burnside; 241-1137; map:GG7; $; no alcohol; no credit cards; local checks only; breakfast, lunch Mon–Sat.*

Pho Hung ★½ When both your doctor and your mother recommend soup, Pho Hung will fill their prescription. For $5, you can immerse yourself in a curative bowl —"tureen" might be more accurate—of Vietnamese beef soup thick with noodles, vegetables, cilantro, and beef, and choose from a row of Asian hot sauces waiting to boost the megatonnage. The soup comes in different styles, but the basic message is the same; and while there's little else on the menu, you'll never leave hungry. ■ *4717 SE Powell Blvd; 775-3170; map:HH4; $; no alcohol; no credit cards; checks OK; lunch, dinner every day.*

Pho Van ★½ Another great place to get pho, the beefy noodle soup of Vietnam, Pho Van is packed with devoted fans morning, noon, and night (hours are 9:30am to 8pm). There's a take-out menu if you can't wait. Not in the mood for soup? The menu has other options, including a delicious noodle-charbroiled shrimp combination. ■ *1919 SE 82nd Ave; 788-5244; map:II3; $; beer only; DIS, MC, V; no checks; lunch, dinner every day.* &

Pizzicato ★½ These yupscale gourmet pizzerias tower over their megachain competitors and over many local pizza places that have been in business a lot longer. Credit Pizzicato's success to the imaginative pairings of fresh ingredients on pies (red potatoes and prosciutto, for instance), as well as classics—like pepperoni—done with respect. There's a caesar salad that's garlicky good, and a daily special, which you can buy by the slice for lunch at several of the locations. The best bet may be the simplest: the luscious pizza Margherita is little more than crust, cheese, and tomato sauce, but it's divine. ■ *1749 SW Skyline Blvd (and branches); 221-8784; map:HH8; $; beer and wine; AE, MC, V; checks OK; dinner every day.*

▼

Top 200 Restaurants

▲

Plainfield's Mayur ★ Plainfield's has been in business for two decades—much longer than any other Portland Indian restaurant—but its longevity doesn't distinguish it as much as do two other factors: its formality (china, crystal, and the absence of a messy lunch buffet) and its wine list (with wines dating back to the 18th century). The tandoori dishes, roasted in authentic style in a huge oven, are highlights, but don't miss the biryanis, fragrant rice concoctions served with intriguingly edible silver foil—much as the maharaja might have had centuries ago. ■ *852 SW 21st Ave; 223-2995; map:GG7; www.plainfields.com; rich@plainfields.com; $$; full bar; AE, DC, MC, V; no checks; dinner every day.* &

Portland Brewing Co.'s Brewhouse Taproom and Grill ★½ There's nothing "micro" about this microbrewer's showpiece brewpub, in northwest Portland's industrial zone. Huge copper kettles greet you at the entrance, but there's plenty of space for diners to pull up a seat in the main room; in the smaller, quieter dining room to the back; or outside on the inviting patio. Beer is the thing here, but the food is a good match for the brew: sausages, onion rings, steamers, beer-battered fish and chips, salads. The atmo is nice: a bit Old World, but cleaner and better lit than the Hofbrauhaus ever was, and big enough to accommodate a macro crowd. (Call if you're not sure how to find the place; it's easy to get lost in this area.) ▪ *2730 NW 31st Ave; 228-5269; map:FF7; $-$$; beer and wine; AE, MC, V; local checks only; lunch, dinner every day.* &

Pumpernickles Many who frequent this neighborhood cafe never even glance at the menu. Instead, they order their coffee at the counter and take in the lavish spread of homespun desserts and pastries—fruit cobblers, bread pudding, coffee cake, muffins, and cookies. While the sweets hold the greatest appeal, the "take out or hang out" menu delivers simple, honest fare: bagels and granola for breakfast; soup, salad, and sandwiches for lunch. A recent expansion doubled the seating area and added a quirk—video poker machines in the back. ▪ *344 NE 28th Ave; 230-2349; map:FF5; $; beer and wine; MC, V; checks OK; breakfast, lunch every day.*

Red Electric Cafe ★½ This is a soup-and-sandwich spot that redefines the genre: order a cup of creamy tomato soup and you'll find it comes with pesto-graced crostini. Put that cup of soup next to a grilled mozzarella and tomato sandwich on Grand Central's toasted Como bread, and you won't begin to miss the bag of chips or the floppy pickle that often graces such an order. The special of the day might be sloppy joes or a meat loaf sandwich, and there's cold beer or fresh lemonade to go along with the half-dozen burgers. Breakfasts—the standards—are delicious and hearty. The once-close quarters were expanded late in 1997; now there's room to spread out—and it still feels cozy. A real find. ▪ *6440 SW Capitol Hwy; 293-1266; map:JJ7; $; beer and wine; DIS, MC, V; checks OK; breakfast, lunch, dinner Tues–Sat, brunch Sun.* &

Red Hills Provincial Dining ★★½ In many ways, Red Hills is an ideal wine-country stop. You'll be received warmly by jovial co-owner Alice Halstead in this country-house-turned-restaurant, while chefs Nancy and Richard Gehrts preside in the kitchen. The simple dinner menu of a half-dozen items changes weekly, and the choices are all intriguing. Penne with olives, capers, and Montrachet cheese is perfectly balanced, beef tenderloin is thick and succulent, pork medallions on white beans are simple but flavorful. You get the idea: only the best of European country cooking. And all the details are just right, whether it's bread dusted with fresh rosemary or a crisp salad of greens or lightly cooked vegetables. Desserts are interesting, too, like a rich, chewy fennel cake or raspberry-filled chocolate cake. Add to this an outstanding wine list, with a huge selection from all over the world, and you have a meal you'll want to linger over. ▪ *276 Hwy 99W, Dundee; 538-8224; $$; beer and wine; MC, V; checks OK; lunch Tues–Fri, dinner Tues–Sun.*

Red Star Tavern and Roast House ★★½ The folks who came up from San Francisco to open the Fifth Avenue Suites Hotel in 1996 had a shrewd idea: they hired Mark Gould, formerly of Atwater's and one of the most creative young chefs in Portland. Although he's since moved on, Gould left his mark at Red Star: the kitchen uses a wood grill to cook up huge, family-size platters of pork loin, duck, and other meats, and everything from oysters and mussels to heavily laden flat breads passes through the oven. The smokiness can be a bit pervasive, but portions are sizable and the atmosphere is entertaining—the tone reflects the interior's giant workingman murals of the restaurant's bounty. A great place for breakfasts too. ■ *503 SW Alder; 222-0005; map:H4; $$; full bar; AE, DC, MC, V; no checks; breakfast Mon–Fri, lunch, dinner every day, brunch Sat–Sun.* &

Riccardo's Ristorante ★ Owner Richard Spaccarelli is a serious enophile, as his more than 300 bottles of Italian-only wine (and Riccardo's own wine shop across the way) attest. The rising kitchen is strong on veal dishes, from an impressively meaty veal chop (with a lively brandy demiglace) to a pungent, tender saltimbocca. The menu also includes juicy lamb chops and a half-dozen mostly meatless pastas. Dishes can be a bit uneven, but the service has sharpened pleasantly. This is one of the few places around where you can chase your pasta with a glass of grappa— or a selection of them. The outside dining area blossoms in nice weather. ■ *16035 SW Boones Ferry Rd, Lake Oswego; 636-4104; map:MM8; $$; full bar; AE, DC, MC, V; checks OK; lunch Mon–Fri, dinner Mon–Sat.* &

Rich's ★ Housed in a historic brick building, Rich's is a popular spot in Tualatin. Part of the appeal is in the range of dishes— from a bistro menu that includes mid-priced and -portioned entrees (including a fisherman's stew) to a daily list that features some wonderful items. You might find a roasted half chicken stuffed with prosciutto, garlic, and sage under a crust of Asiago cheese, or a tasty red pepper linguine tossed with basil, kalamata olives, shiitake mushrooms, grilled leeks, and Sonoma Jack cheese. Two *can* eat for relatively little here (there are plenty of offerings for under $10)—but prices, like the menu and the dress code, range from the modest to the extravagant. ■ *18810 Boones Ferry Rd, Tualatin; 692-1460; map:MM9; $$; full bar; AE, DC, MC, V; checks OK; lunch Mon–Fri, dinner every day, brunch Sat–Sun.*

The Ringside ★★ Sure, lots of people speak well of the fried chicken or the fish, and there really is a mean seafood caesar. But after more than 50 years, the only real question for most fans of the Ringside is which cut: the New York, the filet mignon, or the prime rib? People come here for beef, and that's what they get, in large, juicy slabs. In this territory these steaks are hard to beat;

for texture, color, flavor, and character, they're everything you could want from a hunk of steer. Still, it's the plump, light, slightly salty onion rings, made with Walla Walla sweets, that single-handedly made the Ringside famous; an order is essential. The dignified black-jacketed and bow-tied waiters are eminently professional, and the wine list is substantial—especially if you're looking for something to go with beef. ▪ *2165 W Burnside; 223-1513; map:GG7; $$; full bar; AE, DC, MC, V; checks OK; dinner every day.* ⅍

Roland's ★★ The best reason to go to Gresham since MAX. Roland Blasi's traditional continental cuisine—sizable portions and strong flavors, gathered from his cooking odyssey through four continents—has taken root in Gresham. Roland's is a very personal restaurant in feel and menu; Blasi draws ideas from the full range of European cooking, and comes up with some of his own. So you're offered not only a pungent gypsy chicken, but also a heartwarming pasta Angelo made with Italian sausage, and a deep, fragrant onion soup. ▪ *155 SE Vista, Gresham; 665-7215; $$; beer and wine; MC, V; local checks only; dinner Tues–Sat.* ⅍

Ron Paul Catering and Charcuterie ★★ In some ways, this operation's ambitions are growing with the addresses—the latest of which is **Ron Paul Express**, a take-out spot downtown (507 SW Broadway, 221-0053). The Ron Paul restaurants are reaching toward wine dinners and upscale cooking classes, but the core here stays the same: a range of distinctive dishes such as barbecued chicken, spinach-mushroom lasagne, pan-fried oysters, Sichuan noodle salad, and some of the best specialty breads in town (try the rich, dark walnut wheat). The ever-changing dinner menus have gotten considerably more advanced, from elaborately prepared chops and fish to cassoulet. Desserts, from rhubarb pie with a filo crust to ultrarich Black Angus Cookies to a carrot cake with ricotta and raisins, rank high. Quality control here is an obvious priority: the kitchen smokes the sausages, mixes the pâtés, and cures the salmon—which, on the homemade bagels, brightens one of Portland's more inviting weekend brunches. ▪ *1441 NE Broadway; 284-5347; map:FF5; $$; beer and wine; AE, MC, V; checks OK; continental breakfast Mon–Fri, lunch every day, dinner Mon–Sat, brunch Sat–Sun.* ▪ *6141 SW Macadam Ave; 977-0313; map:JJ6; $$; beer and wine; AE, MC, V; checks OK; continental breakfast Mon–Fri, lunch every day, dinner Mon–Sat, brunch Sat–Sun.* ⅍

Rustica ★ This cheerful, expansive trattoria, with its open kitchen and Italian street scene fresco all over the back wall, has become a favorite with families in northeast Portland. Prices are reasonable, with most pastas around $10, and some dishes— notably the carbonara and the scampi—are vivid and impressive. Lunchtime adds pungent panini: crusty sandwiches such as grilled eggplant with smoked mozzarella or nifty grilled sausages with caramelized onions and aioli. Either time offers one of the great desserts of the Pacific Slope: an ice cream sandwich of creamy gelato between two crisp Florentine cookies with a chocolate sauce drizzle. With its big sweeping picture windows on bustling NE Broadway, the restaurant's name may be rustic, but its appeal is decidedly urban. ■ *1700 NE Broadway; 288-0990; map:GG5; www.citysearch.com/pdx/rustica; $$; full bar; AE, DIS, MC, V; local checks only; lunch Mon–Fri, dinner every day.* &

Ruth's Chris Steak House ★★½ It's possible, of course, to order something here besides steak. There is chicken, and a catch of the day, and oversize, $20-a-pound lobsters. But it would really be missing the point. Ruth's Chris is about steak, and the real choice is among filets, T-bones, and New Yorks. The steaks—served in solitary splendor on snow-white platters—are fit for royalty, especially the outsize porterhouse for two. They're also expensive, especially considering that everything—potato, vegetable—is à la carte. But if you and your wallet are prepared to take on some serious beef, garlic mashed potatoes, and creamed spinach, Ruth's Chris will come through splendidly and provide all the other steakhouse accoutrements: solid onion rings, crab-stuffed mushrooms, cheesecake, and an extensive red wine list, although with limited Northwest options. You might want to avoid the New Orleans–style appetizers, a vestige of this national chain's Crescent City roots. Just think beef—and you'll still be thinking it the next day as you work through your doggy bag. ■ *309 SW 3rd Ave; 221-4518; map:I5; $$$; full bar; AE, DC, MC, V; no checks; dinner every day.* &

Saigon Kitchen ★★ The two branches of this restaurant are among the best of Portland's seemingly endless supply of Vietnamese eateries. The menu—more than 120 items long—features Thai dishes as well as the predominantly southern Vietnamese offerings. Standouts are the spicy soups—try the sour catfish concoction with pineapple(!)—and the stews and ragouts, which go well with white or fried rice. The service is brisk and efficient at both busy locations. If the cheerful, enthusiastic waiters bring you a dish you didn't order, consider this: their unintentional error might be the perfect subliminal suggestion because when it comes to food, you can't go wrong here. ■ *835 NE Broadway; 281-3669; map:FF5; $; beer and wine; AE, MC, V; no checks; lunch, dinner every day.* ■ *3829 SE Division St; 236-2312; map:HH5; $; beer and wine; AE, MC, V; no checks; lunch, dinner Mon–Sat.*

Salvador Molly's Sun Spot Cafe ★★ [KIDS] Who would've thought? A couple of years ago when it opened, Salvador Molly's seemed little more than a bright spot in a tired little strip mall off the Beaverton-Hillsdale Highway. But before long, fans had passed the word along that this place was outrageously fun; pretty soon the "dining room" had spread outside to a charming covered balcony, and diners were queuing at the door. They come for the new Latin cuisine: Willapa Bay corn-crusted oyster tacos, mouth-sizzling jerk grilled chicken, jambalayas studded with shrimp and sausage, and the never-disappointing tamale-of-the-day. And they come for the mood, which is just plain good. Nobody's in a hurry (and if you are in a hurry, you're sure to be disappointed), but that's part of what makes this place happen. What's the rush? Sip a margarita, crack a few peanuts, enjoy the wait. ■ *1523 SW Sunset Blvd; 293-1790; map:II7; $–$$; full bar; AE, DC, MC, V; checks OK; lunch, dinner Tues–Sat.* &

Sammy's Restaurant and Bar ★½ There have been a number of notable restaurants on this site in the last 10 years, but Sammy's seems to have the staying power that eluded its predecessors. When Sam Pishue, founder and longtime successful proprietor of Opus Too, decided to open another restaurant, he stayed with what he knew. As a result, the best things here are hot off the grill—steaks, chops, and seafood—although the menu is flecked with pastas and Greek specialties. Subtlety may not be a strong point, but the meats are good, the room is comfortable, and the artfully assembled bar is popular and crowded. Sunday brunch is a particular success, especially on warm weekends when brunchers spread out on the tables that stretch along NW 23rd, and the atmosphere of urban sophistication makes the just-baked cinnamon twists taste even better. ■ *333 NW 23rd Ave; 222-3123; map:GG7; $$; full bar; AE, DC, DIS, MC, V; no checks; lunch, dinner every day, brunch Sat–Sun.*

Saucebox ★★★ When Chris Israel, proprietor of Zefiro, opened up this sleek, small, slacker-black place, he seemed to be thinking in terms of a hangout—a place for Portland's gilded youth to drink deep into the night. But somewhere along the way, Saucebox turned into one of the city's most alluring restaurants—from the plate of salty, chilled soybeans that's delivered to your table as you peruse the menu, to the music that begins around 10 each night (there's live Afro-jazz on Thursdays). The small, carefully assembled pan-Asian menu runs to noodles, chicken dumplings, and a Thai curry, with a few more substantial elements such as steamed fish in a banana leaf and an intense, fragrant Javanese grilled salmon fillet, crisped in soy, garlic, and ginger. Hardly anything costs more than $10—and it's still a good place for that drink. ■ *214 SW Broadway; 241-3393; map:J4; $; full bar, AE, MC, V; local checks OK; lunch Tues–Fri, dinner Tues–Sat.* &

Sayler's ★½ This place—or, rather, these places—could be called Portland's low-profile steak houses; they don't have all the high-protein hoopla of the downtown beef palaces. But for

decades now, Sayler's has been setting out solid, reasonably priced steaks, and the crowds continue to come. The kitchen serves the basics here—steak and baked potato on a sizzling black iron platter—but the basics are done admirably, especially the filets. Fish and fried chicken are also available, but steaks are really the point, especially when they're served in an environment that's this relaxed. And the good value extends to Sayler's best and best-known deal: a 72-ounce sirloin absolutely free—if you eat it all in an hour. ■ *10519 SE Stark St; 252-4171; map:H9; $$; full bar; AE, DIS, MC, V; checks OK; dinner every day.* ⅃
■ *4655 SW Griffith Dr (just across from Beaverton Town Square), Beaverton; 644-1492; map:II9; $$; full bar; AE, DIS, MC, V; checks OK; dinner every day.* ⅃

Shakers ★★ What can you say about a place that produces turkey burgers that you really *want* to eat, instead of just feel you should? Or that cures its own corned beef for a Reuben that boasts more meat than mess? Or where both of those lunch triumphs play a clear second fiddle to legendary breakfasts: Scottish oats served with a pitcher of milk; thick challah-bread French toast; blue-corn pancakes? The original owner—and inspiration—returned after a hiatus in the mid-'90s; the battalions of Americana salt and pepper shakers never left (there are now about 25,000 sets). In the booming, redeveloping Pearl District, lots of locals consider Shakers their oyster. ■ *1212 NW Glisan; 221-0011; map:L2; $; beer and wine; no credit cards; checks OK; breakfast, lunch Wed–Sun.*

Sheldon's Cafe at the Grant House ★★ The 1849 Grant House, named for Ulysses S. Grant, doubles as a folk art museum and a cafe where American cuisine is emphasized. Its location at Fort Vancouver, with veranda and herb garden, is quite charming. For lunch, soups, salads, quiches, sandwiches, and regional specialties, including the favorite deviled eggs and house-smoked meats, are the bill of fare; for dinner, a Northwest bistro menu features pasta, salmon, Willapa Bay oysters, and grilled duck breast. Apple crisp and praline gingerbread tempt for dessert. And, frankly, we'd come back anytime for the free regional folk art exhibit. ■ *1101 Officers Row, Vancouver, WA; (360)699-1213; map:BB5; $$; beer and wine; MC, V; checks OK; lunch, dinner Tues–Sat.*

Square Peg ★½ Portlanders love the thrill of discovering the little cafe off the beaten path, happening on an unexpected meal when the original intention was a simple cup of coffee. Sleek, modernistic Square Peg, located on the northern end of the North Park Blocks, is one such treasure. Mornings begin here with cappuccino and pastry, while lunch might be small, tasty sandwiches or one of several different salads: mixed greens, tabbouleh, or green lentil. The roasted-tomato soup with Marsala

Restaurants

▼

Top 200
Restaurants

▲

63

and thyme could warm you on the chilliest of days; the vegetarian lentil is another soup to hope for. The lunch menu is available through the dinner hour, and there are a few evening specials as well: pizza, mussels, and polenta—made singular with flavors of roasted mozzarella, green curry, and portobello mushrooms. ■ *422 NW 8th Ave; 224-0511; map:K3; $; beer and wine; MC, V; checks OK; breakfast, lunch, dinner Mon–Sat.* &

Swagat ★★ This Beaverton tract house across from Target looks as if it should produce Rice Krispies treats, not great Indian food. But somehow, people enter the door and—at least spiritually—never leave. Moving from the pillowy *dosas*—giant pancakes wrapped around a filling of curry or lentils—diners slip eagerly into tandoori dishes with a barbecue bite, spinach paneer laced with cheese cubes and fire, or a spicy, buttery Chicken Makhani. It's hard to spend much money here even at dinner, but the lunch buffet is the best deal. The vindaloos may be vibrant, but the atmosphere is low-key; the feeling is Beaverton, not Bengal. In late 1997, Swagat expanded to a large, flashy outpost on Portland's NW 21st Avenue at Lovejoy; it finally gained a location as hot as its tandoori. ■ *4325 SW 109th Ave, Beaverton; 626-3000; www.swagat.teleport.com; $; beer and wine; AE, DIS, MC, V; checks OK; lunch, dinner every day.* ■ *2074 NW Lovejoy St; 227-4300; map:GG7; www.swagat.teleport.com; $; beer and wine; AE, DC, MC, V; checks OK; lunch, dinner every day.*

▼

Top 200 Restaurants

▲

Sweetwater's Jam House ★★½ After starting out in a tiny outpost in the Hollywood district, this lively Caribbean spot has moved to larger (and unquestionably cooler) digs in the refurbished Belmont Dairy. In the process, it's lost none of its fire—peppered shrimp and goat curry could cauterize your taste buds—or its fun, with terrific barbecued ribs and jerk chicken and zippy, fruity chicken skewers. Sides are stunning, from dark, molasses-infused corn bread to ethereal coconut rice, and three of them (including the not-for-Thanksgiving curried pumpkin) come together for the veggie-flashy Rastafarian plate. There is also an extensive list of Caribbean rums, and a wicked list of things the bar does with them. ■ *3350 SE Morrison St; 233-0333; map:GG5; $; full bar; AE, MC, V; no checks; dinner every day, brunch Sun.*

Tad's Chicken 'n' Dumplings [KIDS] A down-home country restaurant, 20 miles east of Portland as you head up the Columbia Gorge, this decades-old Oregon institution is popular with kids, bargain-hungry families, tourists—and fanciers of chicken. Steaks, prime rib, salmon, and halibut are also on the menu. Sit at a window table where you can watch the bottle-green river, and top off your meal with ice cream or homemade pie. The place is usually packed, particularly for Sunday dinner. ■ *943 SE Crown Point, Troutdale; 666-5337; $; full bar; AE, MC, V; checks OK; dinner every day (early dinner Sun).* &

Tapeo ★★½ Northwest Portland may be a bit too drizzly to evoke Spain, but the menu and atmosphere here can get you close. Thirty different tapas—small plates designed for casual munching—and a list of 20 different sherries can make you feel trans-Iberian, especially in a place with small tables and a general sense of no hurry at all. The idea is to start by combining a few cold tapas—maybe some marinated trout, or ham and cheese on thick toasted bread—with some hot items, such as pork tenderloin with goat cheese and ham or the *zarzuelita*, seafood in brandy, almonds, and cinnamon. Then, after some sipping and some conversation, and some wiping off the empty plates with crusty bread, retrieve the menu and explore a bit further. As in a sushi bar, the bill can mount up, but it will record some striking flavors. Come summer, tables outside make NW Thurman seem even more southern European. ■ *2764 NW Thurman St; 226-0409; map:GG7; $$; beer and wine; DIS, MC, V; checks OK; dinner Mon–Sat.* &

Taqueria Chavez ★ Sandwiched between a McDonald's and a used car lot, this unassuming taqueria makes authentic Mexican food: hand-patted tortillas and knock-your-sombrero-off chile sauces that warm the heart and stomach lining of those who eat here. Your choice of *birria* (a deliciously spiced and tender shredded beef), chorizo (sausage), tongue, pork, or chicken fills the small tacos that are topped with onions and cilantro. Rely on the person behind the counter to guide you through the menu, past the familiar burritos—which, though good, don't compare to the tamales. ■ *5703 SE 82nd Ave; 777-2282; map:II3; $; no alcohol; no credit cards; no checks; lunch, dinner every day.*

Tara Thai II ★ Tigard suffered from a deficit of Thai food until Tara Thai House of Beaverton branched out, a couple of years back, to this spot on the neon-wracked Pacific Highway. (The menu contains Laotian dishes as well.) The multilevel dining room at Tara Thai II is a bright and inviting spot; the noise level seems as comfortable for two as it does for 10. Food is happy too: salad rolls are fresh and plump, and prawns done in garlic sauce with black pepper, ginger, and onion give your mouth a nice spice explosion. Tom kah gai—the chicken soup made with coconut milk and ginger—is as rich as expected; a little goes a long way. From the list of Lao specialties, try the grilled beef, served with a peppery dipping sauce. Order a Thai beer to go with the spice, or a sweet Thai iced tea. The Beaverton location features a similar menu. ■ *11475 SW Pacific Hwy, Tigard; 293-2040; map:KK9; $$; full bar; AE, DIS, MC, V; local checks only; lunch Mon–Fri, dinner every day.* & ■ *4545 SW Watson Ave, Beaverton; 626-2758; $$; beer and wine; DIS, MC, V; checks OK; lunch Mon–Fri, dinner every day.*

Tennessee Red's ★½ You can smell this southeast Portland storefront a block away—the question is, which of its five barbecue sauces are you smelling? With its powerful smoke pits, Tennessee Red's can gild chicken, beef and pork ribs, pork loin, and brisket with Texas, Carolina, Memphis, and Arkansas sauces—plus an Oregon version with hazelnuts. The meat is juicy and deeply smoky, and the possible sides extend from corn bread to beans and rice to intense mashed potatoes. There are also a number of ambitious barbecue sandwiches, which require both large appetites and large hands—and a certain indifference to the cleanliness of your shirt. Most of the barbecue heads out the door, but if basic tables and chairs and lots of aroma fit your idea of ambience, you can consume your barbecue before it even thinks about cooling down. ■ *2133 SE 11th Ave; 231-1710; map:HH6; $; beer; MC, V; local checks only; lunch, dinner Mon–Sat.* &

Thai Little Home ★ It's not as fancy as similar joints across the river in Portland, but here Serm Pong and his family prepare fresh, home-cooked Thai food that Vancouver locals like just fine. *Yum nuer* (sliced beef salad with cucumber, seasoned with chile and lime juice) rivals the popular *pra koong* (shrimp with chile paste, lemongrass, and lime juice); and we've enjoyed both *mee krob* (crisp Thai noodles) and chicken satay at the beginning of meals. Service is friendly, informed, and fast. ■ *3214 E Fourth Plain Blvd, Vancouver, WA; (360)693-4061; map:BB5; $; beer and wine; AE, MC, V; local checks only; lunch Mon–Fri, dinner Mon–Sat.*

Thai Orchid ★★ It's a weekday evening, but there's a stream of glossy youthful Portlanders flowing into this low-profile Burnside storefront—maybe for the Evil Jungle Noodles. Owners Na and Penny Saenguraiporn consistently produce reasonably priced and more than reasonably spiced Thai food. The place looks so mild, you may be surprised by both the size and range of the menu and its powers of heat generation—a fact not lost on faithful take-out customers. Entrees, especially a seafood in chile sauce and a deep-fried whole fish, tend to be more interesting than appetizers. Beef salad is pungent and mouth-clearing—and now it's clearing mouths at a second outpost in West Linn. ■ *2231 W Burnside St; 226-4542; map:GG7; $; beer and wine; MC, V; checks OK; lunch Mon–Fri, dinner every day.* &■ *18740 Willamette Dr, West Linn; 699-4195; map:NN5; $; beer and wine; MC, V; checks OK; lunch Mon–Fri, dinner every day.* &

Thai Restaurant ★½ If you look quickly, you might think it's still a fast-food restaurant. But when you taste the Emerald Pork and its spinach and peanut sauce, the Panang Nuea—beef in a blast of fiery red curry—or the sizzling salad of grilled shrimp with chile and lemongrass, you may be transported, culinarily speaking, far away from this fast-food strip location. ■ *14211 SE*

McLoughlin Blvd, Milwaukie; 786-0410; map:MM4; $; beer and wine; MC, V; no checks; lunch, dinner Mon–Sat. &

Thai Touch ★ Thai Touch looks like a lot of other Thai restaurants in Portland: a bevy of banquet chairs, wall-to-wall carpet, and a modest attempt at decorating. What it lacks in ambience, however, it makes up for in exciting cooking. One taste of the red curry—tender chicken in a spicy broth of chile-infused coconut milk—and you'll wonder why you haven't been here before. The menu is quite long, listing both the familiar (tom kah gai soup, phad Thai noodles, green curry) and the vernacular, such as "The Ocean," a spicy medley of shellfish and vegetables. Lunch is a good bargain: for $3.95, you get your choice among four featured entrees, plus an appetizer and soup or salad. ■ *4806 SE Stark; 230-2875; map:GG4; $; no alcohol; MC, V; no checks; lunch, dinner Tues–Sun.*

Thai Villa ★½ The heat thermometer here ranges from "calm" to "volcano" (with little in between). A popular Lake Oswego restaurant, Thai Villa specializes in pungent soups served swirling in a moat around a pillar of flame, and a wide range of seafood dishes. The chef is handy with basil, garlic, and subtle hints of sweetness, and the prices are reasonable, especially on a cost-per-tingle basis. It's a good thing this place sits near the Lake Oswego fire department, because someday someone is going to take an innocent bite of "volcano" *gang galee* (chicken curry with potatoes) and self-combust. ■ *340 N 1st St, Lake Oswego; 635-6164; map:KK6; $; beer and wine; MC, V; no checks; lunch Mon–Fri, dinner every day.* &

Thanh Thao ★½ This Hawthorne-area Thai/Vietnamese restaurant does a brisk take-out business, which may be the way to go, since getting a table is no easy work. It's also a good place to be a regular, because that's the only way you'll work your way through the extensive menu before the year 2000. Some of the food is very good: on the short Thai menu the chicken coconut soup is silky-smooth, punctuated with snow peas, mushrooms, and bites of chicken, and the phad Thai noodles, topped with crunchy bean sprouts and bits of peanuts, are fine (in fact, noodle dishes—Thai or Vietnamese—are usually a sure bet). You'll find some ordinary dishes here (like peanut chicken), but all are generous. In the realm of more exotic fare, the menu satisfies with such things as squid with pineapple, tomatoes, mushrooms, and celery, and a curried goat dish. ■ *4005 SE Hawthorne Blvd; 238-6232; map:GG4; $; beer and wine; AE, MC, V; checks OK; lunch, dinner Wed-Mon.* ■ *8355 SE Powell Blvd; 775-0306; map:HH3; $; beer and wine; AE, DIS, MC, V; checks OK; lunch, dinner every day.*

3 Doors Down ★★★ In just a few years, this dinner spot has made a real impact on the Hawthorne neighborhood—first because its deft mingling of Northwest seafood and Italian instincts offers a lively, inviting local option, and second because its no-reservations policy often leaves a line of hungry diners out on the street. Fans come for the bountiful seafood Fra Diavolo, shrewdly grilled salmon on polenta, and the half-dozen firm and flavorful pastas. The small, spare storefront, three doors down from Hawthorne Boulevard (hence the name), has a warm atmosphere—if a considerable noise level—and a way with garlicky steamed clams. There are occasional slips, but the odds are in your favor, especially if you start with the outsize antipasto of tender marinated eggplant and finish with the intense chocolate mousse cake or the walnut torte with a zinfandel sabayon. ■ *1429 SE 37th Ave; 236-6886; map:GG5; $$; beer and wine; AE, DC, MC, V; checks OK; dinner Tues–Sat.* &

Three Square Grill ★½ This determinedly down-home neighborhood place, in the Hillsdale Shopping Center just a few doors from Nature's, has built a strong local following with its brunches and lunches: deft omelets and French toast in the morning, and unusual sandwiches—pulled pork barbecue, for instance—and intricate hash dishes at noon. Three Square has also gotten attention for its particularly nifty mashed potatoes and its other interesting sides, but the news here now is an ambitious drive at dinner. Prices remain neighborhood-reasonable, but the menu features items such as cassoulet, and an evening's specials might include roast pork tenderloin with bing cherry sauce or Oregon sea bass Grenobloise. The customers are still happy; they just have more options. ■ *6320 SW Capitol Hwy; 244-4467; map:JJ7; www.citysearch.com\pdx\threesquare; $$; beer and wine; MC, V; checks OK; lunch Tues–Fri, dinner Tues–Sat, brunch Sat–Sun.* &

Tiger Bar ★ The question isn't whether you're hungry enough to eat here; it's whether you're cool enough. If you think you can carry it off, put on lots of black and lots of attitude and drop by— the place doesn't really fill up until 10:30pm or so—for some creative, highly reasonable Asian food. What sticks out here are the satays, a half-dozen choices from tiger prawns (with a coconut-tamarind sauce) to lamb chunks (dusted with five spices and accompanied by a Vietnamese pineapple dip). Pastas are uncertain, but curries are lively, and nothing will cost you too much. Aside from the just-ready-for-prime-time age level, the Gen X ambience is marked by continuously playing TV sets hung on the walls. Especially with the sound off, they really can't compete with the satays. ■ *317 NW Broadway; 222-7297; map:N4; $$; full bar; AE, DIS, MC, V; local checks only; dinner every day.* &

Tina's ★★½ Owners Tina Landfried and husband David Bergen work their magic in a small, squat building by the side of the road: a vest-pocket herb-and-salad garden outside, plain white walls inside. As for the food, there's a spirit of innovation and creativity. The half-dozen entree choices are on the chalkboard: try rabbit risotto or grilled pork tenderloin in port-garlic sauce. Soup might be a flavorful cream of cucumber with dill and cilantro, and the green salad is simple and absolutely fresh. Tina's offers a good selection of local wines by the glass, all reasonably priced. There's not much elbow room, but it's a terrific place to relax and unwind after a wine-country day; lots of local winemakers do. ■ *760 Hwy 99W, Dundee; 538-8880; $$; beer and wine; AE, MC, V; checks OK; lunch Tues–Fri, dinner every day.* &

Toulouse ★★ If the sole appeal of Toulouse was as Portland's only steady source of the southern French bean stew known as cassoulet, it would be a gain for the city. But the place also offers impressive items from its fiery wood oven, such as rich pork chops, vividly moist chicken, and a dazzling veal chop with a Madeira sauce. The menu makes successful forays into other parts of the European continent for dishes such as gravlax and pasta with wild mushrooms. Desserts, such as tarte Tatin and silken vanilla crème brûlée, are memorable. The big warm room, with an almost equally outsize bar next door, is rapidly becoming a downtown hangout, and warm weather promises a backyard cigar patio. ■ *71 SW 2nd Ave; 241-4343; map:I6; $$; full bar; AE, MC, V; no checks; lunch Tues–Fri, dinner Tues–Sun.* &

Tribeca ★½ Chefs change at Tribeca, but the crab cakes persist— which is a fortunate thing. This comfortable corner restaurant on Portland's rising Restaurant Row has gone through several makeovers, and the newest seems a bit livelier and spicier, with offerings such as barbecued duck confit and chipotle-and-honey-infused chicken. You'd probably also want to check out the tequila-and-lime-cured gravlax, and the bar's a promising place to encounter the tequila directly. Desserts have been consistently interesting, and the ambience can seem a bit gentler than some of the other places on the row. ■ *704 NW 21st Ave; 226-6126; map:GG7; $$; full bar; AE, MC, V; local checks only; dinner every day.*

▼
Top 200
Restaurants
▲

Trio ★½ Located in a low-key residential neighborhood of northeast Portland, Trio has three different intriguing dining spaces—and manages to fill them all with interesting food. A semi- elaborate dining room, a bistro-style bar area, and a pastoral backyard garden are all endearing places to dine. Staffed by alumni of the popular Cafe des Amis, Trio changes its menu constantly, creating a certain inconsistency but offering up some striking creations as well, such as a chipotle-and-molasses-rubbed pork loin or a balsamic-glazed salmon. And in the bistro area, with its impressive bar at the back of the room, a cherry-chocolate cake or a roast duck salad roll with hoisin sauce can make the pleasant surroundings seem even more lovely. ■ *4627 NE Fremont; 249-3247; map:FF4; $$; full bar; AE, DIS, MC, V; local checks only; dinner Tues–Sat.* &

Typhoon! ★★½ Bo Kline does a Thai cuisine with more colors than curry. From openers of *miang kam* (spinach leaves that you can fill with a half-dozen ingredients) and beggar's purses of succulent shrimp, the menu ranges into a kaleidoscope of curries, inspired seafood dishes, and pungent Thai noodle dishes. (The King's Noodles, with chicken and most of the spices you can think of, has fanatic devotees.) Scored into a checkerboard grid, a fried fish blossoms into a pine cone. Kline has a particularly deft hand with shrimp and fish, allowing the seafood's delicate flavors to surmount ginger, garlic, basil, and some spices that could cook a flounder by themselves. The atmosphere is hipper than that of many Thai restaurants, with colorful plates decorating each place setting, and an indoor-outdoor option when the weather allows. The restaurant also offers 50 different Asian teas—but with these chiles, you might want to stick to beer. ■ *2310 NW Everett (in the Everett Market); 243-7557; map:GG7; $; beer and wine; AE, DC, MC, V; no checks; lunch Mon–Sat, dinner every day.* ♿

Umenoki ★ ½ When a Japanese restaurant hangs a samurai sword over the sushi bar, it's serious. And Umenoki is. A quick, skillful sushi chef does remarkable things with yellowtail and mackerel, especially when he combines them in a trademark roll called Saba Street. There's a mountainous roll of tuna and smoked salmon called—appropriately—Red Mountain, and California rolls and Umenoki's own San Francisco roll benefit from fresh real crabmeat instead of surimi. Hot dishes include crisp, greaseless tempura and specials such as New York steak teriyaki. Umenoki is a very comfortable, traditionally decorated Japanese restaurant—all blond wood and paper screens—but the sushi can have the impact of the samurai sword. ■ *2330 NW Thurman St; 242-6404; map:FF7; $$; beer and wine; MC, V; no checks; lunch Mon–Fri, dinner Mon–Sat.* ♿

▼
Top 200 Restaurants
▲

Vista Springs Cafe ★ [KIDS] Portland Heights neighbors pack this place for gourmet pizzas; microbrews or huge, thick milk shakes; and sandwiches or pasta. Even if the pizzas lack some of the spark that pizza fiends have learned to expect in the late '90s, they're loaded with all the right toppings: olives, prosciutto, Thai chicken, sun-dried tomatoes, feta cheese—and you can always put together your own combination. The red-ceilinged, low-lit room has a velvety feeling—with booths along the walls and strings of twinkling lights hung about. A welcoming spot; nice folks, too. ■ *2440 SW Vista Ave; 222-2811; map:HH7; $; beer and wine; AE, DIS, MC, V; checks OK; lunch, dinner every day.* ♿

Waterzooies Northwest ★ ½ Seafood is the pride of Waterzooies, where they skillfully smoke their own salmon out back. The salmon is part of the seafood sampler appetizer, a wise choice as a starter, and from there you might move on to another oceanic dish, such as sautéed halibut cooked with steamer clams and enlivened with pesto, or sautéed snapper coated in pecans and bathed in a delicate orange sauce (apparently a centuries-old recipe—you'll soon understand why it's still around). There are non-fish options too: the grilled half chicken is marinated in a garlicky black bean sauce and served on rich wild-mushroom polenta.

Among the dessert offerings might be a bread pudding jazzed up with sour cherries and crème fraîche or a wedge of caramely chocolate heaven. Housed in a bright turn-of-the-century home on NW Thurman Street, Waterzoies is simply decorated with oak chairs and white tablecloths; color is supplied by the art hung on white walls. The shaded garden in the back is a popular place to dine during summer months. Our only warning: Beware the noisy, battery-powered pepper grinder during the salad course, which could discourage even the most ardent pepper-lover from partaking. ■ *2574 NW Thurman St; 225-0641; map:GG7; $$$; full bar; MC, V; local checks only; lunch Tues–Fri, dinner Tues–Sat.* &

Widmer's Gasthaus ★ The giant brewing vats loom over the kitchen at this restored industrial-area hangout, and that's not accidental. But the careful craftsmanship that raised Widmer Brewing from two yeasty rooms in northwest Portland to a nationally known maxi-microbrew also surfaces in both the cooking and the restoration of the space. The old Albina relic of a building is now a haven of polished wood, copper, and glass, and the dining space keeps growing. The food is simple German and American—sausages, sauerbraten, goulash, and thick sandwiches—but it's tasty and substantial. The atmosphere is equally warm, and both the cuisine and the ambience benefit considerably from a six-beer sampler, in miniature mugs, extending from black *bier* to fruity Widberry. Your crowd might want to think of it as an appetizer, with a pitcher of lemon-laced Hefeweizen as the entree. ■ *955 N Russell St; 281-3333; map:DD7; $; beer and wine; AE, DIS, MC, V; local checks only; lunch, dinner every day.* &

Wild Abandon ★½ In its quiet neighborhood setting, this small dining room may surprise you with its rich and quirky appointments: dramatic paintings and murals, golden hands that emerge from the walls to hold candles, and white tablecloths. The menu looks like a typing student's C-minus assignment (there's a startling lack of capital letters), but otherwise it reads well: you might start your meal with a cocktail and a plate of grilled prawns served with red pepper–cilantro aioli, and follow that with the grilled pork tenderloin, skillfully finished with a pomegranate-ginger glaze. Each day there's a house-made ravioli; any day you can get an excellent caesar. Desserts—especially the exotic fruit sorbets (maybe strawberry-rhubarb mint)—are a sweet finish. Wild Abandon is a romantic, understated place to have dinner, and you'll probably like it so much that you'll want to try the luscious omelets at Sunday brunch. ■ *2411 SE Belmont; 232-4458; map:HH5; $$; full bar; AE, DIS, MC, V; local checks only; dinner every day, brunch Sun.* &

Wild Heron Cafe ★ [KIDS] One of the region's nicer juice bars is in Lake Oswego, left over from the days when this place was run by the crew at Nature's. The restaurant changed hands a few years ago, but you can still get fruity and/or veggie drink concoctions with names like Ruby Tuesday or Lighter Shade of Pale—blended while you wait. The juice is orchard fresh, and the food is fine too: three meals a day with highlights such as French toast made with braided cardamom bread, a chicken burger made with Wild Heron's own chipotle black bean chicken sausage, and a rich risotto primavera. Desserts are encased in glass at the entry, lovely to look at and almost as good to eat (try the double lemon cheesecake). The expansive dining room, though located in a bland Lake Oswego shopping mall, has a casual, eco-hip feel about it, with plenty of space for families, power lunchers, and even romance-seekers. ▪ *333 S State St, Lake Oswego; 635-3374; map:MM5; $$; beer and wine; AE, MC, V; checks OK; breakfast, lunch, dinner every day.* &

Wildwood ★★★½ Wildwood goes from strong to stronger, as chef/owner Cory Schreiber hones his skills and delves deeper into Northwest cuisine. Schreiber, who found fame as a chef in San Francisco, returned to his hometown to open Wildwood in 1994, and to fill his huge, wood-fired oven with regional ingredients and his own imagination. Lately, that could mean Muscovy duck breast with sweet onion potato cake and huckleberries, or grilled Columbia River sturgeon with leek and smoky bacon risotto. Regular oven specialties include skillet-roasted mussels, designer pizzas such as duck confit and apple, and seductive, elegantly presented desserts like banana bread pudding with caramel sauce. In its open, boisterous style, Wildwood feels a bit like San Francisco, but it tastes like Oregon—and usually the best of Oregon (it's named for the trail in Forest Park). If there's a salad on the menu that features fried oysters and pancetta on an herbed crêpe, make it your starter. Free parking in the lot next to the building. ▪ *1221 NW 21st Ave; 248-9663; map:GG7; www.wildwoodpdx.com; $$$; full bar; AE, MC, V; checks OK; lunch, dinner every day, brunch Sun.* &

Winterborne ★★½ On what had been a distinctly Northwest fish place, small and precise, the Alsatian chef Gilbert Henry has made a distinct impression: there can't be many local restaurants offering *choucroute aux poissons*. But aside from the sauerkraut, Gilbert has upheld both Winterborne's high reputation and many of its specialties; for instance, you can still dine on the delicate sautéed oysters or the potent Death by Chocolate. The menu also includes another Henry specialty, Basil Thai Prawn—substantial shellfish laced with garlic, ginger, and coconut milk. And he brings new continental inspirations to Northwest seafood; this chef can stretch a halibut from Astoria to Alsace. Winterborne is a tiny place of perhaps a dozen tables, and guests feel the warmth and care that such a size allows. ▪ *3520 NE 42nd Ave; 249-8486; map:FF4; $$; beer and wine; AE, MC, V; local checks only; dinner Wed–Sat.* &

Wu's Open Kitchen ★ [KIDS] The flames leaping high behind the windows in the back of the restaurant are firing the large woks in the kitchen, and you can watch the cooks deftly preparing dishes while you wait for dinner. Chef Jimmy Wu's extended family helps run this place, serving a variety of spicy and not-so-spicy dishes from all over China (but the cooks reckon on the American palate—the hot dishes won't wilt too many taste buds). Seafood is fresh, vegetables are crisp, sauces are light, service is speedy and attentive. Kids will feel right at home, and parents will appreciate the modest prices. Prepare for a wait on weekends— Wu's is popular with locals. There is a second restaurant in Tigard. ■ *17773 SW Lower Boones Ferry Rd, Lake Oswego; 636-8899; map:MM8; $; full bar; DIS, MC, V; no checks; lunch, dinner every day.* &■ *12180 SW Scholls Ferry Rd, Tigard; 579-8899; map:KK9; $; full bar; DIS, MC, V; no checks; lunch, dinner every day.* &

Yen Ha ★½ With 160 items, Portland's most extensive Vietnamese menu (and one of its oldest) offers a range of possibilities that invite intricate exploration. One shortcut—which isn't that short—is Yen Ha's signature specialty: seven courses of beef, including soup, meatballs, skewers, and a delicate wrapping (with vegetables and spices) in rice paper. You might also try a messy, tangy whole Dungeness crab, a game hen with coconut rice, or one of the remarkable preparations of frogs' legs. Some local Vietnamese have been heard to mutter that the menu (and the spicing) has become a bit Americanized, but the crowd is consistently multicultural. The ambience is Formica and Budweiser; concentrate on your beef. ■ *6820 NE Sandy Blvd; 287-3698; map:FF3; $; beer and wine; AE, MC, V; no checks; lunch, dinner every day.* &

Top 200
Restaurants

Zefiro ★★★★ After starting—and dazzling—with a Mediterranean menu, the restaurant that many consider Portland's most exciting has been migrating steadily toward Asia. Chef/proprietor Chris Israel, after his own Asian interludes, has brought back Eastern inspirations—although the creativity is still all his, with nightly offerings ranging from a Vietnamese quail salad to clams sautéed in black bean sauce. But the menu never forgets its Riviera roots; diners may still encounter an intense Tuscan beef stew, a Moroccan lamb mixed grill, or a vibrant Spanish seafood-and-squid-ink risotto. Signature dishes include a crisp, perfect caesar salad for two featuring crunchy canoes of romaine. Desserts never disappoint. The food is complemented by one of the city's liveliest atmospheres, and the feeling that there might be someone rather famous at the next table. Zefiro's bar area (a good bet if you arrive without a reservation) is prime territory for scoping out Portlanders, and also for cool and trendy martinis. (In a different direction, the atmosphere is now balanced by

Zefiro's own ice cream parlor, the hazelnut-gelati-toned Zero's, next door.) Zefiro's has even managed to do something about the noise level, but the buzz about it is still louder than ever. ■ *500 NW 21st Ave; 226-3394; map:GG7; zefiro@teleport.com; $$$; full bar; AE, DC, MC, V; local checks only; lunch Mon–Fri, dinner Mon–Sat.* &

Zell's: An American Cafe ★★ If you're truly inconsolable about founder Tom Zell's departure, you can comfort yourself with a Bloody Mary—one of the few noticeable menu changes. Otherwise, just go straight to one of the best breakfasts in this time zone: fresh fruit waffles, a range of pancakes (try the ginger if they're available), and inspired eggs. To the trademark chorizo-and-peppers omelet has now been added a Brie-and-tomato effort and, if you're lucky, scrambled eggs with smoked salmon, Gruyère, and green onions. Expect a warm welcome here, even on chilly weekend mornings when you may be forced to wait outside for a table: the awning is outfitted with heating elements, and you can get a hot cup of coffee and a heartening view of the feathery scones. Of course there is a lunch menu, with thick burgers, vegetarian sandwiches, and fresh fish specialties, but the breakfasts are tough to beat. ■ *1300 SE Morrison St; 239-0196; map:GG5; $; beer and wine; AE, MC, V; checks OK; breakfast, lunch every day.*

▼

Top 200 Restaurants

▲

NIGHTLIFE

Nightlife Index

Nightlife Index: *Type*   **77**

Reggae/World Beat
Aladdin Theater
Berbati's Pan
La Luna
The Red Sea

Rock 'n' Roll, Live
Aladdin Theater

Berbati's Pan
The Crystal Ballroom
The Green Room
Key Largo
La Luna
Laurelthirst Public House
Roseland Theater

Spanish Coffee
Huber's

View
The Bar (at Atwater's)
Harborside Pilsner Room

LOCATION

Downtown
Anne Hughes Coffee Room
   (in Powell's Books)
The Bar (at Atwater's)
Bar 71
The Benson Hotel
Berbati's Pan
B. Moloch/The Heathman
   Bakery and Pub
Brasserie Montmartre
Bush Garden
Captain Ankeny's Well
Cassidy's
The Crystal Ballroom
Downtown Deli and Greek
   Cusina
Embers
Fellini
Harvey's Comedy Club
The Heathman Hotel
Higgins Bar
Huber's
Jake's Grill/Jake's Famous
   Crawfish
Key Largo
The Lotus Cardroom
McCormick & Schmick's
   Seafood Restaurant
Moody's
Panorama
Pazzo Ristorante
Quest
Rialto Poolroom Bar and
   Cafe
The Rock Bottom Brew
   Pub
Roseland Theater
Sandoval's
Satyricon
Saucebox
Starbucks
1201 Cafe & Lounge
Upfront FX
Veritable Quandary
Virginia Cafe
Wilf's

Goose Hollow
Goose Hollow Inn

Hawthorne
Bar of the Gods
Biddy McGraws
Cafe Lena
Coffee People
Common Grounds
   Coffeehouse
The Lucky Labrador
   Brewing Company
Mount Tabor Pub and
   Cinema
Space Room (at the Brite
   Spot)

Northeast
E. J.'s
Laurelthirst Public House
Ponderosa Lounge at
   Jubitz Truck Stop
Torrefazione Italia
XO Restaurant and Lounge

North Portland
The Alibi

Northwest
The Brazen Bean
Coffee People
The Green Room
Gypsy
L'Auberge
Papa Haydn
Portland Brewing Co.'s
   Brewhouse Taproom
   and Grill
Torrefazione Italia
Uptown Billiard Club
Wildwood Bar
Zefiro

Old Town/Skidmore
Alexis
Berbati's Pan
Brewsisters Pub
Captain Ankeny's Well

Hung Far Low
Jazz de Opus
Key Largo
La Patisserie
McCormick & Schmick's
   Seafood Restaurant
Quest
The Red Sea
Rialto Poolroom, Bar and
   Cafe
Sandoval's

Pearl District
Bridgeport Brew Pub
The Crystal Ballroom
Giant Steps
Portland Brewing Co.
   (Flanders Street
   Brewery and Pub)
Wilf's

Raleigh Hills
Dublin Pub

RiverPlace
Harborside Pilsner Room

Sellwood
Rock 'n' Rodeo

Southeast
The Aladdin Theater
The Egyptian Club
The Grand Cafe/Andrea's
   Cha Cha Club
Horse Brass Pub
La Luna
Living Room
Nor'Wester Brew Pub
Papa Haydn
The Pied Cow
Produce Row Cafe
Pub at the End of the
   Universe
Rimsky-Korsakoffee House
Utopia Dessert and Coffee
   House

Nightlife

BARS, PUBS, AND TAVERNS

Alexis If you've got ouzo on the brain, and the idea of a professional tummy tumbler (i.e., belly dancer) is appealing, check out Alexis on weekend nights. Have a flaming drink with some flaming cheese and help heat up this windowless bar in Old Town. (See also review in the Restaurants chapter.) ■ *215 W Burnside; 224-8577; full bar; map:J5.*

The Alibi You are lured here, hypnotized by the gallant pageantry of neon that throws a glow over Interstate Avenue. One doesn't need an alibi to go to the Alibi—it is simply one of Portland's best untouched landmarks, where the service is sharp and all the waitstaff wear palm trees on their shirts. Karaoke hosts Steve and Denise lead a wholesome lung-powered jamboree starting at 9pm on Thursday and Saturday nights. Tip: Saturday nights are really busy, so if you're itching to bust a move, try the Thursday-night fest. ■ *4024 N Interstate Ave; 287-5335; full bar; map:EE6.*

The Bar (at Atwater's) You've got to get dressed up sometimes. You *want* to get dressed up sometimes, and there's no better reason to get swell than the lavish view from Atwater's highly situated, high-class space on the 30th floor of the US Bancorp Tower. Pay homage to Portland's signature bridge-over-water vista while imbibing a perfectly mixed drink. Wednesday through Saturday, catch live jazz with some of the city's better performers, including local god-of-bass Leroy Vinegar. (See also review in the Restaurants chapter.) ■ *111 SW 5th Ave, 30th floor; 275-3600; full bar; map:J4.*

Bar of the Gods Brought to you by the creators of the 1201 Club, Bar of the Gods is a smallish hole-in-the-wall that's been spackled a bit: think dive meets beehive. Expect a full bar, a tasty global menu, pinball machines, and a swank back-porch area that's perfect for giving your honey a nibble on the ear. ■ *4801 SE Hawthorne Blvd; 232-2037; beer and wine; map:HH4.*

Bar 71 This is the kind of place where you'll feel most comfortable if you own a cellular phone and have given it a pet name. Attire usually reflects the after-work suit 'n' heels crowd and is yuppie-trendy on weekend nights. Go just for drinking, or drinking and dancing Thursday through Saturday. Brought to you by the fine folks who run the Lotus, the Gypsy, and Toulouse Restaurant. ■ *71 SW 2nd Ave; 241-0938; full bar; map:J5.*

Biddy McGraws If you're looking for an Irish Spring–freshened, sweater-wearing hangout, keep looking. But if a sweaty, smoky, jigging joint fits the bill, then Biddy McGraws is your place. You'll swoon to hear half the patrons using a genuine shipped-over-from-the-land-o'-the-green brogue. And these folks haven't brought just the good times over from the old country, they've brought their political beliefs, too—the walls are plastered with posters urging sentiments such as "All-Party Peace Talks." You can get your Guinness as well as a full spectrum of drafts and hard cider. Catch musicians going crazy-Celtic on some nights, and watch the crowd explode into a toe-to-the-sky frenzy. ■ *3518 SE Hawthorne Blvd; 233-1178; beer and wine; map:GG5.*

▼

Bars, Pubs, and Taverns

▲

B. Moloch/The Heathman Bakery and Pub This used to be a casual, cafeteria-style setup where you could get a half sandwich and a pint of brewed-on-the-premises Widmer. You can still get fresh Widmer, or choose from the carefully drafted Northwest wine list, but now there's table service, and the menu is a bit more spendy (although pizza from the wood-burning brick oven is still favored by many; see review in the Restaurants chapter). Still, if you're on your way to the Schnitz, the art museum, or the performing arts center, B. Moloch's location on the Park Blocks, its fishbowl glass windows, and its outside seating on sunny days can't be beat. ■ *901 SW Salmon St; 227-5700; beer and wine; map:G2.*

Brewsisters Pub Though primarily for the womyn-to-womyn crowd, this airy Old Town pub welcomes all. The large selection of bottled and tap beer is a plus, as is the back porch that is perfect for outdoor guzzling and eating on warm days. ■ *53 NW 1st Ave; 274-9901; beer and wine; map:J6.*

Captain Ankeny's Well Named after the Portland sailor who left his stamp in Old Town, this pizza-and-potables pit stop has become a home for a different kind of traveler: on any given day you can catch a gaggle of bike messengers hanging around the outdoor tables or staring out of the glass-walled bar. (Bonus: Bike messengers have a unique fashion sense; you may pick up some trendy tips.) Captain Ankeny's offers a full bar, but is best known for its wide variety of beers (20 on tap, 20 in bottles), the $2 pints on Wednesdays, and the $1.50 slice-of-pizza deals—and the fact that you can order up a pitcher as you watch downtown Portland passing by. ■ *50 SW 3rd Ave; 223-1375; full bar; map:J5.*

Cassidy's The dim, turn-of-the-century environs are conducive to heavy thoughts and heavier conversation. But it's a night-owl place, too; you can knock 'em back here until 2am. ■ *1331 SW Washington St; 223-0054; full bar; map:J1.*

Downtown Deli and Greek Cusina By day it's a Greek deli, but every Friday and Saturday night the upstairs bar gets crazy. Arrive before 9:30pm to watch the transformation: at first the musical trio seems to be dozing off, but before long the host peps things up by giving Greek dancing lessons. By midnight the floor is packed with as many as 100 people caught up in frenzied dancing, ouzo drinking, and plate smashing (a dollar a plate). ■ *404 SW Washington St; 224-2288; full bar; map:H4.*

Dublin Pub One of the darkest bars in town is also one of the more popular with the beer-swilling-'n'-shoe-tapping set. Choose from 104 beers on tap and listen to bagpipers and Celtic balladeers in the early evening; later there are usually live tunes that you don't need a kilt to dance to. ■ *6821 SW Beaverton-Hillsdale Hwy; 297-2889; beer and wine; map:II7.*

▼

Bars, Pubs, and Taverns

▲

Fellini How did Portland get so lucky? This place combines some of the best cheap bar food around (coming in for dinner isn't such a bad idea, either) with a full bar and plenty o' beer on tap. Fellini is situated next to the punk club Satyricon, so expect the thumpy fuzz of booming bass to mix with your sloe gin fizz. Warning: The place is small, so be willing to order some food before you plunk yourself down at one of the tables (see review in the Restaurants chapter), or you may annoy one of the already annoyed, but adorable, waitstaff. ■ *121 NW 6th Ave; 243-2120; full bar; map:K4.*

Goose Hollow Inn For decades, the Goose was a hotbed of political debate and discussion. And though its owner, former mayor J. E. "Bud" Clark, handed over the tavern to wife Sigrid years ago, it remains a social institution. Join the hundreds who came before you and surreptitiously carve your initials into the dark wooden booths, or sink your teeth into one of the thick Reuben sandwiches that have made this place as much a classic as did the "Expose Yourself to Art" poster on the wall. ■ *1927 SW Jefferson St; 228-7010; beer and wine; map:GG6.*

The Green Room The appealing thing about the Green Room is the combination of food (the menu indulges both vegetarians and meat eaters) and ambience (arty, funky, smoky living room). There are bean-and-rice burritos, hamburgers, bowls of house-made granola, and banana splits. And whether you're in the mood for a cold Redhook ESB, a soothing chai tea, or a jolt of espresso, they've got it all—along with framed art for sale on the walls and live music (blues or jazz) every night. The patio, a great spot during warm weather, is fenced off by a bank of doors. ■ *2280 NW Thurman St; 228-6178; full bar; map:GG7.*

Gypsy   The company that runs the Gypsy, the Lotus, Toulouse Restaurant, and Bar 71 is called Concept Entertainment. The concept here is thus: take a well-loved, enlarged-liver bar and totally reconstruct it so it looks like a cleaner, more-retro-than-retro, well-loved enlarged-liver bar. The kids who head into the city from the outlying 'burbs seem to like it a lot. There's a dineresque section with comfy booths (see review in the Restaurants chapter), and a bar section with a decent jukebox. Occasionally there's live music. ■ *625 NW 21st Ave; 796-1859; full bar; map:GG7.*

Harborside Pilsner Room   This is perhaps the best waterfront drinking-with-a-view spot in Portland. The crowd tends toward quick-draw cellular packers and those who adore them, but the beer selection is large—Full Sail itself is brewed right next door—and you can get a decent mixed drink as well. Park yourself either inside near one of the floor-to-ceiling windows, to look out onto the RiverPlace esplanade, or outside, to behold the scene on our own green Willamette. ■ *0309 SW Montgomery; 220-1865; full bar; map:C5.*

The Heathman Hotel   The three bars in the Heathman are among Portland's most chic: there's the cool ambience of the Marble Bar, where symphony crowds rendezvous after the performance and executives convene for lunch; the high-ceilinged Lobby Lounge, as formal as a Tudor drawing room, with a fire blazing in the hearth and live music (jazz, piano) seven nights a week; and, upstairs, the Mezzanine Bar, where art shows from the Elizabeth Leach Gallery decorate the walls. ■ *SW Broadway and SW Salmon Sts; 241-4100; www.holog.com/heathman; full bar; map:G2.*

Horse Brass Pub   In true British pub tradition, one of the more appealing aspects of the Horse Brass is that patrons of all ages inhabit the wooden benches. Toss back a pint of Guinness—or, for that matter, a glass of Portland's own Hair of the Dog—with the elder statesman on your left, and you may receive a few choice words to live by. You can count on that world-renowned English cuisine (yes, they really do have bangers, as well as Scotch eggs and kidney pie). The Horse Brass features festive music every now and again. ■ *4534 SE Belmont; 232-2202; full bar; map:GG4.*

Huber's This is supposedly Portland's oldest bar, and it's certainly one of the more interesting, but even something that worked so well for so long has found a way to improve. A fabulous rendezvous spot for famous, flaming Spanish coffees and turkey sandwiches (two great tastes that actually taste great together) finally overcame its only flaw—the small number of tables, which inevitably led to a long wait. Voilà—Huber's has expanded. Now expect the place to hold twice the number of patrons as before amid an open kitchen, a new skylight, and a lower ceiling. (See also review in the Restaurants chapter.) ▪ *411 SW 3rd Ave; 228-5686; full bar; map:H4.*

Hung Far Low This small, dark bar in the back corner of a brightly lit restaurant (which, by virtue of its name, has made the pages of *National Lampoon*) is the place to meet friends pre-concert and post-dancing downtown. Economically disadvantaged subculture types come for the strong, cheap drinks and the sassy but stern waitresses. ▪ *112 NW 4th Ave; 223-8686; full bar; map:L5.*

Jake's Grill ▪ Jake's Famous Crawfish The Grill, located in the exquisitely refurbished Governor Hotel, does its father establishment, Jake's Famous Crawfish, proud. Career dressing dominates, but all walks of Portland life gravitate here after work to see the original 1909 mosaic tiled floor, slow-turning fans, gold-framed mirrors, and big-game heads staring down at the plates of onion rings on the bar. Jake's Famous Crawfish is much the same, but with a little less elbow room. Check out either spot for a happy-hour bar menu featuring great cheap eats. (See also review in the Restaurants chapter.) ▪ *Jake's Grill: 611 SW 10th Ave; 241-2100; full bar; map:I2.* ▪ *Jake's Famous Crawfish: 401 SW 12th Ave; 226-1419; full bar; map:I1.*

▼

Bars, Pubs, and Taverns

L'Auberge On Sunday evenings you might come for the free classic movies and popcorn, but the rest of the week you'll come for this bar's understated elegance. In winter, settle into plush fireside seats; in summer, the patio out back is pleasant. And comfort isn't the only draw: the bartenders are great conversationalists, and the food, prepared in the notorious L'Auberge kitchen, is outstanding (see review in the Restaurants chapter). Order from an ample bistro menu, and on Sundays try the famous hamburgers, which have caused more than a few vegetarians to rethink their platform. This is a sweet place for dessert, too. ▪ *2601 NW Vaughn St; 223-3302; full bar; map:FF7.*

Laurelthirst Public House With places like Laurelthirst in the 'hood, there's never any reason to confront the parking problems downtown. Tell the whole gang to meet you at this casual watering hole with a beautiful, antique wooden bar and comfortable booths. The Laurelthirst has zero pretension—and a sense of humor to boot. On the billiards side, you can cram around a small table and catch up on gossip. In the main section, live bands—blues, rock, acoustic—keep the karma flowing and get people dancing. ■ *2958 NE Glisan St; 232-1504; full bar; map:GG5.*

Living Room   People think of La Luna as a place to check out live, alternative rock shows, but this comfy bar atop the club is a stop all its own. Drink beer (or wine if you must), play pool, eyeball the oft-changing, sometimes interesting art show on the walls, or chat up one of the bartenders. Occasionally the Living Room holds special events, and sometimes there's a DJ at work; every Monday is Queer Night. La Luna recently opened a restaurant, and now you can order food from the bartender to be delivered to your booth (see review under Clubs and Lounges in this chapter). ■ *215 SE Pine St; 241-LUNA; www.monqui.com; beer and wine; map:GG5.*

McCormick & Schmick's Seafood Restaurant   The piano bar here continues to pack in the architects and advertising execs, who come after work for the astoundingly low-priced bar menu. Thick Cajun burgers and rotating pasta dishes can feed the hungry for $1.95 (1:30pm to 6:30pm weekdays; 9:30pm to close every night; see review in the Restaurants chapter). You may need a pencil and paper to converse; this brass-and-oak bar is often packed and noisy. ■ *235 SW 1st Ave; 224-7522; full bar; map:H5.*

Mount Tabor Pub and Cinema   A movie theater marquee is the gateway to this multifaceted place: kind of a one-stop shop for nightlife, albeit in somewhat dingy surroundings. Live bands, mostly alternative rock, play the intimate music room. A separate pub features big-screen TVs. And there are really cheap movies as well—but only for drinking-age patrons. ■ *4811 SE Hawthorne Blvd; 238-1646; beer and wine; map:GG5.*

Pazzo Ristorante   The smoked hams and braids of garlic hanging above the bar lend a festive atmosphere to this downtown nightspot. The lighting is flattering enough, but the bar is exposed to the busy street, so if you prefer a quieter atmosphere, take your drinks next door to the adjoining Hotel Vintage Plaza—where there's real wood burning in the fireplace. That the bar food is especially tasty is no surprise, given the accolades Pazzo's kitchen receives (see review in the Restaurants chapter). ■ *627 SW Washington St; 228-1515; pazzo@teleport.com; www.pazzo.com; full bar; map:I3.*

Produce Row Cafe   You certainly don't have to change out of hiking clothes to hunker down at a rough-hewn table on the Produce Row patio and contemplate the selection of 200 bottled beers, 29 drafts (mostly micros), and fresh cider. Next door to the fruit and produce warehouses underneath Martin Luther King Jr. Boulevard, the Row, much-loved since it opened 19 years ago, is a friendly spot for all, from punks, to moms and pops, to Ultimate Frisbee freaks. There's live music—jazz and more—on Monday nights. ■ *204 SE Oak St; 232-8355; beer and wine; map:GG5.*

Pub at the End of the Universe   It's a hard place to find if you don't live in the neighborhood or if you didn't go to Reed College, but this pub is worth a little crosstown navigation. Students and locals yuk it up, play some pool, avoid being bull's-eyed by the continuous dart games going down, and get downright comfy in this lounge-away-from-home atmosphere. ■ *4107 SE 28th Ave; 238-9355; beer and wine; map:GG5.*

Space Room (at the Brite Spot)   In Portland it's become common for subculture types to discover a tacky neighborhood bar of old-time drinkers and turn it into their own. The Space Room at the Brite Spot is a textbook case: during the Ronald Reagan years, the clientele was decidedly middle-aged—except for a single table in the corner, where an isolated group of punks looked up from their cheap and effective Long Island iced teas only long enough to plug another Patsy Cline tune at the jukebox. For years now, this dark and smoky dive—lit by the red Saturn lamps above the bar—has been made up of almost 100 percent twentysomethings, still coming for the economical, strong drinks. ■ *4800 SE Hawthorne Blvd; 235-8303; full bar; map:GG5.*

▼

▲

Veritable Quandary   The narrow, galley shape of this exposed-brick-and-dark-wood bar encourages body contact. By day, you rub up against corporate types and politicos who come for the efficient business lunches; by night, a dressed-up crowd moves in and transforms the VQ into a sultry late-night spot. Steel yourself for some brazen once-overs when you enter. Outside seating means you can wear your sunglasses while you're scamming. ■ *1220 SW 1st Ave; 227-7342; full bar; map:E4.*

Virginia Cafe   The VC is almost a guarantee for a good time, and the cheap drink specials grow addictive. Comfy in a worn-shoe way, the place is popular, and at times it's nearly impossible to find a seat. Among the diverse clientele are students from the Pacific Northwest College of Art, slumming local business folk, and moms who've been shopping the sales at Meier & Frank. ■ *725 SW Park Ave; 227-0033; full bar; map:H2.*

Zefiro   At this small bar adjoining one of Portland's favorite restaurants (see review in the Restaurants chapter), you can find bliss with a glass of wine or an infused vodka cocktail, a plate of Zefiro's signature crusty bread (served with olives) or one of the excellent desserts, and a very good friend. Huge windows onto hip NW 21st Avenue give Zefiro a fishbowl feeling, so it's not exactly the place for a tête-à-tête. You go to be seen—and heard: yups and artists carry on at full volume, and despite noise-dampening efforts, it's still plenty loud. ■ *500 NW 21st Ave; 226-3394; full bar; map:GG7.*

Bridgeport Brew Pub The folks hanging at Bridgeport always look a little cleaner and PhD-ish than the rest of the world. Maybe it's because smoking is a no-no inside one of Portland's oldest microbreweries, and drinking that great Bridgeport brew—say, Blue Heron Amber Ale—has a brain-enhancing effect. Who knows? The Pearl District locale near cobblestone streets and transient-filled loading docks is the essence of P-town—especially on a night with a little haze. Friendly strangers share the long tables in this cleaned-up warehouse, savoring the beer and sumptuous fresh-made pizza. ▪ *1318 NW Marshall St; 241-7179; beer and wine; map:O1.*

The Lucky Labrador Brewing Company The Lucky Lab is a fun place to flock for a fresh pint and a sandwich. It's another smoke-free microbrewery situated in a clean, warehousey space, where you sit bench to bench with friendly imbibers. If you're dotty about canines, be sure to check out the dozens of doggy pictures that decorate the walls. The Lucky Lab personifies the young, smart, liberal-minded, upwardly mobile quotient of Portland; they even named a beer for Erik Sten when he ran for City Council. ▪ *915 SE Hawthorne Blvd; 236-3555; www.luckylab.com; beer and wine; map:GG5.*

▼

Brewpubs

▲

McMenamins The reigning Princes of Good-Time Portland are two brothers who own a brewpub empire. Mike and Brian McMenamin opened their first pub in 1974 and went on to master the definitive Portland market hereafter known as hippie-meets-yuppie. The dozens of McMenamins brewpubs throughout western Oregon were founded with the same sensibility: let the microbrew flow, let the french fries fling (some of the best skinny with-the-skins-on kind you'll find anywhere), let the freak flag fly. While there's certainly some sense of formulaic calculation to this equation, the Princes made sure their pubs weren't all cookie-cutter. They took into consideration where each pub was located and the architecture already placed there. So the Corbett neighborhood's **Fulton Pub and Brewery** (*0618 SW Nebraska St; 246-9530; beer and wine; map:HH7*) has a flower-trimmed beer garden out back. The **Blue Moon Tavern** (*432 NW 21st Ave; 223-3184; beer and wine; map:GG7*) exchanged its pool tables for more hofbrau tables to fit comfortably the growing throngs on NW 21st Avenue. The **Market Street Pub** (*SW 10th Ave and Market St; 497-0160; full bar; map:E1*) has a more upscale urban approach: it's situated in a condominium complex and serves alcohol as well as microbrews.

The McMenamins are also open to innovation. They created two movie pubs, where for a mere dollar you can watch a second-run flick while drinking a brew. Even poor artsy types, who normally wouldn't associate with Eddie Bauer Portlanders, like this

invention (they're the ones sneaking in their own candy). At the
Mission Theater and Pub (*1624 NW Glisan St; 223-4031; beer and wine; map:GG6*), you can recline on a comfy couch while watching a double-header. The **Bagdad Theater and Pub** (*3710 SE Hawthorne Blvd; 230-0895; beer and wine; map:GG5*) has something for all your desires: a beautiful old theater with matinees on the weekends that you can bring kids to; an attached pub featuring an expansive menu; outdoor seating; and a port and cigar room called **Greater Trumps**, just around the corner.

The latest maneuver à la McMenamins is up near Powell's Books on W Burnside. **Ringler's Annex** is a cigar bar wedged into a pie-cut place at the corner of SW 12th and SW Stark (*1223 SW Stark St; 525-0520; full bar; map:J1*). This place is not typical McMenamins fare: The basement bar is dark, lit predominantly by dripping candles, and covered wall-to-wall with an intricate tile mosaic. You may hear opera booming out of the sound system or the sad wail of Tom Waits. There's a full bar and an interesting menu. This place is as hip as your chunkiest pair of black shoes or your skinniest tie. Up the street is **Ringler's** (*1332 W Burnside St; 225-0543; beer and wine; map:J1*), a spacious place that stares out onto Burnside. Inside are pool tables, an interesting and affordable menu, more of that mosaic-style artwork, and lines snaking out the door on weekends.

Perhaps the biggest triumph of all, though, is the recent opening of the revamped **Crystal Ballroom**, a huge, live entertainment venue that is so embued with Portland history that the McMenamins commissioned an entire book to be written about its background. (See review under Clubs and Lounges in this chapter.)

Finally, check out the amazing McMenamins Web site (www.mcmenamins.com), which features a program that will draw a map from your house to any one of their establishments, or e-mail the brothers at hipster@mcmenamins.com.

Nor'Wester Brew Pub Willamette Valley Brewing serves up its Nor'Wester line of microbrews, exclusively, in this watering hole under the Morrison Bridge. The beauty of Nor'Wester is that despite its converted warehouse location and heavy wooden motif, it feels clean, fresh, and outdoorsy. Even the air is clean; smoking here ain't kosher. For distraction, there are darts, backgammon, and checkers. ▪ *66 SE Morrison; 232-9771; beer and wine; map:G8.*

Portland Brewing Co.'s Brewhouse Taproom and Grill Portland's warehouse districts have no lack of good drinking establishments, and this spot continues the tradition in a large space dominated by two huge, shiny copper kettles. It's tough to decide between the good-for-the-novice Portland Ale; the aromatic, spiced Winter Ale; or the prize-winning MacTarnahan's Ale—all brewed on the premises. (See also review in the Restaurants chapter). Another Portland Brewing venture, the expanded **Flanders Street Brewery and Pub** (*1339 NW Flanders; 222-5910; beer and wine; map:L1*) has more than just spacious booths and tables aplenty to offer; a full menu is at your fingertips, and live music (usually blues) plays Wednesday through Saturday. ■ *2730 NW 31st Ave; 228-5269; www.pcrtlandbrew.com/Portland; beer and wine; map:GG7.*

The Rock Bottom Brew Pub   They boldly came north from Boulder, Colorado, in 1995 with a gutsy idea: to bring a chain of Rocky Mountain brewpubs to the very city in Oregon known for starting the microbrew trend. Most Portlanders scratched their heads and doubted whether such outsiders could go up against the homegrown competition, but Rock Bottom hasn't just survived, it has thrived. In fact, way back in the early days a former local TV news reporter was arrested after allegedly impersonating a police officer to get to the head of the long weekend line. The popularity has waned a little since all the opening brew-ha, but Rock Bottom is still a popular place for the downtown business set, who come for the good beer and for food that's better than one might expect. ■ *206 SW Morrison St; 796-2739; full bar; map:H5.*

CLUBS AND LOUNGES

Aladdin Theater   An astute promoter pulled off magic worthy of a genie at this spot. The Aladdin, formerly a notorious porn parlor, became a concert hall featuring nationally known acoustic, ethnic, and genre-blurring acts. The touring artists who appear here today appeal to the crowd that once loved rock 'n' roll and now flocks to mellower, more highbrow popular music. Here they can enjoy it in a comfortable midsize space with seats and no smoking. ■ *116 SE 11th Ave; 234-9698; beer and wine; map:HH5.*

The Benson Hotel   It's always fun to have a drink in one of your town's nicest hotels—you can pretend you're from some foreign port, just in for the weekend. This is where Bill Clinton usually stays when he's in town; perhaps he too had a drink in the opulent Benson lobby court while pretending to be a visiting dignitary from Pakistan. The lobby is dark, lined with imported Russian walnut, and furnished with sinkingly comfortable black leather chairs. The Benson offers 28 different kinds of martinis and jazz seven nights a week. ■ *309 SW Broadway; 228-9611; www.holog.com/benson; full bar; map:I3.*

Berbati's Pan   In a New York second, this quaint little Greek spot, known both for its food and for its back dining room that buzzes like a bar, expanded into the next building over, creating an intimate live-music venue. Then it expanded even more, so that the live-music venue also has its own snack bar. Berbati's Pan reflects the bright side of Portland's burgeoning nightlife scene: give the people what they want, but don't do it fly-by-night. You're as likely to see a sex cabaret here as you are a national music act like Throwing Muses—or, for literary types, a Poetry Slam. Check out Club Love on Wednesday nights, when a DJ plays acid jazz to your dancing heart's content. (See also review in the Restaurants chapter.) ▪ *231 SW Ankeny; 248-4579; berbati@teleport.com; full bar; map:J6.*

Brasserie Montmartre At this dressed-up, downtown spot you might catch a few Blazers hanging out late-night in their extra-long finest, or see a few head-over-high-heels couples doing their best crayon scribblings on the paper tablecloths (prize-winning drawings decorate the walls). The columnous, high-ceilinged decor is splendid, and the jazz is free. The Brasserie is packed with the professional crowd after work and into the evening; late-night partiers straggle in for early-morning eggs, served up until 3am on weekends. (See also review in the Restaurants chapter.) ▪ *626 SW Park Ave; 224-5552; full bar; map:F1.*

Bush Garden You might not expect to find such a scene in the middle of a serene Japanese restaurant (complete with low tables), but this is one of the most jamming karaoke spots around, Monday through Saturday nights. Bold college students, good-time Asian businessmen, and lovely Nordstrom clerks take turns fulfilling their secret rock-star dreams on the stage. There's no charge to wail along with the video. It's fun if you're up there belting it out, and it's equally (if not more) amusing just to sip a sake and watch. (See also review in the Restaurants chapter.) ▪ *900 SW Morrison; 226-7181; full bar; map:H3.*

The Crystal Ballroom The icing on the McMenamin brothers' cake, this refurbished dance-parlor-cum-rock-club-cum-whatever is a sensory experience to sink your feet into. Notice first the floating dance floor that can make you feel slightly seasick during a particularly raucous rock show, but light on your feet during a ballroom dance soiree. Notice next the attention to detail; artistic motifs abound on the walls, re-creating the room's past incarnations as a dance parlor, soul shack, and hippie hangout. Notice then the size—the Crystal offers one of the larger open-space club atmospheres in town. The offerings are eclectic: an alternative rock show one night, a neo-hippie band the next, and then a ballroom dancing night complete with lessons. Every so often during a break in the activities, the McMenamins marching band comes tromping through the audience, buzzing a trombone by your ear. ▪ *1332 Burnside St; 778-5625; hipster@mcmenamins. com; www.mcmenamins.com; full bar; map:J1.*

The Egyptian Club Hey, ladies! Get funky at this Sapphic social club that comes complete with DJ dancing Thursday through Sunday, a wet T-shirt contest every Memorial Day, free pool on

Tuesday nights, and lots of Ellen DeGeneres talk always. ▪ *3701 SE Division St; 236-8689; full bar; map:HH5.*

E. J.'s   Yet another room of ill repute goes straight. Well, sort of. This former strip joint was stripped of its dance poles and has become Portland's hottest punk club of the moment. Local indie bands like to play here for the over-21 crowd, and out-of-town underbelly bands on tour also like to make a pit stop at this dark room with a low stage. Bonus: foosball, a fireplace, and huge, cheap meals. ▪ *2140 NE Sandy Blvd; 234-3535; beer and wine; map:HH5.*

Embers   The brightness of this awesome disco has been somewhat diminished by the new dance clubs around town, but nothing can extinguish the Embers. The music mix is more Spice Girls and Ace of Base than house and industrial; gay and straight mix under the high-tech, pulsing lights and within the throbbing beat. If you're shy, fuel up for discoing with a few Firecrackers: shots of cinnamon schnapps with a float of Tabasco on top. Don't miss the fabulous drag shows. ▪ *110 NW Broadway; 222-3082; full bar; map:J4.*

The Grand Cafe/Andrea's Cha Cha Club   The Grand Cafe is a strange place indeed. The sprawling interior is lined with mirrors and the color red. Occasionally the menu stretches into the stratosphere to include such delicacies as ostrich meat or bull's balls, which you can nibble while checking out the karaoke action. Downstairs in a smallish, wood-paneled basement party room, Andrea's Cha Cha Club is home to some of the happeningist Latin dance throwdowns around. You can get lessons, if you so choose, or jump right in with the big kids and pump your pelvis to recorded salsa music. ▪ *832 SE Grand Ave; 230-1166; full bar; map:GG6.*

Harvey's Comedy Club   The only continuous comedy club in town, Harvey's has all the intimacy of an auditorium, but the comedy is often first-rate, including some big national names. And the joke's on you, pawns of nicotine—Harv's is a non-smoking establishment. ▪ *436 NW 6th Ave; 241-0338; full bar; map:L4.*

Jazz de Opus   The lighting is low and the mood is mellow in this sedate bar where tempting smells waft through from the mesquite bar next door at Opus Too. Check out the live jazz every night of the week. ▪ *33 NW 2nd St; 222-6077; full bar; map:J6.*

Key Largo   This brick-lined Old Town establishment has seen its heyday, but the faithful and the curious alike are drawn to its dependable personality. Key Largo doesn't get sucked into what's trendy, but sticks with your basic rock and R&B; occasional national acts and benefit performances are part of the lineup. ▪ *31 NW 1st Ave; 223-9919; full bar; map:J6.*

▼

Clubs and Lounges

▲

La Luna Way back in the '80s, two Portlanders went into business as "Monqui," promoting punk rock bands at tiny clubs in bad neighborhoods. They stuck with alternative music and were in the right place late in that decade when everyone started listening to the Seattle sound. Monqui bought the former Pine Street Theater and gussied it up to showcase national acts. Nowadays these big names still play, but local bands get their spotlight, too. Monday is Queer Night, and ever present are forays into the world of ambient and electronica (check local music calendars). Upstairs is the Living Room (see review under Bars, Pubs, and Taverns in this chapter). ▪ *221 SE 9th Ave; 241-LUNA; www. monqui.com; beer and wine; map:GG5.*

The Lotus Cardroom The lines around the block have vanished since the Lotus's boom days a few years back, but sailors, the all-in-black set, and curious types from the 'burbs still check each other out in this converted den of iniquity. In the barroom, some of the city's most beautiful women and sleaziest men knock back drinks; in the middle restaurant section they nibble on the remarkably good appetizers, including the happy-hour $1.95 food specials; and in the back they mob in a sweaty frenzy to a rotation of retro, '90s, new wave, disco, and '80s music. On weekends expect a cover. ▪ *932 SW 3rd Ave; 227-6185; full bar; map:G4.*

Moody's This place has been through more incarnations than David Bowie. First it was a heavy metal club. Then it was an alt-rock club with dancing upstairs. Then it was just dancing. Then it was back to live music and dancing. Now it's just dancing again. Last time we checked, you could groove to '80s music on the spacious upstairs dance floor, or hustle downstairs for '70s sounds on the equally spacious ground deck. ▪ *424 SW 4th Ave; 223-4241; full bar; map:H4.*

Panorama No Portland dance club will ever capture the essence of a Manhattan disco, but Panorama sure tries. It is one of *the* places in the city. Sophisticated grown-ups, young rebels, and lots of suburban slummers see and get seen in the murky light, multiple bars, and fantasy decor of this once gay and now almost-completely-straight-on-weekends club. Next door (accessible for the same cover price) is the Brig, which used to be *the* place for gay men to meet and dance. Now the flocks from Panorama nest at the Brig as well to take in the DJ mix of disco and new wave from the '70s and '80s, techno, trance, house, and progressive tunes. ▪ *341 SW 10th Ave; 221-7262; full bar; map:I3.*

Ponderosa Lounge at Jubitz Truck Stop There's more testosterone pumping through this truck stop than there would be on a battlefield, but the dance floor at the Ponderosa Lounge—lined with lit-up tailgates—offers burly drivers, cowboys, and others an outlet for their hormones and relief from highway stress. Live country western bands play seven nights a week. If that's not entertainment enough, you'll find pool tables and video games off to the side. Handily, there's a motel and weigh station next door. ■ *33 NE Middlefield; 283-1111; full bar; map:CC6.*

Quest All-ages dance clubs seem to come and go in Portland, but Quest is solid as a rock. The kids who stand patiently in weekend lines to disco down '90s-style range from suburban cherubic to urban slick. Some of Portland's most wizardly DJs spin industrial, house, hip-hop, and retro Wednesday through Sunday. This place is smokier than most, but heck, if you can't drink, you gotta indulge somehow. ■ *126 SW 2nd Ave; 497-9113; no alcohol; map:I5.*

The Red Sea One of the more internationally and racially diverse crowds in town throbs in sweaty, cathartic unison on the expanded dance floor in this oddly shaped, right-angle hideaway behind an Ethiopian restaurant. By now regulars must be sick of playlist staples by Peter Tosh and the same old soca tunes, but the newer, esoteric world-beat numbers that flow out of the speakers are nirvana for booty shakers. Amazing international acts play here to small audiences. The drinks are stiff and the vibes and tunes continue even after the bartender stops pouring. ■ *318 SW 3rd Ave; 241-5450; full bar; map:I5.*

Rock 'n' Rodeo For the folks who were country before country was cool, as well as those just off the Garth Brooks bus, this large club under the Sellwood Bridge is it. R'n'R draws a varied crowd for nightly classes and cowboy disco, with '50s rock 'n' roll mixed in. Even if you don't have a poodle skirt and stomping boots, you can get into the swing. Partners two-step, but line dancing (if you don't know about the cowboy hustle, you really have been under a rock) is one of the main attractions here. ■ *220 SE Spokane St; 235-2417; full bar; map:JJ5.*

Roseland Theater Once a two-story Apostolic Faith church, the Roseland is now a comfortable midsize concert hall for out-of-town acts. It's smoky, boozy, and noisy with heavy metal, rock, and folk music (some shows are for all ages). Whether you dance or not, be prepared to sweat, especially in the balcony, which commands an excellent view of the stage. A recent remodel has made the Roseland more homey than its former black-box interior was. ■ *10 NW 6th Ave; 224-2038; beer and wine; map:J4.*

Sandoval's On Saturday nights gawkers stand three deep on the sidewalk, marveling through the windows of this Mexican restaurant at the salsa dancers inside as they slither and sway. The Caribbean and Latin American patrons who flock to this club take Latin rhythms very seriously, putting up with 20-minute waits for beer and cramped space on the dance floor to move to hot salsa bands from Portland, Eugene, and Seattle. ▪ *133 SW 2nd Ave; 223-7020; full bar; map:I6.*

Satyricon This little punk club is one of the nation's longest-lived underground music venues, although with the increased club competition in town, it is no longer the only place to catch the subterranean buzz bands of yesterday, today, and tomorrow. Still, it feels like home, and the lore more than lingers. Satyricon, showing its age perhaps, even underwent a facelift worthy of the consciously hip Fellini bar and restaurant next door. ▪ *125 NW 6th Ave; 243-2380; full bar; map:K4.*

Saucebox Gen X marks the spot at this pan-Asian restaurant-cum-bar-cum-danceteria, opened not so long ago by the magicians at Zefiro. Expensive but perfect cocktails can be had alongside tasty appetizers such as sweet potato spring rolls (see review in the Restaurants chapter). When the kitchen closes, tables are pushed out of the way for the dance-prone, and the DJ mixes hot house wax. Occasionally there's live music too. ▪ *214 SW Broadway; 241-3393; full bar; map:J3.*

1201 Cafe & Lounge This was the hippest cocktail joint in town a few years ago. Today you're not square to be there, but expect a wider range of musical acts than Pink Martini. The 1201 still has its Sinatra-esque swank, but occasionally it showcases so-so rock acts to draw in the nearby PSU crowd. Cocktails, of course: martinis or the house specialty, the Avalanche. ▪ *1201 SW 12th Ave; 225-1201; full bar; map:F1.*

▼
Clubs and
Lounges
▲

Up Front FX Cover the waterfront and cover all the bases by stepping into this club that houses two drinking areas and a huge dance floor. House music is in da house, and on the weekend you'd better dress to impress. ▪ *833 SW Naito Pkwy; 220-0833; full bar; map:F5.*

Wilf's The gold-flecked red velvet wallpaper fell victim to Wilf's remodel, but this piano bar in the train station has retained its Victorian-style look. They make an excellent Cosmopolitan here—served in its own beaker, nested in a bowl of ice. Jim Schroeder coaxes tunes from the '40s and '50s out of the ivories. ▪ *800 NW 6th Ave (Union Station); 223-0070; full bar; map:M4.*

XO Restaurant and Lounge You might walk in and think you're in the wrong place—late at night the restaurant part of this operation has all the action of a graveyard. But head to the expansive bar in the back, and you have found it: the most serious karaoke spot in town, with some 2,000 songs to choose from (you too can be Courtney Love howling about Miss World). These people *practice*—one can almost imagine them at home wailing into bathroom mirrors. ▪ *3902 NE Sandy Blvd; 288-3635; full bar; map:GG5.*

BILLIARDS

Rialto Poolroom Bar and Cafe With 16 pool tables at your disposal, there's a good chance you'll get a game going without much of a wait here. But hold on to your 8-ball, there's more: the Rialto has gotten into the gambling habit (more than the usual ghastly glow of video poker) by including off-track betting with video monitors showing the races. What's more, they mix an honest, straight-to-your-gut drink at this place. ■ *529 SW 4th Ave; 228-7605; full bar; map:I4.*

Uptown Billiard Club Uptown Billiards is a rare find for all those pool-playing freaks who happen not to like clouds of cigarette smoke hazing away their corner shot: it's a smoke-free cueing center in northwest Portland's tony zone. With 10 handsome handmade replicas of 19th-century French billiards tables, exposed brick walls, and a generous supply of pool stools, this is a place where you can focus on the sport without too many other distractions. Once a month there is a cigar night, but afterward the room is completely aired out—to bring it back to its pristine state. ■ *120 NW 23rd Ave; 226-6909; full bar; map:GG7.*

COFFEE AND DESSERT

▼
Billiards
▲

Welcome to the 21st century: safe sex and plenty of espresso. It used to be that folks dashed into coffeehouses in this city for a quick pick-me-up. Of course, they still do—but now there's an added element: romance. Hang out in a Portland coffeehouse and you'll soon hear people trying out pickup lines over cappuccino the way they used to exchange glances over gimlets at the neighborhood bar. Whether it's an innocent afternoon latte and a cookie or a sultry evening of americanos and tiramisu, Portland abounds in choices. If it's truly dessert you are after, remember that many of Portland's finer restaurants offer sweets in the bar or, after the rush, in the dining room (call ahead to confirm).

Anne Hughes Coffee Room (in Powell's Books) It doesn't seem to matter what's going on—gorgeous weather, a major holiday—the Anne Hughes Coffee Room is never empty. At the tables grouped near the magazine stands, patrons gather to read, write, or stare pensively out the window. The coffee is good, as are the housemade cookies and the pastries brought in mostly from the Neighborhood Baking Company. The coffee room keeps the same hours as the bookstore—and it's a good thing; Powell's just wouldn't be the same without it. ■ *1005 W Burnside; 228-0540, ext. 234; map:J2; every day.*

The Brazen Bean See review in the Restaurants chapter. ■ *2075 NW Glisan; 294-0636; map:GG7.*

Cafe Lena   This art-cluttered poetry den pays homage to poets both dead and alive. The open mike on Tuesdays and the scheduled poetry readings on Saturdays draw an eclectic crowd with bohemian tendencies. You can hear the strumming of an acoustic guitar during weekday dinners, and eavesdrop on conversations revolving around anarchy, feminism, and Bukowski any day of the week. The espresso drinks are fine and the house coffee divine; sweets run the gamut from layered cakes to oversize cinnamon rolls. ▪ *2239 SE Hawthorne Blvd; 238-7087; map:GG5; Tues–Sat.*

Coffee People   Jim and Patty Roberts (yes, those are their smiling faces on the logo) have come a long way since selling coffee beans out of wooden barrels in their original NW Westover shop; in fact, their company was sold to a larger organization in 1997. The Greater Portland enterprise totals some 19 outlets, including 9 drive-through Motor Mokas and a gig at PDX called Aeromoka (perfect for catching a high-flying buzz *before* boarding). CP's lengthy menu includes almost every kind of coffee concoction you could dream up, as well as Prince Puckler's ice cream from Eugene and a selection of pastries from various Portland bakeries. The cookies are old-fashioned favorites—chocolate chip, snickerdoodle, peanut butter—and are made in-house. The coffeehouses in northwest Portland and in the Hawthorne district provide stylish backdrops for a late-night rendezvous. ▪ *533 NW 23rd Ave (and branches); 221-0235; map:GG7; every day.* ▪ *3500 SE Hawthorne Blvd; 235-1383; map:GG5; every day.*

Common Grounds Coffeehouse   When the Stark Raving Theatre breaks for intermission, this delightful coffeehouse fills with a crowd primed for a quick fix of caffeine and sugar. Torrefazione—the house brew—makes a perfect cafe au lait when served in a deep green earthenware cup. Most desserts fall in the category of a sweet little something—lemon bars, brownies, shortbread cookies, and Florentines with chocolate and candied ginger. For literary couch potatoes, Common Grounds is heaven—an excellent magazine rack, sofas to lounge on, tables to write at, and coffee served in the increasingly rare nonpaper mug. ▪ *4321 SE Hawthorne Blvd; 236-4835; map:GG4; every day.*

Giant Steps   This gem of a coffee bar in the heart of Portland's Pearl District combines neighborhood friendliness with coffee nirvana. Regulars belly up to the bar to shoot the breeze, sip a perfectly rendered cappuccino, and devour pastries made by dessert wizard Linda Faes, formerly of Panini. The coffeehouse doubles as an art gallery, with work by local artists lining the walls and drawing in the crowds on First Thursday, when there's also live music. ▪ *1208 NW Glisan; 226-2547; map:L2; every day.*

Higgins Bar   See review in the Restaurants chapter. ■ *1239 SW Broadway; 222-9070; map:E2; every day.*

La Patisserie   This second-floor, dark-paneled eatery and espresso bar above Jazz de Opus was one of the first of its kind. In the era of hip and swank coffeehouses, the Patisserie appears dated (as in "totally '80s"), but it's still a fun place to hang out for both the under- and over-twenty crowd. The desserts are good, as is the espresso, but given the wide choice of Allann Brothers coffees brewed to order—by the cup or pot—it is worth trying something new. The Celebes, for example, is wonderfully rich and tasty, especially paired with a slice of French silk pie. ■ *208 NW Couch St; 248-9898; map:J6; every day.*

L'Auberge   See review under Bars, Pubs, and Taverns in this chapter. ■ *2601 NW Vaughn St; 223-3302; map:FF7; every day.*

Papa Haydn   See review in the Restaurants chapter. ■ *701 NW 23rd Ave; 228-7317; map:GG7; every day.* ■ *5829 SE Milwaukie Ave; 232-9440; map:II5; every day.*

The Pied Cow   This is where Jeannie—as in *I Dream of Jeannie*—would hang out now if she were into '70s self-parody; the front room of this colorful Victorian bears a strong resemblance to her bottle, with its bay window dressed in beads, lace curtains, and low couches with pillows covered in leopard-print fabric. Neo-hippies, retro-bohemians, and bookish types come here to read the *New York Times*, play cards, and ponder over a cup of coffee—is it half full or half empty? This is the ultimate coffeehouse: the food is cheap, the cappuccinos are delicious, and there's always a chocolate dessert that's satisfyingly rich. Add to that an excellent tea list (try the Redwood Chai) and a delightful courtyard lit by candles and lanterns, and there's no better place to while away a summer evening. ■ *3244 SE Belmont; 230-4866; map:GG5; Tues–Sun.*

Rimsky-Korsakoffee House   Laughter and music from the resident piano greet the ear at the threshold of this grand old mansion. The place is nearly always filled with young lovers, who share ice cream sundaes (Rasputin's Delight is a favorite) or the decadent mocha fudge cake. The Cafe Borgias are exceptional: coffee, chocolate, and orange harmoniously mingle in one cup. You might drive right by this place—there's no sign marking its presence—but once inside, with a string trio playing in the background and a proper cup of coffee to sip, you may not want to leave. ■ *707 SE 12th Ave; 232-2640; map:FF6; every day.*

Starbucks   See Coffees and Teas in the Shopping chapter. ■ *Pioneer Courthouse Square (and branches); 223-2488; map:H3; every day.*

Torrefazione Italia   This is Portland's own little Italy. The terracotta tile floors, warm yellow walls, and hand-painted earthenware, not to mention the frequently overheard dialect and rich smell of dark-roasted coffee—well, put another notch in the belt

▼
Coffee and Dessert
▲

for Mediterranean vogue. Located near the end of Coffee Row on NW 23rd Avenue, this is a popular hangout for neighborhood locals, Eurobabes, and Italian wannabes. Classic hard, sweet biscotti go perfectly with a foamy cappuccino or cup of coffee, fresh roasted from the Seattle shop. On balmy days the breeze blows through the plate-glass windows, which are open to the street. The eastside shop offers the same delicious coffee—with less of the poser element. ■ *838 NW 23rd Ave; 228-1255; map:GG7; every day.* ■ *1403 NE Weidler; 288-1608; map:FF5; every day.*

Nightlife

Utopia Dessert and Coffee House The coming of Zupan's Market to SE Belmont has brought a general upgrade to the neighborhood. While this is mostly positive, what Belmont doesn't need is another Starbucks. Thankfully, there is still a place for unpretentious, one-of-a-kind neighborhood coffeehouses like Utopia. In this small storefront that opens up to a surprisingly large room in back, neighborhood regulars coalesce over homemade scones, cheesecake, and slices of espresso fudge cake. Any coffeehouse worth its weight in arabica boasts a good cup of house coffee, and Utopia's (from Portland Roasting) is gratifyingly strong. Of the espresso concoctions, the Cappuccino del Sur wins top honors—a delicious combination of espresso, orange syrup, Spanish chocolate, and steamed milk. On weekends there's live acoustic music in back. ■ *3320 SE Belmont; 235-7606; map:GG5; every day.*

▼

Coffee and Dessert

▲

Wildwood Bar See review in the Restaurants chapter. ■ *1221 NW 21st; 248-9663; map:GG7; every day.*

Zefiro Bar See review under Bars, Pubs, and Taverns in this chapter. ■ *500 NW 21st Ave; 226-3394; map:GG7; Mon–Sat.*

The Arts

ART IN PUBLIC PLACES

Public art is everywhere in this city—thanks to the patronage of its citizens and a program that requires all new large-scale commercial and public building construction to include art in the budget. Every City of Portland office building, lobby, and park boasts its signature mural, sculpture, painting, relief, or fountain. With artwork spread out across the city, it's best not to cram a tour into an afternoon. Choose a few arty blocks, stop for a soda along the way, and enjoy.

No matter where you plan to wander, however, the first place to hit is the **Portland/Oregon Visitors Association** (222-2223), open Monday through Saturday during business hours (10am–2pm Sun), at SW Naito Parkway and Salmon Street (map:F5); there you can pick up a free map of the city's public art offerings. Following are some public art highlights around the city.

The famous **Portland Building** (map:F3) is a provocative landmark. The first major work by architect Michael Graves, it has been described with adjectives ranging from "brilliant" to "hideous." Kneeling above its entrance on SW Fifth Avenue is Raymond Kaskey's monumental *Portlandia*. In 1985, locals cheered as the nation's second-largest hammered-copper sculpture (only the Statue of Liberty is larger) was barged down the Willamette River, trucked through downtown, and hoisted to a ledge three stories up. Most Portlanders have forgotten that *Portlandia* is fashioned after Lady Commerce, the figure on the city seal.

Directly across the street from *Portlandia* is Don Wilson's abstract limestone sculpture *Interlocking Forms.* Nearby is **City Hall** (1220 SW Fifth Ave, map:F3), whose east courtyard contains the oldest of Portland's artworks: petroglyphs that were carved into basalt rock near Wallula, Washington—estimated to be some 15,000 years old. One of the city's most familiar landmarks is the bronze *Elk* by Roland Perry, set in the fountain on SW Main Street between SW Third and Fourth Avenues (map:F3), which once served as a watering trough for both horses and humans and remains the primary watering hole for the Portland Police's Mounted Patrol. The **Justice Center** (between SW Second and Third Aves, and Madison and Main Sts, map:F4) houses a fine 19th-century Kwaguilth carving of an eagle and an array of contemporary pieces. At the entrance are Walter Dusenbery's untitled travertine sculptures representing the various paths to justice. Near them is a wall of stained-glass windows by Ed Carpenter.

On SW Yamhill Street between Third and Fourth Avenues (map:G4), the **sidewalk** speaks, thanks to author/artists Katherine Dunn and Bill Will. Engraved in the right of way are thought-provoking phrases and quotes, ranging from a Pablo Picasso quip to "Step on a crack, break your mother's back." Look up, too. The faces of Lee Hunt's work *A Human Comedy* peer out from above the awnings of Copeland Sports. Across the parking lot to the north is Gary Hirsch's *Upstream Downtown,* 18 colorful aluminum fish that decorate the south side of the parking structure at SW Third and Alder. Finally, backtrack a bit to catch John Young's *Soaring Stones* on SW Fifth between Yamhill and Taylor Streets.

The centerpiece of downtown is **Pioneer Courthouse Square** (map:H3), where Portlanders gather any (and every) hour of the day. The amphitheater-style design of the square is well suited to people-watching. Just before noon the *Weather Machine*, a shiny sphere atop a 25-foot pole, plays a musical fanfare and sends forth one of three creatures, depending on the day's weather. When it's clear, you'll see the sun figure Helia; on stormy days, a dragon; and on gray, drizzly days, a great blue heron. Equally popular is the bronze sculpture by J. Seward Johnson, *Allow Me*, a life-size replica of a businessman with an umbrella.

Across the square is a garish purple ceramic-tile fountain and waterfall by Will Martin, which dampens, so to speak, the noise of the surrounding streets. At SW Yamhill and Morrison Streets, behind the historic **Pioneer Courthouse** building, look for Georgia Gerber's delightful bronze animals gathered around small pools of water (map:G3).

The **Transit Mall** on SW Fifth and Sixth Avenues (map:F3) is lined with sculptures, including Kathleen McCullough's limestone cat (a children's favorite) and Norman Taylor's notorious *Kvinneakt*, the nude that Portlanders know as former mayor Bud Clark's accomplice in the "Expose Yourself to Art" poster.

Some of Portland's best privately financed artwork is set inside the **Pacific First Federal Center** (SW Broadway between Taylor and Yamhill Sts, map:G2): Larry Kirkland's suspended woven panels cascade into the lobby, catching the changing light throughout the day. More of Kirkland's work, including an intricately carved staircase and an enormous golden light fixture on the second floor, can be found a few blocks up at the refurbished **Central Library** (SW 10th between Taylor and Yamhill Sts, map:H2).

In the Sculpture Mall on the north side of the **Portland Art Museum** (1219 SW Park Ave, map:F2), look for the Barbara Hepworth sculpture *Dual Form* and works by Lee Kelly and Clement Meadmore.

A modern application of trompe l'oeil effects can be seen from the South Park Blocks between SW Madison and SW Jefferson Streets. The Richard Haas murals on the south and west walls of the **Oregon History Center** (1200 SW Park Ave, map:F2) depict figures from Oregon history: Lewis and Clark, Sacajawea, fur traders, and pioneers who journeyed westward on the Oregon Trail. For another artistic rendering of the Lewis and Clark expedition, visit the lobby of **The Governor Hotel** (SW 10th Ave at Alder St, map:I2), where artist Melinda Morey's sepia-toned murals cover the south wall.

Fountains abound in southwest Portland—here are three to consider. The most popular may be the ever-changing Salmon Street Springs, in Waterfront Park where SW Naito Parkway and SW Salmon Street meet (map:F5). To the southwest, in front of the Civic Auditorium (on SW Third Ave between SW Market and SW Clay Sts, map:D3), is the Ira Keller Fountain, better known as "Forecourt Fountain." It is a cool resting place in the middle of downtown—a full city block of waterfalls and pools built specifically with summer splashing in mind. In Old Town stands the 1888 bronze and granite Skidmore Fountain (SW First Ave and Ankeny St, map:J6); two bronze caryatids hold an overflowing bowl above their heads.

For a different perspective on Portland's public art, take a MAX ride across the river. The **Oregon Convention Center** (NE Martin Luther King Jr. Blvd and Holladay St) is home to one of the state's most impressive public art collections. From the sound garden, created with bronze bells and chimes donated by Portland's Pacific Rim sister cities, to local artist Lucinda Parker's painting *River Song*, the works at the Oregon Convention Center define the spirit of the state's people. The vision is universal, as seen in Kristin Jones and Andrew Ginzel's *Principia*, a pendulum hanging in the center's north tower above a 30-foot halo of suspended rays and a circular blue terrazzo floor inlaid with brass and stones; provincial, as in a series of 30 etched and color-filled plaques noting key events and figures in Oregon history, by Terrence O'Donnell, Dennis Cunningham, and John

Laursen; and witty, as in Elizabeth Mappelli's enameled-glass panels of Oregon waterfalls, installed above men's-room urinals. Particularly telling and provocative is Seattle artist Buster Simpson's outdoor installation facing NE Martin Luther King Jr. Boulevard. The work in progress is a nurse log pulled from Bull Run Reservoir; seedlings sprout from the irrigated, decaying wood, generating a bit of forest in the middle of the city.

While in northeast Portland, don't miss the works scattered around the **Lloyd Center** mall, including Larry Kirkland's fountain *Capitalism.* [KIDS] At the Rose Garden stadium, children love *Essential Forces*, which may or may not qualify as art: a computerized fountain emits some 500 jets of water—a gift to the city from Trail Blazer owner and high-tech tycoon Paul Allen.

GALLERIES

[FREE] Portland's galleries are flourishing—due in part to the success of **First Thursday**, when most galleries stay open late on the first Thursday of each month to welcome visitors to their shows. The Portland Art Museum joins in with free admission, beginning at 4pm.

▼

Art in Public Places

▲

Galleries can be found in every corner of the city and suburbs, but many cluster in two areas: **downtown** and in the **Pearl District**. Downtown, numerous galleries line the streets of the Yamhill and Skidmore historic districts, between SW Naito Parkway and SW Third Avenue. The Pearl District, once an aging industrial center north of Burnside between NW 10th and NW 14th Avenues, is steadily turning warehouses and storefronts into galleries, artists' lofts, and art-oriented businesses. (See Major Attractions in the Exploring chapter.)

Alysia Duckler Gallery This intimate and stylish gallery, tucked into the burgeoning Pearl District, features small shows of consistently fine quality. Located as it is among furniture and gift boutiques, Alysia Duckler makes a fine stop on a leisurely stroll. ■ *512 NW 9th Ave; 223-7595; map:K3; Tues–Sat.*

The Art Gym Once a gymnasium, this 3,000-square-foot space at Marylhurst College is a well-respected showcase (and testing ground) for the work of the Northwest's rising stars and established artists. Christine Bourdette, Lee Kelly, Lucinda Parker, Tad Savinar, and Mel Katz have all shown here. The Art Gym (in the B. P. John Administration Building) occasionally mounts major retrospectives, but there is always a place here for the experimental. Group and alumni shows and student thesis presentations round out the year of exhibits. ■ *Marylhurst College, 10 miles south of Portland on Hwy 43, Marylhurst; 699-6243; map:NN5; Tues–Sat.*

Augen Gallery As one of the largest and most comprehensive galleries in Portland, Augen caters to the tastes and budgets of a diverse clientele with a variety of art—from prints by Robert Motherwell and Jim Dine to paintings by regional artists. Monthly exhibits occupy the central space on the main floor. ■ *817 SW 2nd Ave; 224-8182; map:H5; Mon–Sat.*

Blackfish Gallery During the last 15 years, Blackfish has gained a loyal following among Portlanders, and it is a fixture on the First Thursday circuit. Housed at the edge of the Pearl District, at the sign of the wooden fish, Blackfish is the country's oldest artists' cooperative, primarily displaying the latest works of its 24 members in monthly shows. Media, as varied as the members' styles, run from figurative sculpture and weaving to abstract painting. ■ *420 NW 9th Ave; 224-2634; map:K3; Tues–Sat.*

Blue Sky Gallery and Nine Gallery These two galleries share a space in the Pearl District. Blue Sky, which opened in 1975, displays outstanding contemporary and historical photography. The contemporary selections often show considerable wit, in distinct contrast to the seriousness of more traditional photography shows. The Nine Gallery, in an adjoining room, is a cooperative run by 10 local artists who take turns dreaming up installations. ■ *1231 NW Hoyt St; 225-0210; map:L2; Tues–Sat.*

Butters Gallery, Ltd. This classy Pearl District gallery features monthly exhibits by nationally known—as well as local—artists, including painters David Geiser and Frank Hyder from, respectively, New York and Philadelphia, sculptor Ming Fay, and Portland painter Ted Katz. Highlights might include exhibits by West Coast artists in glass. ■ *223 NW 9th Ave; 248-9378; map:K3; Tues–Sat.*

Contemporary Crafts Gallery The oldest nonprofit gallery in the nation (established in 1937) is undergoing a renovation that will, for the first time, allow its permanent collection to be on view (beginning sometime in 1998). Perched on a hillside in a building that affords spectacular city views from its decks and windows, the gallery presents shows reminding us that the line between craft and art is a hard one to distinguish. The fabulous international glass shows, featuring premium sculptural and decorative pieces, rival those of any gallery anywhere. The ceramics go far beyond functional. ■ *3934 SW Corbett Ave; 223-2654; map:HH6; Tues–Sun.*

Elizabeth Leach Gallery This airy space in the historic Hazeltine Building is well suited to large-scale sculpture, of which all too little is seen in Portland galleries. But the excellent exhibits here are equally strong in two-dimensional works. Northwest contemporary painting and photography get top billing—you'll find such figures as Lee Kelly, Henk Pander, Christopher Rauschenberg, Norie Sato, and Terry Toedtemeier. ■ *207 SW Pine St; 224-0521; map:I5; Mon–Sat.*

Froelick Adelhart Gallery Once part of the Augen Gallery, and still connected to it, this attractive, long space boasts an unusually strong roster of artists in both sculpture and two-dimensional media. The room lends itself well to solid, generous one-person shows featuring a number of excellent artists once associated with the celebrated Jamison-Thomas Gallery. Not to be missed. ■ *817 SW 2nd Ave; 222-1142; map:H5; Tues–Sun.*

Interstate Firehouse Cultural Center A performance space, gallery, and workshop space make up the body of this multifaceted arts showcase, located in a refurbished 1910 firehouse. The emphasis is on the work of the city's artists from all heritages, and often the IFCC scores with shows not likely to be seen at other venues. The Kwanzaa celebration in December is a major event. ■ *5340 N Interstate Ave; 823-2000; map:EE6; Mon–Sat.*

Laura Russo Gallery Laura Russo maintains a strong commitment to artists from the Northwest, and she represents many of the most respected ones. Russo does not shy away from the controversial and experimental. This handsome, bright, must-visit gallery is one of a handful with space enough for large-scale works. ■ *805 NW 21st Ave; 226-2754; map:FF7; Tues–Sat.*

Littman Gallery and White Gallery The Littman Gallery has earned an excellent regional reputation for its engaging photographic exhibits and has long been a regular stop for gallery-goers. Down the corridor from the Littman is the space known as the White Gallery, where primarily two-dimensional works are displayed. ■ *Smith Memorial Center, Portland State University; 725-5656; map:D1; Mon–Fri.*

Oregon College of Art and Craft In every corner of the Oregon College of Art and Craft—on the grounds, in the modern but rustic structures, in each classroom—there is eye-pleasing design and detail. The Hoffman Gallery is entered through a gate of elaborate, swirling wrought iron. Featured (predominantly Northwest) artists work in various combinations of fiber arts, ceramics, glass, metal, and wood. Occasionally the gallery exhibits traditional crafts from Third World countries. The adjacent sales gallery displays and sells beautifully crafted gifts. Before leaving OCAC, stop at the Hands On Cafe (see review in the Restaurants chapter). Your visit's incomplete without a look at the rest room. ■ *8245 SW Barnes Rd; 297-5544; map:GG9; every day.*

Photographic Image Gallery This is the place to go for fine prints by such well-known photographers as Phil Borges and Galen Rowell. Exhibits rotate monthly, featuring contemporary photographers from all around the country, including Portland's own

Christopher Burkett, Edward Thomas, and Karry Thalmann.
There is a small but excellent selection of books and cards as
well. ▪ *240 SW 1st Ave; 224-3543; map:I5; Mon–Sat.*

Pulliam Deffenbaugh Gallery The diversity and quality of the
contemporary art selections featured here are often stimulating
and rewarding. The gallery prefers figurative, expressionistic
works from Northwest artists such as painters Guy Anderson,
Joseph Goldberg, Max Grover, Kay French, and Ken Kelly, and
printmaker Yuji Hiratsuka. ▪ *522 NW 12th Ave; 228-6665;
map:L2; Tues–Sun.*

Quartersaw Gallery Always willing to take a chance on the
untried, this vital little gallery has created a forum for those getting a start in the local arts market and remains a haven for some
established artists—Michele Biehler, Jef Gunn, Mary Josephson,
Thomas Prochaska. Paintings dominate the shows, which
emphasize the figurative, in styles from the relatively representa-
tional to the relatively abstract. Small-scale pieces are effectively
displayed in the tiny front gallery; the two back rooms are
reserved for larger works. ▪ *528 NW 12th Ave; 223-2264;
map:L2; Tues–Sat.*

Quintana Gallery The only Portland gallery dedicated to His-
panic and Native American arts, this downtown establishment
casts a wide net, coming up with such contemporary works as
exquisite Pueblo pottery as well as American Indian–inspired
fine-art paintings and sculptures, carved masks, and storage vessels. Totems from Northwest Coast tribes—Haida, Kwaguilth,
Tlingit—are well represented here, as are Native Alaskan arts,
Inuit prints, and Edward Curtis's photography. ▪ *501 SW
Broadway; 223-1729; map:K4; Mon–Sat.*

MUSEUMS

American Advertising Museum [KIDS]Who could forget Burma
Shave signs, Will Vinton's California Raisins, and Texaco's sign of
the flying horse? All-American artifacts are preserved at AAM—
the first museum of its kind in the world. Time-line displays chart
the development of advertising from the 15th century to the present. Memorable moments from radio days replay continuously—not just commercials but broadcasts that marked the
course of history: FDR's final oath of office, CBS's Bob Trout
announcing the end of World War II. Video recordings of the all-
time best TV commercials can keep you glued in place all day.
Periodic rotating exhibits bring Portland some of the best print
and broadcast advertising around. Admission varies, depending
on the current exhibit. At press time, the museum had plans to
move to a temporary location—call ahead to confirm address.
▪ *New Market Theater Building, 50 SW 2nd Ave; 226-0000;
map:J5; Wed–Sun.*

Children's Museum [KIDS] This museum is not really a museum; it's a play and learning center for children up to age 10. The "please touch" exhibits include a child-size Thriftway, complete with shopping baskets, canned goods, and a checkout line; a water room with no shortage of H$_2$O; and a bistro where your 3-year-old can serve you rubber pizza. Upstairs is the Medical Center, where kids can fix broken bones, bandage wounds, and perform surgery on willing teddy bears. The basement Clayshop is open most Wednesdays. Admission is $4 for everyone, 1 and up. To avoid big crowds of wee people, try Mondays or Thursday afternoons, when the museum is closed to groups. ▪ *3037 SW 2nd Ave; 823-2227; map:HH6; every day.*

End of the Oregon Trail Interpretive Center [KIDS] Under the Paul Bunyan–size covered wagon in Oregon City is this new museum that houses a mixed-media dramatization about life 150 years ago—"The Spirit Lives On"—as well as costumed history interpreters who teach Oregon Trail 101 (do you know how eggs were transported before egg cartons?). Admission is $4.50, less for children and seniors, and you'll want to call ahead to check show times; you won't be allowed in unless you're in the tour, except to see a few exhibits and the well-stocked museum store. ▪ *1726 Washington St, Oregon City; 657-9336; every day.*

▼

Museums

Oregon History Center See Major Attractions in the Exploring chapter. ▪ *1200 SW Park Ave; 222-1741; map:F2; Tues–Sun.*

▲

Oregon Museum of Science and Industry (OMSI). See Major Attractions in the Exploring chapter. ▪ *1945 SE Water Ave; 797-OMSI; map:HH7; every day.*

Portland Art Museum See Major Attractions in the Exploring chapter. ▪ *1219 SW Park Ave; 226-2811; map:F2; Tues–Sun.*

World Forestry Center [KIDS] The talking tree inside the World Forestry Center in Washington Park is strictly for children: the 20-foot-high fir tells them (literally) about its natural functions. The exhibits focus on old-growth stands in the Northwest, specimens of petrified wood, and tropical rain forests (in cooperation with the Smithsonian Institution). One fixture is a monumental tiger sculpture carved from a 1,000-year-old tree for the 1988 Summer Olympics in Seoul. Fighting wildfires is another big theme. Periodic shows feature Oregon woodworkers and carvers and exhibits of wooden toys. Admission is $3.50 for adults, $2.50 for children and seniors, free for 5 and under. ▪ *4033 SW Canyon Rd (Washington Park); 228-1367; map:HH7; every day.*

FREE PUBLIC PERFORMANCES/PERFORMANCE ART

[KIDS] [FREE] One of the best venues for free concerts is **Pioneer Courthouse Square**, where numerous events take place during the summer. The longest-running music series is **Peanut Butter**

and **Jam**, noon-hour concerts that feature local and national acts.
There's also occasional after-work jazz and special concerts. Call
for upcoming events (223-1613).

[FREE] For two decades now, **Shakespeare in the Park** has
been another summer fave. It's a community theater effort that's
high-spirited, popular, and free of charge—ragtag, but fun too.
There are more than a dozen performances each summer in
parks around the city. Check the theater sections of the *Oregonian* or *Willamette Week*. Also happening in summer—and
outside—is Arts in the Arboretum, a festival of performance art,
music, and dance held one Sunday in July at Hoyt Arboretum
(see the Calendar chapter for details).

Often unusual and always original **performance art** blossoms
inside theatres in Portland as well. Below are two of the top companies that put on performance art shows regularly.

Imago Is it dance, is it theater, or is it comedy? All three, actually, and sometimes it's film and music to boot. This innovative
company mounts original productions that blend elements of all
of the above into fascinating and unique stage productions. In
four or five shows per season, Imago can be counted on to
intrigue and entertain. It's an Oregon-born and -bred company
unlike any other in the country. ■ *17 SE 8th Ave; 231-9581;
map:GG6.*

▼

Portland Institute for Contemporary Art Kristy Edmunds's cutting-
edge organization brings to enthusiastic Portland audiences the
best of the national and international avant-garde, from NEA
tweaker Karen Finley to harrowing diva Diamanda Galas to
raconteur Spalding Gray. A typical season might feature Ann
Carlson, Richard Foreman, the Hassidic New Wave, and dance-
meister Rinde Eckert. In the autumn, a social-season high point
is PICA's Dada Ball, which has become an essential Portland tradition in just a few short years. Exhibitions and performances
take place all over town; call to see what the next item on PICA's
varied menu might be. And in 1999, look for PICA's new exhibition and office space in the Weiden & Kennedy building in the
Pearl District. ■ *242-1419.*

THEATER

Artists Repertory Theatre One of the finest small theaters in
town features Portland's best actors and directors under the salu-
brious influence of artistic director Allen Nause. The focus is on
American plays, especially brand-new and relatively new ones. A
sparkling black-box theater has given ART a dream space to
work in; the stage and seating can be reconfigured for each play,
further stretching the creative experience. ■ *1516 SW Alder St;
241-1278; map:G1.*

Northwest Children's Theater [KIDS] Sometimes a dose of Winnie the Pooh for the holidays is just the ticket—and here's the place to get that ticket. NCT presents several plays each year and runs a theater school for the city's youngest thespians. ■ *Northwest Neighborhood Cultural Center, 1819 NW Everett St; 222-4480; map:GG7.*

Oregon Children's Theater Company [KIDS] Everyone from Stuart Little to Willy Wonka to the Velveteen Rabbit comes to life in the hands of this talented group. A handful of plays each year are produced at Portland Community College's Sylvania campus and at Civic Auditorium. Call for schedules and locations. ■ *228-9571.*

Portland Broadway Theater Season Still in its infancy, PBTS is fast becoming a big shot on the local theater scene. Such shows as *Rent*, *Big*, and Faye Dunaway's *Master Class* are hitting a variety of Portland stages and quickly selling out. Tickets are sold through the Portland Opera. ■ *Various locations; 241-1802.*

Portland Center Stage Formerly connected with Ashland's Oregon Shakespeare Festival, Portland's largest, poshest theater company is always professional and occasionally distinguished, on a par with the country's best regional theaters. The excellent production values alone (sets, lights, costumes) guarantee a satisfactory experience, and seasoned actors from across the United States light up the stage. Comedies seem to play better than serious dramas—the lighter the better. ■ *Intermediate Theatre, Portland Center for the Performing Arts, 1111 SW Broadway; 248-4496; map:G2.*

Portland Repertory Theater For years, the city's oldest Actors' Equity company drew a loyal audience for dependable productions of drawing-room comedies and "theme" plays (about politics, aging, and so forth), along with American naturalistic classics (Inge, Miller). In recent years, under artistic director Dennis Bigelow, the Rep has widened its repertoire to include new plays, zany plays, very literary plays, and weird plays, all to good effect. Recent highlights include *Little Shop of Horrors*, Tom Stoppard's *Arcadia*, and August Wilson's *Two Trains Running*. ■ *25 SW Salmon St; 224-4491; map:F5.*

Stark Raving Theatre Portland's scrappiest little theater—and one of its riskier and most innovative—has been hanging on by a shoelace for years with gritty, in-your-face productions of everything from Shakespeare to dramas and monologues by young local playwrights. Check the reviews: chances are, if a show sounds good, it might just be the best theater ticket in town. The Starkers pull in the drama awards formerly reserved for more conservative and richer companies, and the quality has gone up without any sacrifice to the integrity of the uncompromising productions. ■ *4319 SE Hawthorne Blvd, behind Common Grounds Coffee Shop; 232-7072; map:GG4.*

Tears of Joy [KIDS] This Vancouver, Washington–based company has been around a long time, thrilling audiences with its over-the-top puppet-enhanced tellings of classic tales and original works alike. Tears of Joy was one of only a few local arts groups to receive NEA funding recently; everything they do is a class act. Portland performances are held in the Winningstad Theater at the Portland Center for the Performing Arts. ▪ *Winningstad Theater, 1111 SW Broadway; 248-0557; map:G2.*

Tygres Heart Shakespeare Company Director Jan Powell's seven-year-old troupe often comes up with interesting concepts—a *Taming of the Shrew* with an all-female cast, a *Comedy of Errors* set in Maine. The repertoire is "all Shakespeare, all the time," but there's always an idea operating and imagination at work, and these can come together to good effect, with innovative staging and a brisk, entertaining pace. ▪ *Winningstad Theater, 1111 SW Broadway; 222-9220; map:G2.*

DANCE

Arte Flamenco Dance Company [KIDS] This small company comes the closest you will find to *puro flamenco* in Portland. They can most often be found dancing, singing, and playing in the informal settings of taverns, nightclubs, and festivals, but they also offer several full-length concerts throughout the year, in which their colorful costumes, wild music, and soulful dancing can reach an audience of all ages with the timeless drama of Spain's premier folk art. Call to inquire about the next fiesta, and take the kids. ▪ *647-5202.*

Dance

Northwest Afrikan American Ballet This company appears in local college tours and as a regular feature of the Rose Festival. Typically, a dozen athletic dancers, clad in the gorgeous fabrics of West Africa and bangles of the Caribbean, re-create village dance festivals celebrating marriage, coming of age, harvest time, and the passing of the seasons. To the irresistible beat of a virtuoso drum contingent, the dancers jump, slide, shimmy, and shake in unison, then square off in bouts of solo fireworks. Not to be missed. ▪ *287-8852.*

Oregon Ballet Theatre This energetic company of talented dancers relies on youth and daring to satisfy the cravings of Portland's classical ballet fans. Director James Canfield concentrates on his own choreography and that of visiting artists, and he supplements new pieces with reworkings of American classics by the likes of Agnes DeMille, Jerome Robbins, and George Balanchine. Canfield takes plenty of chances; in 1996 he choreographed to the music of Pink Floyd's *Dark Side of the Moon.* Of course, there's the obligatory holiday run of *The Nutcracker,* but it was entirely remade in 1993 (from costumes to choreography to characters)—and has met with resounding critical praise. ▪ *Civic*

Auditorium, SW 3rd Ave between SW Market and SW Clay Sts; 227-6867; map:D3.

Oslund and Company/Dance Artistic director and choreographer Mary Oslund Van Liew puts a concert together when the spirit moves her, which is several times a year. And when she does, she does it right, with some of Portland's best modern dancers, excellent scenery and lighting, and quirky, original dancing to live, newly composed music. The spirit of these evenings is both postmodern and avant-garde; the collaboration of musicians, poets, visual artists, and filmmakers puts Oslund in the best tradition of innovative collaborative art. Check the dance listings in the *Oregonian* or *Willamette Week.*

CLASSICAL MUSIC

Chamber Music Northwest A talented group of musicians recruited from New York's Chamber Music Society of Lincoln Center and other Big Apple ensembles puts this 28-year-old, monthlong summer festival in a class with the best in the nation. In two dozen concerts ranging from solo recitals to evenings for small orchestra, the music runs from Bach to Bartók and from chamber music staples (Brahms, Schubert, Beethoven) to surprises of the repertoire. The variety of the programs is extensive and the range of music broad. Especially with difficult and unusual pieces, the players go far beyond the routine festival standard and show their joy in working together. Call for locations. At various times throughout the year, artistic director David Shifrin brings in other touring chamber groups as well; watch for these in the *Oregonian* or call for information. ▪ *223-3202.*

▼

Dance

▲

Choral Cross-Ties Conductor Bruce Browne, who also leads the Portland Symphonic Choir (see Oregon Symphony Orchestra on next page), has put together a superb 24-voice professional chorus. In repertoire ranging across four centuries, his polished singers—soloists in their own right—move with ease from the Renaissance to the 1990s, from motets to love lyrics. Call for performance schedule. ▪ *736-3374.*

Oregon Repertory Singers More than 20 years of innovative concerts have given Gilbert Seeley's 50-voice ensemble a reputation for creative programming. Seeley specializes in new commissions and neglected classics (such as Frank Martin's *Mass*) and in intriguing combinations of pieces, but he is also a gifted orchestral conductor. The group's collaborations with the Portland Baroque Orchestra and other ensembles (on works by Haydn, Bach, Mozart, and Handel) are high-quality programming staples. Russian guest conductor Vladimir Minin's transcendent renditions of Rachmaninoff's *Vespers* have been a highlight of more than one recent season. ▪ *St Philip Neri Catholic Church, SE 18th Ave and Division St; 230-0652; map:HH6.*

Oregon Symphony Orchestra In recordings and concerts, conductor James DePreist has made a name for himself with his colorful renditions of the large orchestral masterpieces of the late 19th and early 20th centuries: works by Rachmaninoff, Richard Strauss, Tchaikovsky, and Respighi. An all-star roster of visiting soloists and recitalists—from Kathleen Battle, Yo-Yo Ma, and James Galway to Ray Charles, Bobby McFerrin, and Mel Tormé—supplements the symphony's offerings; the Portland Symphonic Choir chimes in a couple of times each year, and a pops series fills out the 39-week season. ■ *Arlene Schnitzer Concert Hall, 1037 SW Broadway; 228-1353; map:G2.*

Portland Baroque Orchestra One of America's premier baroque orchestras has gained enormous stature in recent years under the baton of English superstar violinist Monica Huggett. The Portland early-instrument experts tackle music written between 1600 and 1825 in performances designed to re-create the sound of period ensembles. Visiting soloists on trumpet, cello, violin, harpsichord, and recorder, plus a crack 24-voice chorus, conspire in brisk versions of Monteverdi, Bach, Handel, Telemann, Vivaldi, Mozart, Haydn, and Beethoven. Call early for tickets; many concerts sell out in advance. The season runs from October through April. Some concerts are in St. Anne's Chapel at Marylhurst College in Lake Oswego. ■ *Trinity Episcopal Cathedral, 147 NW 19th Ave; 222-6000; map:FF6.*

Literature

OPERA

Portland Opera Over the years, Portland's homegrown opera company has lived up to its self-composed description: "anything but stuffy." Staples of the repertoire—Verdi, Mozart, Puccini— are juxtaposed with a season-ending Broadway offering, such as *Porgy and Bess* or *Show Boat*, and occasional premieres and less-heard 18th- and 19th-century works. It's the only operatic game in town, and tickets go quickly, so call ahead. ■ *Civic Auditorium, 222 SW Clay St; 241-1802; map:D3.*

LITERATURE

In the beginning, there was Powell's—open 365 days a year and rumored to have broken up the marriages of people who spent too much time in its endless aisles. But although it is the nation's largest literary institution, Powell's—in the Portland book community, at least—is just the tip of the iceberg. The city boasts dozens of independent new-book shops and probably just as many, if not more, dealers in used and rare books (not to mention the bookstore chains, which in this decade have arrived in full force). No less staggering is the fact that more than 70 percent of Multnomah County residents hold active library cards.

Why does Portland have such a voracious hunger for the written word? Perhaps it's the weather, the sort that doesn't exactly make you want to head for the tennis courts. Among the local booksellers, **Powell's** (1005 W Burnside, 228-4651; map:J2) is especially influential: it underwrites dozens of literary projects and events, from book-talk programs on local radio to films at the Northwest Film Center. More evenings than not, readers flock to its Purple Room for appearances or readings by local and national authors.

It's no surprise, then, that bookish events are big news here. Portland is one of the few cities in the country to have its own nonprofit literary organization. Under the direction of Julie Mancini, **Literary Arts** (227-2583) enriches readers and writers in three ways: through fellowships, book awards, and the hugely popular **Portland Arts and Lectures Series.** Created in 1984, the series, which runs during the school year, surprises even the nation's best-known authors with the enthusiasm of its audience. Fiction writers such as Grace Paley, John Updike, and Toni Morrison—as well as essayists, scientists, playwrights, and poets—take the stage not only to read from their work, but also to talk about the writing life. This series, and its spin-off in Seattle, may be the finest of its kind in the United States.

Many other bookstores, including Annie Bloom's, Looking Glass, and Borders, host **writers on tour** (see Books and Magazines in the Shopping chapter). **Open-mike readings** are regularly scheduled at coffeehouse venues on both sides of the river. Check calendar listings in the local newspapers.

Check the newspapers, too, for the location of the next **Poetry Slam.** Poetry as competition, as spectator sport, as interactive art form, is alive and well in this entertaining, amusing, and sometimes moving event in which poets recite their stuff to a noisy crowd of aficionados, who then choose a winner. Local competitors head to regional and even national slams. Often there's a monthly slam at Berbati's Pan (31 SW Ankeny, 248-5479); call to find out when the next one is scheduled.

Portland is home to a number of notable writer support groups. For a yearly membership fee, professional writers can exchange tips on taxes, pay, risky publications, and fair editors through **Northwest Writers Incorporated** (222-2944). The **Mountain Writers Series** is one of the largest poetry reading series in the country, offering readings, workshops, and lectures by Pulitzer Prize winners and other distinguished writers. The series maintains an office at 3624 SE Milwaukie Avenue (236-4854), where you can hear readings, read a literary journal, attend a talk by an accomplished writer or poet—or just hang out. And you need not be a full-time student to take advantage of Lewis and Clark College's **Northwest Writing Institute** (768-7745), with its substantial list of courses and workshops.

For a city of its size, Portland has quite a few movie screens. While still small, the number of art and novelty film venues is growing, making it possible to see a variety of films that the studio-bound theaters fail to book. For complete movie listings, check the entertainment section of the *Oregonian* or the film reviews in *Willamette Week*.

Broadway Metroplex This is one of the newer links in the ever-growing Act III Theatres chain (which has all but a monopoly on first-run movies in Portland). There are some nice touches: old Portland theater marquees hang in the lower lobby, continuous classic film footage entertains the queue, and there's a coffee bar. And it is downtown. By the way, don't hang up when you call this theater (or any of the other Act III houses) and reach the *Oregonian*'s automated information service; punch in the extension, and eventually you'll get what you called for. ▪ *1000 SW Broadway; 225-5555, ext 4607; map:G3.*

CineMagic A rep house, CineMagic serves up the classics, but it's not so much retro as eclectic: you might see *The Sound of Music, A Clockwork Orange, Lawrence of Arabia,* or *Fantasia.* A jukebox in the lobby features movie soundtracks. And that's real butter on the popcorn. ▪ *2021 SE Hawthorne Blvd; 231-7919; map:GG5.*

Cinema

Cinema 21 Portland's best movie house is one of a dying breed—the single-screen neighborhood theater. This spacious repertory-style house is equipped with a balcony, a crying room (for the kids, not the three-hanky movies), and rocking-chair seats, plus air conditioning that really works. Films range from outrageously bad B movies to longer runs of recent art-house releases to lefty documentaries and the occasional premiere. Pick up one of the theater's three-month calendars—and watch for the annual festival of animation. ▪ *616 NW 21st Ave; 223-4515; map:FF6.*

KOIN Center Cinemas Hollywood releases, foreign films, and art-house movies appear on KOIN's six screens (two of which are minuscule). Get there early or take a bus—parking in the KOIN Center neighborhood can be a problem. Parental bonus: Crying rooms are available in two of the theaters. ▪ *SW 3rd Ave and SW Clay St; 225-5555, ext 4608; map:E3.*

L'Auberge Restaurant [FREE] Every Sunday night at 8:30, this fine French restaurant changes its mood and shows a classic film in its bar to a crowd of hushed spectators. There's free popcorn after the movie begins and a special Sunday menu for film buffs. ▪ *2601 NW Vaughn St; 223-3302; map:FF6.*

Lloyd Cinemas   With 10 screens in the mall and 10 across the street, the Lloyd Center is the biggest movie site in the city. Both theaters are owned by the Act III theater chain. The films are traditional Hollywood fare, but the Lloyd Cinemas building is remarkable for such features as its long, neon-lit interior boulevard and lux espresso bar. ▪ *Lloyd Mall, upper level; 225-5555, ext. 4601; map:FF5.* ▪ *Lloyd Cinemas, 1510 NE Multnomah Blvd; 225-5555, ext 4600; map:FF5.*

Mission Theatre and Pub (and others)   What may well be Portland's favorite movie theater chain isn't actually a movie theater chain at all: it's a group of McMenamins brewpubs that show movies. Admission to these pubs is $1, and no one under 21 is allowed. At the beloved **Mission**, the original brewpub/movie venue, you can sip a pint of ale (and maybe have a Communication Breakdown burger to go with it) while you watch a recent release. If the film is especially good, the place remains more or less quiet.

At the **Bagdad Theatre and Pub** (3710 SE Hawthorne Blvd, 230-0895, map:GG5), moviegoers *under* 21 are invited to join their elders during the weekend matinee. Farther afield, you can catch movies at *Edgefield* (in the Power Station, 2126 SW Halsey, Troutdale, 669-8754; see Breweries in the Exploring chapter). ▪ *Mission Theatre, 1624 NW Glisan St; 223-4031; map:GG6.*

Cinema

▲

The Movie House   Here's a first-run art house owned by the big guys, Act III. It's a charming, uncomfortable old theater with inscrutable Egyptian decorations on the walls. In the upstairs lobby, board games and card tables are thrown together, and there's an outdoor balcony for summer. The staff is exceptionally congenial. ▪ *1220 SW Taylor St; 225-5555, ext 4609; map:I1.*

Northwest Film Center   A steady menu of art films, independent features, and documentaries is offered at the center, along with guest filmmakers showing their recent work. This nonprofit corporation, a branch of the Portland Art Museum, also presents the annual Portland International Film Festival, which shows dozens of new films from every corner of the world, and the Northwest Film and Video Festival, highlighting local work, in November. (See the Calendar chapter.) ▪ *1219 SW Park Ave; 221-1156; map:F1.*

Roseway Theater   The city's best-preserved throwback to the days of spacious neighborhood cinemas is this northeast Portland gem. High-ceilinged and elegant, with generous legroom, comfy seats, wide aisles, and a classy, gleaming lobby, the Roseway shows second-run imports and American films of quality. Go for the sheer pleasure of the place—especially if you haven't seen the movie they're offering. ▪ *NE 72nd Ave and Sandy Blvd; 287-8119; map:FF4.*

Exploring

MAJOR ATTRACTIONS

DOWNTOWN
Between the Willamette River and I-405,
SW Market and SW Stark Sts (map:E2–I6)

Portland has good reason to be proud of its downtown. While most cities in America have allowed the malling of suburbia to drain the life from the downtown core, the City of Roses has not. Whatever the season, you will see people taking to the streets downtown: during the day it's a thriving business and retail center; at night, restaurants, hotels, and festivals of one sort or another attract tourists and residents alike. A good way to see the downtown is to walk, and a good place to start your tour is the **Portland/Oregon Visitors Association** (POVA), in the World Trade Center (26 SW Salmon St, 222-2223; map:F5; open daily). Get yourself a copy of **Powell's Walking Map of Downtown Portland**, free at all Powell's bookstores (see Books and Magazines in the Shopping chapter), and keep an eye out for the green-jacketed **Portland guides**, employees of the Association for Portland Progress, who roam the downtown core in pairs just to answer questions about the city.

Portland's downtown owes its lived-in feel in part to its "living room": the Will Martin–designed **Pioneer Courthouse Square** (map:H3). The city's first public school occupied this site, as did its most magnificent hotel, bits and pieces of which are to be found in the present structure. An eyesore of a parking garage stood here after the hotel was demolished, until the city resolved to turn it into public space, with the help of a clever funding campaign: most of the square's 45,000 bricks bear the names of individual contributors who chipped in to pay for the project. It now hosts political rallies, concerts (many at no charge), flower shows during the Rose Festival, and people-watching daily. Underneath the bi-level square is the **Tri-Met Customer Service Office** (for information regarding the bus system or MAX, the light-rail system, call 238-7433 or see the Essentials chapter). [FREE] Incidentally, public transportation is free in the downtown core. **Public rest rooms** and **Powell's Travel Store** are also located in the square. Next to the **Starbucks** at the northwest corner is the **weather machine**, which at noon announces a forecast with fanfare. Adjacent to the meeting place are two big department stores and a bank (**Meier & Frank** at SW Sixth Ave and Morrison St, **Nordstrom** on SW Broadway between Morrison and Yamhill Sts, and **Wells Fargo** in the American Bank Building on SW Morrison St between Sixth Ave and Broadway), and of course the stout **Pioneer Courthouse**, with a gracefully refurbished post office on the main floor.

Not far from the square are downtown's two principal shopping complexes. (A minimum $25 purchase at major downtown retailers buys one or two hours of **free parking** at many downtown public parking lots. Look for the **Smart Park** signs.) Two blocks east is **Pioneer Place** (228-5800), centered at SW Fifth Avenue and SW Yamhill Street, which encompasses two city blocks and is anchored by **Saks Fifth Avenue** (850 SW Fifth Ave). Among the highly touted retail shops in the airy four-level pavilion are those familiar to other Rouse development projects such as Seattle's Westlake Center and New York's South Street Seaport: the San Francisco–based cookware store Williams-Sonoma; established clothing shops such as Eddie Bauer, Banana Republic, and J. Crew; and the eclectic Sharper Image and Museum Company. While you're here, take a stroll down SW Yamhill Street between Third and Fourth Avenues where, courtesy of the city's public art program, the sidewalk is peppered with catchy phrases and quotes, selected in part by Portland novelist Katherine Dunn. To the west of Pioneer Courthouse Square is the **Galleria** (SW Morrison St, between SW Ninth and SW 10th Aves), a splendid five-story terra-cotta building with three floors of retail shops. Down the street from the Galleria, on SW 10th Avenue between SW Yamhill and SW Taylor Streets, is the **Multnomah County Central Library**. Beautifully restored in the mid-1990s at a cost of $24 million, it is an architectural gem worth a visit even if you're not feeling bookish. The **Friends Library Store**, a gift shop for bibliophiles, is just off the lobby, and there's even a Starbucks cafe on the main floor.

A few blocks away are some of Portland's signature buildings. To the north is the tallest, the **US Bancorp Tower** on SW Fifth Avenue between W Burnside and SW Oak Streets, known to locals as "Big Pink" and offering a terrific view from **Atwater's** restaurant on the 30th floor. South on Broadway between Salmon and Main Streets is another pink-tinted and affectionately

▼

Major Attractions

Downtown

▲

nicknamed structure, **1000 Broadway**—"the Ban Roll-on
Building"—which houses a deli, retail space, and a set of cinemas, the **Broadway Metroplex**.

The most controversial of downtown's architectural landmarks is Michael Graves' love-it-or-hate-it postmodern **Portland Building** (1120 SW Fifth Ave), on which crouches **Portlandia**, the second-largest hammered-copper statue in the world (the Statue of Liberty is the biggest). City offices are located here and next door at the lovely **City Hall**, which has undergone a total renovation. Closer to the river, the bold brick **KOIN Center** (SW Clay St and SW Third Ave), like a blue-tipped pen, has left its indelible mark on Portland's skyline; inside are six cinemas and offices for its namesake, KOIN-TV. [KIDS] Kitty-corner to KOIN, across SW Third Avenue and SW Clay Street, are the 18-foot cascades of the **Ira Keller Fountain**, designed specifically with summer kid-fun in mind. **Public rest rooms** are located on the main floor of the Clay Street parking garage, between SW Third and SW Fourth Avenues.

A peaceful component of Portland's downtown is the elm-lined oasis known as the **South Park Blocks** (although new construction on Yamhill and Taylor Streets is altering the mood a bit). Sandwiched between SW Park and SW Ninth Avenues, the blocks are reserved almost entirely for public use and are fronted by public institutions such as the **Portland Art Museum** (between SW Jefferson and SW Main Sts), the **Oregon History Center** (between SW Jefferson and SW Madison Sts), and the **Portland Center for the Performing Arts** and **Arlene Schnitzer Concert Hall** (between SW Madison and SW Salmon Sts). The blocks are capped by **Portland State University** (see Portland Art Museum/Oregon History Center/Park Blocks in this chapter).

Major
Attractions

RiverPlace/
Tom McCall
Waterfront
Park

RIVERPLACE/TOM MCCALL WATERFRONT PARK
On the west side of the Willamette River from the Marquam
Bridge to the Steel Bridge (map:A5–M5)

It is a rare city that has both the planning sense and the political will to reclaim territory taken over by the automobile, but that is precisely what Portland did at the eastern edge of its downtown. In the early '70s, Portlanders decided they didn't like the way the city had grown—an expressway called Harbor Drive impeded access to the otherwise scenic Willamette River. So the Portland Development Commission did what the locals asked: it took the road away and replaced it with a showcase riverfront park. The southern end is occupied by **RiverPlace** (map:C5), a complex that includes the elegant **RiverPlace Hotel**, the tony **RiverPlace Athletic Club**, a sporty marina, condominiums, and a short promenade lined with specialty shops. Farther to the south, where an old Pacific Power and Light plant used to stand, there's covered parking, more shops, apartments, and the efficient **Stanford's Restaurant and Bar**, where you can have a fax machine brought to your table. South of RiverPlace stands a recently completed development that brings together apartment buildings with the new world headquarters for Pacific Gas Transmission—thus establishing an attractive "mixed-use" neighborhood.

Tom McCall Waterfront Park (named for the governor credited with giving Oregon its reputation as a "green" state) has become indispensable. Its showpiece sweeping lawns are the hardest-working turf in the city; from Cinco de Mayo through Labor Day, it's rare to find a weekend when something (the Rose Festival, park concerts, the Bite) isn't going on here (see the Calendar chapter). The riverside promenade is shared by anglers, walkers, runners, bladers, and cyclists, and in the summer, many cool off with a dash through the **Salmon Street Springs fountain** at the foot of SW Salmon.

The old visitors center, in the country's first plywood building (smack in the middle of the park), is now **McCall's Waterfront Cafe** (248-9710). The promenade stretches north under the Burnside Bridge, passing on its way the mast of the USS *Oregon* at the **Battleship Oregon Marine Memorial**. Beyond it lies the **Waterfront Story Garden**—a whimsical tribute by artist Larry Kirkland to storytellers of all ages, complete with etchings in granite and cobblestone of animals, queries ("What do you remember?"), and "safe havens" like a tropical paradise. Next, the walkway passes 100 Japanese cherry trees in the **Japanese-American Historical Plaza**, which commemorates the Japanese-American internments during the Second World War. Memorable quotes by Oregonians who were interned are set in boulders along the pathway. To the north, at the foot of the Steel Bridge, sits the **Friendship Circle**, a sculpture that emits the sounds of a Japanese flute and drum, and honors the strong sister-city relationship between Portland and Sapporo, Japan. The park ends just beyond, but the walkway continues north to **Albers Mill**, off Front Avenue, recently renamed Naito Parkway, where every Saturday morning during the growing season vendors sell produce, flowers, plants, and fresh pies at the **Portland Farmers Market**.

If you can't take in the entire 2-mile stretch of Waterfront Park all at once, at least check out the neighboring **Mill Ends Park**, located in the SW Naito Parkway median at Taylor Street. A plaque at the site tells how a hole for a lamppost became the smallest park in the nation; despite its size, weddings are occasionally held at the spot.

PORTLAND ART MUSEUM/OREGON HISTORY CENTER/PARK BLOCKS
Along Park Ave: SW Jackson St to SW Salmon St, then W Burnside to NW Glisan St (map:C1–L3)

If Pioneer Courthouse Square is the heart of the city, the **Park Blocks** are its green backbone: a mostly calm, 25-block stretch running parallel to Broadway from Portland State University on the south end to NW Glisan Street on the north. The entire elm-arched strip was set aside in 1852 as a park (although in 1871 eight blocks ended up in private hands, and they continue to be developed). Today it's one of the city's favorite strolls.

The **South Park Blocks** begin in a pedestrians-only zone on the PSU campus and continue north for 12 blocks, hedged neatly along the way with student apartments alongside upscale condominiums. They continue to the doorstep of the private Arlington Club on SW Salmon Street, where nearby the **B. Moloch/ Heathman Bakery and Pub**, bustling **Coffee People**, and health-conscious **Macheezmo Mouse** occupy the high-demand retail space.

Sculpture abounds in the South Park Blocks (see Art in Public Places in The Arts chapter). Tipped-over granite monoliths adorn the three-church block between SW Columbia and Jefferson Streets, and Theodore Roosevelt and his horse guard the next block north, overlooked by the well-executed *trompe l'oeil* mural gracing the Madison Street wing of the **Oregon History Center** (1200 SW Park Ave, 222-1741; www.ohs.org). **[KIDS]** The center is the headquarters of the Oregon Historical Society and houses a bookstore, archives, a library, and a museum, all open to the public. The archives consist of manuscripts, oral histories, and more than 2 million photographs, prints of which are available for purchase; the museum hosts a variety of exhibits on Portland and Oregon history. Admission is $6 for adults, $3 for students, and $1.50 for children 6–12. Seniors get in free on Thursdays.

Across the park, the multifaceted **Portland Art Museum** (1219 SW Park Ave, 226-2811; www.pam.org/pam/) comprises not only its own three levels of galleries but also the **Northwest Film Center** (running film series in the museum's Berg Swann

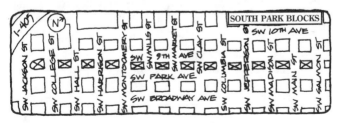

Auditorium) and the **Rental/Sales Gallery**, holed up in the North Wing next door.

Designed by Portland's venerable architect, the late Pietro Belluschi, the art museum is a landmark structure on the Park Blocks, with changing exhibits of classic to contemporary art, including the occasional touring blockbuster (*Tombs of China* or Chihuly glass). Its permanent holdings—Northwest Coast Indian art, tribal art of Cameroon, prehistoric Chinese artifacts, modern European and American sculpture and painting—span 35 centuries. Admission is $6 for adults, $4.50 for seniors and students 16 and over, and $2.50 for children 2–15. The museum is open Tuesday through Sunday; on the first Thursday of every month from 4pm to 9pm, two can enter for the price of one. There are regular lectures and tours, and every Wednesday from October through April, PAM lets down its hair after work and warms up with two hours of live music in the sculpture court, from 5:30 to 7:30. Tickets for **Museum After Hours** are $6, $3 for museum members.

A somber statue of Abe Lincoln stands outside the museum's North Wing. On the east side of the block is the **Portland Center for the Performing Arts** (1111 SW Park Ave, 796-9293); be sure to view the Henk Pander mural *Portland Town* through the glass on the west side of the building. Just across SW Main Street (this block is closed during concerts) is the larger **Arlene Schnitzer Concert Hall**, aka "The Schnitz," a plush and ornate theater that's home to the Oregon Symphony and the Portland Arts and Lectures Series (see Literature in The Arts chapter). Purchase tickets for events at either location through the Portland Center for the Performing Arts.

▼

**Major
Attractions**

*Portland
Art
Museum/
Park Blocks*

▲

The Park Blocks only seem to end on SW Salmon Street. Skip over the ugly parking garages and various storefronts between SW Salmon and SW Washington Streets to **O'Bryant Square** (named for Portland's first mayor, Hugh Donaldson O'Bryant), with a jet engine–like fountain encircled by brick steps, a good spot to catch noontime rays in summer. The five blocks from W Burnside to NW Glisan comprise the **North Park Blocks**, home to walking paths, basketball courts, and playground equipment. Bordering the park are retail shops, lofts, and the granite colonnade and courtyard of the majestic Italian Renaissance **U.S. Customs House**.

*NORTHWEST PORTLAND
North of W Burnside between NW 18th Ave
and NW 27th Ave (map:FF7)*

The streets of this district are lined with elegant old houses and grand apartment buildings. For thousands of Portlanders, "Northwest" means home, but for nonresidents it mostly means shopping and dining along two of the most bustling avenues in

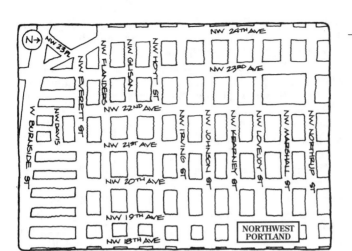

NORTHWEST PORTLAND

the city. Lively, urbane **NW 23rd Avenue** purposefully combines elements of funk with high fashion, making for a smart street scene, while two blocks away, **NW 21st Avenue** has more exceptional restaurants in a six-block stretch than any other area of the city.

In block after block along NW 23rd—from W Burnside to NW Thurman Street—there's a wealth of cosmopolitan attractions (it helps in orienting yourself to know that the streets of northwest Portland are named in alphabetical order from south to north: Burnside, Couch, Davis, and so on). Down the avenue, many Victorian homes have been remodeled into small retail enclaves, and attractive new developments have also been built, nosing out less sightly structures. "Trendy-Third," as it's affectionately been tagged, draws an eclectic crowd: neighborhood first-graders on miniature mountain bikes weave among open-mouthed tourists; determined shoppers busily compare goods in the many "interiors" stores; and the cafe crowd lingers at tables along the sidewalk. It's easy to pass a day here. **Parking** can be tough; your best bet for spaces is on the east-west cross streets. Or take Tri-Met (238-7433).

Chances are, if you're out exploring you'll probably start somewhere in the middle of NW 23rd Avenue; a good way to see it all is to walk up one side and down the other. The southern end is occupied by the **Uptown Shopping Center** (W Burnside and NW 23rd Ave), which is bisected by W Burnside. The **Town Pharmacy** (2334 W Burnside, 226-6211) has been an institution for 40 years, while the classy, well-stocked **Zupan's Market** (2340 W Burnside, 497-1088) is relatively new. North of Burnside in the Uptown are more shops; check out the fabulous take-out at **Elephant's Delicatessen** (13 NW 23rd Pl, 224-3955); **Phil's Uptown Meat Market** (17 NW 23rd Pl, 224-9541), where special

Major Attractions

Northwest Portland

orders are no problem; the district's utterly dependable **Uptown Hardware** (27 NW 23rd Pl, 227-5375); and **Foothill Broiler** (33 NW 23rd Pl, 223-0287), a top-drawer cafeteria.

Nearby is the playful **Twist** (30 NW 23rd Pl, 224-0334), offering colorful earthenware, glassware, and furniture, and **Smith & Hawken** (26 NW 23rd Pl, 274-9561), which elevates gardening to an art form. A bit to the north is the big clapboard **Westover Place**, where you'll find the city's original—and many say best—bento spot, **Big Dan's West Coast Bento** (2346 NW Westover Rd, 227-1779).

When it comes to lunch here, options abound. Pizza? Decide only whether your slice will be classic East Coast style (**Escape from New York Pizza**, 622 NW 23rd Ave, 227-5423) or a little more tarted-up (**Pizzicato**, 505 NW 23rd Ave, 242-0023, or **La Macchia**, 2340 NW Westover Rd, 226-8082). Get a thick corned beef sandwich and all the pickles you can eat at **Kornblatt's Delicatessen** (628 NW 23rd Ave, 242-0055); a towering, intense Autumn Meringue at **Papa Haydn West** (701 NW 23rd Ave, 228-7317); or a scoop of Black Tiger (espresso ice cream) at the mod **Coffee People** (533 NW 23rd Ave, 221-0235). On hot days, you can sip cold drinks alfresco at **Sammy's Restaurant and Bar** (333 NW 23rd Ave, 222-3123), or stop at **Macheezmo Mouse** (811 NW 23rd Ave, 274-0500) for a nonalcoholic Cactus Cooler—if you're lucky, there will be an open table on the sidewalk. Coffee flows freely up and down the avenue, but the best place to linger over an Americano and few biscotti is **Torrefazione Italia** (838 NW 23rd Ave, 228-2528). Farther down the avenue at NW Pettygrove Street is the home of **Clear Creek Distillery** (1430 NW 23rd Ave, 248-9470), which rivals European brandy makers with its pear and apple eaux-de-vie and its grappa.

Even Martha Stewart would have a ball shopping 23rd Avenue, where shops offer every "necessity" for the home. Standouts among these are **Restoration Hardware** (315 NW 23rd Ave, 228-6226), for upscale fixtures and accessories; **Kitchen Kaboodle** (NW 23rd Ave and Flanders St, 241-4040), for everything from lawn furniture to egg timers; **Urbino** (638 NW 23rd Ave, 220-0053), for gorgeous Italian pottery; **Itchy Fingers** (517 NW 23rd Ave, 222-5237), for fanciful switchplates and other metalwork; and **The Compleat Bed & Breakfast** (615 NW 23rd Ave, 221-0193), for elegant linens. Longtime NW 23rd resident **Dazzle** (704 NW 23rd Ave, 224-1294) brims with kooky artifacts.

Fashion is the other shopping focus in this neighborhood, from stylish undergarments meant for few to see (**Jane's Obsession**, 728 NW 23rd Ave, 221-1490) to stylish spectacles that help you to see (**Reynold's Optical**, 625 NW 23rd Ave, 221-6539). The venerable **Elizabeth Street** (635 NW 23rd Ave, 243-2456) has women's cotton sportswear and rayon dresses, and at **Zelda's Shoe Bar** (633 NW 23rd Ave, 226-0363), you're bound to find footwear to suit. Hip, hand-knit children's clothes hang down-

stairs at **Mako** (732 NW 23rd Ave, 274-9081), and next door is
Wild West Clothing (740 NW 23rd Ave, 222-6666), which has a
more varied stock than the name suggests. **Mimi and Lena** (823
NW 23rd Ave, 224-7736) is one of the nicest dress shops in town.
Shoes, too.

Music Millennium (801 NW 23rd Ave, 248-0163) is to CD
junkies what Powell's Books is to literary folk, and **Child's Play**
(907 NW 23rd Ave, 224-5586) is a wall-to-wall toy store. In the
shadow of the Good Samaritan Hospital sits the hospitable
Twenty-Third Avenue Books (1015 NW 23rd Ave, 224-5097).

Down on NW 21st the restaurant scene shows no sign of
fading. Some of the bustling eateries in the stretch between NW
Flanders and NW Lovejoy Streets are **Bastas** (410 NW 21st Ave,
274-1572), for outstanding pasta; **Zefiro** (500 NW 21st Ave, 226-
3394), where the food competes with the patrons for attention;
Tribeca (704 NW 21st Ave, 226-6126), for trendy but not intimi-
dating dining; **Caffe Mingo** (807 NW 21st Ave, 226-4646), for
well-prepared Italian fare in a setting at once romantic and convivial; and **Delfina's** (2112 NW Kearney St, 221-1195), the neighborhood's classiest place to order pizza. Two of the hottest
restaurants in town, cutting-edge **Wildwood** (1221 NW 21st Ave,
248-9663) and diminutive **Paley's Place** (1204 NW 21st Ave, 243-
2403), are farther up the avenue.

If you're dining in, stock up at **City Market** (735 NW 21st Ave,
221-3007), where the finest pasta, seafood, fruits, vegetables, and
meats are gathered under one roof, and stop at **Liner & Elsen
Ltd.** (202 NW 21st Ave, 241-9463), for the perfect bottle of wine.

After dark, cinema lovers ease into the rocking chairs that
serve as seats at one of Portland's favorite movie houses,
Cinema 21 (616 NW 21st Ave, 223-4515), for art-house and foreign flicks.

For additional information on establishments listed above,
see the Restaurants and Shopping chapters.

PEARL DISTRICT
North of Burnside to Marshall St between NW Eighth Ave
and NW 15th Ave (map:K2–N1)

In the last 10 years, warehouses and wholesalers' storefronts in
the aged industrial Northwest Triangle district have taken on
new lives. Welcome to the **Pearl District**, Portland's urban
renewal zone of the moment. Construction and renovation continue along the cobblestone streets; when the dust finally clears,
the area will be substantially transformed—and considerably
more populated. Empty spaces have been turned into clean-lined
art galleries, antique showrooms, furniture stores, bookstores,
and lofts for upscale urban dwellers.

The Pearl is *the* place to gallery-browse, especially on the
First Thursday of each month, when galleries throw open their
doors to show off their collections. The Pearl District boasts
more than two dozen galleries (see Galleries in The Arts

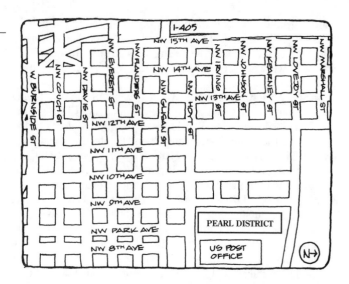

chapter); among the better are **Blackfish Gallery** (420 NW Ninth Ave, 224-2634), a local cooperative; a photography gallery, **Blue Sky** (1231 NW Hoyt St, 225-0210); the impressive **Butters Gallery** (223 NW Ninth Ave, 248-9378); the little **Quartersaw Gallery** (528 NW 12th Ave, 223-2264), always willing to take a chance on the untried, with frequent success; and the **Pulliam Deffenbaugh Gallery** (522 NW 12th Ave, 228-6665), a real force in regional contemporary art. In the same block, **Morrison Books** (530 NW 12th Ave, 295-6882) focuses on art books in fine and rare editions.

Newer in the Pearl District are a handful of "functional art" galleries and hot furniture stores. Among them: **P. H. Reed** (1100 NW Glisan St, 274-7080), for a variety of stylish, contemporary furniture and lighting designs; **Kaboom** (1115 NW Glisan St, 223-1465), for sofas and chairs the Mad Hatter might have chosen; **Lux Lighting** (1109 NW Glisan St, 299-6754), for lamps that have life even when they're turned off; and **Full Upright Position** (1101 NW Glisan St, 228-6190), for chairs—and nothing but.

[FREE]The art of beer making is not as much of a newcomer to the neighborhood: pedestrians venturing near NW 11th Avenue and W Burnside have been greeted by the smell of hops since Henry Weinhard moved his brewery here in 1904. Now **Blitz-Weinhard Brewing Company** (1133 W Burnside St, 222-4351) takes up five city blocks. Free 45-minute tours are followed by samples; call ahead for the schedule. Two other breweries are nearby: Portland Brewing Company's **Flanders Street Brewery & Pub** (1339 NW Flanders St, 222-3414) and **Bridgeport Brewery & Pub** (1313 NW Marshall St, 241-7179). (For the scoop on these breweries and brewpubs, and others outside the

Pearl District, see Breweries later in this chapter and Brewpubs
in the Nightlife chapter.)

Next door to Blitz-Weinhard is **Powell's Books** (1005 W
Burnside, 228-4651), featuring a city block's worth of new and
used books. A visit to this literary institution is a tour in itself, so
finish by resting your feet in the **Anne Hughes Coffee Room**, in
the southwest corner of the store. You can also get your coffee
fix at the jazzy **Giant Steps** (1208 NW Glisan St, 226-2547), displaying art on loan from local galleries. For more substantial
fare, stop in for breakfast at **Shakers** (1212 NW Glisan St, 221-
0011)—be prepared for a long wait on Sunday morning—or
lunch at **Little Wing** (529 NW 13th Ave, 228-3101), with its huge
array of cookies for dessert.

Nearby are a few of the district's interesting retail outlets:
Hanna Andersson (327 NW 10th Ave, 321-5275), for colorful
cotton kids' clothing; **Aubergine** (1100 NW Glisan St, 228-7313),
for fine women's clothing; **Dieci Soli** (304 NW 11th Ave, 222-
4221), for April Cornell linens and Italian pottery; and **Dehen
Knitting Company's Factory Outlet Store** (324 NW 10th Ave,
222-3871)—the place to buy that letter jacket you could only earn
in high school.

SATURDAY MARKET
Under the Burnside Bridge at SW First Ave, 222-6072 (map:J6)

Nearly 20 years ago a group of Portland artists assembled the *Saturday
Market*
beginnings of what has become a lively attraction—possibly the
largest outdoor craft market in the country. From March through
December, every Saturday and Sunday and for a week before
Christmas Eve, nearly 300 craft and food booths cluster under
the Burnside Bridge (for protection from Portland's notorious
rain) to peddle handmade items ranging from stained glass to
huckleberry jam, sweaters to silver earrings. The food booths
are often a few bites beyond what you'd expect from a cart. On
any given weekend (and especially around holidays or during the
summer), musicians, jugglers, magicians, face painters, and
clowns please the crowd, and recently a group of local writers
and composers staged a serial street opera.

You can reach the Saturday Market via bus, rail, or car. [FREE]
Tri-Met (238-7433) is free in the heart of downtown (Fareless
Square). MAX light rail—also free within Fareless Square—runs
to the market every 15 minutes or so. Get off at Skidmore Foun-
tain, right in the thick of things under the Burnside Bridge.
Street parking is free on Sundays, but with a $25 purchase at the
Market you can also get two hours of free parking at the Smart
Park garage on NW Davis Street and Naito Parkway.

While in the area, wander through the year-round stalls in the
nearby **New Market Village** and the **Skidmore Fountain** buildings (see Skidmore/Old Town/Chinatown in this chapter).

The map shows streets including NW HOYT, NW GLISAN ST, NW FLANDERS ST, NW EVERETT ST, NW DAVIS ST, NW COUCH ST, W BURNSIDE ST, SW ANKENY ST, SW OAK ST, SW PINE ST, SW ASH ST, with avenues NW 8TH AVE, NW BROADWAY, NW 6TH AVE, NW 5TH AVE, NW 4TH AVE, NW 3RD AVE, NW 2ND AVE, NW 1ST AVE, FRONT AVE, the WILLAMETTE RIVER, STEEL BRIDGE, and OLD TOWN.

SKIDMORE/OLD TOWN/CHINATOWN
*Between Naito Pkwy and Fourth Ave from SW Oak St
to NW Glisan St (map:H5–L5)*

Once part of the city's commercial core, the restored brick buildings of the **Skidmore** and **Old Town** districts, just north of the
present downtown, now abound with art galleries, good restaurants, and nightclubs. Demarcated by antique street signs, Old
Town runs predominantly north of W Burnside between SW
Naito Pkwy and Fourth Avenue; Skidmore spills over just south
of Burnside. Here lawyers, architects, and artists dominate the
work force, but the perpetually unemployed consider the area
prime turf, too. On weekends, a craft market bustles 10 months
out of the year underneath the Burnside Bridge (see Saturday
Market in this chapter).

At the center of the Skidmore district is the city's most gracious fountain, **Skidmore Fountain** (where two women dis-
pense the gift of water in drinking troughs for both man and
beast), in cobblestone **Ankeny Square**. Across the square, the
Skidmore Fountain Building has been remodeled as a mall
with a number of tourist-oriented shops. [KIDS] [FREE] At the east
end of the square, the **Jeff Morris Fire Museum** (55 SW Ash
St) provides what is basically a window view of vintage fire
engines; take a peek, it's free.

West of Ankeny Square is a courtyard with an overflow of
tables from the eateries inside the **New Market Village**, a magnificent brick and terra-cotta building dating back to 1872. A

column-lined atrium with two rows of tables displays three levels of decent boutiques, jewelry shops, florists, and a number of inexpensive eateries. There are two additional wings to the south and west of what was once the New Market Theater. Public bathrooms are available, but they're locked, so you'll need to ask one of the merchants for a key.

Driving around Portland, it's easy to forget that this is a port city. You can regain a watery perspective at the **Oregon Maritime Center and Museum** (113 SW Naito Pkwy, 224-7724). The museum exhibits model sailing ships, Liberty ships, sternwheelers, and navigational instruments, and is open weekends; admission is $4 for adults (less for seniors and students), and children under 8 are free.

Hungry yet? Why not down a few mollusks at the 92-year-old **Dan and Louis Oyster Bar** (208 SW Ankeny St, 227-5906)? Or, at the foot of SW Ankeny Street on SW Second Avenue, there's **Berbati** (19 SW Second Ave, 226-2122), an excellent, casual Greek restaurant, and **Berbati's Pan** (231 SW Ankeny St, 248-4579), its connected nightclub.

Just south, along SW Second and SW First Avenues, are a handful of galleries. In the historic Hazeltine Building, the **Elizabeth Leach Gallery** (207 SW Pine St, 224-0521) is a large, airy space representing many of Portland's well-known painters and photographers. **First Avenue Gallery** (205 SW First Ave, 222-3850) leans toward fresh and technically accomplished Northwest contemporary artists. **Photographic Image Gallery** (240 SW First Ave, 224-3543) exhibits excellent prints from master photographers. After a day's gallery-hopping, stop in at **McCormick & Schmick's Seafood Restaurant** (235 SW First Ave, 224-7522) for some of the best happy-hour eats in town, or **Kells Irish Restaurant & Pub** (112 SW Second Ave, 227-4057) for Celtic music and a creamy pint of stout.

Down the middle of SW First Avenue runs the MAX light rail, transporting people from downtown to the east side as far as Gresham. Cross north under the Burnside Bridge to the carefully restored historic district of Old Town—and the last free eastbound stop on MAX. At the corner of NW First Avenue and W Burnside is a store where everything is **Made in Oregon** (10 NW First Ave, 273-8354). The popular **Oregon Mountain Community** (60 NW Davis St, 227-1038) stocks a good variety of outdoor sports clothing and equipment—for sale and for rent.

There are still more great places to eat in Old Town. From the upstairs windows of **La Patisserie** (208 NW Couch St, 248-9898), watch the activity in the streets with the octagonal One Pacific Square building in the background. Upon closer inspection, you'll find a plaque on the side that notes the high-water mark of the flood on June 7, 1894 (about 3 feet above the present sidewalk level). **Opus Too** (33 NW Second Ave, 222-6077) is known for its excellent grilled fish. Next door, lights are low in **Jazz de Opus**

Major
Attractions

*Skidmore/
Old Town/
Chinatown*

(33 NW Second Ave, 222-6077), a good choice for late-night drinks. **Obi** (101 NW Second Ave, 226-3826) creates innovative renditions of maki, and **Uogashi** is one of the most strikingly designed Japanese restaurants in Portland (107 NW Couch St, 242-1848). There's also the formal **Couch Street Fish House** (105 NW Third Ave, 223-6173).

Portland's diminutive **Chinatown** blends into Old Town at about NW Third Avenue; the main serpent-adorned entrance to Chinatown is on NW Fourth Avenue. In 1989, the area north of Burnside between NW Third and NW Sixth Avenues was designated a National Historic District, now the oldest and, technically, the largest in Oregon. It's still small enough that fiery red-and-yellow lampposts are needed to remind you of your whereabouts, though. Trucks unload bok choy at the back door of **Fong Chong** (301 NW Fourth Ave, 220-0235), which is half Oriental grocery, half restaurant—and Portland's finest dim sum parlor, a Sunday morning favorite.

THE GROTTO
NE 85th Ave and Sandy Blvd, 254-7371 (map:EE3)

Out-of-towners sometimes introduce longtime Portlanders to the **Sanctuary of Our Sorrowful Mother**, commonly known as the Grotto. Tended by members of the Order of the Servants of Mary (the Servites), the Grotto is both a religious shrine and a lovely woodland garden. Mass is held daily year-round in the chapel; from May to September, Sunday Mass faces the Grotto itself, a fern-lined niche in the 110-foot-tall cliff, which houses a marble replica of Michelangelo's *Pieta*. Throughout the 58-acre grounds, rhododendrons, camellias, azaleas, and ferns shelter religious statuary, providing both the prayerful and the plant lover with ample material for contemplation, while giant sequoias tower above. Upper-level gardens and a panoramic view of the Cascades and the Columbia River are reached via a 10-story elevator ride ($2). Noteworthy events include the 10-night Festival of Lights in December and an outdoor ecumenical Easter sunrise service.

PITTOCK MANSION
3229 NW Pittock Dr, 823-3624 (map:FF7)

Henry Pittock had the advantage of watching over Portland from two perspectives: from behind the founder's desk at the *Daily Oregonian* and, in his later years, from his home 1,000 feet above the city. The stately **Pittock Mansion**, built in 1914, stands on 46 acres that look across northeast Portland to Mount Hood. The house stayed in the family until 1964, when the entire property was sold to the City of Portland for $225,000. Today the Pittock Mansion is open to visitors from noon to 4pm every day.

Inside, a graceful staircase sweeps from the basement to the second story; another, less conspicuous stairway leads to the servants' quarters on the top floor. The 22 rooms, furnished with antiques, include an oval parlor and a Turkish smoking room. Regular tours are conducted in the afternoon, and the manicured grounds around the mansion and Pittock Acres (with numerous hiking trails) are open to the public until dark. The gatehouse (once the gardener's cottage) is home to the Gate Lodge Restaurant, serving lunch and afternoon tea every day but Sunday; call to inquire about special, seasonal events (823-3627). Admission is $4.50 for adults, $4 for seniors, $2 for kids 6–18, and free for children 5 and younger.

WASHINGTON PARK
SW Park Pl at Vista Ave, 823-5112 (map:GG7)

There are some 280 parks in Portland. At 4,683 acres, Forest Park is the most sprawling and primitive, while the 24-square-inch Mill Ends Park (SW Naito Pkwy and SW Taylor St) is decidedly the city's smallest. Washington Park may well be the most civilized.

A substantial portion of the 546-acre plot, originally purchased by Portland's founders in 1871, is currently home to the well-kept trails of the **Hoyt Arboretum** and the inspiring **Vietnam Veterans' Living Memorial**, as well as to the more formal **International Rose Test Garden**, the elegant **Japanese Garden**, and the lush **Rhododendron Gardens** (see descriptions, which follow). In the northern end of the park, hiking trails meander through the woods.

[KIDS] Also in the park is the **Washington Park Zoo**, famed for its successful breeding of Asian elephants (see description, which follows). The westside light-rail line, MAX, stops at the zoo; those who arrive by car take a chance with overflow parking, especially on the weekend. In the vicinity of the zoo is the educational **World Forestry Center** (4033 SW Canyon Rd, 228-1367; see Museums in The Arts chapter).

One-way roads wind through Washington Park, and in warm-weather months a narrow-gauge train runs through the zoo to the Rose Garden (see Train and Trolley Tours in this chapter). Other facilities include four lit tennis courts, an outdoor amphitheater, covered picnic areas, and an archery range.

▼

**Major
Attractions**

*Washington
Park*

▲

Hoyt Arboretum [KIDS][FREE] Sweeping views, 10 miles of trails, and more than 700 species of trees and shrubs—all neatly labeled—make up Washington Park's 175-acre tree garden. It's an international collection of woody plants, including the nation's largest assortment of conifer species. Blossoms dust the Magnolia Trail in spring; a three-quarter-mile section of the Bristlecone Pine Trail is paved for wheelchair access. In the arboretum's southwest corner is the **Vietnam Veterans' Living Memorial**, an inspiring outdoor cathedral commemorating the Oregon victims of that war. Maps are available at the arboretum's Visitor Center (9am–4pm), and weekend guided walks (April through October) begin there. The one-day July festival called

Arts in the Arboretum is a stroll-through celebration of everything from dance to calligraphy. ■ *4000 SW Fairview Blvd; 823-3654.*

International Rose Test Garden [FREE] Whether to obtain a blossom-framed snapshot of Mount Hood or to scrutinize a new hybrid, this is an obligatory stop for any visitor to the Rose City. The garden (established in 1917) is the oldest continually operating testing program in the country. Thanks to its 10,000 plants—some 500 varieties—and a knockout setting overlooking downtown Portland, it's an unmatched display of the genus *Rosa*.

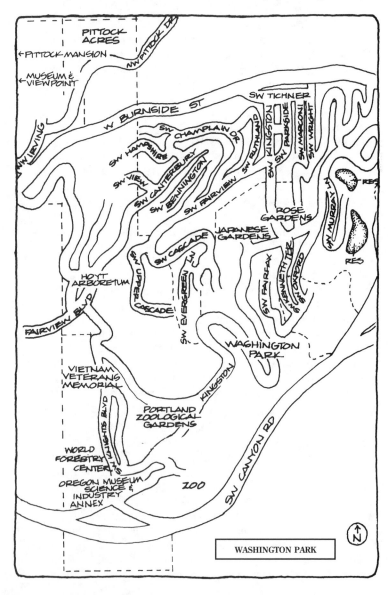

The garden's 4½ acres are a riot of blooms from June through October, from dainty half-inch-wide miniatures to great, blowsy 8-inch beauties. Fragrant old-garden varieties fill the gap between the parking lot and the Washington Park tennis courts. ■ *400 SW Kingston Ave; 823-3636.*

Japanese Garden In 1988, the Japanese ambassador to the United States pronounced this the most beautiful and authentic Japanese garden outside of Japan. An extraordinarily peaceful spot, it actually comprises five gardens: the traditional Flat Garden, the secluded and flowing Strolling Pond Garden, the Tea Garden with a *chashitsu* (ceremonial teahouse), the stark Sand and Stone Garden, and a miniature Natural Garden. In contrast with the exuberant rose blossoms down the hill, this is an oasis of lush greenery, winding paths, and tranquil ponds. Flowering cherries and azaleas accent the grounds come spring; in summer, the Japanese irises bloom, and in autumn, the laceleaf maples glow orange and red. Eaves and posts of the Japanese pavilion frame the Flat Garden to the west and Mount Hood to the east. A shop in the garden stocks books on such topics as the art of Japanese flower arranging and traditional tea ceremonies, and one on Portland's garden itself. Hours are 9am–8pm June through August, 10am–6pm the rest of the year. Admission is $5 for adults; $2.50 for seniors, students, and children over 5. ■ *611 SW Kingston Ave; 223-1321.*

Major Attractions

Washington Park Zoo [KIDS] What began over a century ago as a seaman-turned-veterinarian's menagerie on SW Third Avenue and SW Morrison Street has since grown into an outstanding 64-acre zoo in Washington Park, winning awards for exhibits showcasing the lush flora and fauna of the Cascades as well as the colony of endangered Peruvian Humboldt penguins, well protected (and thriving) here. In 1962, Packy—the first Asian elephant born in the Western Hemisphere—blazed the trail for the pachyderm breeding program. Now, some two dozen newborns later, the elephant grounds have been enlarged, allowing for excellent viewing opportunities. The zoo has a complex chimpanzee exhibit, featuring an arena architecturally designed with the natural behavior of the chimps in mind. The eight-year-old African savanna exhibit features black rhinoceros, giraffes, impalas, zebras, and birds. The one-third-acre African rain forest delights zoo-goers with hourly rainstorms and more than two dozen animal species, including the naked mole-rat. Other unique environments include the extreme climates of Alaska and the microscopic world of insects. Over the next couple of years, the feline and bear grottoes will be upgraded and a new Oregon habitat exhibit installed.

Washington Park

During warm-weather months you can catch the small steam train that chugs through the zoo and down to the Rose Garden. On the second Tuesday of each month, zoo admission is free after 3pm; regular admission is $5.50 for adults, $4 for seniors, and $3.50 for kids 3–11. Crowds throng to the grassy outdoor amphitheater during summer evenings, when there are jazz and blues concerts on Wednesdays and Thursdays, respectively, and occasional children's concerts. Around Halloween look for ZooBoo—a scary extravaganza—and, in December, for the Zoo Lights Festival, an incandescent holiday tradition (see the Calendar chapter). ■ *4001 SW Canyon Rd; 226-ROAR.*

HAWTHORNE DISTRICT
Along SE Hawthorne Blvd from SE 17th Ave
to 43rd Ave (map:GG4–GG5)

The lengthy strip that is Hawthorne Boulevard might well be considered Portland's own little Haight-Ashbury. And while those who worship the late great Jerry Garcia might feel right at home here among the purveyors of tie-dye and Grateful Dead records, an increasing number of upscale retail shops and eateries are locating here as well. As commercial activity creeps east and west along the boulevard, this district—just southeast of downtown—may come to resemble a funkadelic, four-lane version of NW 23rd Avenue.

Even on Hawthorne, the counterculture has taken a back seat to the coffee culture. Espresso can be quaffed at such corporate coffeehouses as **Starbucks** (3639 SE Hawthorne Blvd, 234-1757) and **Coffee People** (3500 SE Hawthorne Blvd, 235-1383), or in the cozier confines of the très comfy **Common Grounds Coffeehouse** (4321 SE Hawthorne Blvd, 236-4835) or the popular **Cup and Saucer** (3566 SE Hawthorne Blvd, 236-6001). For an ice creamy pickup, try the Coffee Olé at **Ben & Jerry's** (1248 SE 36th Ave, 234-2223).

Nowadays, the bustling boulevard offers a good representation of international cuisines. The wonderfully idiosyncratic **Bread and Ink Cafe** (3610 SE Hawthorne Blvd, 239-4756) serves up one of the city's finer hamburgers and a luscious cassata for dessert. Just down the street is **Nick's Famous Coney Island Restaurant** (3746 SE Hawthorne Blvd, 235-4024), otherwise known as Yankee Stadium West, where the chili dogs draw 'em in. **3 Doors Down Cafe** (1429 SE 37th Ave, 236-6886) offers Italian-inspired fare in a warm, bistro-style setting. **Garbonzos** (3433 SE Hawthorne Blvd, 239-6087) is a bright lunch spot serving falafel, *shawarma,* baba ghanouj, and other Middle Eastern favorites, and **Thanh Thao** (4005 SE Hawthorne Blvd, 238-6232) is known for its Thai and Vietnamese dishes (see the Restaurants chapter).

If pizza and a brewski with a movie is your thing, try the McMenamins' brightly colored **Bagdad Theater and Pub** (3702 SE Hawthorne Blvd, 232-6676 or 230-0895). Around the corner is

Greater Trumps (1520 SE 37th Ave, 235-4530), where you can sit back in luxury with port and a cigar, and down the boulevard is the classy Hawthorne Street Ale House (3632 SE Hawthorne Blvd, 233-6540), where Bridgeport is the brew on tap. Book and music shoppers won't be disappointed by this neighborhood. Powell's on Hawthorne (3723 SE Hawthorne Blvd, 238-1668) and Powell's Books for Cooks & Gardeners (3747 SE Hawthorne Blvd, 235-3802) are outposts of the venerable downtown bookstore; the latter stocks a variety of cooking- and gardening-related accessories and gifts in addition to new and used books. With the recipe for culinary inspiration in hand, step next door to Pastaworks (3739 SE Hawthorne Blvd, 232-1010) to choose from a gala assortment of fresh pastas, cheeses, prepared antipasti, and imported foodstuffs.

Birds of many feathers will flock for a bath and a nibble at your house if you stock up at the Backyard Bird Shop (3572 SE Hawthorne Blvd, 230-9557). Presents of Mind (3633 SE Hawthorne Blvd, 230-7740) is crowded with cards, gifts, and pretty wrapping paper. Handcrafted pottery and the works of local artists fill the Graystone Gallery (3279 SE Hawthorne Blvd, 238-0651), and a fine collection of guitars, violins, flutes, and drums make a musical display at Artichoke Music (3526 SE Hawthorne Blvd, 232-8845). Escential Lotions & Oils (3638 SE Hawthorne Blvd, 236-7976) specializes in custom-scented skin and bath products, and The Third Eye (3950 SE Hawthorne Blvd, 232-3EYE), "your Grateful Dead HQ," will keep you in patchouli oil and incense—and might be just the place to find that bootleg Dead tape from '73 missing from your definitive collection.

An eclectic array of antiques, vintage furnishings, and various flea-marketable odds and ends are bought and sold at Sorel Vintages Limited (3713 SE Hawthorne Blvd, 232-8482), and Ruby's Antiques (3590 SE Hawthorne Blvd, 2239-9837) offers a plethora of pretty gifts, including antique linens, Victorian-inspired cards and wrapping paper, and antique reproduction glassware. Colorful cotton and rayon clothes can be found at El Mundo for Women (3556 SE Hawthorne Blvd, 239-4605), designer shoes make their imprint at Imelda's (1431 SE 37th Ave, 233-7476), and moms-to-be and their offspring can dress stylishly with clothes from Generations (4029 SE Hawthorne Blvd, 233-8130). Every fashionable traveler knows about the Perfume House (3328 SE Hawthorne Blvd, 234-5375), where you can buy perfumes from around the globe.

Closer to the river are the nouveau-beat hangout Café Lena (2239 SE Hawthorne Blvd, 238-7087), where you can take in music and poetry readings (and, of course, coffee), and the nouveau-Mex Chez Grill & Chez's Lounge (2229 SE Hawthorne Blvd, 239-4002).

Major
Attractions

Hawthorne District

MULTNOMAH VILLAGE
*Along SW Capitol Hwy from SW 28th Ave south to the overpass
over Multnomah Blvd, and vicinity (map:II7)*

Hidden among the hills and vales of southwest Portland is a jewel of a district known to most as Multnomah Village (although some old-timers insist on calling it by its name when it was an independent town: simply Multnomah). Although **antique shopping** is the big draw here (more than a dozen stores), there are enough other shops and hangouts—including the requisite Starbucks (7737 SW Capitol Hwy, 245-1961)—to give the village destination status for just about anyone.

The antique shops are sufficiently close together along SW Capitol Highway that browsing and window shopping are easy (many—but not all—are clustered near the SW 35th Avenue intersection). The **Multnomah Antique Gallery** (7784 SW Capitol Hwy, 245-3175) features the antiques of some 30 dealers; **Wooden Craftsman Antiques** (7868 SW Capitol Hwy, 245-8681) specializes in furniture restoration; and **Auntie's Attic** (7784 SW Capitol Hwy, 244-0496) stocks quilts, dolls, kitchenware, and other collectibles.

For more contemporary finds, slip into **Annie Bloom's Books** (7834 SW Capitol Hwy, 246-0053), one of the finer bookstores in the city. Colorful Haitian wall hangings (created from steel drums that have been pounded flat) and other unusual gifts are at **Topanien** (7832 SW Capitol Hwy, 244-9683). Climb the steps to **Mary Ann's** (7779 SW Capitol Hwy, 246-9787) for fanciful picture frames and gift wrap. East on SW Capitol Highway is a multipurpose neighborhood treasure, the **Multnomah Art Center** (7688 SW Capitol Hwy, 823-ARTS). Beyond the MAC, at **Bibelot–Curious Works of Art Gallery** (7642 SW Capitol Hwy, 244-8483), there's a wide array of artwork—goofy to serious.

Good eats, too. One longtime favorite is **Fat City Cafe** (7820 SW Capitol Hwy, 245-5457), with its fresh cinnamon rolls and square breakfasts. Two happy, all-day neighborhood restaurants are **Marco's Cafe and Espresso Bar** (7910 SW 35th Ave, 245-0199) and **O'Connor's** (7850 SW Capitol Hwy, 244-1690), the latter a late-night spot as well.

OREGON MUSEUM OF SCIENCE AND INDUSTRY (OMSI)
1945 SE Water Ave, 797-4000 (map:A9)

[KIDS] The 219,000-square-foot Oregon Museum of Science and Industry (OMSI), with its spectacular view of downtown from the east bank of the Willamette, is a delightful diversion no matter the weather—and it's not just for kids. The facility features six immense exhibit halls, a planetarium that doubles as a theater in the round, Oregon's first IMAX theater, a riverfront cafe, and a naval submarine, the USS *Blueback*, which is permanently docked for tours (admission is $3.50 extra).

You can't miss this angular brick showpiece, domed with a copper cap topped by a Ferrari-red smokestack and a glass pyramid atrium. The 18½-acre industrial location (formerly owned by Portland General Electric Company, which donated the land) is appropriate for a museum where science and industry are the emphasis: the Marquam Bridge soars just above, a PGE substation still operates at one corner of the property, and moth-balled train cars are parked along the eastern edge.

Inside, you can poke around an old turbine, stand on a plat-form and feel an earthquake, touch a tornado in the Natural Science Hall, observe nutrient cycling in the Greenway, or cruise the Internet in the Information Science Area. A favorite is the Space Science Hall, simulating what life might be like on the space station *Freedom*. The numerous hands-on exhibits are pop-ular with people of all ages, but for the very young—and their grateful parents—there's a children's room with tennis balls to feed into a pneumatic tube, a Lego table, and live reptiles. In the planetarium are educational shows exploring the stars, planets, and galaxies, and occasional laser-light extravaganzas. Traveling exhibits—*Dinosaurs of the Gobi*, for example— prove educational as well as entertaining. Museum admission is $9.50 for adults, $8 for seniors and children 4–13; Omnimax (the IMAX theater) admission is an additional $5.50 for adults, $4 for seniors and children. Memberships are available.

RIVER CRUISES
Columbia and Willamette Rivers

[KIDS] Before the arrival of railroads and paved roads, people could hail a steamboat just about anywhere between Portland and Eugene, Astoria and The Dalles. **Stern-wheelers** still navi-gate the waters of the Columbia and Willamette Rivers and offer some relief from today's crowded highways—but also, more importantly, give patrons an opportunity to see the region from a riverine viewpoint.

From its summer base about 45 minutes east of Portland, the stern-wheeler *Columbia Gorge* (a triple-deck paddle wheeler) voy-ages through the dramatic Columbia River Gorge. Sound a bit touristy? There are plenty of Portlanders who've taken the scenic trip several times and still love it. In mid-October, the 147-foot vessel returns to Portland, where it's used for wedding recep-tions and company outings. Holiday dinner-and-dance and lunch, brunch, and dinner cruises are very popular. Operated by the same company, the 139-foot *Cascade Queen* stern-wheeler leaves RiverPlace Marina on weekend days for brunch and dinner excursions up and down the Willamette River. Fares for both ships range from $12.95 to $36. The monthly schedule varies, so call ahead; 223-3928.

The *Rose*, a 92-foot stern-wheeler replica, sails from the OMSI dock on the east side of the Willamette. The downriver trip gets quite industrial, passing shipyards, grain terminals, 7 of Portland's 12 bridges, and perhaps the world's largest dry dock. The more scenic direction is upriver toward Milwaukie, passing Sellwood, Oaks Park, Johns Landing, and gracious old homes on the bluffs overlooking the Willamette. The 130-passenger, double-deck stern-wheeler is often privately chartered, but public cruises are available; prices are $25 for brunch, $35 for dinner. Call for schedule; 286-7673.

For a more modern-day river experience, visit **Rose City Riverboat Cruises**. Their 49-passenger *Yachts-O-Fun* provides a good outing for all ages (those big engines churn up more excitement than the stern-wheeler). Aim for the upriver trip (toward Oregon City), as downriver sights, again, tend toward the industrial. Adult fares range from $10.50 for the hour-long downtown moonlight cruise to $35 for the two-hour dinner trip to Lake Oswego; there's also a Sunday brunch cruise ($25). Open April through October (charters year-round), with annual excursions during the Christmas parade of lighted boats. Reservations are recommended (required for dinner trips). Departs from OMSI; 234-6665.

The *Portland Spirit* and its sister craft, the *Willamette Star,* offer fine dining and evening cruises from their berth near the Salmon Street Springs in Tom McCall Waterfront Park. Sunset and City Lights dinner cruises cost $46, with a $5 discount for seniors and children. A midday lunch tour costs $24 ($16 for kids). Evening dance cruises are available Saturday night for $10, and a river city tour on Saturday or Sunday also costs $14, again with a $5 discount for seniors and children. Charters are available; call 224-3900.

BREWERIES
Citywide

In Portland there are almost as many places to drink beer as there are to drink coffee—and it's *good* beer, too. The Northwest in general—and Portland in particular—is the national center for craft breweries: small, independent companies that turn out specialty beers, generally in small batches and according to traditional methods. Aficionados argue that Northwest brews are distinctly different from even the best imports. They claim that the western barley, hops from the Willamette and Yakima Valleys, and Cascade water give local concoctions their particular character.

The "local" brewery (actually opened by a company in Wisconsin) that enjoys big commercial status is Portland's own **Blitz-Weinhard Brewing Company** (1133 W Burnside St, 222-4351). **[FREE]** Blitz's 45-minute tours (Tues–Fri only; noon, 1:30pm, and 3pm) show how their successful beers have been made for more than 100 years. Sample local favorite Henry Weinhard's Private Reserve (aka Hank's) after the tour.

You can't miss the gleaming copper kettles at the **Portland Brewing Company's Brewhouse Taproom and Grill** (2730 NW 31st Ave, 228-5269), although the location in northwest Portland's industrial zone isn't simple to find. Once you make it, though, the rewards are great: some of the best brew in the city is made here. Sample the ever-popular MacTarnahan's Ale, Zig Zag River Lager, Haystack Black Porter, or Oregon Honey Beer with grilled Copper River salmon in season, halibut fish and chips, or steamed clams cooked in beer. At the **Flanders Street Brewpub** (1339 NW Flanders St, 222-5910), there's a smaller menu but the same beer. There's entertainment, too: local bands play live music Thursday through Sunday nights.

Through picture windows behind the bar, you can watch the brewers at **Bridgeport Brewery & Pub** (1313 NW Marshall St, 241-7179) at work. The comfortable pub, with its library of periodicals and exceptionally good pizza, encourages lingering over Blue Heron Ale, India Pale Ale, Bridgeport Ale, and seasonal brews. In the summer the best tables are out on the loading dock under ropes of leafy green hops.

Head to the waterfront along the RiverPlace esplanade for **Full Sail Brewing Company**'s Portland brewery. Tours are by appointment only (222-5343), but you can see the works from the adjoining pub (**The Harborside Pilsner Room**, 0309 SW Montgomery, 220-1865) and sample 12 beers, including their best-selling Amber Ale, Golden Ale, and Nut-Brown Ale.

Widmer Brewing Company is one of the finer Portland breweries, which may be why Anheuser-Busch recently purchased a minority interest in the company. Corporate or not, Widmer brews the city's favorite hefeweizen in its facility on an industrial byway in North Portland. The attached, attractive beer hall, the **Widmer Gasthaus** (955 N Russell St, 281-3333), is a fine place to sample Widmer suds with a plate of sausage and kraut or a pretzel.

A new brewery that's garnered attention on the international level is **Hair of the Dog** (4509 SE 29th Ave, 232-6585), producing sublime bottle-conditioned strong beer. British beer writer Michael Jackson has pegged their Adam beer as one of his personal favorites. It's a small operation, but the beer makers at Hair of the Dog are happy to give tours (call ahead for directions).

Technically, the **McMenamins** joints all over town are not breweries, they're brewpubs. The difference? A brewery is exactly what it claims to be—sometimes with a pub or tasting room attached. A brewpub is more of a novelty—a brewery that makes its beer only for a particular bar or, in the case of McMenamins, a group of bars. Most will give tours by prior arrangement only, though there's always a place to get a peek at the process. Of the dozens of McMenamins pubs in Portland and other Oregon cities, only a handful have in-house breweries. In Portland, try the **Fulton Pub and Brewery** (0618 SW Nebraska

St, 246-9530) or the original **Hillsdale Brewery and Public House** (1505 SW Sunset Blvd, 246-3938). **Cornelius Pass Roadhouse and Brewery** (Sunset Hwy and Cornelius Pass Rd, Hillsboro; 640-6174), in a huge, inviting farmhouse, is favored by the techies who work in the neighborhood. There are also a number of popular brewpubs in town that aren't owned by the McMenamin brothers, including the **Alameda Brewhouse** (4765 NE Fremont St, 460-9025) and the **Lucky Labrador Brewpub** (915 SE Hawthorne Blvd, 236-3555). See also Brewpubs in the Nightlife chapter, and the review for Alameda Brewhouse and Cornelius Pass Roadhouse and Brewery in the Restaurants chapter.

One way to sample brews from several different places and not have to drive along the way is to take the **Portland Brew Bus** (273-9206; www.brewbus.com). For $29.95—including beer, snacks, and tours—the bus takes you to at least three breweries, where you can sample a lot of beer and learn how it is made. Scheduled tours are Saturday afternoons, although you and some friends can schedule a group gig almost anytime you're thirsty.

ANTIQUING IN SELLWOOD
SE 13th Ave from Malden to Clatsop Sts (map:JJ5)

At the east end of the Sellwood Bridge is Portland's antique territory—13 blocks of antique and collectible shops. Sellwood, once a separate town on the east bank of the Willamette, was annexed to Portland in the 1890s, and it is proud of its past: shop owners have placed signs on their buildings identifying their original uses and construction dates. The better part of a day can be spent browsing in this old neighborhood, now a repository of American country furniture, lace, quilts, toys, hardware, china, jewelry, and trinkets.

Particularly noteworthy are **1874 House** (8070 SE 13th Ave, 233-1874), crammed with brass and copper hardware, light fixtures, and architectural fragments; and **R. Spencer's** (8130 SE 13th Ave, 238-1737), with fine art and collectibles. **The Raven** (7805 SE 13th Ave, 233-8075) features all things military. The **General Store** (7987 SE 13th Ave, 233-1321) is housed in the 1905 Caldwell Grocery, whose back wall is the exterior of an old caboose from the Spokane, Portland, and Seattle Railway. The **Sellwood Antique Mall** (7875 SE 13th Ave, 232-3755) is one of the better of these malls in town.

Follow SE 13th Avenue across Tacoma Street to **Old Sellwood Square** (8235 SE 13th Ave). The **Webfoot Bookman** (239-5233) retails old books on Oregon and the West, and **Jonathan's** (233-1489) deals in estate jewelry and Victorian silver.

To restore your energy, stop in at **El Palenque** (8324 SE 17th Ave, 231-5140) for Portland's only Salvadoran cuisine, or head north to neighboring Westmoreland, where you can find some of the most exciting food in the city at **Fiddleheads** (6816 SE Milwaukie Ave, 233-1547), sip wine and nibble superior snacks at Caprial's Bistro and Wine (7015 SE Milwaukie Ave, 236-6457), or check out the exotic menu at BJ's Brazilian Restaurant (7019 SE Milwaukie Ave, 236-9629).

GARDENS

Portland has been called the gardening capital of the United States. That may or may not be true, but there's no disputing the fact that it is a fantastic place to get your hands dirty. The Willamette Valley's mild climate makes for a long growing season that supports a variety of plant life about which most American gardeners only fantasize, and the diversity, expertise, and wild enthusiasm of the local green thumbs make it fertile ground in more ways than one.

Accomplished Portland gardeners are not a recent phenomenon. In 1889 the nation's first rose society was established here, soon followed by the first primrose and rhododendron societies. By the 1920s, Portland boasted more garden clubs than any other city in the nation; they now total more than 20.

This predilection for plant life means that visitors will encounter gardens in unexpected places. Small bamboo, butterfly, and lily gardens, for example, are tucked between exhibits at the Washington Park Zoo (see Washington Park in the Major Attractions section of this chapter). There are more than 120 named varieties of camellias on the University of Portland campus. A third-floor courtyard in Good Samaritan Hospital includes a rose garden; the Kaiser Permanente Clinic in Rockwood (669-3900) maintains a sinister garden of common poisonous plants, designed to alert parents to backyard dangers.

Gardens

The Community Gardens Program (823-1612) took root in Portland in the 1970s; it has spread to 21 neighborhood locations. Both year-round and summer 20-by-20-foot plots are available; some gardens have waiting lists. For those who would rather look than dig, the Friends of Portland Community Gardens has established a demonstration site at Fulton Garden (SW Second Ave and SW Miles St) featuring raised beds, irrigation and composting methods, heirloom seeds, and new plant varieties. A backyard wildlife habitat cozies up to the Clinton Garden (SE 18th Ave and SE Clinton St), and a demonstration orchard spreads its limbs next to the Gabriel Garden (SW 41st Ave and SW Canby St).

The following gardens are among the city's horticultural highlights—all free and open daily, unless otherwise noted.

Berry Botanic Garden Berry's quarter-acre rock garden is more than an extraordinary accumulation of alpine plants; it is also part of this Dunthorpe garden's nationally recognized effort to preserve endangered plant species. The primrose collection, for example, contains several varieties that are threatened in their native habitats. Three other plant groups (lilies, rhododendrons, and Northwest natives) are featured on the 6½-acre Mrs. Rae Selling Berry estate. Groups may schedule tours with volunteer guides who explain the connection between the lush woodland, streamside plantings, and berry-seed bank. During the warm-weather months, the garden is open every day, from 9am to 5pm (or so); call ahead to tell them you're coming and to get directions. Admission is $2 for nonmembers. ▪ *11505 SW Summerville Ave; 636-4112; map:JJ6.*

Crystal Springs Rhododendron Garden Kodachrome was invented for places like this. Normally, this nationally acclaimed garden near Reed College is a peaceful green retreat for bird-watchers and neighborhood strollers. In April, May, and June, however, Crystal Springs becomes an irresistible magnet for color-happy camera and video buffs, as some 2,500 rhododendrons, azaleas, and companion plants blaze on the 7-acre grounds. Japanese maples, sourwood trees, and fothergillas paint the garden in fall, and the spring-fed lake, home to a sizable colony of waterfowl, is a year-round attraction. Although the garden is free to view on Tuesdays and Wednesdays, a $2 admission fee is charged Thursday through Monday, March through Labor Day. The annual plant sale and show are held on Mother's Day, when loads of Portlanders traditionally promenade through at peak bloom, and Crystal Springs is *the* spot for a spring wedding. Finally, check out the elegant new gatehouse, completed in 1997. ▪ *SE 28th Ave, one block north of Woodstock Blvd; 771-8386; map:II5.*

Elk Rock: The Garden of the Bishop's Close This 13-acre estate at the edge of the exclusive Dunthorpe neighborhood serves as the headquarters of the Episcopal Diocese of Oregon, which explains the name: "close" is an English term for an enclosed place or garden—especially one adjoining a church, where monks used to march in peace. This garden's genesis, however, dates back 75 years to the collaboration between its owner, Scottish grain merchant Peter Kerr, and New York landscape architect John Olmsted, son of Central Park designer Frederick Law Olmsted. Together they created an exquisite terraced garden facing Mount Hood and overlooking pristine Elk Rock in the Willamette River. Both native and rare plants are featured, including a multitude of madrones and 70 varieties of magnolia. Other highlights are lily ponds, a landscaped watercourse fed by a natural spring, a large rock garden, a formal boxwood-hedged terrace, and some of the finest specimens of wisteria you're likely ever to see. Tread respectfully. Open daily. ▪ *11800 SW Military Lane; 636-5613; map:JJ6.*

Home Orchard Society Arboretum Adjacent to the John Inskeep Environmental Learning Center (at Clackamas Community College) is a dazzling assortment of fruit-bearing plants. The Home Orchard Society cultivates dwarf fruit trees, with terrific samplings

of apple and pear varieties. If you've been wanting to add a blueberry bush to your yard—or a kiwi vine, persimmon, papaw, or
plum-apricot cross—this is the place to decide on the variety. The
hours are 8am to 3pm on Saturdays, March through October, or
call to arrange a tour. ▪ *19600 S Molalla Ave, Oregon City; 631-*
3574; map:OO3.

Hoyt Arboretum See Washington Park in the Major Attractions
section of this chapter.

International Rose Test Garden See Washington Park in the Major
Attractions section of this chapter.

Japanese Garden See Washington Park in the Major Attractions
section of this chapter.

John Inskeep Environmental Learning Center What was once an 8-
acre plot of ravaged land—the wastewater lagoons and parking
lots of a berry-processing plant—is now home to shady paths,
ponds, and wildlife habitat in an urban setting. The learning
center at Clackamas Community College demonstrates environmentally sound solutions to landscape problems, incorporating
recycled plastic "logs" in footbridges and utilizing solar- and com-
post-heated greenhouses in the nursery. [KIDS] Kids flock to the
birds of prey exhibit—featuring an owl, three eagles, and several
hawks—and to the ponds, home to muskrats and ducks. The ▼
observatory's 24-inch refractor telescope is open during cloud- **Parks and**
less Friday and Saturday evenings. ▪ *19600 S Molalla Ave,* **Waterfront**
Oregon City; 657-6958; map:OO3. ▲

Leach Botanical Garden The emphasis on native Northwest
plants in this garden is fitting: one of the garden's creators discovered two genera and 11 species in Northwest wildernesses.
Well-known amateur botanist Lilla Leach and her husband, John,
began their 5-acre garden along Johnson Creek in the early
1930s; today it encompasses more than 14 acres and 1,500
species of wildflowers, shrubs, native irises, and ferns; recently,
bog and rock gardens have been added. [KIDS] The Leaches'
1930s manor house is used for children's nature study classes; it
can be rented for weddings and meetings. Open every day but
Monday, with tours at 2pm Wednesdays and 10am Saturdays. ▪
6704 SE 122nd Ave; 761-9503; map:HH1.

PARKS AND WATERFRONT

Blue Lake Park [KIDS] Although there is a 3-acre natural wetlands area here, most of Blue Lake Park is unabashedly developed, with plenty of parking, swimming, boat rentals, volleyball
courts, paved paths, playfields, and other facilities. Metro's
Regional Parks and Greenspaces Department holds a summer
concert series here featuring everything from country to
Caribbean; admission to the concert area is $3.50 for adults and

$1 for teenagers. There is weekly kids' entertainment too, with puppets, comedy, and music. Park admission is $3 for cars, and free for walkers and cyclists (no pets). Groups and families are entitled to discounts. ■ *Blue Lake Rd at N Marine Dr and NE 223rd Ave, Troutdale; 797-1850 or 665-4995.*

Council Crest Park   Set atop one of the tallest peaks in the Tualatin Mountains, Council Crest Park is valued for its nearly panoramic views of the Coast Range and the Cascades. Park at the top, especially popular at sunset. The Marquam Hill Trail crosses through the Douglas firs and maple forest on the northwest side of the hill. ■ *Top of Marquam Hill, a 10-minute drive southwest of downtown—follow SW Vista Ave from W Burnside, then continue on SW Talbot Rd; map:HH7.*

Elk Rock Island   Each spring, high waters on the Willamette impede access to this pristine island, but at other times you can step from Milwaukie's Spring Park across the gravel-scrubbed bedrock to the island. Great blue herons feed in the little bay between the island and Milwaukie's Spring Park. Migrating Canada geese graze on the shelf of grass on the island's west side. A sublime natural rock formation cascades out of the oak forest on the northwest end, while the deepest waters of the Willamette (home to many sturgeon) slice by. Local lore attributes the name to Native Americans driving elk over the bluff and floating them to the island for processing. Watch for poison oak if you've a notion to wander into the woods. ■ *SE 19th Ave and Bluebird St, Milwaukie; map:KK4.*

▼

Parks and Waterfront

▲

Forest Park   In 1948, after more than 40 years of citizen effort, 4,200 acres of forestland were formally designated Forest Park. The land had survived logging, wildfire burns, subdivision into private lots, and an aborted scenic-road project. Now expanded to 4,683 acres, it is the largest city park in the nation. The forest wilderness includes 50 miles of trails and 30 miles of gated roadways for mountain biking along northwest Portland's Tualatin Mountains, and is an easy 10-minute drive from downtown. Leif Erickson Drive, an 11-mile gravel road that stretches from NW Thurman Street to Germantown Road, is all that remains of an ambitious real estate agent's 1914 plans for a subdivision. Now closed to cars, the popular hiking, running, and mountain-biking lane is paved for a short stretch near NW Thurman Street; its rough section parallels the Wildwood Trail (see Hiking in the Recreation chapter). An indispensible reference to the park is Marcy Cottrell Houle's *One City's Wilderness: Portland's Forest Park*, which includes maps, park history, and flora and fauna checklists. ■ *Boundaries: north of W Burnside to NW Newberry Rd, west of NW St. Helens Rd (Hwy 30) to SW Skyline Rd; 823-4492; map:DD9–FF7.*

Hoyt Arboretum   See Washington Park in the Major Attractions section of this chapter.

Kelley Point Park   This is an isolated park across the channel from Sauvie Island at the convergence of the Willamette and Columbia Rivers. Biking, hiking, and wildlife viewing are best in the spring and fall. An easy 15-mile trail skirts the lake. In the summer, Kelley Point is inundated with picnickers and sun-bathers. Despite abundant wildlife, the slow-moving waters are polluted, and water experts advise against swimming and fishing. As in all urban-area parks, leave your valuables at home and lock your car. ■ *N Suttle Rd off west end of N Marine Dr; map:AA9–BB6.*

Mary S. Young State Park   Along the Willamette River, this sub-urban refuge is stalwartly defending itself from surrounding development. The 160-acre park has baseball diamonds, soccer fields, picnic spots, 2 miles of dense forest trails, and a half-mile bike path. The state maintains it in as close to its original natural condition as possible. ■ *Hwy 43, just south of Marylhurst College, West Linn; map:MM5.*

Oxbow Park   In the oxbow bends of the Sandy River Gorge, old-growth forests and wildlife thrive (in part because no dogs are allowed—not even on a leash). Formally the park covers over 1,000 acres, but the ecosystem appears to extend upstream to the Sandy River Preserve (owned by The Nature Conservancy) and downstream to the YMCA camp. In October the park hosts its annual Salmon Festival, focusing on the spawning salmon (see the Calendar chapter), and in December there's a two-day fly-fishing festival. One of the state's finer winter steelhead fisheries is in the Sandy River, with 4 miles of access in the park's bound-aries. About 15 miles of hiking trails follow the river and climb the ridges, and more than half are open to horses. The park includes 45 camping sites, probably the closest public camp-grounds to Portland proper. Call the park for information on spe-cial Sandy River fishing rules and guided raft trips. Year-round interpretive hikes, programs, films, and lectures are available to groups and the public; call for reservations. ■ *8 miles east of Gre-sham via SE Division St and Oxbow Pkwy, Gresham; 663-4708 or 797-1850.*

▼

**Parks and
Waterfront**

▲

Portland Audubon Society Sanctuary   See Bird-Watching/Wildlife Viewing in the Recreation chapter. ■ *5151 NW Cornell Rd; 292-6855; map:FF7.*

Powell Butte   Plenty of horses, mountain bikes, and hikers share the trails in this park, and on days with perfect weather, the trails can be downright crowded. From the meadows at the 630-foot summit, you can see north to Mount St. Helens and south to Mount Jefferson. A 2-mile loop circles the volcanic mound on the way to the top. Watch out for poison oak. ■ *SE Powell Blvd and SE 162nd Ave; map:JJ1.*

Rooster Rock State Park On a warm weekend, all 1,800 parking spaces for this mile-long sandy beach are full. The familiar Crown Point viewpoint rises on the other side of I-84. There's a logged-off swimming hole in the Columbia River, a boat launch, and docks for boats and anglers. On the far east end, a separate beach has been designated "clothing optional." When the east wind is blowing, windsurfers crowd the beaches; call Micro Forecasts, (800)934-2278, for Columbia River wind and weather information. Park admission is $3 per car. ▪ *Take I-84 east to exit 25; 695-2261.*

Sauvie Island Wildlife Management Area The hinterlands of Sauvie Island offer great birding opportunities, but in the past two decades, both human and car traffic in this area have tripled. To finance toilets, parking, an interpretive center, and maintenance, the Oregon Fish and Wildlife Commission charges $3 daily and $10.50 annually for car-park permits for this 12,000-acre state wildlife preserve. Walton Beach, one of the few sandy beaches on the Columbia, is located at the end of the paved portion of NW Reeder Road. Warrior Rock Lighthouse is a 3-mile hike from the north unit parking facility. Non-wildlife-related activity is discouraged; open fires are prohibited, and there are no picnic facilities. (See Day Trips in the Outings chapter.) ▪ *At confluence of Willamette and Columbia Rivers (10 miles northwest of Portland via Hwy 30), on north end of Sauvie Island; 621-3488; map:AA9.*

▼

Parks and Waterfront

▲

Silver Falls State Park Silver Falls, a 1½-hour drive southeast of Portland, can't really be considered a *Portland* park. But it's certainly a park Portlanders love visiting to see the (at least) 10 waterfalls that drape Silver Creek Canyon. South Falls, the most spectacular, is a short walk from the lodge and main parking area. Farther up Highway 214, parking is available within a few hundred yards of Winter Falls, North Falls, and Upper North Falls. The essence of Silver Falls State Park, however, is best taken in from the 7-mile Silver Creek Canyon Trail, constructed in the 1930s by the Civilian Conservation Corps. A conference center makes this a favorite meeting and retreat spot. Lots of other trails: 4 miles for bikes, 3 miles for joggers, and 12 miles for horses. More than 100 campsites offer overnight accommodations; 53 sites have electrical hookups. ▪ *20024 Silver Falls Hwy SE, Sublimity Park; 873-8681.*

Smith and Bybee Lakes In industrial north Portland, this designated natural area, encompassing nearly 2,100 acres of lakes and wetlands, is yet another haven where urbanites can hike, watch wildlife, and listen to birds call. (The bird blinds offer a good place to spy on wildlife, especially blue herons in the slough.) The newly constructed trails make up a portion of Portland's Forty-Mile Loop Trail (see Day Trips in the Outings chapter).

• *North Portland Peninsula between Delta and Kelley Point Parks; map:CC7–CC8.*

Springwater Corridor A true gem among Portland parks, the abandoned Springwater rail line—also known as the Bellrose Line—is a favorite pedestrian and mountain-biking path, and its popularity will only increase as word of its existence gets out. It's an important link in the Forty-Mile Loop Trail (see Day Trips in the Outings chapter). • *16½ miles, from Sellwood east to Boring.*

Tom McCall Waterfront Park See RiverPlace/Tom McCall Waterfront Park in the Major Attractions section of this chapter.

Tryon Creek State Park Like Forest Park, the Tryon Creek canyon was threatened with a housing project. Thanks to the Friends of Tryon Creek State Park, a citizens' group organized to raise money to buy the land, it is now a park consisting of 645 protected acres between Lewis and Clark College and Lake Oswego. There are 14 miles of intersecting trails, including the paved half-mile Trillium Trail—the first all-abilities trail in an Oregon state park—and a 3-mile bike trail along the park's border with Terwilliger Boulevard. The Nature Center features a bookstore, exhibits, and a meeting room (see Meetings, Conferences, and Receptions in the Essentials chapter). And a Trillium festival is hosted in April, when these delicate flowers blossom (see the Calendar chapter for details). • *11321 SW Terwilliger Blvd (1 mile off Hwy 43), Lake Oswego; 636-9886; map:KK6.*

ORGANIZED TOURS

MOTOR TOURS

ART: The Cultural Bus Aka Tri-Met bus 63, ART hits all the city's cultural hot spots: the Portland Art Museum, Oregon History Center, OMSI, and the Washington Park Zoo, to name a few. Wildly designed by beloved Portland artist Henk Pander and his sons, Arnold and Jacob, ART is itself a masterpiece. Prices are the same for all Tri-Met buses. • *238-7433 for information (or see the Essentials chapter for information on the Tri-Met system).*

Evergreen–Gray Line of Portland This touring agency offers several bus-tour choices, including a northern Oregon Coast tour ($42) and three Portland city tours year-round (two half-day tours for $22 each, and a combination of the two for $38). From late March through mid-October, two 4½-hour tours take in Timberline Lodge and Mount Hood ($28) and Multnomah Falls and the Columbia River Gorge ($28); one deluxe tour makes the whole loop for $38; and for the same price they offer a bus-and-boat tour of the gorge, including a stretch on the stern-wheeler. Pickup can be arranged from any major hotel. Reservations required. • *285-9845.*

Portland Parks and Recreation Historical Tours These educational day trips sponsored by the Outdoor Recreation Department of Portland Parks and Recreation cover a gold mine of historic places: the Oregon Trail, Lewis and Clark's route to Astoria, the Columbia Gorge, Portland cemeteries, and even a literal gold mine—Bohemia. Portland historian and writer Dick Pintarich leads the popular van tours. Most span the entire day (8am to 7pm), give or take a few good stories. April through October only. Reservations required. ■ *823-5132.*

WALKING TOURS

Peter's Walking Tours [KIDS] Former elementary school teacher Peter Chausse offers walking tours of the downtown area, any day of the week. A knowledgeable and enthusiastic guide, Chausse focuses on the city's art, architecture, and history. A two-hour, 2-mile tour costs $10 for adults, $5 for teens, and nothing for children. Call to reserve a time. ■ *665-2588.*

Portland Public Art Walking Tour Request the map at the Regional Arts & Culture Council (309 SW Sixth Ave, Suite 100), the Portland Art Museum (1219 SW Park Ave), the Oregon Convention Center (NE Martin Luther King Jr. Blvd and NE Holladay St), the main lobby of the Portland Building (1120 SW Fifth Ave), or the Portland/Oregon Visitors Association (SW Naito Pkwy and SW Salmon St). See Art in Public Places in The Arts chapter for more information on public art and architecture. ■ *823-5111.*

▼

**Organized
Tours**

Motor Tours

▲

Urban Tour Group [KIDS] [FREE] For more than 25 years, schoolchildren and adults alike have learned Portland history from UTG volunteers. Teachers, round up the kids—school groups are free. Private tours cost $5 per person ($25 minimum); reservations are a must. Tourists can choose one of three stock tours, or have one custom-made. ■ *227-5780.*

Waterfront Bridge Walks There are few cities that offer such diverse bridgework as Portland, and fewer yet that feature tours by such a lively and devoted guide as Sharon Wood, whose *Portland Bridge Book* was published in 1989. Schedule one of her tours, such as the annual July Fourth Bridge Walk, by calling the Portland Parks and Recreation Department. Wood also offers private tours; call her office (222-5535). ■ *823-5132.*

BOAT TOURS
See River Cruises in the Major Attractions section of this chapter.

TRAIN AND TROLLEY TOURS

Metro Washington Park Zoo Railway [KIDS] The zoo railway boasts the only surviving railroad post office in the country, so mailing a postcard while you're on board is a must. A round-trip ticket to ride the train from the zoo to the Rose Garden costs $2.75, $2 for seniors and children 3–11 (in addition to zoo admission). You'll get a dose of history and some nice scenery along the 35-minute loop; the winter route is shorter. At Halloween and Christmas, special railroad-related events are planned. ■ *Metro Washington Park Zoo; 226-ROAR.*

Molalla Miniature Train—Pacific Northwest Live Steamers [KIDS]

[FREE] All-volunteer hobbyists drive these miniature trains along a seven-tenths-mile route noon to 5pm every Sunday, May to October. Passengers can bring their own lunches and relax in the shaded picnic area, admiring the fine, detailed antique trains. ■ *Southeast of downtown Portland; (503)829-6866.*

Mount Hood Scenic Railroad [KIDS]

The restored Pullman cars of the Mount Hood Railroad chug from Hood River to Parkdale, April through December, linking the Columbia Gorge to the foothills of Mount Hood. Tickets are $21.95 for adults, $18.95 for seniors 60 and over, and $13.95 for children 2–12. The line has recently added two new runs: a Saturday dinner train for $67.50 and a Sunday brunch for $55. The spring run gives rail riders spectacular views of blossoming orchards; in December the Christmas-tree train gives riders the chance to chop down their own tree, haul it on the train, and visit with Santa. Call to get a full list of seasonal events. ■ *(541)386-3556 or (800)872-4661.*

Samtrack [KIDS]

A bright red-and-white train allows you to take in the riverine scenery between OMSI and the legendary Oaks Amusement Park near the Sellwood Bridge. The open-air train runs every day but Monday, departing SE Spokane Street on the hour and OMSI on the half hour, June through Labor Day. The round trip takes about an hour, but allow time to get lost at either OMSI or the amusement park. Round-trip fare is $4 for ages 5 and up ($3 one way) and $1.50 for kids 1–4. ■ *659-5452.*

Vintage Trolley [KIDS][FREE]

Four oak-paneled and brass-belled trolleys—replicas of the city's old Council Crest trolley—follow the MAX route (catch the trolley at any light-rail station), from Lloyd Center to the downtown turnaround at SW 11th Avenue and back. Top speed is 35 miles an hour, and the round trip takes about 40 minutes. The trolley is free, and operates from 9:30am to 3pm on weekdays, and 10am to 6pm Saturday and Sunday. Vintage Trolley is owned by PGE and operated by Tri-Met. ■ *323-7363.*

Willamette Shore Trolley [KIDS]

The Willamette Shore Trolley has been running along the river from downtown Portland to Lake Oswego for nine years, keeping the track warm for eventual mass transportation development. Two trolleys, one built in 1902 in Blackpool, England, and another 1932 model from Portland, run for 7 miles from RiverPlace to the State Street terminal in Lake Oswego (call for current schedule). Round-trip tickets are $6 adults, $5 for seniors, $3 for children under 12. Charter runs are available for large groups; everyone should call for a reservation ■ *222-2226.*

Organized
Tours

*Train
and
Trolley
Tours*

Whether you're a resident or a visitor, here are suggestions for spending one day—or as many as three days—enjoying the best of Portland. Specifics on most of the places in boldface type may be found in the appropriate chapters (Restaurants, Shopping, The Arts, Lodgings, Exploring, etc.) throughout this guide.

ONE DAY

If you have just one day in Portland, you'll want to get downtown and stay there—it's one of the most interesting and lively urban cores in the nation. Ideally, you'll spend the night at either the **Heathman Hotel** or the **Hotel Vintage Plaza**.

Morning: King salmon hash at the **Heathman Restaurant and Bar** is a tasteful—and tasty—way to begin your day. If coffee and a pastry are more your style, head to **Pazzoria Bakery and Cafe** (just next door to **Pazzo Ristorante**). After breakfast, stretch your legs with a walk in **Tom McCall Waterfront Park** or along the elm-lined **South Park Blocks**.

Afternoon: Stop for a sandwich at the **Red Star Tavern & Roast House**, or order a pizza, dressed in upscale ingredients, at **B. Moloch**. Book lovers should then go on to **Powell's Books**; art lovers to the **Portland Art Museum**; history buffs to the **Oregon History Center**; and shoppers to **Pioneer Place**, **Nike Town**, or (if it's a weekend day) the **Saturday Market** in **Old Town**.

▼

Itineraries

▲

Evening: One excellent place to snag a reservation is **Higgin's**, where local ingredients receive reverential treatment. Bring the evening to a close with a view of the city lights from the bar at **Atwater's**, 30 stories up in the US Bank Building.

TWO DAYS

After a day spent downtown, you could easily linger for another day in the **Pearl District** and **Northwest Portland**.

Morning: Excellent breakfasts are the norm at **Shakers**, or for lighter fare drop into **Torrefazione**. After breakfast, explore the pastoral side of the city at the **Washington Park Rose Garden**, especially during summer months, or the **Japanese Garden**, both dramatic any time of year. For a bit more of a workout, hike into **Forest Park** via the **Wildwood Trail** or **Leif Erickson Drive**.

Afternoon: For outstanding Thai food, stop in at **Typhoon!** or make your way down NW 23rd Avenue for a salad and voluptuous dessert at **Papa Haydn**. Spend the afternoon browsing the boutiques along NW 23rd or NW 21st Avenues, and then hit the **Pearl District**, along NW Glisan Street. **Art galleries** abound in the Pearl; pick up a guide at the **Laura Russo Gallery** while you're still on NW 21st Avenue—or just wander among the

Pearl's warehouses; you're bound to find something interesting. Stop to rest and drink a glass of India Pale Ale at **Bridgeport.**

Evening: You have your pick of excellent restaurants, all within a few blocks of one another. For variety you might have drinks and appetizers at **Zefiro**, and move on to dinner at **Wildwood**. Go from there to the quiet and romantic bar at **L'Auberge** for a sliver of poached lemon cheesecake, the fireplace, and a mug of something warm, or head over to the loud, lively bar scene at **Bima**.

THREE DAYS

Spend two days in the city, and one day on the road. Head to the **Columbia River Gorge** for stunning views, and don't forget a jacket: you will probably feel the famous east wind.

Morning: Have breakfast in Troutdale at **Edgefield** (in fact, you might book a bed-and-breakfast room the night before your gorge day). Then get off the I-84 freeway and head east on the **Historic Columbia River Highway** (Highway 30). Stop at **Crown Point** for the sweeping vista 725 feet above the river; you might visit any one of the many waterfalls along the way for a hike (one option is powerful Multnomah Falls, the second-highest falls in the country).

▼

Afternoon: Make your way to **Hood River** for lunch. Take a picnic down to the **Columbia Gorge Sailpark/Marina** and watch the brightly outfitted board sailors flit across the water. On your way back to town, save time for a stop at the **Bonneville Dam**, with its underwater windows for viewing the fish ladders, and the **Bonneville Fish Hatchery**, where the sturgeon are as long as alligators and almost as prehistoric-looking.

Evening: Head back toward Portland for dinner. You might try one of these old favorites: **Jake's Famous Crawfish, Bread and Ink Cafe**, or **Indigine**. Or if you're in the mood to splurge on your last night in town, reserve a table at gracious **Genoa.**

ONE DAY WITH KIDS

Morning: Breakfast at the **Original Pancake House** is popular with everybody—allow plenty of time to be seated (although service from that point is snappy). Depending on the ages of the children and everyone's interests, you might spend the rest of the morning at the **Washington Park Zoo**, the **Oregon Museum of Science and Industry**, or **Fort Vancouver National Historic Site** (north just over the I-5 bridge in Vancouver, Washington).

Afternoon: Get a look at Portland from the Willamette River; the *Portland Spirit* offers excursions for all ages and leaves from the dock near the **Salmon Street Springs**. (If the *Spirit* is booked, try another company; many other **river cruises** are available.)

I

Evening: Take the whole clan out to **Alexis** for a Greek feast, complete with belly dancing; or to **Pizzicato** on NW 23rd Avenue if pizza is the only thing everyone can agree on. After dinner, **Ben & Jerry's** on **Hawthorne Boulevard** features all the frozen treats any family could want, and the funky shops of the Hawthorne area afford great window-shopping.

BEACH DAY

You *can* see the Oregon Coast in a day trip from Portland; we just recommend you take longer in order to gain a sense of its beauty—from craggy cliffs constantly battered by the surf, to tide pools swimming with aquatic life, to the wide, windswept beaches. If we had only 12 hours, though, here's what we would do.

Morning: Start early and head west on Highway 26 toward **Seaside**—skip it, though, and go directly south on Highway 101 to **Cannon Beach**. Have a late, great breakfast at the **Midtown Cafe**. Walk this idyllic town's wonderful beach; it's a good stroll even during high tide and, graced by its signature Haystack Rock offshore, is always picturesque. Plenty of shops and galleries to look into, too.

Afternoon: Grab a bag of picnic supplies in Cannon Beach and drive south to **Oswald West State Park**, where you can walk through an old-growth forest to a massive cove with tide pools. Linger among the rocks; lose yourself in the pounding of the surf. Then head farther south to Manzanita for dinner.

Evening: Reserve a table at the **Blue Sky Cafe** in advance. After dinner, take one last stroll on the maybe moonlit—and hopefully not rain-lashed—beach. Then hit the road; it's a solid two hours back to Portland.

SHOPPING

Shopping

DOWNTOWN

Unlike many big cities in this country, Portland has successfully encouraged retail in its **downtown core**. The result is something you don't often witness elsewhere in the United States: people actually come in from the suburbs to shop. A few big department stores (Nordstrom, Meier & Frank, Saks) and the Pioneer Place mall attract the lion's share of attention, but a large number of boutiques, specialty shops, and chains also entice shoppers. (For shopping highlights in the downtown area, see the Exploring chapter.)

NEIGHBORHOODS

Shoppers flock in droves to **NW 23rd Avenue** (from W Burnside north to NW Thurman St; map:GG7) for chic apparel, arty gifts, myriad housewares, and a coffee stop on practically every block (see the Exploring chapter). Down toward the river is the restored **Skidmore/Old Town** (between Naito Pkwy and Fourth Ave from SW Oak to NW Glisan Sts; map:H5–L5), which has a few good shops, a couple of dependable Greek restaurants, and some fine galleries. On weekends, Skidmore livens with the Saturday Market (again, see the Exploring chapter for details).

Southwest of town is the charming **Multnomah Village** (just off SW Multnomah Blvd on SW Capitol Hwy; map:II7), with a quaint, small-town personality revolving around several eateries, an excellent bookstore, a few arty shops, and about a dozen antique stores (see Major Attractions in the Exploring chapter). Alongside the Willamette is the Water Tower at **Johns Landing** (between the Ross Island and Sellwood Bridges on SW Macadam Ave, open every day and weekday evenings; map:II6), with three stories of shops, including imported and specialty-size clothing retailers and jewelers. Cross the Sellwood Bridge into the city's southeast corner; **Sellwood** (SE Tacoma St and SE 13th Ave; map:II5) is inundated with stores selling country antiques (see Major Attractions in the Exploring chapter).

The **Hawthorne** area (SE Hawthorne Blvd between about SE 30th and SE 45th Aves; map:GG5) has that thrown-together look— great for browsing. Scavengers can spend hours pawing through secondhand record shops and vintage clothiers, just down the street from an Italian foods specialty shop, a top-drawer cookbook store, and natural-fiber boutiques (see the Exploring chapter). To the north, **NE Broadway** (east from NE Seventh Ave; map:FF5) has experienced a renaissance of its own, with clothing, kitchenware, and book shops; a good wine store; a brewpub; and more than a half-dozen better-than-average restaurants.

SUBURBAN MALLS

Long a fixture of Portland life, the **Lloyd Center** (east across the Broadway Bridge, bordered by NE Broadway and NE Multnomah, and NE Ninth and NE 16th Aves, open daily; map:FF5) remains the state's largest mall. A multimillion-dollar renovation in the last decade put a glass roof over the entire structure (including the ice rink); these days there are three levels with nearly 200 shops. Nordstrom is the foremost anchor store; Meier & Frank and J.C. Penney are also there. Lloyd Center's proximity to downtown (connected by MAX light rail), as well as to the Oregon Convention Center and the Rose Quarter, have all helped give this formerly faltering mall a new life.

The west side is crawling with malls. Between Beaverton and Tigard is the largest, **Washington Square and Square Too** (just off Hwy 217, open daily; map:II9). A food court, lots of specialty shops, and the essential Nordstrom (the newest in town) are the big draws.

Beaverton Town Square (off SW Canyon Rd and SW Beaverton-Hillsdale Hwy off Hwy 217, open daily; map:HH9), marked by its clock tower, and the **Beaverton Mall** (take SW Walker Rd exit off Hwy 217, open daily; map:HH9) are smaller westside shopping stops.

Back across the river lie **Mall 205** (take the SE Stark St exit off I-205, open daily; map:GG3) and the booming **Clackamas Town Center** (take the Sunnyside Rd exit from I-205, open daily; map:KK3), best known as the place Tonya Harding learned to skate. Up north is **Jantzen Beach Center** (just off I-5 at Jantzen Beach, open daily; map:BB6), which stands out from the crowd with a 72-horse merry-go-round in the center of the mall ($1 a spin).

ACCESSORIES AND LUGGAGE

The Coach Store With strong lines and classic silhouettes, Coach bags have an understated elegance. Choose carefully from the overwhelming selection, because these leather goods never go out of style and will probably last forever. Handbags, briefcases, and luggage, plus accessories, from mini-belt bags to writing portfolios. ▪ *Pioneer Place; 294-0772; map:G4; every day.* ▪ *Washington Square; 968-1772; map:JJ9; every day.*

John Helmer Haberdasher The real substance here is hats—and lots of 'em. There's also tried-and-true men's clothing (since 1921) and classic umbrellas, ascots, suspenders, and gloves. Three generations of experienced salespeople will help, if you ask, with tips on knotting a bow tie. ▪ *969 SW Broadway; 223-4976; map:G2; Mon-Sat.*

Portland Luggage Competitively priced Portland Luggage has been in business almost 60 years. A purist's delight, this shop carries fine leather luggage and business cases, and is unencumbered by the exotic gifts that most luggage stores seem to stock. ▪ *421 SW Stark; 226-3255; map:I4; Mon-Sat.* ▪ *Beaverton Town Square; 641-3456; map:HH9; every day.*

ANTIQUES

▼
Antiques
▲

Give antique lovers a free afternoon and a handful of good shops to poke through, and it doesn't really matter if they bag their intended prey—it's the thrill of the hunt that counts. As the ever-increasing number of antique malls, colonies, and villages indicates, dealers who cluster together provide especially appealing hunting grounds.

In Portland, the biggest such browsers' mecca is **Sellwood**, where about two dozen antique stores—plus a generous leavening of country and gift shops—line a 12-block stretch of SE 13th Avenue (see the Exploring chapter).

Another popular territory, southwest Portland's **Multnomah Village**, has the look of a small-town Main Street—which is just what it was until Portland swallowed it up many years ago. Today there are a dozen or so vintage stores within a sedate 2½-block stretch of SW Capitol Highway (map:II7). (See the Exploring chapter.)

The **Pearl District** (north of W Burnside between Broadway and NW 18th Ave) continues to be gentrified into lofts and art galleries, but the area is also home to more and more large antique furniture shops. NW 23rd Avenue, SE Hawthorne Boulevard, and downtown Portland contain other notable concentrations of collectibles.

Four of the better **antique malls** in town are the Sellwood Antique Mall (7875 SE 13th Ave, 232-3755; map:JJ5), Stars Northwest (305 NW 21st Ave, 220-8180; map:II5), and its cousins, Stars (7027 SE Milwaukie Blvd, 239-0346; map:II5) and Stars & Splendid (7030 SE Milwaukie Blvd, 235-5990; map:II5).

In addition, Portland is home to a handful of **flea markets**, frequent estate sales, and several **annual antique shows**. The granddaddy of them all is Don Wirfs's accurately named America's Largest Antique and Collectible Sales (Expo Center— 282-0877; map:GG6). For one weekend in March, in July, and in October, 1,250 dealers fill 6 acres (indoors) at the Expo Center— wear walking shoes. In November, at the Oregon Convention Center, a fourth Wirfs show joins the lineup. Dickering is the order of the day; by late Sunday many tables sport sale signs (few vendors want to cart home their goods).

Finally, there are a number of **antiques publications** (available at most large antique stores) that list fairs, markets, malls, and so forth—great resources.

Amsterdam Trading Company "The bigger, the better" seems to be the motto here, especially when it comes to the cache of teak tables and desks (both antique and new). There are also pine armoires and dressers, red lacquer Chinese cabinets, teak folding chairs, wire chandeliers, and vintage leather suitcases from England so fetching you'd never check them through. ▪ *536 NW 14th Ave; 229-0737; map:J1; Tues-Sat.*

▼

Antiques

▲

1874 House See Hardware in this chapter. ▪ *8070 SE 13th Ave; 233-1874; map:II5; Tues-Sat.*

End of the Trail It's almost a mini-mall in itself: behind the unprepossessing storefront is a warren of some 14 rooms. There's little furniture for sale, but you'll find every sort of collectible—from salt and pepper shakers to marbles to Chinese opium bottles. One room is devoted solely to militaria and another to American Indian artifacts. The enormous postcard collection (numbering upwards of 100,000) attracts enthusiasts from all over the country. ▪ *5937 N Greeley St; 283-0419; map:EE6; every day.*

The General Store Tough to miss—it's attached to a vintage red caboose. Margie Waite's been in the antique business for years, and her selection (and her refinishing techniques) shows it: Victorian and Early American walnut, mahogany, pine, and oak furniture. The especially large furniture—perhaps a dining room table that seats 12 or a high-backed bed frame—is relegated to the upstairs room behind the caboose. ▪ *7987 SE 13th Ave; 233-1321; map:II5; Tues-Sun and by appointment.*

Geraldine's You could drive up Thurman every day and never notice this little antique shop tucked between a pottery gallery and a Spanish restaurant. Once you discover it, however, you'll frequent Geraldine's to peruse the ever-changing display of attractive furnishings: English pine dressers, freestanding full-length mirrors, iron bed frames, and garden gates. Tucked in here and there are bed linens, wire baskets, and other curiosities. ■ *2772 NW Thurman; 295-5911; map:GG7; Mon-Sat.*

The Handwerk Shop See Furniture in this chapter. ■ *8317 SE 13th Ave; 236-7870; map:JJ5; Thurs-Sun and by appointment.*

Hippo Hardware and Trading Company See Hardware in this chapter. ■ *1040 E Burnside; 231-1444; map:GG5; Mon-Sat.*

Hollywood Antique Showcase Antique malls seem to be the wave of the future, and northeast Portland's Hollywood district is home to one of the city's largest. More than 70 dealers fill over 10,000 square feet. On the main level are collectibles, from Depression-era glass to jewelry, while the basement showcases good-quality furniture and home accessories. ■ *1969 NE 42nd Ave; 288-1051; map:FF4; every day.*

Jerry Lamb Interiors and Antiques This surprisingly large Pearl District showroom (the place looks dinky from the outside) only enhances interior designer Jerry Lamb's displays of Oriental antiques—especially porcelains—and fine furniture. There are embroidery and woodblock prints from China or Japan, and hundreds of porcelain pieces—Imari, blue and white Canton, celadon, and Rose Medallion—are stocked. ■ *416 NW 10th Ave; 227-6077; map:K3; Tues-Fri.*

Antiques

Partners in Time Everything here is pine—mostly antique European pine from England, Austria, Holland, and Germany, though there are a small number of new pieces done in period style. In addition to the furniture (armoires, tables, chairs, benches, dressers, nightstands), you'll also find Oriental rugs of all ages plus decorative objects (Turkish pots, painted wooden boxes, and papier-mâché trays) and gift items (books, soaps, candlesticks). ■ *1313 W Burnside; 228-6299; map:J1; every day.*

Portland Antique Company At one of the Northwest's biggest antique retailers, you'll find both the ordinary (a table with four chairs) and extraordinary (an ornate wooden confessional or a British telephone booth). New shipments from England and other parts of Europe arrive weekly, yielding sturdy, sometimes reasonably priced English oak tables, armoires, and dressers. There's also an ever-growing cache of Indonesian cabinets and hutches (which have become popular for hiding the television). A similar assortment can be found at the new shop on SE Clinton and 26th, which is smaller but equally crowded. ■ *1314 and 1211 NW Glisan St; 223-0999; map:L1; every day.* ■ *2601 SE Clinton; 239-5124; map:HH5; every day.*

Rejuvenation House Parts See Furniture in this chapter. ▪ *1100 SE Grand Ave; 238-1900; map:EE5; every day.*

Richard Rife French Antique Imports In 1966, Richard Rife established his business in Portland, and since 1983 he has specialized in fine French furniture, garnering a reputation for quality and knowledgeability. Most pieces date to the Belle Epoque (1871–1914), with an abundance of Louis XV–style and Louis XVI–style armoires and buffets. ▪ *300 NW 13th Ave; 294-0276; map:K1; Tues-Sat.*

Sellwood Peddler Attic Goodies A little bit of everything is crammed into this 5,000-square-foot space, with emphasis on Native American items, vintage clothing and jewelry, glassware, china, sterling flatware, and quilts. There's also a fair amount of furniture. The back room is full of dusty tools and salvageable house parts. ▪ *8065 SE 13th Ave; 235-0946; map:II5; every day.*

APPAREL

See also Department Stores in this chapter.

▼

Antiques

▲

Aubergine Located in the Pearl District, this gallerylike store features clothing suited to professional women ages 25 to 50 who want to look elegantly casual. Owners Margaret Block and Tanya Doubleday regularly travel to New York in search of unique designs. Hand-spun sweaters, beautifully styled leather goods, and elegant-but-not-too-pricey jewelry finish the store's collection. ▪ *1100 NW Glisan St; 228-7313; map:L1; Mon-Sat.*

Bella Luna The seventies intersect the nineties in this ultrahip retro-biased clothing store tucked into NW 23rd. Big floral prints, skin-tight numbers in chartreuse polyester, long swingy skirts, sheer and sexy dresses—Marcia Brady never looked so good. Also worth trying on: Angelheart and Flax linen dresses and trousers, breezy scarves, fun and funky accessories. ▪ *610 NW 23rd; 248-0191; map:GG7; every day.*

Changes—Designs to Wear An extension of the Real Mother Goose, this shop carries clothing designed by regional and national artists. Goose management is always on the prowl for the new and the wonderful, so there are often great surprises: blocked silk shirts, burned velvet scarves, hand-woven suits cut to flatter real women's bodies. This is a great destination for window shoppers as well as collectors. ▪ *927 SW Yamhill St; 223-3737; map:H2; Mon-Sat.*

CP Shades The look from this San Francisco–based company is at once casual and sophisticated—very Portland. The hues are earthy and the fabrics down-to-earth (rayon, textured cottons, velvet). Look for wide-legged pants, elegant tunics and vests, free-form dresses; loose-fitting linen is a specialty. ▪ *513 NW 23rd Ave; 241-7838; map:GG7; every day.*

Divine Designs This shop caters to brides and their wedding parties, but it's also a great source for perfectly tailored cocktail dresses—Nicole Miller to Donna Karan—dressy shoes, unusual handbags, French and Italian lingerie, and classic casual wear. ▪ *437 NW 23rd Ave; 827-0667; map:GG7; every day.*

Easy Street Here's where you'll find glitzy evening dresses and spunky accessories to wear with them. Mothers of the bride and groom favor this shop, which has been dressing women for special occasions for 18 years. ▪ *16337 SW Bryant Rd, Lake Oswego; 636-6547; map:MM7; Mon-Sat.*

Elizabeth Street This classic Portland boutique carries dresses, suits, and casual wear cut on the edge of style. There are enough hats, belts, bags, jewelry, watches, and inexpensive sunglasses here to punch up an entire wardrobe—and killer jeans to boot. ▪ *635 NW 23rd Ave; 243-2456; map:GG7; every day.*

Eye of Ra See Imports in this chapter. ▪ *5331 SW Macadam Ave (Johns Landing); 224-4292; map:HH6; every day.*

Girlfriends Tailored to the young and slender, this shop carries a solid collection of fashion T-shirts, chic dresses, sweaters, and trousers, as well as pajamas and stockings (not to mention soaps, scents, dishes, and candles). Shoppers' companions can rest on a sofa, sampling coffee, candy, and newspapers provided by the savvy management. ▪ *904 NW 23rd Ave; 294-0488; map:GG7; every day.*

Helen's of Course Owner Helen Gell practically defines Portland retail. In business for decades, she graciously entertains all who enter her store, taking a personal interest in their fashion needs. Escada suits stand out here among other designer goods; there are cocktail dresses, evening gowns, fabulous handbags, and shoes to live for. In-store tailoring is exceptional. ▪ *9875 SW Beaverton-Hillsdale Hwy, Beaverton; 643-8402; map:HH9; Mon-Sat.*

Irving's The owners of Elizabeth Street and Zelda's Shoe Bar teamed to open this savvy men's shop. You'll find great denim, outerwear, and a branch of Zelda's for men that carries just the right lugsole shoe—or Harley boot—for the occasion. ▪ *2322 NW Irving; 243-5300; map:GG7; every day.*

J. Crew This is the home of wholesome, tailored clothing for men and women. J. Crew carries a variety of consistently wonderful men's cotton shirts and trousers as well as simple, contemporary women's wear. Look here for the little black dress, the chic-cut miniskirt, the perfect shell, or the bag no one (but other Crew shoppers) has. Two big sales, in January and June. ▪ *Pioneer Place; 228-2739; map:G4; every day.*

John Helmer Haberdasher See Accessories and Luggage in this chapter. ▪ *969 SW Broadway; 223-4976; map:G2; Mon-Sat.*

▼ Apparel ▲

Katee Haddad This local fashion designer has been experimenting for years in Portland with innovative women's clothing ideas. She's young and has a great sense of humor, which is reflected in her apparel—short hand-dyed silk dresses, velvet tie-dyed tops, and sleek wedding dresses. Haddad is now connected in a second-floor walk-up space to Wild Iris, a jewelry shop specializing in handcrafted sterling silver necklaces, bracelets, and rings set with semiprecious beads. Iris owner Leslie O'Conner and Haddad enthusiastically work together to coordinate their merchandise. ▪ *604 NW 23rd; 228-1852; map:GG7; Thurs-Sun and by appointment.*

La Paloma In the unassuming Hillsdale Shopping Center (home of such culinary hot spots as Nature's, Noah's Bagels, and Pizzicato) lies one of the city's best finds for women's natural-fiber clothing, imaginative accessories, silver jewelry from Southeast Asia, Mishi 100 percent cotton separates (with socks dyed to match), sweaters, and Indonesian batik and ikat clothing. Local women who love the style and comfort of ethnic clothing shop here religiously. ▪ *6316 SW Capitol Hwy (Hillsdale Shopping Center); 246-3417; map:II7; every day.*

Mario's For more than 60 years, men demanding the best in designer fashion have shopped Mario's. Armani, Donna Karan for Men, Canali, and Zegna suits keep elegant company here with fine sweaters, topnotch cotton shirts, and tasteful Friday casual wear. ▪ *921 SW Morrison St (The Galleria); 227-3477; map:H2; every day.*

Matisse A lush and funky closet of a store, Matisse carries one-of-a-kind rayon and silk dresses created by local independent women designers along with plenty of romantic accessories for dash. ▪ *2223 NE Broadway; 287-5414; map:FF5; every day.*

The Mercantile Owner Victoria Taylor loves fashion, and her store seems at once a gallery of her favorite up-to-the-minute styles and an elegant, comfortable shopping destination. Clothing here suits mature women looking for tailored, upscale style as well as young professionals looking for sophisticated, "now" fashion. Here is everything from evening wear to soft sportswear, and a fine collection of eclectic accessories and household objects. ▪ *735 SW Park; 227-7882; map:H2; every day.*

Merry's Barefoot Boutique Merry Colvin, mistress of Merry's Barefoot Boutique, was a New York model for half of her life, then a Mexico-based environmental activist, and then a Lake Oswego city councilwoman. Everything in her store reflects her personality and her philosophy: clothing should flow, wear comfortably, look fantastic, and cost almost nothing. Imported dresses, trousers, and shells coordinate with ethnic belts, bags, and jewelry, including gems to wear on the feet. ▪ *366 N State St, Lake Oswego; 636-3806; map:LL6; Tues-Sat.*

▼

Apparel

▲

Mimi and Lena   Named for the grandmothers of the two shop owners, Mimi and Lena caters to the customer who prefers the atmosphere of a small boutique. Contemporary dresses range from simply casual to bridesmaid dressy. Interesting sweaters and hats by Portland's Hillary Day are displayed like museum pieces. Mimi and Lena recently merged with Suzan for Shoes, and now offers a large collection of unusual sandals, boots, flats, and pumps. ■ *823 NW 23rd Ave; 224-7736; map:GG7; every day.*

M. Sellin Ltd.   Formerly El Mundo for Women, M. Sellin on Hawthorne carries natural-fiber clothing cut to wear easy and still look sophisticated—classic Northwest style. Designer lines include Eileen Fisher and Flax; sizes range from petite to plus. Thirty different styles of shoes decorate store shelves near a good selection of linen handbags, ethnic jewelry, stockings, scarves, and scrunchable hats. ■ *3556 SE Hawthorne Blvd; 239-4605; map:GG4; every day.*

Norm Thompson   We'd be remiss in not telling you about Norm Thompson's two stores—in northwest Portland and at the airport. The clothes range from conservative to rigid and are of standard quality, but devotees appreciate the predictability of the designs. From comfy big polo dresses to slacks and pastel shirts, from sturdy luggage to shoes, slippers, and gift foods, everything here is beautifully displayed. ■ *1805 NW Thurman St; 221-0764; map:GG7; every day.*

Phillip Stewart   Hidden away in Goose Hollow, Phillip Stewart's men's store is one beautifully tailored secret. Fine wool jackets, cashmere sweaters, and beautiful flannel trousers are displayed like treasured objects through the main floor of this historic-house-become-shop. Expect more than 200 choices of fabric for custom shirts and excellent, if traditional, men's furnishing advice from Stewart, a man dedicated to polished dressing. ■ *1201 SW 19th St; 226-3589; map:GG6; Mon-Sat.*

The Portland Pendleton Shop   Believe it or not, Pendleton has dusted off its look at the end of the 20th century. The shop, in the Standard Insurance Building, offers the most complete collection of Pendleton clothing anywhere in Oregon, including petite sizes, skirt-and-shirt matchables, and summer silk and rayon combinations. Of course, it wouldn't be Pendleton without the wool chemises and blankets, endearingly familiar to virtually every Northwesterner. ■ *900 SW 5th Ave; 242-0037; map:F2; Mon-Sat.*

Sheba House of Elegance   You wouldn't expect to find elegant Ethiopian attire behind this red brick colonial storefront on Broadway. But Assefash Melles has lined her clean, white shop walls with floating, dramatic ethnic pieces from Africa, Indonesia, and Portland. The Portland styles are ethnic inspirations by local designers. There's some alternative office wear here, plenty of caftans, and alternative evening looks as well as great jewelry. Private showings over catered lunch in the upstairs rooms are available by appointment. ▪ *2730 NE Broadway; 287-6997; map:FF5; every day.*

Urban Outfitters   Styles here are young, trendy, and pure urban decay. Expect anything from olive-drab underwear to floral chiffon dresses, camouflage trousers to earth-tone T-shirts, picture frames, pasta of provoking shapes, and alien autopsy dolls. The store fizzes with counterculture energy. Adults: Beware of the blaring sound system. ▪ *2320 NW Westover Rd; 248-0020; map:GG7; every day.*

BAKERIES

Beaverton Bakery   Beautiful (and delicious) wedding and birthday cakes are what BB is best known for, but the crusty monastery whole-wheat loaf, onion-cheese faugasse bread, and apple-cinnamon loaf are addictive staples. Lines are often long at the larger Broadway store; take a number, or pick up a cake at any number of local markets. ▪ *12375 SW Broadway, Beaverton; 646-7136; map:HH9; every day.* ▪ *8775 SW Cascade Ave (Cascade Plaza), Beaverton; 646-7816; map:JJ9; every day.*

▼
Apparel
▲

B. Moloch/Heathman Bakery and Pub   Since the remodel in 1997, it's become much easier to buy bread and do take-out at B. Moloch. Every day there's a very sour San Francisco sourdough along with a wheat-onion bread, bier brot, and usually a pesto bread. In the mornings you can count on cinnamon rolls, bran muffins, and chocolate chip or blueberry scones. ▪ *901 SW Salmon St; 227-5700; map:G1; every day.*

Gabriel's Bakery   There's no shortage of baked temptations for residents of northwest Portland, but at least the offerings here are healthful. The dietary staff at nearby Good Samaritan Hospital can appreciate the 15 varieties of egg- and fat-free breads, but in truth, it's the muffins—from cornmeal-rum-currant to pumpkin-apple-raisin to peach-almond—that sell out first. A second location resides on NE Broadway. ▪ *2272 NW Kearney St; 227-4712; map:GG7; every day.* ▪ *1411 NE Broadway; 287-9921; map:FF5; every day.*

The German Bakery   This is the only place in town to find traditional German breads, butter cookies, and pastries. Sit at one of the several tables and sample some desserts: creamhorns, Black Forest and Bienenstich cakes, and German tea cookies. ▪ *10528 NE Sandy Blvd; 252-1881; map:FF2; Tues-Sat.*

Goldberg's Bakery, Deli, and Catering   Goldberg's might not make it in New York, but the light and dark rye, half-dozen bagel varieties, bialys, challah, and ubiquitous iced cinnamon roll satisfy

local noshers. Old-fashioned service and a decent deli, too.
■ *4516 SW Vermont St; 246-4201; map:FF3; Tues-Sat.*

Grand Central Baking Company   The spacious, airy spot is a great place to start the morning with a jammer, apricot scone, or slice of pumpkin bread. Specialty breads, such as fresh herb, olive, or walnut-thyme, are sold only at the bakery, although Grand Central's rustic Italian baguettes and hearty sour white, among others, are also sold at better grocery stores throughout the city. There's a branch in Multnomah and one near the Lloyd Center, too. ■ *2230 SE Hawthorne Blvd (and branches); 232-0575; map:GG5; every day.*

Great Harvest Bread Company   Looking to buy the freshest loaf of bread in town? Go where the wheat is ground, and the flour milled, daily. Breads of substance, character, and a healthy amount of fiber are harvested at this Montana-based franchise. Free samples of the whole crop are always available, as well as warm bread by the slice slathered with butter. In the morning, long lines form for no-cholesterol bran muffins, and you'll want to try the sweet, gooey cinnamon rolls—at least once. ■ *810 SW 2nd Ave (and branches); 224-8583; map:F4; Mon-Sat.*

JaCiva's Chocolates and Pastries   Behind the retail area, Jack Elmer, Swiss-trained chocolatier and pastry chef, and his wife, Iva Sue, craft fine Swiss chocolates sold across the country. With their own recipes they create chocolates that Grandma would envy (she'd also smile at the money left over in her pocketbook). They also stock the shop with billowy éclairs and exquisitely decorated cakes (perhaps a chocolate mousse dome?), as well as less dramatic coffee cakes, Danishes, and muffins. There's even a room where brides and grooms can sample wedding cakes (pictures and "dummy cakes" help you decide). Call for directions to the westside location. ■ *4733 SE Hawthorne Blvd; 234-8115; map:GG4; Mon-Sat.*

Bakeries

Marsee Baking   Something for everyone: bagels, baguettes, hearty Italian breads, tarts, cakes, cookies, pastries—you name it, they bake it. The original Marsee, at the north end of NW 23rd Avenue, is in the part of the neighborhood that's more neighborly than slick, and was remodeled to accommodate longer lingering; new branches (recently in Lake Oswego and NE Broadway) continue to sprout. ■ *1323 NW 23rd Ave (and branches); 295-4000; map:FF7; every day.*

Noah's Bagels   While transplanted New Yorkers claim that it's hard to find a good bagel so far from home, many take refuge in this bright shop on Hawthorne—and at the many other Noah's throughout the city. In addition to above-average bagels in both the usual and less usual flavors—onion, poppyseed, pumpernickel, jalapeño, banana-nut—there's also a variety of cream cheese shmears, several kinds of lox (including Oregon and New York style), rugelach, and, as it should be, good, strong house coffee. ■ *3541 SE Hawthorne Blvd (and branches); 731-8855; map:GG5; every day.*

Pearl Bakery From the irresistible pastries and incredible breads to the light-filled room and pretty blue bags—everything the Pearl does, it does well. The artisan breads—Pain Poolish, Levain, and Ciabatta—are leavened by traditional methods, hand-formed and baked in the huge ovens in the back; people who work in the neighborhood set their watches to the time when their favorite loaf comes out of the oven. Such pastries as the chocolate croissant and brioche galette—puff pastry baked with a custard center and golden raisins—are positively habit-forming. ■ *102 NW 9th Ave; 827-0910; map:K3; Mon-Sat.*

Ron Paul Catering and Charcuterie The extraordinary dome-puff éclairs and chocolaty-rich Black Angus cookies sold here are only two examples of good baking in Portland. Fresh-baked breads may include buttermilk cheddar, whole-wheat walnut, or spinach-herb. The bakery is only part of what Ron Paul's offers—there's also a world of take-out and a great sit-down restaurant (see review in the Restaurants chapter). The new **Ron Paul Express** downtown (221-0052) specializes in gourmet-to-go: pastries, breads, sandwiches, and lunch-fare entrees. ■ *1441 NE Broadway (and branches); 284-5347; map:FF5; every day.*

Three Lions' Bakery & Cafe Three Lions' bakeries continue to pop up in unexpected places, the most recent on SE 42nd and Division (236-5089). Croissants of all sorts are standouts, as are the scones, focaccia bread, and cookies. Beautiful cakes, such as the lemon gâteau and French fudge cake, can be found gracing dessert menus at other restaurants around town. Take note: On Fridays or Saturdays (depending on the individual store), between 4pm and 6pm, everything is half price. ■ *1138 SW Morrison St (and branches); 224-3429; map:I2; Mon-Sat.*

BODY CARE

Aveda Lifestyle Store and Spa If you're familiar with Aveda products, you know what to expect: natural, richly scented products for your skin and hair. The entire Aveda line—makeup, cleansers, hair care products—is available at the front of this attractive space in the Fifth Avenue Suites Hotel; full spa service is available in back. ■ *500 SW 5th Ave; 248-0615; map:I5; every day.*

The Body Shop This British company has a social conscience: its line of body products are not tested on animals. They also support "community trade"—purchasing their ingredients from international communities that are trying to sustain natural resources. Makeovers and gift baskets are among their services;

everything is clean and tasteful. ▪ *Pioneer Place; 226-7141; map:H4;*
every day. ▪ *Clackamas Town Center; 653-8384; map:KK3; every day.*

Boutique Alternare   Facial products from Germany, homeopathic remedies, Chinese vitamin supplements, and pet care products are just some of what's available at this dreamy retail shop and spa. After your full-body treatment, you can order a fresh juice at the bar in the back—and go home feeling like a peach. ▪ *1444 NE Broadway; 822-8200; map:FF5; every day.*

The Perfume House   The ultimate in olfactory stimulation: Chris Tsefelas's Perfume House has been praised by the likes of Yves St. Laurent and Jean Patou as the finest in the world. You can sniff exquisite scents, from rare Russian perfumes to "Corina" from the Patrician House, introduced at the 1962 Seattle World's Fair and considered one of the greatest perfumes ever created. Prices range from $2 for a sample-size vial to $8,500 worth of L'Air d'Or. ▪ *3328 SE Hawthorne Blvd; 234-5375; map:GG5; Mon-Sat.*

BOOKS AND MAGAZINES

Annie Bloom's Books   More than just a neighborhood bookstore for the citizens of Multnomah, this cozy shop attracts readers from all over the west side. They come for the fiction and the excellent selection of children's literature, which surrounds a colorful play area at the back of the store. The Judaica section is also strong, and special orders are no problem. Just try the armchairs here—as inviting as Grandma's lap—with a cup of tea on the house. Well-read clerks will suggest their latest favorites. Magazines, cards, and puppets, too. ▪ *7834 SW Capitol Hwy; 246-0053; map:II7; every day.*

Books and Magazines

Barnes & Noble   With six locations in the Portland-Vancouver area, these megabookstores place a savvy emphasis on comfort. There are plenty of chairs and writing desks for perusing the goods before you buy, and when you do buy, you'll find that markdowns are standard. ▪ *1231 NE Broadway (and branches); 335-0201; map:FF5; every day.*

Bertha Station   With a thoughtful selection of magazines and journals, a smooth cup of espresso, and cigars too, this Hillsdale shop has attracted wanderers who come from far beyond the neighborhood. But the periodicals alone are a good reason to pop in. ▪ *6446 SW Capitol Hwy; 246-6225; map:II7; every day.*

Borders Books and Music   A sunny operation that combines books, music, and coffee, this store—part of a national chain—presents itself as a community-oriented, user-friendly shop in the downtown core. Situated in the historic Mohawk Building, two blocks from Pioneer Place, Borders provides many services and a stunning collection of new titles on every subject, drawing in even the most loyal nonchain devotees (it's hard to say no to a 10 percent discount on hardcovers). The music selection is expansive, with hookups for prepurchase listening. ▪ *708 SW 3rd Ave (and branches); 220-5911; map:G4; every day.*

Broadway Books When the Barnes & Noble superstore blew into the neighborhood in 1993, it might have knocked this young shop off its feet. But that didn't happen, in part because Broadway Books had already become an integral part of its neighborhood. Together, Gloria Borg Olds and Roberta Dyer have been in the book biz in Portland for more than three decades, and they provide personal, educated service. There's a sizable selection of biographies and memoirs, the shop's specialty, but also fiction, Judaica, and African-American literature. They're pros at the special order, so if the book you want isn't in stock, they can get it for you—pronto. ▪ *1714 NE Broadway; 284-1726; map:FF5; every day.*

Cameron's Books and Magazines At Portland's oldest used-book store, it's actually old magazines that account for most of the trade. Vintage glossies are kept well organized in the back room to preserve them in good condition. A hodgepodge collection at very good prices. ▪ *336 SW 3rd Ave; 228-2391; map:H4; every day.*

A Children's Place This may be as close to heaven on earth as your pint-size bookworm will get. Kids and adults alike love the selection, which varies from classics to gimmicks, and it's an excellent resource for educators, who receive a discount. If you're gift-buying, the helpful clerks seem to have no problem finding a book that's just right among the hundreds of volumes that pack the place—whether the recipient wants a book to chew on (lots of cardboard titles) or to thumb through. ▪ *1631 NE Broadway; 284-8294; map:FF5; every day.*

Future Dreams The stuff of Future Dreams is one part sci-fi and one part comic art. New and used magazines, books, and comics range from favorites to esoteric, hard-to-find titles. There is also a reservation service for new volumes. ▪ *1800 E Burnside; 231-8311; map:FF5; every day.* ▪ *1424 NE 103rd Ave; 255-5245; map:EE2; Thurs-Sat.*

The Great NW Book Store Good karma, good books, good people. With 150,000 titles in stock, GNW boasts the largest exclusively used-book inventory in the city, and so it makes sense that they would also offer appraisals among their services (one of the few bookstores in town to do so). The strengths are Western Americana, first-edition modern and older literature, and sports—specifically baseball, mountain climbing, and golf. There's a rare-book room full of treasures, too. Book buying by appointment. ▪ *1234 SW Stark St; 223-8098; map:J2; every day.*

Hanson's Books A clean, well-lighted (and well-organized) place, Hanson's is the literary equivalent of a plain brown wrapper. This used-book shop offers decent deals on large, glossy art and design books, an excellent variety of hard- and softcover literary fiction, and couches and tables where you can pore over your treasures. ■ *814 NW 23rd; 223-7610; map:GG7; every day.*

Hawthorne Boulevard Books Roger and Ilse Roberts invite the public into their Hawthorne home to browse their used and antiquarian books. They're particularly fond of classic literature and American history. A fireplace (when lit) makes it tough to leave. ■ *3129 SE Hawthorne Blvd; 236-3211; map:GG5; Tues-Sun.*

In Other Words Another bookstore on the book lover's miracle mile-and-a-half that is Hawthorne Boulevard, IOW distinguishes itself with a community-oriented, feminist approach. All the books are written by women. The nonprofit store provides its patrons with feminist, gay/lesbian, and holistic literature not available at mainstream retail venues, as well as "women-positive" videos to rent. The atmosphere is cheerful and calming, with a wonderfully dreamy painting in the public rest room. ■ *3734 SE Hawthorne Blvd; 232-6003; map:GG5; every day.*

Laughing Horse Books Politically progressive and environmentally oriented publications and programs are the focus of this bookstore-coffeehouse collective. Community potlucks focus on social change—health care in Guatemala, war-tax resistance, and rain-forest protection struggles; call for a schedule. Open-mike poetry on Wednesdays, too. ■ *3652 SE Division St; 236-2893; map:HH5; Mon-Sat.*

Looking Glass Bookstore This much-loved shop—now over a quarter century old—with a sky-lit and polished tri-level interior is probably one of the nicest-looking bookstores around. But it's more than a pretty place, with a selection of titles other stores might skip over: offbeat comic books and contemporary graphic arts, as well as science fiction (plus notable psychology, health, and modern literature sections). Ask to be put on the mailing list for the holiday catalog. ■ *318 SW Taylor St; 227-4760; map:G3; Mon-Sat.*

Morrison Books David Morrison has made a name for himself in two ways: by selling high-quality, used books on art, architecture, and design, and also by speaking out against bigger, monopolizing bookstores. His shop in the Pearl District is smaller than the original one off Hawthorne, but boasts the largest collection of used photography books in the city, as well as a fine cache of rare and out-of-print titles. ■ *530 NW 12th Ave; 295-6882; map:K2; every day.*

Murder by the Book The genius locus of Murder by the Book manifests itself as a trinity: mystery, thriller, and spy fiction. Look for Kate Fanslar in the Cherchez la Femme section and more than 50 Northwest mystery writers in On the Homefront (many signings, too). New and used volumes to buy, sell, barter, and kill for—so to speak. ■ *3210 SE Hawthorne Blvd; 232-9995; map:GG5; every day.*

Books and Magazines

The Nature Store at Portland Audubon Society On the edge of Forest Park, within the Audubon sanctuary, resides this resource center and gift shop. Inside, there's the cool odor of birdseed and a treasure trove for Northwest naturalists: field guides, natural history books, binoculars, and more. About one-third of the book inventory is children's books; there are also stuffed animals, model insects, and jigsaw puzzles. ▪ *5151 NW Cornell Rd; 292-6855; map:FF8; every day.*

New Renaissance Bookshop Two adjacent Victorians house approximately 15,000 titles and a varied selection of paraphernalia to help people take that next spiritual step, whether it be recovery, growth, business prosperity, or self-transformation. Browsers must pay homage to the multiple shelves of tarot books. The top floor houses a meditation room and a small selection of used books. Lectures, tarot readings, or discussions led by "intuitive counselors" are also part of the scene. In the interest of the younger set, the play area has been expanded and there are holographs, science toys, and books on children's spirituality. ▪ *1338 NW 23rd Ave; 224-4929; map:FF7; every day.*

Oregon History Center Museum Store Books remain the emphasis at this store operated by the Oregon Historical Society, despite the broad nonbook inventory (T-shirts, jewelry, calendars, and other tourist take-home items). The bookstore sells a fine selection of regional history books, perhaps the best in the state, including the society's own quarterly journal. If a book won't do, there's a substantial collection of maps and postcards depicting early Oregon. Upstairs, an extensive photo library offers reproductions of historical photographs. ▪ *1200 SW Park Ave; 222-1741; map:F2; every day.*

▼

Books and Magazines

▲

Pegasus Books These six stores stock trading cards (sports and otherwise), comic books, lead miniatures, Japanese toys, and, yes, sci-fi and fantasy lit. The spin-off stores sport the totally hip names "It Came From Outer Space" and "Planet X." ▪ *4133 NE Sandy Blvd (and branches); 284-4693; map:FF5; every day.*

Periodicals Paradise In business for nearly a decade, this Fred Meyer of used magazines continues to thrive. With close to a million issues in stock, Periodicals Paradise may be the biggest store of its type in the West. Issues published within the past year sell for 75 percent off the cover price. ▪ *3366 SE Powell St; 236-8370; map:HH5; every day.*

Portland State University Bookstore Not just for students, the cooperatively run PSU Bookstore has been the city's major supplier of textbooks for more than 40 years; however, the stock of children's, computer, business, fiction, and reference books attracts even Ivy League alumni. Test and study guides, too. ▪ *1880 SW 6th Ave; 226-2631; map:C1; Mon-Sat.*

Powell's Books National chains can open as many "superstores" in town as they please, but Powell's will always be top dog in Portland. Even those who prefer smaller, more intimate book-stores find themselves lured to Powell's out of sheer gluttony. With a million volumes filling a city block at the main Burnside store, it is most definitely the largest bookstore in the country. (Tourists should plan at least an afternoon here, if just to say they've been.)

The store provides maps to guide buyers through its dozens of sections, from Automotive to Zen. Tucked into the maze are a rare-book room, the Anne Hughes Coffee Room, and a children's book room. Several times each week, touring authors of national repute read from their work in the Purple Room. There's even a **parking garage** (enter on NW 11th Ave), and a parking lot (on the east side of NW 10th, between Burnside and Couch).

With branches at such local outposts as Rejuvenation House Parts (a home improvement store) and Portland Nursery, Powell's influence stretches far and wide. There are also the Powell's offspring, each with its own specialty. **Powell's Travel Store** (*SW 6th Ave and Yamhill St, 228-1108*), in the southeast corner of Pioneer Courthouse Square, carries guidebooks to everywhere. On your way out of town at the airport, check out **Powell's Books at PDX** (249-1950), which stocks mostly new volumes. A few blocks from the main store, **Powell's Technical Bookstore** (*33 NW Park Ave, 228-3906*) has the city's best selec-tion of computer, electronics, and engineering books. The newly redone **Powell's Books in Cascade Plaza** (*8725 SW Cascade Ave, Beaverton; 643-3131*) has an excellent children's selection. Finally, **Powell's on Hawthorne** (*3723 SE Hawthorne Blvd, 238-1668*) carries a healthy selection of new and used general titles, while two stores down, **Powell's Books for Cooks and Gardeners** (see below) specializes in—what else?—cookbooks and gardening guides. ▪ *1005 W Burnside (and branches); 228-4651; map:J2; every day.*

Powell's Books for Cooks and Gardeners Optimally located next door to Pastaworks (see Markets and Delicatessens in this chap-ter), this shop is a delight. Cookbooks are the thing here: new, used, coffee table, rare, and remaindered. There are lots of cool things for the kitchen, too—colorful dishes and table linens, mixing bowls, retro refrigerator magnets, whisks, and lots of whatnot you simply can't live without. Noted cookbook authors pass through for signings and demonstrations; local chefs also give demonstrations here. Finally, there's a large gardening sec-tion, replete with accessories such as chimes and pots—and, of course, books galore. ▪ *3747 SE Hawthorne Blvd; 235-3802; map:GG5; every day.*

Reed College Bookstore Heavily academic, and no wonder: the bookstore is right in the middle of this liberal-arts campus. The buyers here know they can't compete with general stores, so instead they fatten their shelves with humanities and a surprisingly substantial natural sciences collection. ▪ *3203 SE Woodstock Blvd; 777-7287; map:II4; Mon-Sat (Mon-Fri when school's out).*

Rich's Cigar Store One hundred years ago, Rich's was just another newsstand/tobacco-seller in Portland. Now it's one of the few left, carrying a huge and thorough selection of magazines, foreign newspapers and magazines, and, yes, tobacco. The Northwest Portland store doesn't have the same charm as the downtown location, which has less than it used to since it moved across the street into a new space (one that formerly housed a McDonald's). ▪ *820 SW Alder St; 228-1700; map:I2; every day.* ▪ *706 NW 23rd Ave; 227-6907; map:FF7; every day.*

RiverPlace Book Merchants With its strong fiction and regional literature sections, RiverPlace Book Merchants has attracted a strong local following to its sunny, lively boardwalk. The shop is smaller than when it was Book Port, but still smart. ▪ *0315 SW Montgomery St (RiverPlace), Suite 340; 248-5674; map:C5; every day.*

Title Wave Bookstore Ever wonder where old library books end up? More than 20,000 volumes from the Multnomah County Library sell for bargain prices here at the old Albina Library. The volunteer staff organizes the books (including encyclopedia sets) by—what else?—the Dewey decimal system. There are also magazines, CDs, books on tape, and videos. ▪ *216 NE Knott St; 248-5021; map:FF5; Mon-Sat.*

Tower Books Lots of best sellers, coffee table books, and popular fiction, but some surprises, too: a strong computer book section, a good selection of books related to the Pacific Northwest (including university press books), and an international newspaper and magazine stash. This is one link in a nationwide chain, and they offer a 10 percent discount on all titles. Buy records, tapes, and CDs at good prices next door at Tower Records. ▪ *NE 102nd Ave and Halsey (Gateway Shopping Center); 253-3116; map:FF2; every day.*

Twenty-Third Avenue Books Bob Maull's friendly demeanor is part of what makes this northwest Portland store so appealing. It's just what a bookstore should be: low-key and well organized, with a strong sense of its authors. Contemporary fiction predominates the original store space, while the adjoining room makes lots of space for lovely gardening and design books. ▪ *1015 NW 23rd Ave; 224-5097; map:FF7; every day.*

US Government Bookstore One hundred percent government issue, with books on subjects from aviation to natural resources. The store gets a lot of traffic from G-men, but it's a fascinating place for civilians, too. ▪ *1305 SW 1st Ave (Jefferson-Columbia Square); 221-6217; map:E3; Mon-Fri.*

Water Tower Books Regular customers know that this shop, with its gift-book leanings, is not limited to coffee table editions of Monet and Georgia O'Keeffe but extends to in-depth photographic treatments of, say, endangered wildlife. A respectable sampling of general books, with a good mystery section, but no trashy fiction. ▪ *5331 SW Macadam Ave (Johns Landing); 228-0290; map:II6; every day.*

CAMERAS

Advance Camera Repair If they can't fix it at this Raleigh Hills shop, the knowledgeable, efficient staff will help you send your camera to someone who will—like the manufacturer. The good selection of secondhand cameras is worth a look before you consider buying elsewhere. ▪ *8124 SW Beaverton-Hillsdale Hwy; 292-6996; map:II8; Mon-Sat.*

Camera World At its fancy new location, Camera World offers a huge selection for all your camera needs, with the best prices around. It's probably a good idea to know what you want before you go in, since the salespeople are eager to sell you anything. Mail-order service is available. ▪ *400 SW 6th Ave; 222-0008; map:I3; every day.*

▼

Candies and Chocolates

▲

Citizens Photo At this well-stocked shop full of quality lighting and equipment, each salesperson has a specialty. Not the cheapest, but the equipment and service are topnotch. ▪ *709 SE 7th Ave; 232-8501; map:FF5; Mon-Sat.*

Tymers Camera Shop Tymers customers range from the novice to the professional who'll cross the river in search of chemicals and camera equipment. A very friendly staff with lots of advice; also a print and blueprint shop. ▪ *1601 Broadway, Vancouver, WA; (360)796-0215; map:AA6; Mon-Sat.*

CANDIES AND CHOCOLATES

Candy Basket Since 1977, Dick Fuhr has been perfecting the art of candy making and has come up with some delectable confections. He indulges at times, making such items as caramel cars in 20 different models. The retail store is located in front of the factory, and sports a working chocolate fountain. ▪ *1924 NE 181st Ave; 666-2000; map:FF1; Mon-Sat.*

Godiva Chocolatier This is the nation's candy shop: a chocolate-only chain with links in many major cities. But quantity hasn't reduced the quality. The gold-tinted store is stocked with beautifully sculpted chocolate starfish, seashells, and flowers, as well as an irresistible assortment of truffles and chocolate-nut concoctions. Ice cream, too. Expensive, but worth it. ▪ *Pioneer Place; 226-4722; map:H4; every day.*

JaCiva's Chocolates and Pastries See Bakeries in this chapter. ▪ *4733 SE Hawthorne Blvd; 234-8115; map:GG4; Mon-Sat.*

Moonstruck Chocolatier One thing about selling chocolates is that you don't need a lot of space—just enough room to ogle and queue. The small retail shop showcases probably the prettiest chocolates in town—and the tastiest. Some Moonstruck truffles—many hand-dipped—are spiked with such heavenly fillings as raspberry Chambord, Clear Creek pear brandy, and Grand Marnier; others, like the cinnamon latte and bittersweet chocolate truffles, are equally intoxicating and worthy of addiction. Recently Moonstruck opened another wee shop in the Portland airport. ▪ *608 SW Alder; 241-0955; map:H4; every day.*

Simply Irresistible Kids love this little candy shop in Westmoreland for the jars of gummies, jelly beans, licorice, and sour candies; adults swoon with nostalgia. Everything is made out of house except for the fudge—and what fudge it is! There are usually several varieties of flavors and colors, such as the pink bubble-gum fudge studded with marshmallows. There's also sugar-free candy, Umpqua ice cream, and Italian sodas. ▪ *1620 SE Bybee; 231-2960; map:II5; every day.*

▼

Candies and Chocolates

▲

CARDS AND STATIONERY

Jelly Bean Owner Jeanie Breall has been selling it all in her shop since 1978: from squeaky-clean standard greetings to seriously risqué cards. Some of the funniest cards going keep 'em laughing in her aisles, as do slogan T-shirts, bumper stickers, and personal novelties. ▪ *721 SW 10th Ave; 222-5888; map:H2; Mon-Sat.*

Papyrus The selection of boxed cards here could tie you up for the better part of a lunch hour. This link in a chain of stationery stores features a high-quality, unusual (but not bizarre) collection of greeting cards—plus journals, writing paper, gift wrap, and all sorts of mailable items. ▪ *810 SW Broadway; 294-1139; map:G3; Mon-Sat.*

Present Perfect This downtown destination for gift wrapping offers cheery papers sold by the sheet, laminated gift bags, bows, and ribbons—even a roll of tape and scissors for last-minute wrapping jobs. Stationery here also hits a higher plane; the knowledgeable staff can help you wade through a mammoth selection of cards for every mood and occasion. Creative party invitations and matching favors will get any celebration rolling. ▪ *Pioneer Place; 228-9727; map:G4; every day.*

Rice Paper Shelby Rice's shop in Multnomah stocks for the connoisseur: beautiful handmade and imported papers for writing letters, covering books, doing calligraphy, and so forth. In addition, there are elegant invitations, journals, and artists' books. The store shares space with Wisteria's—a lovely gift boutique. ■ *7808 SW Capitol Hwy; 452-3181; map:JJ7; Mon-Sat.*

Urban Dreams Today it's high art and pop culture icons as well as a great collection of Albert Einstein greetings. Tomorrow? There's always a unique collection of cards, postcards, posters, T-shirts, and gift wrap. ■ *Lloyd Center (and branches); 284-1151; map:GG5; every day.*

Wham! Lots of pop culture cards, but toys too. Remember sea monkeys and potato guns? And what about Gumby, the original yogi? ■ *617 NW 23rd Ave; 222-4992; map:GG7; every day.*

CHILDREN'S CLOTHING

Bambini's Children's Boutique A fun (if expensive) place in the Lake Grove Shopping Center to outfit your bambini, newborn to preteen, with clothing as whimsical as the youngsters themselves. It's the only store around stocking Maine Madhatter sweaters and Tickle Me for girls or Tackle Me for boys. Also, gifts for the new baby: silver rattles, picture frames, crib toys, and mobiles. ■ *16353 SW Bryant Rd, Lake Oswego; 635-7661; map:KK6; Mon-Sat.*

Gap Kids ■ Baby Gap These wee clothes are just like the grown-ups' Gap fashions. Charming school dresses, trendy-colored sportswear (how does your rug rat look in chartreuse?), groovy baseball hats, plus the basics: sturdy jeans and overalls, good cotton T-shirts and turtlenecks, and socks to complement them all. Prices are competitive and, given that a new line comes in every two months, there are great deals to be found on the sale rack. Recently a layette setup was added to the repertoire—from cute newborn onesies to bumpers and crib sheets. ■ *Pioneer Place (and branches); 228-8115; map:G4; every day.*

Generations As befits its SE Hawthorne Boulevard location, this store carries both tie-dyed and undyed cotton clothing and accessories, but mainstream brands like Cotton Caboodle, Flapdoodles, and Newsport Kids are its bread and butter. Items range from soft gowns for newborns to cute jacket-and-pant ensembles for boys and girls up to size 8. There's a small selection of used items in the back of the store, plus good-as-it-gets maternity wear. ■ *4029 SE Hawthorne Blvd; 233-8130; map:GG5; Mon-Sat.*

Gymboree You'll see the same colors—blue, green, red, and pink—reworked from season to season, which is good news if your child insists on dressing herself while you stand by helplessly, hoping she chooses a top and a bottom that don't clash.

Most of these togs are made of prewashed cotton, in sizes from NB to 7. There's also a small selection of wooden toys and some terrific baby blankets. ▪ *Pioneer Place (and branches); 224-2075; map:G4; every day.*

Hanna Andersson Hanna Andersson—best known around the country for its catalog of Swedish-style cotton clothing for kids and moms—is one of Portland's brighter retail success stories; with colors this vivid, how could it be anything but? The quality of Hannas (as the goods are known) is usually very high, and the styles are irresistible. Buy bargain-priced irregulars and last season's stock at the spacious outlet store in Lake Oswego's Mountain Park neighborhood. ▪ *327 NW 10th Ave; 321-5275; map:L2; every day.* ▪ *7 Monroe Pkwy (Oswego Town Square), Lake Oswego; 697-1953; map:LL7; every day.*

Lads and Lassies Frocks and Britches This shop offers more than just beautiful infant-to-preteen clothes—the sales staff will treat your kids like heirs to the throne. The toy and book departments rival those of fine toy stores, as does the doll collection. ▪ *Beaverton Town Square; 626-6578; map:HH9; every day.*

Mako Lots of cotton—a great selection of rainbow-hued leggings and T-shirts—and everyday prices. There's practical rain gear, cotton sweaters hand-knit by Mako herself, colorful bathrobes, flashy underwear, a fanciful sock collection, and shelves of toys, puzzles, and bath accessories for kids. ▪ *732 NW 23rd Ave; 274-9081; map:GG7; every day.*

Old Navy Some call Old Navy "budget Baby Gap"—the styles are similar, but the clothes cost a third to half the price. When it comes to basics—denim overalls, cotton print shirts and dresses—you can't go wrong here. The bare-bones setting lacks visual appeal, but that's not out of character given its mall location. There are also clothes for bigger kids and adults. ▪ *1752 Jantzen Beach Center; 289-9086; map:BB6; every day.* ▪ *Clackamas Promenade; 659-2638; map:KK3; every day.*

Second to None Tucked into the Hillsdale Shopping Center, this children's shop features a good selection of used clothing (often name brands like Guess, Gap, and Hanna Andersson) and colorful new cottonwear and polar fleece jackets. Costumes for dress-up, too. Unfinished and hand-painted wooden toy chests and child-size chairs, American Girl clothes and accessories (some custom made), and used car seats set this store apart from other consignment shops. ▪ *6308 SW Capitol Hwy (Hillsdale Shopping Center); 244-0071; map:II8; Mon-Sat.*

Water Babies We expected swimwear when we first visited this store, and we found it—plus all-cotton undies and bright pile jackets and all layers in between. This longtime Sellwood store is overflowing with clothes and accessories for newborns to preteens, as well as a thoughtful selection of cloth and wooden toys.

Both you and your child will appreciate the sale room, which houses good buys—and a rice (as opposed to sand) box. ▪ *8085 SE 13th Ave; 232-6039; map:JJ5; Tues-Sat.*

COFFEES AND TEAS

The Bean Another coffeehouse and coffee merchant, Cafe Splendid (formerly Captain Beans) roasts and retails a changing variety of beans, many of which are sold here. Located in Ladd's Addition, this spot makes a great hangout on a lazy Sunday afternoon. ▪ *1720 SE 12th Ave; 232-8338; map:GG6, every day.*

British Tea Garden ▪ Tea Time on Hawthorne Shop here for a tea party: there's plenty of plum cake, English tea biscuits, gooseberry preserves, Terry's York Chocolate Oranges, and, yes, tea. Scones with Devonshire cream and a hot pot of Earl Grey are perfect in the middle of a hectic day (there are plenty of tables). On bright afternoons, explore the secret garden behind the British Tea Garden; at Tea Time on Hawthorne, sample traditional British fare on weekend evenings, when the dining room stays open until 9. Ask to be put on the mailing list to receive the monthly newsletter of special events such as tea leaf readings or children's and literary teas. ▪ *725 SW 10th Ave; 221-7817; map:H2; every day.* ▪ *3439 SE Hawthorne Blvd; 231-7750; map:HH5; every day.*

Coffee Merchant You can't buy a cup of joe here; they give it to you. Four brews are always hot for sampling, and a wide assortment of beans come roasted or unroasted (for those who like to roast their own). There's also a good selection of teas. Dave and Linda McCammon and the staff on NE Broadway have created a relaxed environment for perusing cookbooks and the collection of coffee and tea accoutrements, or selecting your bean of the week. Doris Glasser (a former employee of the McCammons) owns the store on Hawthorne: same coffee, same idea. ▪ *1637 NE Broadway; 284-9209; map:FF5; every day.* ▪ *3562 SE Hawthorne Blvd; 230-1222; map:GG5; every day.*

▼

Coffees and Teas

▲

Coffee People What began as a simple coffee shop has burgeoned into an empire—and, in this city at least, has become a serious Starbucks competitor. The stylish superstores on NW 23rd Avenue and in the Hawthorne district attract a crowd morning, noon, and night. The product in most of the Coffee People outlets is the same: a gazillion different espresso concoctions, pastries, and cookies (some of the best in town), ice cream, and noncoffee alternatives such as steamers and sodas. There are 60 different varieties of coffee beans, as well as cups, pots, and gadgets. The original CP, **Motor Moka** (525 NE Grand; map:FF6), maintains a strong following (so strong, in fact, that it's often quicker to get out of your car). ▪ *533 NW 23rd Ave; 221-0235;*

map:GG7; every day. ▪ 3500 SE Hawthorne Blvd (and branches); 235-1383; map:GG5; every day.

Kobos Company Long before it was hip to peddle specialty coffee—24 years ago, in fact—Kobos was in the bean business in Portland, roasting their own and selling it from their original Johns Landing location. Now there are seven outlets around the city, each with an espresso bar; the most recent shop is in the building that houses the roasting plant and corporate offices (2355 NW Vaughn). Kobos also offers one of the best selections of loose teas in town, and the larger stores house an excellent collection of kitchenware. ▪ 5331 SW Macadam Ave (Johns Landing) and branches; 222-5226; map:JJ6; every day.

Starbucks A few years ago this Seattle-based megachain injected itself into the bloodstream of Portland coffee lovers; now it seems as if every time you turn around, a new Starbucks is opening (there are already some 50 stores in the metropolitan area). One of the more recent additions—and perhaps the most novel—is a small coffee bar in the reading room of the Multnomah County Library. What Starbucks offers is this: sleek interiors, consistent coffee, good service, and shelves of must-have coffee products and toys for the consumer. The Rose City's first Starbucks, on the northwest corner of Pioneer Courthouse Square, is probably Portland's favorite. ▪ Pioneer Courthouse Square (and branches); 223-2488; map:H3; every day.

Torrefazione Italia See Coffee and Dessert in the Nightlife chapter. ▪ 838 NW 23rd Ave; 228-1255; map:GG7; every day. ▪ 1403 NE Weidler; 288-1608; map:FF5; every day.

DEPARTMENT STORES

Fred Meyer It was 1922 when Fred G. Meyer opened shop at SW Fifth Avenue and Yamhill Street, pioneering the cash-and-carry concept, self-service, and prepackaging. Today that business has grown to 225 stores in 17 states, including the famous "one-stop shopping" stores, where you can find just about anything. These superstores, which boast hundreds of thousands of food and non-food items in dozens of specialty areas, include everything from produce to lumber to computers to fine jewelry to apparel. Often good wine buys, too. ▪ 3030 NE Weidler St (and branches); 232-8844; map:FF4; every day.

Meier & Frank The Meier and Frank families started a grand Portland tradition in 1857 when they opened this multifloored department store on SW Fifth and Morrison. Now eight enterprises, the Meier & Frank chain is owned by the St. Louis–based May department-store company. The original store offers a full complement of services: a beauty salon, a bridal registry, picture framing, jewelry repair, a travel agency, and a photography studio. It's the "everyperson's" department store, specializing in good-looking, moderately priced merchandise, from fine china to men's and women's fashions—and plenty of it. Sale shoppers take heed: Meier & Frank markdowns are sometimes considerable. The Washington Square store—among the bigger M&Fs—carries Baccarat crystal. ■ *621 SW 5th Ave (and branches); 223-0512; map:H3; every day.*

Nordstrom Portlanders are convinced they can't live without Nordie's. Much of this developing success is owed to Nordstrom's famous emphasis on service. The "At Your Service," or concierge, booths located on each of the store's main floors provide visitors with maps and brochures in eight languages. An extremely helpful sales staff follows current fashions and knows the merchandise they're selling (and they dress to emphasize that point). Nordstrom started business as a shoe store in 1901, and shoes are still its specialty at all locations, with a tremendous range of styles and prices, and an impressive stock of hard-to-find sizes. Women's fashions are displayed in numerous well-defined departments, ranging from sophisticated to playful and everything in between. Men can be outfitted to Nordstrom Ivy League specifications in five distinctively different shops.

Keep an eye out for the famous sales—the anniversary sale in July and the half-yearly sales for women (June and November) and for men (June and December)—notorious for great deals and outrageous crowds. The downtown location was Oregon's first, but the Washington Square branch may be the most elegant. ■ *701 SW Broadway (and branches); 224-6666; map:H2; every day.*

Saks Fifth Avenue The Northwest got its first taste of this distinguished New York–based department store when its 47th branch opened, in downtown Portland, in 1990. The beautiful display windows that line SW Fourth and Fifth Avenues give just a tantalizing hint of what's inside. The intimate, tasteful interior feels more like a large boutique than a department store, with two levels of American and European designer wear for men and women, supplemented by Saks's own private-label merchandise.

From elegant special-occasion dresses to cutting-edge sportswear, Saks offers top quality, style, and taste. Sales help is attentive, and if they don't have your size, they'll gladly order it for you. The 5th Avenue Club offers customers personal shopping services, including wardrobe consultation and gift selection, at no extra charge. Now an integral part of Portland's social fabric, Saks quietly offers the upper-end merchandise that makes the society columns. Sales, however, are frequent, and Saks's own label offers some of the best values anywhere on both shoes and apparel. ■ *850 SW 5th Ave; 226-3200; map:G4; every day.*

DISCOUNT AND FACTORY OUTLETS

Act II Exclusive Resale Boutique   There are labels in this high-brow, low-key store that scream "no one can afford me." You can. Armani, Donna Karan, Valentino, and St. John take a sharp mark-down here. ▪ *1139 SW Morrison St; 227-7969; map:I1; Tues-Sat.*

Barbara Johnson Clothing Outlet   If you're a sample size (from 6 to 12), you're in luck, because Barbara Johnson is the place where sales reps unload their merchandise. Women's dresses, suits, blouses, and lingerie are priced 15 percent above wholesale, and well-known brands (Susan Bristol, Carol Anderson, Marisa Christina) hit the racks here one to two seasons ahead of the stores. ▪ *18005 SW Lower Boones Ferry Rd, Tigard; 620-1777; map:MM9; Mon-Sat.*

Bargain Tree   Designer labels from Donna Karan to Liz Claiborne appear regularly here at a percentage of their retail price. Clothing quality is excellent. Stock is unpredictable, so frequent shopping is smart. The store is run by the Junior League, and all proceeds from their sales go to charities serving women and children in crisis. ▪ *838 SW 4th Ave; 227-7413; map:G4; Mon-Sat.*

Bits & Pieces Factory Outlet   NewportLayton Creations, a major manufacturer of home fashions, offers factory seconds and overruns at great prices. Upstairs, the factory produces bedspreads and decorator pillows that are sold throughout the country. The outlet is downstairs, with prices of up to 50 percent off retail on all seconds of bedspreads, plus scraps by the pound and bolts by the yard. ▪ *1420 NW Lovejoy St; 222-1549; map:GG7; Mon-Sat.*

Columbia Gorge Factory Stores   It's not the best outlet shopping in the state, but it's nearby: only 20 minutes east of downtown Portland (exit 17 off I-84). More than 40 stores sell everything from men's clothing (Geoffrey Beene and Levi's) to luggage (American Tourister) to sneakers (Adidas)—at 30 to 70 percent off retail. Lace up your walking shoes because once you start, it's hard to stop. ▪ *450 NW 257th Ave, Troutdale; 669-8060; every day.*

Columbia Knit Factory Outlet Store   The company sews built-to-last rugby shirts for famous national mail-order catalogs. Merchandise is mostly overruns with some seconds, priced up to 50 percent below retail. In addition, the store offers great cotton knits for the entire family. ▪ *5200 SE Harney Dr; 777-7385; map:II4; Mon-Fri.*

Columbia Sportswear Factory Outlet   These outlets are favorites among those who think the best thing about Portland is leaving it behind on the weekends. Trucks deliver irregulars, closeouts, and overstocks of active outdoor apparel and footwear fresh from the factory several times a week. Columbia's own gear is 30 to 50

▼

Discount and Factory Outlets

▲

percent below retail; miscellaneous others are discounted by 10 to 15 percent. The Lake Oswego outlet is three times larger than the Sellwood store. ▪ *8128 SE 13th Ave; 238-0118; map:II5; every day.* ▪ *3 Monroe Pkwy (Oswego Town Square), Lake Oswego; 636-6593; map:LL8; every day.*

Danner Factory Outlet Store   Danner is boots: hunting, military, work, and hiking. First-quality boots sell for brand-new prices; irregulars are up to 50 percent off—not guaranteed to be waterproof. Especially busy on Saturdays and in hunting season. ▪ *12722 NE Airport Way; 251-1111; map:EE2; Mon-Sat.*

Dehen Outlet Store   Dehen could outfit a soda pop commercial with its all-American line—at a fraction of retail. In real life, the company supplies L. L. Bean and many colleges and universities with casual, feel-good sportswear; its hot new business is crafting custom-made varsity lettermen's jackets. In addition to factory overruns, the shop carries an exclusive line of upper-end, inexpensive cotton merchandise. ▪ *924 NW Flanders; 222-3871; map:L2; Mon-Fri (Sat by appointment only).*

Ellington Rucksack Co.   Rugged leather goods and eco-sensitive recycled fabric-and-webbing rucksacks rock the shelves at the outlet for this Portland-based company. Seconds, closeouts, and prototypes take a markdown at this northwest Portland store where parking is a cinch. ▪ *1533 NW 24th Ave; 223-7457; map:GG7; Mon-Fri.*

Hanna Andersson Outlet Store   The Swedish-made children's clothing available by catalog and at the company's only retail outlet downtown is sold here once it's been discontinued. No special purchases or specially manufactured lines, just last season's colorful cotton jumpers, sleepers, and rompers, along with a few irregulars. Great selection of clothes for Mom, too. ▪ *7 Monroe Pkwy (Oswego Town Square), Lake Oswego; 697-1953; map:LL7; every day.*

Jantzen Factory Outlet Store   This formerly employee-only store recently opened to the public. Stop here for end-of-season, irregular, and discontinued sports- and swimwear marked to fly out the door at least 50 percent off. ▪ *NE 17th Ave and Glisan St; 238-5393; map:GG5; Mon-Fri and the first Sat of the month.*

Kutters: An Outlet Store   The $12 men's shirt continues to be Kutters's signature, and with hundreds of men's shirts lining the wall at this off-the-wall "shirt bar," choice is not a problem. Women find a fast-moving selection of overruns, experimental designer lines, and brands that only a seasoned shopper would recognize (labels are snipped). Among some of the better buys: roomy wool coats in big and tall sizes. ▪ *217 SW Ash St; 228-4858; map:I5; every day.*

▼

▲

Nike Factory Store There is the high-tech shoe shrine Nike Town, there are the splashy full-price Nike stores and the employee-only store, and then there's the off-price Nike outlet, where good prices can be had by all. Among the bargains: close-outs and seconds at 20 to 40 percent off regular retail. Everything's guaranteed—even imperfect shoes. ■ *3044 NE Martin Luther King Jr Blvd; 281-5901; map:EE5; every day.*

Nordstrom Rack The Rack carries clearance merchandise from the Nordstrom stores at up to 70 percent off, and supplemental buying adds more career and casual looks at great prices. The downtown basement store fills—and feels—like a tightly packed submarine, while the Clackamas location lets shoppers see the light of day. Look for some astonishing finds among the everyday sales items. Retail clerks maintain sunny Nordstrom smiles. ■ *401 SW Morrison St; 299-1815; map:G4; every day.* ■ *8930 SE Sunnyside Rd (Clackamas Promenade), Clackamas; 654-5415; map:KK3; every day.*

Norm Thompson Outlet Store The same predictable quality and style that's carried in the retail shops can be found at the outlet store—but at 20 to 60 percent off the original price. Watch for frequent sales: the price of select stock is knocked down so far you can't afford *not* to buy. ■ *Columbia Gorge Factory Stores, 450 NW 257th Ave, Troutdale; 665-8416; every day.*

▼
Discount
and Factory
Outlets
▲

Oregon Mail Order Outlet Store It's an understatement to say the inventory here is eclectic. This store stocks clothing, gizmos, and dry goods from three very different catalogs—Norm Thompson, Early Winters, and Solutions—all part of the Norm Thompson family. ■ *3 Monroe Pkwy (Oswego Town Square), Lake Oswego; 697-2931; map:LL7; every day.*

Pendleton Woolen Mills Wool Mill Store This is the drop-off spot for products from the research and development department of the Pendleton Woolen Mills. Prototypes for new products—from Pendleton wool–upholstered furniture to theme blankets—land here at discount prices. A shop annex offers fabric, buttons, elastic, and other sewing goods for as little as $1. ■ *8550 SE McLoughlin; 273-2786; map:JJ5; Mon-Sat.*

FABRIC AND NEEDLECRAFT SUPPLIES

Calico Corners Probably the biggest selection of home fabrics in the city, ranging from mill ends to designer bolts from the United States and Europe, can be found here. The store appeals to do-it-yourself home remodelers, but there's also custom sewing for those not familiar with the details of re-covering their own couches. ■ *9120 SW Hall Blvd, Tigard; 624-7218; map:II6; every day.*

Cheryl's Own Design Fabric Outlet COD, subtitled "The Sports Connection," caters exclusively to sports-oriented tailors. Manufacturers like Nike, Roffe, and Patagonia supply the raw materials. (Where else will you find wool stretch ski-pant fabric or 100 percent cotton cloth for sweats?) There are some custom patterns and factory-excess D-rings, ribbings, and zippers, but no tweed. ■ *12675 SW Broadway, Beaverton; 641-7271; map:HH10; Mon-Sat.*

Daisy Kingdom Fabrics and Trims About a quarter of the two-story store's fabric supply comes from the million yards that the wholesale division designs and prints for international distribution. The second floor here serves as a factory outlet, discounting discontinued items. At the ready-made children's outlet store across the street (207 NW Park Ave, 222-9033), a seconds dress that would retail for $80 might go for $30. The mail-order division, (800)234-6688, retails crafts, fabrics, infant wear, and ready-to-wear. ■ *134 NW 8th Ave; 222-4281; map:K4; every day.*

Famous Labels Fabric Outlet The area's best selection of Lycra, nylon, and cotton swimwear fabrics, including fabric from brand-name apparel makers such as Speedo and Osh-Kosh. Buy by the pound for the best deals. ■ *2155 E Burnside, Gresham; 666-3187; map:FF5; every day.*

In Stitches This shop has been supplying needlepoint enthusiasts for over 20 years. It carries everything from the finest hand-dyed fibers to hand-colored patterns and custom frames, but you won't find prepackaged kits. And they'll turn your handiwork into gorgeous pillows. ■ *25-5 NW 23rd Pl (Uptown Shopping Center); 226-0814; map:I3; Mon-Sat.*

Josephine's Dry Goods Josephine's, the only fabric store in downtown Portland, appeals to the accomplished, upscale seamstress. A fine selection of elegant natural fibers, a generous button selection, and Vogue, New Look, and Burda patterns come together at this fabric boutique. ■ *921 SW Morrison St (The Galleria); 224-4202; map:I2; every day.*

Mill End Store Located in the old Omark building, the Milwaukie Mill End holds 70,000 square feet of fabric—arguably America's biggest fabric display. Although you can still find bargain end-cuts, prices are no longer wholesale cheap. Also in Beaverton. ■ *9701 SE McLoughlin Blvd; 786-1234; map:II5; every day.* ■ *12155 SW Broadway, Beaverton; 646-3000; map:HH9; every day.*

Northwest Wools This shop offers skeins of wool, linen, cotton, silk, and mohair; hand-spun yarns and all the raw materials to spin your own; and looms and spinning wheels. If you don't know how to knit, spin, or weave, classes are available; or they'll do it for you. ■ *3524 SW Troy St; 244-5024; map:II7; Mon-Sat.*

Fabric and
Needlecraft
Supplies

Uncommon Threads Here's an outstanding selection of hand-dyed silks, wools, and cottons in glorious colors. A complete supplier for the knitter and weaver, including Rigid Heddle looms, Uncommon Threads is known for its classes, which include weaving, basic and adventurous knitting, and finishing. ■ *2390 NW Thurman St; 227-0134; map:FF6; Tues-Sat.*

The Whole Nine Yards Painter Amy Estrin brings an artist's eye to the selection of upholstery and drapery fabric here. She and co-owner Jamie Eoff stock some 6,000 square feet of washed Italian chenilles, velvets, tapestries, linens, and silks. There's a fantastic selection of trims; loads of contemporary solid and print sheers; and patient, personalized service. ■ *1033 NW Glisan St; 223-2880; map:L2; Mon-Sat.*

FLORISTS

Alameda Orchids Gary Brown stocks hundreds of orchid varieties (mostly potted plants), ranging in price from $10 to $1,000 (special-order orchids can cost as much as $5,000), but staff members excel in leading you to the right plant. At any one time there are around 150 orchids in bloom in the store—some fragrant, some not. Other varieties of cut flowers are for sale outside on the sidewalk. A smaller shop is situated off the lobby of the Hotel Vintage Plaza. ■ *2438 NE Broadway; 249-0676; map:FF5; Mon-Sat.* ■ *422 SW Broadway (Hotel Vintage Plaza); 223-4944; map:I4; every day.*

Flowers by Dorcas At first glance, Dorcas resembles an upscale gift store—and about 40 percent of its business is, in fact, items besides flowers. But gardeny flowers there are as well, generally arranged in a loose, natural style. Prices are not low, a fact that doesn't seem to faze Dorcas's carriage-trade clientele, but the quality is evident. ■ *525 SW Broadway; 227-6454; map:H4; Mon-Sat.*

Flowers Tommy Luke This high-volume florist's shop is a Portland tradition, with designs from standard FTD to airier English garden arrangements. In addition, there are select gifts, including handblown Blenko vases. ■ *1701 SW Jefferson (and branches); 228-3140; map:G1; every day.*

Gifford-Doving Florists Gifford-Doving (family-owned since 1938) stocks one of the better selections of cut flowers in town, and in the late afternoon, it is one of Portland's busiest florists. Several kinds of greens are usually on hand as well, making this a favorite source for do-it-yourself arrangers. ■ *704 SW Jefferson St (and branches); 222-9193; map:F2; Mon-Sat.*

Linda Loving Florist Linda Loving buys from local growers (or cuts flowers from her own garden) when she can, and her floral arrangements mirror that commitment; they share a fresh-cut beauty. The shop is tiny, but it does a brisk business in cut flowers and conversation. ▪ *3614 SE Hawthorne Blvd; 231-5660; map:GG5; Mon-Sat.*

Northwest Garden and Topiary To enter Laura Williams Mapes's shop on NW 23rd Avenue is to seek shade between two colorful buildings and find birdsong, orange blossoms, and a large selection of cut flowers, annuals, perennials, garden tools, and plant- and flower-inspired gifts. The shop also houses a full-service florist and a plant, statue, and fountain delivery service. The space is so inviting you'll be tempted to spread a picnic blanket and spend the afternoon staring at its trompe l'oeil sky. ▪ *805 NW 23rd Ave; 222-9939; map:GG7; every day.*

Rainyday Flowers Rainyday means tropical flowers and Hawaiian plants. Orchids, anthuriums, gardenia corsages, leis, and Venus's-flytraps are generally on hand, along with bonsai, cacti, and a wide range of less exotic cut flowers. There are outdoor plants, pots, and garden items as well. ▪ *7306 SW Beaverton-Hillsdale Hwy; 203-1904; map:II8; Mon-Sat.*

Richard Calhoun Old Town Florist The florists here favor striking designs of tropical flowers and foliage; silk flowers are equally dramatic. Located in the arty Pearl District. ▪ *403 NW 9th Ave; 223-1646; map:K3; Mon-Sat.*

Sammy's Flowers (Durst's Thriftway) You'll be spoiled for choice with more than 50 varieties of cut flowers at near-wholesale prices, most of them in rows of containers outside along the front of the grocery store. Sammy happily wraps up mixed bouquets— your choice of flowers or hers—for under $15. Drop by on a Friday when the selection is at its best, and you can sometimes find a dozen roses for about $10. Open 24 hours to handle any floral emergency; delivery available. ▪ *2122 NW Glisan St; 222-9759; map:GG7; every day.*

Wildflowers on Hawthorne More aptly called a flower shop than a florist (although they do deliver), this enchanting store sells flowers in many forms. The small but lovely selection of fresh-cut flowers tends toward the wild and seasonal varieties—snapdragons and veronica in the summer, branches of vine maples and rose hips in the fall. There are also bouquets of dried larkspur, lavender, and roses, and handmade wreaths. In the back are shelves lined with jars of herbs, spices, and the delicious herbal tea blends. Don't hesitate to ask for guidance; the staff is both knowledgeable and helpful. ▪ *3202 SE Hawthorne; 230-9485; map:GG5; every day.*

Bader & Fox Sofa Factory New sofas and chairs are manufactured from scratch here, and old pieces are redone. Many customers bring in pictures from magazines; Bader & Fox can re-create those designs, using your fabric or theirs. Detailing is superb, and prices are competitive. Take time to double-check your dimensions; this is custom-made furniture, after all. ■ *3400 SE 122nd Ave; 761-6135; map:HH1; Mon-Sat.*

Full Upright Position The specialty here is modern classic furniture. Located in Pearl District central, this store has a beautiful display of contemporary chairs, sofas, and tables that's practically a Who's Who of modern architecture: Eames, Jacobsen, Breuer, Le Corbusier, Aalto, Starck, and more. Any of it can be special-ordered by the friendly, unpretentious staff. ■ *1101 NW Glisan St; 228-6190; map:L2; Tues-Sun.*

The Handwerk Shop Customers quickly become friends at this welcoming store on the end of Sellwood's antique row offering Mission oak furniture, textiles, and pottery from (or just inspired by) the Arts and Crafts period. Co-owner Brent Willis makes Morris chairs, settles, accent tables, and picture frames in the spirit of designer Gustav Stickley. His wife and partner, Linda, runs the shop and gives design advice to inquiring bungalow owners—and seeks out specialty items like Arts and Crafts stencils. ■ *8317 SE 13th Ave; 236-7870; map:JJ5; Thurs-Sun and by appointment.*

▼

Furniture

▲

The Joinery For a long time, the Joinery was a fine place to find custom-made Mission- and Shaker-style furniture—and it still is. But in this exquisite new showroom/workshop, in addition to tables and chairs, you can now find finely hewn wooden accessories such as mirrors, boxes, and spinning tops from around the world. The furniture has changed, too. Now you can order a granite-topped dining table or an Early American dresser. You might wait three months for your new treasure—but it will be worth waiting for. ■ *4804 SE Woodstock Blvd; 788-8547; map:HH5; Mon-Sat.*

Kaboom George Jetson would be right at home in this loft-size outpost of contemporary furniture and gifts. Whimsical '60s-style sofas and love seats in primary colors share space with affordable mobiles big enough to crowd an airplane hangar. Postmodern gift items include Alessi teapots designed by Phillippe Starck and crystal by Aalto. ■ *1115 NW Glisan St; 223-1465; map:L2; every day.*

Kinion Furniture Company Choose from among 50 samples crafted mainly in cherry (the workshop is in McMinnville). You'll find beautifully made contemporary renditions of Shaker furniture with a little Mission and Arts and Crafts thrown in. Traditional joinery techniques mean the furniture's built to last. ■ *216 SW Yamhill St; 221-1574; map:G4; Mon-Sat.*

Leather Furniture Company   Leather, of course, in such quantities that this store can offer consistently lower prices, higher quality, and more specialized product knowledge than any other furniture store in the area. One shop is in Raleigh Hills; the other is downtown. ■ *6800 SW Beaverton-Hillsdale Hwy; 297-1034; map:II8; every day.* ■ *311 SW Alder St; 224-0272; map:H5; every day.*

P. H. Reed   Upscale upholstered furniture and Italian lighting reach dizzying heights of sophistication at what feels and looks like a gallery. Pieter Reed represents local artists and furniture makers, so you see cast-glass side tables, wrought-iron beds, hand-loomed carpets, and hand-painted wallpapers that are distinctive and timeless—style that won't go out of style. ■ *1100 NW Glisan St; 274-7080; map:K2; Tues-Sun.*

The Real Mother Goose   See Jewelry and Repairs in this chapter. ■ *901 SW Yamhill St (and branches); 223-9510; map:H2; Mon-Sat.*

Rejuvenation House Parts   Now a Portland institution, this store has quietly built a nationwide catalog business around its superior reproductions of turn-of-the-century and Craftsman-style light fixtures and Mission-style furniture. You'll also find salvaged doors, windows, tubs, and sinks. The staff here offers a wealth of advice to do-it-yourselfers and licensed architects alike (by the way, the *Business Journal* listed Rejuvenation as the best company to work for in Oregon). Finally, Powell's Books stocks interior design and building books here. ■ *1100 SE Grand Ave; 238-1900; map:EE5; every day.*

▼

Furniture

▲

Restoration Hardware   See Hardware in this chapter. ■ *315 NW 23rd Ave; 228-6226; map:GG7; every day.*

Scan/Design   A huge selection of Danish imports in traditional teak and rosewood plus more contemporary whitewashed ash with timeless, clean Scandinavian lines. Scan/Design can furnish every room in the house, as well as the office. ■ *10760 SW Beaverton-Hillsdale Hwy, Beaverton (and branches); 644-4040; map:II8; every day.*

Simon Toney and Fischer   David Simon and Bill Toney designed and built custom cabinetry and fine furniture in Portland for 21 years before opening a Pearl District showroom in 1994, with designer and partner Susan Fischer. That's good news to anyone who stops by to see the luminous collection of tables, beds, and cabinetry made from seldom-used, unusual woods—walnut, pear, yew, and chinkapin—many indigenous to Oregon. Each board is hand-picked, and most of the one-of-a-kind pieces have painterly finishes that fuse splashes of color with copper- or silver-leaf beading. The result is astonishingly beautiful—more akin to fine art than furniture. ▪ *545 NW 13th Ave; 721-0392; map:L2; Tues-Sat.*

Urbino Home   The owners of Urbino (see Gifts in this chapter) have taken their signature Old World atmosphere and sophisticated modern taste down the street to this sumptuous outpost of furniture and interior accessories. Fine fabrics, one-of-a-kind lamps and wall sconces, custom-upholstered furniture, and more. ▪ *638 NW 23rd Ave; 220-4194; map:GG7; every day.*

GIFTS

Barn Owl Nursery   See Nurseries and Garden Centers in this chapter. ▪ *22999 SW Newland Rd, Wilsonville; 638-0387; map:QQ9; Wed-Sat.*

Bibelot   This art and craft gallery carries something for gift hunters in every price range—from willow-branch floor lamps to pear-shaped beeswax candles. Vivid colors are everywhere, from the jewelry to the ceramics to the painted furniture. It's in Multnomah, fittingly near the Multnomah Arts Center. ▪ *7642 SW Capitol Hwy; 244-8483; map:JJ7; Tues-Sun.*

Callin Novelty Shop   Behind-the-counter expert magicians can show you how to pull off pranks in style. Callin's sells the props for jokesters of all ages and has everything you ever wanted to buy from the back pages of comic books: sea monkeys, magic rocks, X-ray specs. ▪ *1013 SW Washington St; 223-4821; map:I5; Mon-Sat.*

The Cat's Meow   The purr-fect store for the discriminating cat lover. Owner Pam Gibson ceded management of the premises to the beige-furred, blue-eyed Mr. Muddles and his assistant, the cuddly Ms. Clarity, long ago. Customers can paw through cat jewelry, cat-patterned pajamas, and the latest edition of *Who's Who of Cats.* ▪ *3538 SE Hawthorne Blvd; 231-1341; map:GG5; Tues-Sun.*

Christmas at the Zoo   The Zoo captures a year-round selection of all things Christmas, including European ornaments and handmade collectibles. Beyond the trimmings you'll find puppets and a marvelous menagerie of stuffed animals for the young at heart. ▪ *118 NW 23rd Ave; 223-4048; map:FF7; every day.*

Contemporary Crafts Gallery   See Galleries in the Arts chapter. ▪ *3934 SW Corbett Ave; 223-2654; map:HH6; Tues-Sun.*

Dazzle   The walls at Dazzle suggest the trendy Southwestern style, but the wacky merchandise throws any sort of interior design plan into chaos. Look for colorful objects here from both local and international artists. ▪ *704 NW 23rd Ave; 224-1294; map:GG7; every day.*

Earth Mercantile You can sip complimentary herbal tea while browsing through this Hillsdale store, where the range of products is vast and quirky: diaper wraps, vegetable seeds, wooden toys, toilet paper, T-shirts, stationery, jewelry. The clerks are superfriendly and there's a playroom to keep the kids entertained. ▪ *6345 SW Capitol Hwy; 246-4935; map:II7; every day.*

Friends Library Store When the refurbished Central Library opened in 1997, it not only had a Starbucks, it also had its own gift shop, run by Friends of the Multnomah County Library, with everything for the book lover—bookends, book lights, writing equipment (both costly and not), children's gifts, and jewelry— but no books. Open during library hours. ▪ *801 SW 10th Ave; 306-5911; map:H2; every day.*

Itchy Fingers Gallery From swirling colored-glass objects to postmodern picture frames, vanilla candles to filigree jewelry, this is one great gift shop. Can't find a pink pig light fixture anywhere? It's here, along with a lot of other upscale gimcracks— and a lot of less goofy merchandise that's quite pretty. ▪ *517 NW 23rd Ave; 222-5237; map:FF7; every day.*

Julia's, The Ultimate Collection Julia's boasts a glorious mishmash of everything from Russian lacquered boxes and brooches to ornate sterling silver picture frames. Dollhouse collectors will want to visit just for the miniatures. African and Indonesian wall masks startle, an enormous hand-painted silk scarf decorated with a brightly colored cat delights, and marcasite jewelry shimmers alluringly. ▪ *1016 SW Morrison St; 274-9308; map:I1; Mon-Sat.*

▼

Gifts

▲

Liquid Sunshine They say you can tell who's a native Oregonian because natives never carry an umbrella, but try telling that to the owners of this store. Hundreds of umbrellas in glorious patterns, from Monet paintings and Nicole Miller prints to fanciful dogs or cats, decorate the walls here. ▪ *Pioneer Place; 226-7246; map:H4; every day.*

Made in Oregon Everything sold here is made, caught, or grown in Oregon. You'll find smoked salmon, conversation-piece wooden slugs, Pendleton blankets and clothing, hazelnuts, wines, and, of course, myrtlewood. What do you expect from a company whose first store, meant to appeal to tourists, was at the Portland airport? For a catalog, call 273-8498 (or, from out of state, (800)828-9673). ▪ *921 SW Morrison St (The Galleria) and branches; 241-3630; map:H2; every day.*

The Museum Company Time was, you actually had to visit a museum before you were able to explore the offerings in its gift shop. No longer. Here you can buy statuary from the Metropolitan

Museum, games from the Museum of Modern Art, prints from Boston's Museum of Fine Arts—in short, there are items from museums all around the globe. Jewelry, scarves, ties, toys, stationery—gifts to please most everyone. ■ *Pioneer Place; 223-0069; map:G4; every day.* ■ *Washington Square; 598-9891; map:KK9; every day.*

The Nature Company   This nationwide chain brings the natural world to the city center. Shoppers lose themselves amid the telescopes and globes, mineral samples and fossils, cards and books. Distinctive timepieces (including sundials) and jewelry, too. Five-year-olds will be delirious with joy when they see the collection of dinosaur toys. ■ *Pioneer Place; 222-0015; map:G4; every day.*

The Real Mother Goose   See Jewelry and Repairs in this chapter. ■ *901 SW Yamhill St (and branches); 223-9510; map:H2; Mon-Sat.*

Ruby's   There's a healthy complement of decorative Orientalia and antique furnishings here, but Ruby Knight has a keen eye for giftware: antique reproduction salt and pepper shakers for the housewarming, colorful Fiesta ware for the newlyweds, fine linens and lace for Grandmother (and a pretty selection of Victorian cards and gift wrap to go with them). ■ *3590 SE Hawthorne Blvd; 239-9867; map:GG5; Wed-Sun.*

▼

Gifts

▲

The Sharper Image   Like a toy store for adults, the Sharper Image beckons you to touch the merchandise. Crazy gear with an incidental practical use. ■ *Pioneer Place; 228-4110; map:G4; every day.*

Topanien   This friendly shop in Multnomah has a huge, colorful stock of beeswax sheets for candle-making, plus gifts from the world over for those who are less inclined toward do-it-yourself projects. Tablecloths, vases, wall hangings, toys, and necklaces are among the finds. ■ *7832 SW Capitol Hwy; 244-9683; map:JJ7; every day.*

Twist   This shop evolved from a cooperative business in Eugene that sold rough-hewn pots and mugs. The evolution continues: the gallerylike space in northwest Portland focuses on original jewelry from exclusive designers, delicate glassware, crafts, and some furniture. All Twist wares represent impeccable craftmanship by artists of national repute. The smaller selection at Pioneer Place is geared toward the tourist. ■ *30 NW 23rd Pl; 224-0334; map:GG7; every day.* ■ *Pioneer Place; 222-3137; map:G4; every day.*

Urbino   Amid sunny decor inspired by a Tuscan barn, owners Rob Friedman and Stacey Mattraw have assembled a collection of all things beautiful for home, body, and spirit—artful dinnerware, jewelry, furniture, candlesticks, and more—mostly handcrafted on this side of the Atlantic. Antique toys as well. ■ *521 NW 23rd Ave; 220-0053; map:GG7; every day.*

A-Ball Plumbing Supply A-Ball's surprise-filled windows have amused passing motorists and attracted customers since 1973. This nationally known emporium of posh porcelain sells high-class kitchen fixtures and bathroom fittings to the likes of Olivia Newton-John, Meg Ryan, and Bill Pullman. If you're not in the mood to buy, go in to ogle the $2,600 claw-footed tub. ▪ *1703 W Burnside; 228-0026; map:GG6; Mon-Sat.*

1874 House Architectural remnants that most home owners ripped out decades ago are found at 1874. A jumble of venerable light shades and fixtures, antique and reproduction hardware, old doors, windows, shutters, and mantels all wait to be reinstalled. Younger than much of its contents, this place has been around for more than three decades. ▪ *8070 SE 13th Ave; 233-1874; map:II5; Tues–Sat.*

Environmental Building Supplies Not just another paint store, EBS is the source for hard-to-find floor coverings and finishes—among them, plant-based finishes from Germany and linoleum from Holland—that are both safe for your home and easy on the environment. New are New Zealand wool carpets and sustainable hardwoods. Markus Stoffel and Abigail Mages opened their Pearl District store in 1993, providing a host of products in addition to lots of helpful information about environmentally safe building. ▪ *1331 NW Kearney St; 222-3881; map:N1; Mon-Sat.*

Hardware

Hippo Hardware and Trading Company This is the place that fathers, tinkerers, and movie producers dream of—packed with architectural gems from mantels to vintage nuts and bolts to period light fixtures. A wonderfully quirky staff keeps you smiling as you paw through organized bins of clutter. If you can't find something, ask; if they don't have it, they just might be able to splice, cut, or file something to fit. ▪ *1040 E Burnside; 231-1444; map:GG5; Mon-Sat.*

Rejuvenation House Parts See Furniture in this chapter. ▪ *1100 SE Grand Ave; 238-1900; map:EE5; every day.*

Restoration Hardware Don't come expecting to find nuts and bolts. But do come to find decorative door handles, water features, garden tools, house numbers, sofas, coatracks, lamps, shower curtains, furniture oil, magazine racks, mailboxes, footstools, garden benches, small hammers, pet toys, fireplace tools . . . well, you get the picture. Prices are high; quality is fine. ▪ *315 NW 23rd Ave; 228-6226; map:GG7; every day.*

Uptown Hardware The Northwest district's favorite do-all shop, a family-owned business since 1950, doesn't get into heavy machinery, but it does get into just about everything else. A knowledgeable, service-minded staff caters to do-it-yourselfers, and if you can't find what you need, they'll gladly order it for you. ▪ *27 NW 23rd Pl (Uptown Shopping Center); 227-5375; map:GG7; every day.*

Wacky Willy's A cross between a surplus store, a museum, and a joke shop, Wacky Willy's is a strange and zany place where you can find just about anything, be it 27,000 pieces of Plexiglas or 100 telephones from an office building that's closed down. This place is popular with artists, mechanics, electricians, and hobbyists. If you're looking for something you can't even describe, you just might stumble upon it at Wacky Willy's. ▪ *2374 NW Vaughn; 525-9211; map:J1; every day.* ▪ *2900 SW 219th Ave, Hillsboro; 642-5111; every day.*

Winks Hardware We're not too sure that Jayne Kilkenny's father intended to stock 50,000 items when he opened this hardware store in 1909. But everything from 1,000 sizes of springs to 70 different types of hammers gives Winks a full house. With its impressive assortment of outdated, odd, and useful things, Winks caters to the trade (hence the weekday-only hours), but experienced sales clerks happily share advice with do-it-yourselfers. ▪ *903 NW Davis St; 227-5536; map:K3; Mon-Fri.*

Hardware

Woodcrafters This is where Portland's builders and woodworkers spend their fun money—a friendly warehouse filled with tools, wood stains, and high-quality lumber, mill ends, and hardwood carving blocks. An enormous book section (with back issues of *Fine Homebuilding*) serves as an unofficial library for do-it-yourselfers and craftsmen—and makes this the logical destination after an episode of *This Old House*. Free demonstrations of wood turning and other specialized techniques on most Saturdays. ▪ *212 NE 6th Ave; 231-0226; map:GG6; every day.*

HOME ACCESSORIES

Alder Street Clock Shop One look at this store's gargantuan circa-1905 master clock (salvaged from Meier & Frank), and you know folks here are serious about time. Grandfathers and cuckoos are the specialty, along with various restored European-made clocks and even some music boxes. Sprinkled among the large selection of new anniversary clocks are a few antique showpieces, like an 1880s French marble mantel clock. The knowledgeable, affable staff also takes time to do repairs. ▪ *251 SW Alder St; 227-3651; map:H5; Mon-Sat.*

Ann Sacks Tile and Stone Primarily a showroom for tiles from all over, this store offers many custom lines, some set designs (made to order), and imports from Italy, Spain, Portugal, France, and Mexico. Five years ago Ann Sacks, which got its start in Portland, was purchased by bathroom-fixture giant Kohler; now there are showrooms in seven other cities. Sacks's own collection includes tiles handcrafted in Portland. ■ *1210 SE Grand Ave; 233-0611; map:HH6; Mon-Sat.*

The Arrangement Off the normal retail track, this friendly shop in the Alameda neighborhood overflows with ever-changing decorative items for your home. The staff will work with your colors, fabrics, photos, or whatever to create just the right dried-flower wreath or silk-flower table arrangement to fit your decor. There are plenty of other distractions, too, like jewelry, casual wear, cards, and Radko Christmas ornaments. ■ *4210 NE Fremont St; 287-4440; map:FF4; every day.*

Backyard Bird Shop See Nurseries and Garden Centers in this chapter. ■ *352 B Ave, Lake Oswego (and branches); 635-2044; map:LL5; every day.*

Blue Pear In the old, beloved Jamison Thomas art gallery space now sits this upscale housewares store full of oh-so-delectable treasures: bolts of fabric, heavy dishes, fine tables, commissioned tiles. A must-stop spot on an afternoon tour of the Pearl District. ■ *1313 NW Glisan; 227-0057; map:L1; Tues-Sun.*

The Compleat Bed & Breakfast This is a store where you can indulge in some civilized pampering—you'll find enough luxurious linens and billowy comforters to supply sweet dreams for a lifetime. If it's not on the shelf, pick out fabric—from Waverly or another top line—and they'll make it to order. A large selection of Crabtree & Evelyn toiletries as well. ■ *615 NW 23rd Ave; 221-0193; map:GG7; every day.*

Home Accessories

Dieci Soli In an area where you'd least expect to find gorgeous treasures for your table—a few blocks from the Pearl District art galleries and furniture stores, behind Blitz-Weinhard, and near a shop that sells ball bearings—Dieci Soli carries an enormous selection of hand-painted Italian pottery and fine linens. ■ *304 NW 11th Ave; 222-4221; map:K2; every day.*

Embry & Co. This shop, alongside the Beaverton-Hillsdale Highway on the stretch between Hillsdale and Raleigh Hills, is packed to the rafters with folk art, antiques, furniture, and other homey treasures. The stock changes often, since owner Embry Savage frequently returns from travels abroad with armloads of new merchandise. ■ *4709 SW Beaverton-Hillsdale Hwy; 244-1646; map:HH7; Mon-Sat.*

French Quarter "Crème de la crème" best describes this small shop just off NE Broadway that retails fine linens from Europe. Every square inch of the French Quarter is filled with something to lust after: plush bath mats from Portugal, unbelievably soft flannel (100 percent cotton, unbleached, undyed) sheets, aromatic candles, fancy French soaps and bath salts, colorful towels, downy bathrobes, and dreamy pajamas. At press time a sister store—City of Paris—was setting up shop around the corner. ▪ *1713 NE 15th Ave; 284-1379; map:FF5; every day.*

Geri Miner Ltd.   Ten years on NW 23rd makes Geri Miner an old-timer in this part of town, especially for such merchandise as antique quilts and handmade dolls. This is the only place in the Northwest to find delightful MacKenzie-Childs Ltd. pottery, glassware, and furniture, and the shop can special-order those pieces you might want to add to your collection. New to the store is a beautiful collection of Stonehouse Farm Goods. Handmade hammered sterling and brass jewelry by Jeep Collins of Texas and distinctive complimentary gift wrapping. ▪ *524 NW 23rd Ave; 242-2539; map:FF6; Mon-Sat.*

La Bottega di Mamma Ro'   In the tiny Tuscan town of Lucca, handmade earthenware is fashioned with Old World care. At Portland's Mamma Ro', the first retail outlet of this Italian company, you can find this simple yet sophisticated tableware in rich hues: bright red dinner plates are offset by the handblown glassware in brilliant turquoise and delicious peach. ▪ *940 NW 23rd Ave; 241-4960; map:GG7; every day.*

Pier 1   The Pier 1 chain, which claims to be the largest direct importer of home furnishings in the world, has consistently kept pace with the trends, offering the latest colors and styles at comfortable prices. The Portland stores are no exception. Some of what's here: whitewashed wicker furniture, chintz pillows, rag rugs, pottery lamps, and window shades. In the realm of tabletop accessories, it's tough to beat the selection of colorful, sturdy pottery and the wide assortment of place mats and flatware. Baskets have always been a strong point—if they don't have it, you probably don't need it. ▪ *5331 SW Macadam Ave (and branches); 248-0359; map:HH6; every day.*

Pratt & Larson   With what seems to be miles of tile lining every surface, this is probably the country's largest custom tile manufacturer. It's actually an overblown studio rather than a factory, with local artists in the loftlike space above the showroom creating one-of-a-kind tile art. Michael Pratt, a potter, and Reta Larson, a fabric artist, combine their considerable talents to produce a distinctive line of tiles in colors such as cherry, celadon, and ocher. Accent with imported tile—16th-century-style Portuguese tiles, bird- and floral-motif tile from France, or iridescent slate from India—for stunning results. For bargain tiling, check out the seconds room, where mistakes are practically given away. ▪ *1201 SE 3rd Ave; 231-9464; map:E9; Mon-Sat.*

Storables   Storables got its start in 1981 in Portland by getting others organized. Closet organizers, shelving cut to order, bright-colored grids, and wire basket systems interlock to create order—or at least the appearance of it. Now with stores in both Portland and Seattle, it's come out of the closet and into the bedroom, kitchen, and living room. ■ *2405 W Burnside (Uptown Shopping Center); 221-4500; map:FF6; every day.*

Virginia Jacobs This top-drawer bed and bath shop treats Portlanders to the finer things in life: crisp Palais Royal linens, plush Fieldcrest towels, white goose-down comforters, delicate soaps and scents, and lots of embroidered white linens. Or design your own look with their custom bed-cover fabrics. Not for the budget-conscious. ■ *2325 NW Westover Rd; 241-8436; map:GG7; every day.*

Yardbirds Ltd. See Nurseries and Garden Centers in this chapter. ■ *2200 NE Broadway; 288-9985; map:FF5; every day.*

IMPORTS

Arthur W. Erikson Fine Arts This astonishingly eclectic mélange of ethnographic objects (with a Native American focus) will appeal to the novice and experienced collector alike. A boar's-tusk necklace from New Guinea, 2,000-year-old bronze bracelets from the Mediterranean, and Kashmiri shawls are just a few of the out-of-the-ordinary offerings. ■ *1030 SW Taylor St; 227-4710; map:H1; Wed and by appointment.*

Cargo Whether your space and budget are large or small, you're sure to find something of interest in this lofty Pearl District showroom. Some of the big-ticket items include a Chang dynasty bed or Ming dynasty puppet theater with puppets (for just under $10,000). Folding iron "French" (made in India) chairs, seed baskets from Borneo, Indonesian hutches, Mexican pottery and glassware, and funky doodads and novelties from everywhere else fill this store to the rafters. ■ *1301 NW Glisan; 827-7377; map:L1; every day.* ■ *1210 SE Grand; 238-8150; map:GG6; every day.*

▼
Imports
▲

Carolyn Locke At this shop you'll find a twist on imported clothing: contemporary looks made from imported fabrics. Pair the floral chiffons with collectible silver jewelry from Africa or Thailand. Their stock also includes an abundance of collectibles—folk art pieces such as Indonesian dowry boxes inlaid with shells, and baskets from Africa. ■ *820 NW 23rd Ave; 222-2870; map:GG7; every day.*

Cost Plus Since this much-loved import store from San Francisco opened a branch in Portland, it has quickly become a regular haunt for foodies, who come to stock up on gourmet goods for a song. Beyond the English tea biscuits and Tex-Mex salsas, there's basic furniture, jewelry, and a good selection of kitchen utensils, glassware, and imported pottery. ■ *10108 SW Washington Square Rd (next to Washington Square) and branches; 968-2060; map:JJ9; every day.*

Eye of Ra Robin Busch's longtime Johns Landing spot features vividly hued clothing imported from Southeast Asia, Africa, and India—as well as Mishi cotton basics and clothing from other labels. There's also a wide array of jewelry, ethnic furniture, textiles, and folk art. Trunk shows and sales are scheduled throughout the year. ▪ *5331 SW Macadam Ave (Johns Landing); 224-4292; map:HH6; every day.*

Julia's, The Ultimate Collection   See Gifts in this chapter. ▪ *1016 SW Morrison St; 274-9308; map:I1; Mon-Sat.*

Nostalgic Nomad Trading Company   Portland has other stores of the incense-and-mask ilk, but none as good as this one, which emphasizes Asian crafts and attracts a steady cadre of world travelers looking for inspiration. Ceremonial Buddhist statues and a recirculating fountain at the entrance set a spiritual tone; among the hundreds of tribal treasures you'll find embroidered wall hangings; raw silk scarves; big, thick sweaters; an assortment of beads, including Tibetan turquoise and Kyhmer silver; and an assortment of furniture. ▪ *720 NW 23rd Ave; 228-4388; map:GG7; every day.*

Pier 1   See Home Accessories in this chapter. ▪ *5331 SW Macadam Ave (and branches); 248-0359; map:HH6; every day.*

Scandia Imports   Finnish glassware, gleaming brown stoneware by Arabia, and heavy pewter candelabras from Denmark dazzle at surprisingly low prices. Homesick Scandinavians can buy birthday cards in their native languages, good Swedish mint pastilles, linens, and enough candles for a hundred Santa Lucia nights. ▪ *10020 SW Beaverton-Hillsdale Hwy; 643-2424; map:HH9; every day.*

Signature Imports   With five stores in the state—the latest being downtown on the corner of SW Broadway and Alder—Signature is doing something right. About 75 percent of the merchandise is from Latin America—colorful sweaters, jewelry, and clothing. They carry rough-hewn furniture and gorgeous handblown glass from Mexico, masks from Ghana, and Oaxacan figures. You can shop with a clear conscience—Signature supports cottage industries and has its own knitting co-op in Bolivia, so craftspeople benefit directly from their labors. ▪ *638 SW Broadway (and branches); 222-5340; map:H3; every day.*

Ten Thousand Villages   The creed of this nonprofit organization—"fairly traded handicrafts from around the world"—manifests itself as a store full of eye-catching crafts. Mexican pottery, colorful Haitian metal sculpture, handmade paper from Bangladesh, Vietnamese ceramics, and nesting dolls from India are only some of the Third World countries and crafts represented. A great place to buy gifts, especially for children. ▪ *3508 SE Hawthorne Blvd; 231-8832; map:GG5; Mon-Sat.*

Trade Roots   Pare back the clutter you find at many import stores to the stuff you usually break down and buy, and you have Trade Roots. Folk art includes brightly painted coconut-shell masks from Mexico, Peruvian amulets, and handwoven place mats from Nepal. Gauzy skirts, embroidered vests, batik dresses and other colorful apparel, plus lots of silver jewelry. A small collection of Native American pottery makes this a great place to find a gift for someone who has everything. ▪ *1831 NE Broadway; 281-5335; map:FF5; every day.*

JEWELRY AND REPAIRS

Carl Greve Exclusive designer lines are the specialty at Carl Greve, a family-owned business since 1922. Tiffany also gets top billing; this is where you'll find Oregon's only Tiffany boutique. And above all the glittering jewels, up an elegant curved stairway to the second floor, is a fantasyland of shimmering china, stemware, and housewares—popular with brides and grooms. ▪ *731 SW Morrison St; 223-7121; map:H3; Mon-Sat.*

Dan Marx For more than a century, Portlanders and visitors have been buying from Dan Marx, Oregon's oldest jewelry store. Clean-lined jewelry, gorgeous colored stones and diamonds, and the staff's quiet politeness set the tone. Eighteen-karat gold is used throughout this immaculate little family-owned shop full of small treasures. ▪ *511 SW Broadway; 228-5090; map:H3; Mon-Sat.*

Gary Swank Jewelers Custom designer Gary Swank does on-the-spot creations—bold earrings or necklaces like something from an Egyptian tomb—and he'll set anything from a diamond to a scarab. A good selection of new watches as well as vintage timepieces restored to perfect ticking order are extra lures. ▪ *840 SW Broadway; 223-8940; map:G3; Tues-Sat.*

Goldmark Cal Brockman of Goldmark loves working with customers to create one-of-a-kind jewelry designs. Endlessly fascinated with the variety of colored gemstones, he has been designing, updating, and restyling jewelry for 22 years. ▪ *1000 SW Taylor St; 224-3743; map:H1; Tues-Sat and by appointment.*

Margulis Jewelers David Margulis designs clean, strong pieces in 18- or 22-karat gold as well as platinum, many of which are inspired by classical themes: Heracles-knot bracelets, Celtic-style rings adorned with granulation, and elegant pearl earrings that resemble those in a Rubens painting. This family-owned business was the first to sell estate jewelry in Portland, and it offers pieces culled from around the world. Although it was established in 1932, this is hardly a traditional shop. Sleek, glossy, and very spacious, with a view of Pioneer Courthouse Square. ▪ *800 SW Broadway; 227-1153; map:G2; Mon-Sat.*

The Real Mother Goose A fairy-tale shop with singular art pieces, the Goose recently won the American Crafts Gallery of the Year award. A jewelry designer and goldsmith are on staff here to design wedding rings and other custom pieces; this is also a popular stop for holiday shoppers and travelers seeking choice Northwest gifts. The furniture gallery at the spacious downtown store carries contemporary pieces, in creative blends of fine and sometimes exotic woods. ▪ *901 SW Yamhill St (and branches); 223-9510; map:H2; Mon-Sat.*

Shimeras This shop offers exact copies of designer jewelry from legends like Chanel, Tiffany, and Cartier. Cubic zirconia packs a lot of sparkle, and if you've always longed for, say, a 2-carat marquise cut, your dreams can come true for a few hundred rather than many thousands of dollars. ▪ *0315 SW Montgomery St (RiverPlace); 224-1689; map:D5; every day.*

Zell Bros. In 1912, brothers Julius and Harry Zell opened a small jewelry store near Portland's Union Station. Today, a marble building downtown houses the Zell empire: three floors of jewelry, Swiss watches, sterling silver, china, and crystal. Another reason to visit: the store brought in jewelry artist Tim Green of the now-defunct Collaborations to do custom orders and repair work. ▪ *800 SW Morrison; 227-8471; map:H3; Mon-Sat.* ▪ *9595 SW Washington Square Rd; 620-3610; map:JJ9; every day.*

KITCHENWARE

Boxer-Northwest Co. Follow the crowd in chefs' whites to this no-nonsense restaurant supply store, where you're likely to meet other home cooks scouting for cookware basics at reasonable prices. It's Rexall meets Williams-Sonoma as you wend your way through woks the size of manhole covers, bar stools, and a hodgepodge of dinnerware. Here's the place to buy nuts-and-bolts items like utensils, stockpots, cast-iron frying pans, and serious mixers. Beware, weekend shoppers: the fun can be had only during weekday business hours. ▪ *438 NW Broadway; 226-1186; map:L4; Mon-Fri.*

Cloudtree and Sun Today's home and kitchen standbys— All-Clad, Chantal, and Dansk tableware—share shelf space with one-of-a-kind art pieces, Blenko vases, and kitchen gadgets. Lots of taste and bustle, and gift wrapping is free with a $10 purchase. Cloudtree flows into the lively Main Street Cafe, where people pause, refresh, and shop on. ▪ *112 N Main St, Gresham; 666-8495; every day.*

Kitchen Kaboodle Top-of-the-line cookware, tons of gadgets, and beautiful, reasonably priced tabletop ware make Kitchen Kaboodle a favorite haunt of food enthusiasts. Out-of-the-ordinary accessories, like salt and pepper shakers in the shape of tomatoes, are complemented by purely practical tools and appliances. Most of the stores have furniture, too: cherry dressers, ash side tables, and custom-made couches. Kitchen Kaboodle's biannual sale has been known to turn even the best-mannered into shopping sharks. A new store downtown opened in the fall of 1997. ▪ *8788 SW Hall Blvd (and branches); 643-5491; map:II9; every day.*

Kobos Company David and Susan Kobos founded a coffee-roasting business 25 years ago; now the enterprise has grown to include chefs' tools as well as coffee beans. There are several branches, but the Johns Landing store has the largest assortment of kitchenware, stocking Le Creuset and martini shakers, and, of course, everything it takes to make and enjoy the perfect cup of coffee. Kobos celebrates the bean with espresso machines—both sophisticated and simple—grinders, thermoses, and mugs. ▪ *5331 SW Macadam Ave (Johns Landing) and branches; 222-5226; map:JJ6; every day.*

Pastaworks See Markets and Delicatessens chapter. ▪ *3735 SE Hawthorne Blvd; 232-1010; map:GG5; every day.*

LINGERIE

Jane's Obsession ▪ Jane's Vanity Two elegant lingerie outlets owned by Jane Van Duinen feature the best in European bras, panties, garter belts, nightwear, and accessories. Acquired every January in Paris, elegant bits of silk and lace are displayed on racks, in glass cases, and across the walls. The central downtown store (Jane's Vanity) is pricier than Jane's Obsession, which features younger, trendier attire. ▪ *521 SW Broadway; 241-3860; map:I3; Mon-Sat.* ▪ *728 NW 23rd Ave; 221-1490; map:GG7; every day.*

Victoria's Secret Women have come to expect two things from this store: cotton that isn't frumpy and tasteful lingerie that doesn't cost a fortune. Intimate apparel runs from sports bras to skimpy silk nighties to bear-hug bathrobes. ▪ *Pioneer Place (and branches); 223-9297; map:G7; every day.*

MARKETS AND DELICATESSENS

Anzen Oriental Grocers For all things Japanese—fish and nori for sushi, pickled ginger, live geoduck, fresh yellowfin tuna, and octopus—Anzen is the place. The Beaverton branch has more elbow room, but both locations carry upwards of 10,000 items—prepared deli foods (sushi and bentos among them), plenty of packaged and canned goods (including shelves of various soy sauces), and a large selection of sake and Asian beers. ▪ *736 NE Martin Luther King Jr Blvd; 233-5111; map:FF6; every day.* ▪ *4021 SW 117th Ave, Beaverton; 627-0913; map:HH9; every day.*

Becerra's Spanish and Imported Groceries The groceries come from Mexico, Southern California, South America, and Spain, and Becerra's customers come from as far away as Spokane. Mexican white cheeses are a specialty, as is the store's own beef and pork chorizo. Look here for things you might have a hard time finding elsewhere: quince paste, chipotle peppers, and bottled cactus.

Half the store consists of music and videotapes—in Spanish, of course. ▪ *3022 NE Glisan St; 234-7785; map:FF5; every day.*

Burlingame Grocery See Wines, Beers, and Spirits in this chapter. ▪ *8502 SW Terwilliger Blvd; 246-0711; map:HH6; every day.*

City Market NW Located in the heart of northwest Portland, City Market houses the best specialty markets in Portland: Viande Meats and Sausage, Kruger's Specialty Produce, Pasta-works (pasta, cheese, wine, and gourmet foods), and Newman's Fish Co. Besides a Swiss bank account, there's not much more to ask for. The food is beautiful to look at, touch, and smell; inevitably you'll spend more than you intended. ▪ *735 NW 21st Ave; 221-3004; map:GG7; every day.*

Cost Plus See Imports in this chapter. ▪ *10108 SW Washington Square Rd (next to Washington Square) and branches; 968-2060; map:JJ9; every day.*

The Daily Grind An old-fashioned health food store: no chocolate, no meat, no white sugar, organic coffee only, and healthful muffins and cinnamon rolls in the bakery. A dozen breads include several salt- and wheat-free loaves. Much of the produce is organically grown, including that in the salad bar. ▪ *4026 SE Hawthorne Blvd; 233-5521; map:GG4; every day.*

Edelweiss Sausage Company and Deli See Meats and Seafood in this chapter. ▪ *3119 SE 12th Ave; 238-4411; map:GG5; Mon-Sat.*

Elephants Delicatessen Well-heeled food lovers can Elephax their lunch order (224-4097) for a smoked turkey on pumpernickel spread with homemade herb mayonnaise, to be delivered by noon. The kitchen also bakes numerous breads, voluptuous desserts, and an impressive selection of sumptuous take-home dinner entrees. The remodel in 1997 expanded the space—more gifts, a few tables up front, and a separate area to order drinks and sandwiches—without necessarily making it any easier to move around. ▪ *13 NW 23rd Pl (Uptown Shopping Center); 224-3955; map:FF7; every day.*

Fong Chong & Co. This is one of Portland's busiest Chinese markets, perhaps because of the succulent roasted and barbecued pork and ribs and the Peking duck available for take-out, cooked at the adjoining Cantonese restaurant of the same name. Narrow aisles bulge with sacks of rice, teas, noodles, seasonings, and sauces from China, Hong Kong, and Taiwan. ▪ *301 NW 4th Ave; 223-1777; map:K5; every day.*

Food Front Pony up $150 for a lifetime membership at this cooperative grocery and you'll receive 5 percent off all purchases; if you work eight hours a month, you'll receive a 15 percent discount. Bulk foods for the health-conscious, and trendier fare (Sichuan noodle salad, Vietnamese steamed buns, European chocolates) for the gourmand. The wines are priced conserva-

tively, and there are always two choices in the produce department: organic or non. ▪ *2375 NW Thurman St; 222-5658;*
map:FF7; every day.

Fou Lee Market Oriental Meats and Groceries   In addition to the
wonderful fresh produce—broccoli, rape, long beans, Japanese
and Thai eggplant, lychee, lime leaves, lemongrass, and purple
basil—Fou Lee also houses an extensive meat and seafood section (live, fresh, frozen, and barbecued to go). You can spend
hours here contemplating the myriad of fish sauces, or wander-
ing up and down the aisles looking at noodles, dried mushrooms,
tea, and cookware. If you have need of a huge mortar and pestle,
this is the place to buy it. ▪ *3811 SE Belmont; 239-0215;*
map:GG5; every day.

International Food Bazaar   Exotic smells waft from this multicultural market to the sidewalk above. An amazing range of goods is
sold here: ghee, teas, and lentils from India; olives and feta
cheese from Greece; Pakistani and Indian basmati rice; halal
meat and poultry for Muslims; and kosher pickles from Israel. In
the summer you can take a mezze plate out to one of the sidewalk
cafe tables; any time of the year you can stop in for a cup of hot
chai to go. ▪ *915 SW 9th Ave; 228-1960; map:H2; every day.*

Irvington Market   An attractive market further enhanced by the   ▼
fresh flowers on the sidewalk outside, the Irvington Market shel-   **Markets and**
ters under one roof Kruger's Specialty Produce, Newman's Fish   **Delicatessens**
Co., the Cheshire Cat deli and wine shop, and Torrefazione
coffee. All of these vendors, with exception of the coffeehouse,   ▲
were formerly located down a block at Holladay's Market, now a
ghost of a place. Prices are high, but the quality and service rarely
disappoint. ▪ *1409 NE Weidler; 288-4236 (Kruger's); map:FF5;*
every day.

Kornblatt's   See review in the Restaurants chapter. ▪ *628 NW*
23rd Ave (and branches); 242-0055; map:GG7; every day.

Kruger's Specialty Produce   A few exotics—edible flowers, baby
bok choy, purple potatoes—are mixed among more familiar (and
some organic) produce. Kruger's also sells bulk and packaged
natural foods and gourmet items, from breakfast cereals to dried
pasta in the shape of artichokes or bicycles. Unforgiving prices
guarantee high-quality produce. ▪ *735 NW 21st Ave (City Market*
NW) and branches; 221-3004; map:GG6; every day.

Martinotti's Cafe & Delicatessen   Italy is for lovers, and this shop
is for lovers of Italy. The Martinotti family has developed a decidedly Italian grocery of good tastes, good smells, and good products. See Armand for wine, Dixie for catering, and Frank for
lunch and the latest in microbrews. The wine selection is rich in
Burgundies and Bordeaux futures, and ample in Italian varieties.
Armand tastes before buying, when he can, so he knows his

product. Check out the twice-yearly big-deal sales. For everyday shopping, there are oodles of dried pastas and sundry other items. ▪ *404 SW 10th Ave; 224-9028; map:J2; Mon-Sat.*

Nature's Fresh Northwest! You know the gentry has landed when Nature's opens a store in your neighborhood. This store used to be the place for nitty-gritty-sprouty bulk food and garden supplies, but today the line between health food and other food, including gourmet fare, has blurred. The success of the super-store on SE Division—complete with a juice bar, deli, gifts, fresh flowers, bakery, meat and cheese counters, a playhouse for the kids (not to mention child-size grocery carts), and well-stocked beer and wine sections—has spawned other superstores, one in Vancouver and another that's set to open in August 1998 in Lake Oswego. Nature's offers an excellent range of common and less common produce, much of it organically grown, along with hor-mone- and nitrate-free meats (all of the beef, lamb, and pork is Oregon-raised). Most stores have delis with full-service meat and seafood counters. ▪ *3016 SE Division (and branches); 233-7374; map:HH5; every day.*

Pastaworks Pastaworks is all things Italian: fresh pastas, pesto and mushroom sauces, dozens of olive oils, herbed and aged vinegars, whole-bean coffees, take-home entrees (torta rustica, polenta), delectable desserts, exotic cheeses—and the best (and most expensive) Italian wine section in town. Some bottlings are so esoteric they escape mention even in Italian wine books—so don't hesitate to ask for help from owners Don and Peter. The original Pastaworks on Hawthorne has expanded their inventory of kitchenware; Reidel glassware, Spanish pottery, wooden salad bowls and cutting boards, and top-notch cooking utensils are just some of the things that can turn a quick stop for a loaf of bread into a half hour of browsing. ▪ *735 NW 21st Ave (City Market NW); 221-3002; map:GG7; every day.* ▪ *3731 SE Hawthorne Blvd; 232-1010; map:GG5; every day.*

Sheridan Fruit Co. Founded in 1916, this is one of the last rem-nants of the city's old Produce Row. Neighborhood locals know it for more than well-priced produce, however: there's also a wide and eclectic selection of bulk foods and a full-service meat market. To keep up with the times, Sheridan's has made several changes—an inside espresso cart that brews and sells Tor-refazione coffee, a cooking school with weekly classes taught by well-known local foodies, and improvements in the cheese, meat, and wine departments. Concurrently, prices have crept up and there are fewer good deals to be had. ▪ *408 SE Martin Luther King Jr Blvd; 235-9353; map:GG5; every day.*

Stroheckers You can walk out of here with a carton of milk or a prescription, but this 94-year-old Portland institution is designed primarily for serious gastronomes—with ample cash. From orchids to British bangers, fresh matsutake mushrooms to vintage wines (some with three-digit price tags), Stroheckers has it. An outstanding full-service meat and seafood department (domestic lamb, sport-caught fish, local beef) and a small showcase of Oregon products make West Hillers very proud to have Stroheckers as their neighborhood market. Parking is under the store. ■ *2855 SW Patton Rd; 223-7391; map:GG7; every day.*

Trader Joe's While transplanted Californians danced a jig when the first Trader Joe's opened in Portland, Portlanders approached cautiously. After all, who wouldn't be skeptical of bargain gourmet? The same skeptics now stock their pantry with peanut butter–filled pretzels, their freezers with sun-dried-tomato ravioli, and their refrigerator doors with jars of TJ's Dijon mustard. Good prices on milk and cheese, but the produce section is extremely limited. As good fortune would have it, **Limbo** (774-8008), a fresh, mostly organic produce market and juice bar, resides next door to the southeast Portland store. ■ *4715 SE 39th Ave (and branches); 777-1601; map:II5; every day.*

Wizer's Lake Grove Market More than a thousand specialty items fill the aisles of this neighborhood grocery. Seafood, meats, baked goods, specialty produce, and a full-service deli are among the enticements; the staff wine steward keeps that section well stocked. ■ *16331 SW Bryant Rd, Lake Oswego; 636-8457; map:KK5; every day.*

Wizer's Lake Oswego Foods See Wines, Beers, and Spirits in this chapter. ■ *330 1st St, Lake Oswego; 636-1414; map:KK5; every day.*

Zupan's Market Here's a cross between Fred Meyer and City Market NW, where you can buy toilet paper and fresh lychees in the same stop. The produce section is stupendous—14 different varieties of apples in peak season, fresh water chestnuts, champagne grapes, and seasonal exotic mushrooms. The market is open 24 hours a day, every day except Christmas, and contains a deli, bakery, meat counter, and wine section. Nothing is bargain-priced. ■ *2340 W Burnside (and branches); 497-1088; map:GG7; every day.*

Meats and Seafood

MEATS AND SEAFOOD

Edelweiss Sausage Company and Deli This crowded, nose-pleasing store is famous for its German foods and sundries (as well as those from other European countries) and for its wonderful meat and cheese case—where else can you find butterkase? Stacked chockablock are dozens of varieties of sausages (try the spicy beer version), Black Forest hams, and some of Portland's best bacons. Ask for a taste, or take out a sausage sandwich for lunch. Anyone nostalgic for Germany or Austria will delight in the European chocolates, preserves from Austria, and—be still, my heart—German butter in the freezer. ▪ *3119 SE 12th Ave; 238-4411; map:GG5; Mon-Sat.*

Fetzer's German Sausage and Deli   You don't have to be German to appreciate Fetzer's homemade German bratwurst, blood sausage, bauerschinken, weisswurst, Black Forest ham, and smoked meats. The hams are excellent, but the beef can be overcooked at this lively, stuffed-to-the-rafters store. Game processing and smoking available. ▪ *2485 SW Cedar Hills Blvd, Beaverton; 641-6300; map:HH8; Tues-Sat.*

Gartner's Country Meat Market   Okay, you want a red-meat market? This is the no-flourishes, serious-about-meat store. Busy but truly pleasant counter people staff a large, open preparation and display-case area. Roasts, whole filets, steaks, chops, and house-smoked hams and bacons fill the L-shaped meat case. Smoky, aromatic smells spice the air, and meat saws whir in the background. Enthusiasm and pride imbue the store with a feeling of quality and value. ▪ *7450 NE Killingsworth St; 252-7801; map:EE3; Tues-Sat.*

Meating Place Meat Market and Smokehouse   A display of sports accoutrements invites browsing in this wonderful long, narrow meat store. Quality is good for red meats and poultry (specialties include smoked sausages and hams); the bacon (smoked on the premises) is a treat. The owner cheerfully accommodates requests and queries. ▪ *3172 NW 185th Pl; 645-6811; map:GG9; Tues-Sat.*

▼

Meats and Seafood

▲

Nature's Fresh Northwest!   See Markets and Delicatessens in this chapter. ▪ *3016 SE Division (and branches); 233-7374; map:HH5; every day.*

Newman's Fish Co.   Hands down, Newman's is the best place in town to buy fresh fish. The stores are staffed by knowledgeable, energetic, and pleasant individuals; helping customers learn to buy and prepare fish is a priority of the owners. The variety is noteworthy, and freshness is a given. Admire the fresh whole salmon, the Oregon lox, the beautiful green-lipped mussels, and the scampi (when available). At the Irvington Market location, there's also a small selection of poultry and red meat. ▪ *1409 NE Weidler (Irvington Market) and branches; 284-4537; map:FF5; every day.*

Otto's Sausage Kitchen & Meat Market   This solid, good-natured store is Germanic in spirit, with lots of smoked meats and homemade sausages. The smoked meats are delicious, the stuffed chicken breasts—Florentine, Cordon Bleu, or stuffed with wild rice—are from Otto's own recipe, and the sausages (ground and stuffed in the back room) are out of this world. Don't pass up the hams: smoked or dry-cured. There's an evenly balanced wine selection with excellent French choices and good sparkling

wines. Beers, too. ■ *4138 SE Woodstock Blvd; 771-6714; map:II4;*
Mon-Sat.

Phil's Uptown Meat Market Phil knows meats—and is very accommodating. This small black-and-white-tiled shop, with white porcelain display cases, butcher blocks, and fan-type butcher scales, sells meats and poultry of the highest quality, and there's a small seafood selection, too. Here you can find domestic lamb: leg, rack, chops, and kabobs. Check out the wines on your way in; on your way out, buy a grilled chicken skewer to munch on the way home. ■ *17 NW 23rd Pl (Uptown Shopping Center); 224-9541; map:FF7; Tues-Sat.*

Sheridan Fruit Co. See Markets and Delicatessens in this chapter. ■ *408 SE Martin Luther King Jr Blvd; 235-9353; map:GG5; every day.*

Viande Meats and Sausage Co. Inc. Formerly known as Salumeria di Carlo, the renamed Viande Meats and Sausage Co. carries on with unchanged high standards for quality. Prosciutto-style ham, marinated chicken, fresh sausages (such as the classic Italian pork with fennel, Moroccan-style lamb, Spanish chorizo, and Thai chicken), and a fantastic boneless stuffed pig—porchetta—fill the small case in the front of City Market NW. There's also fresh Oregon poussin, or young chicken, something not commonly sold in retail meat markets. The delicious sausage sandwiches, messy with grilled peppers and onions, are available daily for take-out. ■ *735 NW 21st Ave (City Market NW); 221-3012; map:GG7; every day.*

Nurseries and Garden Centers

White's Country Meats Gresham residents highly recommend this establishment: it's a straightforward, good-quality meat store with its own smokehouse and processing facilities. Expect fresh, honestly trimmed, reasonably priced meats. A variety of roasts, steaks, and ground meats are available; poultry and pork look better than at most other meat counters. ■ *1206 SE Orient Dr, Gresham; 666-0967; Tues-Sat.*

NURSERIES AND GARDEN CENTERS

The mild climate and fertile soil of the Willamette Valley allow Portlanders access to some of the best nurseries in the country. Nurseries that most gardeners know only through mail-order catalogs are just a short drive outside the city limits. Among the most notable are **Swan Island Dahlias**, in Canby (995 NW 22nd Ave, 266-7711), the nation's largest grower of dahlia bulbs, and **Northwoods Retail Nursery**, also in Canby (27635 S Oglesby Rd, 266-5432), for food-bearing plants, from hardy kiwis to persimmons. The businesses listed below provide some of the city's finest garden supplies.

Backyard Bird Shop What's a garden without the birds and the bees? Avid bird-watcher Scott Lukens opened his first bird-feeding shop in an old house in Lake Oswego with feeders in the trees, birdbaths in the yard, and all you need to set up house for your feathered friends—everything from hardware hooks to sunflower seeds as well as bird- and bat-related gift items and books. Now there are eight stores. Individual store managers buy unique items for each store, so all are different. A six-page bimonthly newsletter and myriad free handouts offer tips on everything from bird chow to creating hummingbird-friendly landscapes. ▪ *352 B Ave, Lake Oswego (and branches); 635-2044; map:LL5; every day.*

Barn Owl Nursery One step inside the door and your nose knows: this is herb heaven. Dried herbs and herbal soaps begin the list of fragrant gifts. What sets Barn Owl apart from scores of similar "country" boutiques is the fact that it's also a working nursery. Budding herbalists stroll through the acre of display gardens (open April to July, October to November) and choose from more than 200 varieties of herbs. Seasonal hours; call first. ▪ *22999 SW Newland Rd, Wilsonville; 638-0387; map:QQ9; Wed-Sat.*

The Bovees Nursery Customers can wander under towering firs and among hundreds of types of rhododendrons in the display garden, examining neatly labeled mature samples of prospective purchases. The star rhodies and deciduous azaleas bloom nearly six months of the year, but trees, hardy perennials, and Northwest natives are no less visible. Catalog on request. ▪ *1737 SW Coronado St; 244-9341; map:KK5; every day (closed Jan and mid-Aug through mid-Sept, except by appointment).*

Caprice Farms Nursery Daylilies are for times when yellow and orange alone just won't do. Nearly 280 varieties of these long-blooming beauties—blazing reds, shimmering whites, delicate lavenders—dot the Rogers family's 6-acre nursery. For color selection, visit the nursery in July. Peony lovers should visit during Caprice's open-house weekends in May, when 250 varieties of peonies bloom. Mail-order catalogs are available. ▪ *15425 SW Pleasant Hill Rd, Sherwood; 625-7241; map:PP8; Mon-Sat.*

Cornell Farm The Dutch Colonial house, built in 1926, with its towering monkey puzzle tree and lovely flower gardens, is the centerpiece of this 5-acre nursery. The gardens support 300 varieties of roses. Owner Ed Blatter's folks still live in the house, but the former goat and strawberry farm now grows 700 varieties of perennials and 150 varieties of annuals—garden flowers tended by a sales staff of 12 gardeners. Growing beds are open to the public, and neighbors walk here daily, but give Ed's parents a break—please don't ring the doorbell. Across the road from the Oregon College of Art and Craft. ▪ *8212 SW Barnes Rd; 292-9895; map:HH9; every day.*

Dennis' 7 Dees Nursery and Landscaping Years of appearing as the garden expert on local TV talk shows have made Dennis Snodgrass a familiar face in Portland; his real job, however, is running three garden centers. You'll find the standard array of gardening supplies alongside a smattering of plants ranging from trees to annuals. ■ *6025 SE Powell Blvd (and branches); 777-1421; map:HH4; every day.*

Drake's 7 Dees Nursery and Landscaping Advice for gardeners, landscaping services, and a regular newsletter are only a sampling of this southeast Portland garden center's services. The nursery is newly focused on pools, pond systems, and fish, holding regular seminars on how to install ponds properly in your garden. ■ *16519 SE Stark St; 255-9225; map:GG1; every day.*

Kascho's Garden Center and Nursery On the plus side: this well-established chain has seven greater Portland locations and a broad range of garden goods. On the minus side: there's a sometimes spotty selection at the smaller branch stores, and the staffs' expertise is far from consistent. Ornamental shrubs and spring bulbs are strong points. The main branch is the best. ■ *2500 SE Tacoma St (and branches); 231-7711; map:JJ5; every day.*

Northwoods Nursery Portlanders drive to this Canby location for the astonishing array of plants, many imported from Russia and Asia: kiwis, razzleberry, papaw, Shiro plum, Asian pear, and more, with plenty of advice on how to grow and maintain the exotica. ■ *27635 S Oglesby Rd, Canby; 266-5432; call for hours.*

▼

Nurseries and Garden Centers

▲

Portland Nursery Hands down, this is the city's finest nursery: an abundance of good-quality plants and supplies fills the 5-acre grounds. The perennials are especially bountiful, but many unusual trees and shrubs—witch hazels and Franklinia trees—are stocked as well. The store's reputation owes much to its uniformly knowledgeable and helpful staff, ready to track down the answers to any questions they can't immediately resolve themselves. Powell's Books supplies the gardening lit at the SE Stark Street store, which specializes in roses, trees, and shrubs. The SE Division Street store specializes in ponds and aquatic plants. ■ *5050 SE Stark St; 231-5050; map:GG4; every day.* ■ *9000 SE Division St; 788-9000; map:HH3; every day.*

Tualatin Nursery In just two years, John and Lori Blair have created a shopping destination known for its relaxed atmosphere: there's a children's garden, lovely pathway, and coffee shop that serves espresso and light meals featuring homegrown vegetables. And there are plants—perennials as good as you'll find anyplace in Portland, and annuals with new and interesting foliage. Call during the winter to be sure someone's around. ■ *65 S Dollar St, West Linn; 650-8511; map:OO5; every day.*

Wildwood Garden Furnishings This is a garden store, but surprise! You won't find a plant for sale on the premises—nor a pink flamingo. Owner Ron Colvin opened his Multnomah shop in 1990, and now there's an outdoor garden showroom, too: European in the front, Oriental in the back. The place is brimming with sophisticated and pretty—and spendy—niceties for the garden: tiles and pots, bronzes from Thailand, stylistic animal sculptures, and a huge collection of granite basins, spheres, and lanterns. ■ *7435 SW Capitol Hwy; 452-0301; map:II7; Tues-Sat, Apr-Sept.*

Yardbirds Ltd. This is an eclectic garden-gift store with an ever-increasing inventory of magnets, T-shirts, wind chimes, bird feeders, watering cans, kids' gardening tools, house numbers, goatskin gloves—anything a flower-loving, vegetable-growing fool might love. Park across the street in the free lot. ■ *2200 NE Broadway; 288-9985; map:FF5; every day.*

OUTDOOR GEAR

Alder Creek Kayak Supply If it floats and you paddle it, Alder Creek probably sells it—whether it's a canoe, sea kayak, or river kayak. Demos in the nearby Columbia River are free (and a good way to find out how much you're willing to carry, when you lug your craft back up the dock). The store carries an extensive line of gear, books, and videos and emphasizes group and private instruction and guided tours. ■ *250 NE Tomahawk Island Dr; 285-0464; map:CC6; every day.*

Andy & Bax Sporting Goods Heaps of personality, split three ways between rafting and whitewater equipment, piles of Army and Navy surplus, and family camping and cold-weather gear. From commercial inflatables to information on guides and beginner classes, Andy & Bax is one of Portland's better rafting and whitewater resources. Reasonable prices and some true bargains. ■ *324 SE Grand Ave; 234-7538; map:GG5; Mon-Sat.*

Athletic Department This was the original Nike store at the beginning of the running boom, when both runners and Nike were considered slightly demented. When Nike turned its massive marketing attention to a full line of specialty stores, ex-Nike employee Danny Adams bought this shop. He hasn't changed it much. As far as he knows, it is—along with the Bend branch of the Athletic Department—the only non-Nike-owned Nike-only store in the country. ■ *3275 SW Cedar Hills Blvd, Beaverton; 646-0691; map:HH9; every day.*

Bicycle Repair Collective The Bicycle Repair Collective has only a handful of peers nationwide. It sells parts and accessories, rents work space, repairs bikes, and gives classes on bike repair and maintenance. For $30 a year or $5 an hour, cyclists can tune their bikes and adjust their chains. ■ *4438 SE Belmont St; 233-0564; map:GG4; Mon-Sat.*

The Bike Gallery The Bike Gallery is to cycles what Saks is to clothes. Begun as a small, family-run shop, it's now one of the country's finest bike dealers. All sales are guaranteed, so customer risk is minimal. Branches throughout the city; the Beaverton store also carries Nordic ski gear. ▪ *2625 SW Hall Blvd, Beaverton (and branches); 641-2580; map:HH9; every day.*

Bob's Bicycle Center Bob's started as a small BMX store and is now the largest individual cycling shop in the Northwest. The stock has grown to over 2,000 bikes, everything from BMX to touring, and the store sponsors a mountain-biking race team. Eighteen staff members in one store cater to customer needs, from free bicycle fits to full-service bike repairs. ▪ *10950 SE Division St; 254-2663; map:GG2; every day.*

Columbia Sportswear While Gert Boyle, mother figure and CEO of Columbia Sportswear, has become a national icon through savvy advertising and an insistence that everyone dress warmly, her business has exploded internationally. This is Boyle's flagship store: 16,000 square feet of outdoor apparel and footwear reflecting the latest in high-tech fabrics and technologies. Got a sport? She's got the shoes, the socks, and the practical advice. ▪ *911 SW Broadway; 226-6800; map:H2; every day.*

Costco's SportsNation This recently opened sports megastore includes nine basketball/volleyball courts, a soccer/hockey rink, a SportsNation for kids, child care for toddlers, and a restaurant and bars—and boasts the highest indoor rock-climbing wall (45 feet) in the Portland area (see Climbing in the Recreation chapter). ▪ *18120 SW Lower Boones Ferry Rd, Tigard; 968-4500; map:MM9; every day.*

▼

Outdoor Gear

▲

Countrysport For the fly fisher, Countrysport is a gorgeous store, furnished with antique reels, bamboo fly rods, wicker creels, canoe chairs, and—when they can get them—Rays River Dories, displayed on hardwood floors. Clothing includes waxed cotton rainwear, lamb's-wool sweaters, canvas shirts, and fleece. There's a huge selection of flies, feathers, and thread, and practical gear (float tubes, pontoon boats) as well. Fly-fishing classes and guided tours are available. ▪ *126 SW 1st Ave; 221-4545; map:I7; every day.*

Ebb & Flow Paddlesports Donna Holman is Portland's sea-kayaking expert. Co-founder of OOPS (Oregon Ocean Paddling Society), she's refined her line of sea kayaks and canoes based on 15 years of renting them—if they don't hold up, out they go. The shop is intimate—boats and gear squeezed into a small space—with a warehouse full of boats behind. You can put a kayak on a portage cart, wheel it across the street to Willamette Park's boat ramp, and try out different kinds of paddles to ensure a perfect fit. Whitewater instruction for all levels of experience. ▪ *0604 SW Nebraska; 245-1756; map:JJ6; Tues-Sun.*

Fat Tire Farm This shop, located at NW 27th and Thurman, has the advantage of great access to Forest Park. Mountain biker wannabes can rent a bike and helmet here, load up on equipment, grab a water bottle and a fistful of Power Bars and, on Thursdays at 6pm, take a guided tour through the park. Free park maps available. Mountain bikes, bike accessories, clothes, literature, and miscellany for sale. Friendly, informed staff. Easy parking. ■ *2714 NW Thurman St; 222-FARM; map:GG7; every day.*

Kaufmann's Streamborn Fly Shop Kaufmann's has been Portland's consummate fly shop for more than two decades. The knowledgeable staff can outfit you for fishing on the Clackamas, or they can equip you for specialty fishing trips, local or abroad. Along with one of the finer selections of flies in the country, Kaufmann's offers fishing classes and fly-tying materials. Its free catalog has made the store world-renowned. ■ *8861 SW Commercial St, Tigard; 639-6400; map:KK9; Mon–Sat.*

The Mountain Shop This store may well be the area's best downhill-gear shop. It's certainly the most unabashed, with three floors of ski stuff to help you perfect your style. They also outfit backcountry skiers, and both sell and rent mountaineering and camping gear in addition to skis. ■ *628 NE Broadway; 288-6768; map:FF5; every day.*

▼

Outdoor Gear

▲

Nike Town This highly touted, state-of-the-art store showcases the entire Nike line: all collections, all colors. Fans come not only to buy, but also to be entertained, in a shop that evokes an upscale carnival funhouse: black walls, darkroom doors, catwalks, aqua socks displayed against a wall-size, fish-filled aquarium, a video treadmill in the Running Pavilion. The show stops, however, when it comes to outfitting athletes. The twentysomething clerks—athletes one and all—know what they're talking about. And though you'll never find an item on sale here, there is something for every budget. The Nike store in the Portland airport's retail row (284-3558) packs as much as it can into a small space. Runners can call the Nike hotline for race information (223-RUNS). ■ *930 SW 6th Ave; 221-6453; map:G3; every day.*

Northwest Fitness Supply Northwest Fitness is the largest all-around exercise-gear store in the state. They sell everything from simple barbells to high-tech climbers and treadmills. Try them out; qualified fitness consultants. ■ *1338 NE Sandy Blvd; 231-1330; map:FF5; every day.*

Oregon Mountain Community OMC is a four-season outfitter: in winter, the popular Old Town outdoor store stocks up with skis; in summer, look for packs, tents, sleeping bags, and rock-climbing equipment. Other outdoor clothing and equipment are available year-round. The sales staff has a tremendous amount of outdoor experience. ■ *60 NW Davis St; 227-1038; map:K6; every day.*

Pacesetter Athletics Some of the area's better athletes work in this store, so the merchandise reflects a slightly more technical bias than that of the typical running store. In addition to offering more than 115 models of running shoes, Pacesetter sponsors a 30-person racing team. Customers not as fast or knowledgeable as the staff will like the casual, helpful atmosphere. Student discounts. In Lake Oswego, too. ▪ *4306 SE Woodstock Blvd; 777-3214; map:HH4; Mon-Sat.* ▪ *333 S State St, Lake Oswego; 635-3577; map:LL6; Mon-Sat.*

Play It Again Sports For moms and dads, Play It Again is a great idea. This store targets kids who are growing too fast to wear anything out and beginners who don't want to pay a fortune to try out a sport. You'll find new and used sports equipment (skis to backyard games). The location, next door to Valley Ice Arena, assures a fine stock of hockey and ice-skating equipment—in-line, too. ▪ *9248 SW Beaverton-Hillsdale Hwy; 292-4552; map:HH8; every day.*

REI (Recreational Equipment Inc.) The nation's largest co-op, REI specializes in clothes and equipment for mountaineering, backpacking, downhill and cross-country skiing, cycling, water sports, and walking. The store prides itself on well-priced, technically appropriate gear, though it seems to have slipped into the outdoor fashion market as well—and nowhere is that more apparent than at the Tualatin store. Still, the staff is knowledgeable, congenial, and helpful. A one-time $15 fee earns roughly 10 percent cash back on nonsale purchases. ▪ *1798 Jantzen Beach Center; 283-1300; map:BB7; every day.* ▪ *7410 SW Bridgeport, Tualatin; 624-8600; map:MM9; every day.*

Records, Tapes, and Compact Discs

▲

River City Bicycles Open only since 1994, this bike shop may be the finest in town. With an 11,000-square-foot showroom, which includes an indoor test track, it's certainly the largest. The friendly experts who run River City stock the store with all kinds of riding gear: tricycles, tandems, mountain and road bikes, helmets, shoes, a huge clothing section—you name it. A great place to outfit the family. ▪ *706 SE Martin Luther King Jr Blvd; 233-5973; map:G9; every day.*

Running Outfitters At the foot of the popular Terwilliger Boulevard running route, two blocks from Duniway Park's track, is the city's oldest running-only store (formerly Terwilliger Athletic Gear)—smaller than your garage, but well stocked. Owner Jim Davis is, of course, an avid runner, and his store has an almost cult-like following. ▪ *2331 SW 6th Ave; 248-9820; map:GG6; Mon-Sat.*

RECORDS, TAPES, AND COMPACT DISCS

Birdland Jazz Portland's only exclusively jazz outlet, Birdland features new and used CDs, and is a must-stop for jazz lovers. It's a quiet place, but chat with owner Don Anderson about Charlie

Parker, Miles Davis, or Thelonious Monk. ▪ *1008 SW Taylor St; 274-2738; map:GG5; every day.*

Bird's Suite Bird's Suite is stocked with new and used records, tapes, and CDs as well as cutouts and consignments. It's mostly rock, but there are good jazz and blues selections and a fair-size classical section. A free record search is available. An added plus: the staff is loaded with personality. ▪ *4133 SE Division; 235-6224; map:HH4; every day.*

Borders Books and Music See Books and Magazines in this chapter. ▪ *708 SW 3rd Ave (and branches); 220-5911; map:G4; every day.*

Crossroads This cooperative of 25 vendors in a storefront is modeled after an antiques mall. They specialize in collectibles and hard-to-find records—there's a computerized record-search service available. If you need *Meet the Beatles* on the black label, green label, red label, or Apple label to complete your collection, pay a visit. ▪ *3130-B SE Hawthorne Blvd; 232-1767; map:GG5; every day.*

▼

Records, Tapes, and Compact Discs

▲

Django's This place reminds us a little of the record stores of the '70s: lots of posters for sale (including a wall of Escher prints), incense burning, the Grateful Dead's *American Beauty* on the stereo, and loads of vinyl LPs. But Django's is a lot more than a trip down memory lane; it's a Portland landmark. Owner Bob Dietsche, who teaches a class called Jazz and Existentialism at PSU, stocks lots of used CDs and records in all styles of music. Take heed: The racks get picked over quickly, making some titles difficult to find. ▪ *1111 SW Stark St; 227-4381; map:I2; every day.*

Everyday Music A large space on W Burnside—a short walk from Powell's Books—this store is well stocked with CDs, cassettes, and somewhat fewer LPs (although there is a large bin of LPs, arranged harum-scarum, for under $5). Most everything is used and priced quite fairly. There are several listening stations, and all genres are well represented. Plus, we found almost a dozen Burt Bacharach LPs. ▪ *1313 W Burnside; 274-0961; map:J1; every day.*

Locals Only All types of music from the Pacific Northwest can be found at Locals Only. CDs from platinum acts such as Nirvana and Alice in Chains sit on racks opposite hand-labeled tapes of shows at the Satyricon. Jazz, folk, and other sounds, too. They'll gladly let you listen before you buy. ▪ *916 W Burnside; 227-5000; map:I6; every day.*

Music Millennium Since 1969, the independently owned Music Millennium has stayed competitive with larger record chains. Its stock is truly impressive: an amazing variety of rock CDs, from ABBA to Zuzu's Petals, plus separate areas for collections, oldies, rap, jazz, blues, reggae, country, and New Age. The Burnside store has a separate classical music annex. Big-name musicians coming through town occasionally stop in to meet their fans. ■ *3158 E Burnside; 231-8926; map:GG5; every day.* ■ *801 NW 23rd Ave; 248-0163; map:FF7; every day.*

Ozone Ozone may be across the street from Django's, but in music circles it's in a different stratosphere. Sonic Youth plays in the background, and the catchword is "cutting edge"—everything experimental, industrial, and alternative. Live local and out-of-town bands play and hang out here every weekend. ■ *1036 W Burnside; 227-1975; map:J2; every day.*

Platinum Records This DJ-oriented shop is the place to go for acid jazz, trip-hop, and assorted rave genres. The stock is mostly LPs—not surprising, since DJs don't mix with cassettes. There is also a good selection of DJ equipment, including mixers, PA systems, and even some disco balls. ■ *115 SW Ash; 222-9166; map:I5; every day.*

Reverb New and used LPs are mixed together with a smaller number of CDs and cassettes. Most prices are reasonable, and there are unquestionably a few finds to be had. In addition to rock, there are sections for country, jazz, gospel—and even zither. Check out the extensive collection of Pez dispensers. ■ *3623 SE Hawthorne; 736-9110; map:GG5; every day.*

Roundhouse Records Roundhouse rounds out the ever-growing mecca for music on SE Hawthorne Boulevard. Owner Peter Genest stocks new and used punk, hard-core, and alternative 7-inch singles, LPs, and CDs as well as collectable punk vinyl. There's also an impressive selection of local alternative rock. Want to start your own garage band? Come here to find out what's been done already. ■ *1727 SE Hawthorne Blvd; 238-3913; map:GG5; Mon-Sat.*

2nd Avenue Records Stacks and stacks of boxes containing tapes and CDs of rap, metal, alternative, punk, and rock crowd every square inch of this store. For years, 2nd Avenue Records has been a browser's paradise. If you don't have the time to wade through it all, ask Cathy Hagen or John McNally: they know where to find what you want. ■ *400 SW 2nd Ave; 222-3783; map:H5; every day.*

Sound Addiction This quiet store has a good if eccentric collection of used LPs that range from prerock to postpunk. Owner Don Robinson makes sensible purchasing suggestions and is all too happy to let you use his listening station to hear for yourself. The under-$3 bin is a huge treasure trove for the brave quester who is not afraid to wade through a little El DeBarge. We almost like the faint incense that lingers in the air. ■ *3430 SE Belmont, Suite 104; 238-9670; map:GG5; every day.*

Records, Tapes, and Compact Discs

Tower Records An enormous selection of music—classical, folk, pop, children's, country—at prices that might make you twist and shout. Don't expect much in the way of nuances, though; this is a chain store. ▪ *1307 NE 102nd Ave (Gateway Shopping Center); 253-1314; map:FF2; every day.* ▪ *3175 SW Cedar Hills Blvd, Beaverton; 626-2600; map:II9; every day.*

Turntable Mary's There's only one criterion Mary's music has to meet: 105 to 110 beats per minute. This is Portland's best outlet for techno-house-disco. ▪ *126 SW Stark St; 227-3933; map:I5; Mon-Sat.*

SHOES

Birkenstock Footprints of Oregon Descend the stairs and you're met by the chatter of canaries, Birkie the house cat, and a collection of the world's most comfortable walking shoes. In the last few years, the hipness quotient of Birkenstocks has skyrocketed (there's even Birkie jewelry), but if your tastes run to sleeker designs, there are other options here as well: Finn Comfort, Haflingers, Romika, and Stegmann wool clogs. ▪ *730 SW 11th Ave; 227-4202; map:H2; Mon-Sat.*

▼

Records,
Tapes, and
Compact
Discs

▲

Imelda's Designer Shoes Heads up, shoehorses. Here's a store that prides itself on carrying lines you won't find at department stores, but at prices that allow more than an occasional indulgence. Owner Pam Coven strives for a mix of fashion-forward lines that stops just shy of trendiness, with an emphasis on designer labels such as Franco Sarto and David Aaron. Leather handbags, jewelry, and hosiery too, all a half block away from colorful Hawthorne Boulevard. ▪ *1431 SE 37th Ave; 233-7476; map:GG5; every day.*

J. Cobb Company Robert Cobb couldn't find the shoes he wanted in Portland, so he opened this shop, ordered his faves, and, reluctantly, decided to allow customers to buy them. Nearly a dozen lines of his men's and unisex shoes are imported from Europe, including Soho, Natha, and Brown as well as the tougher Kickers of London, Tattoo, Shelley, and Robert Wayne designs. ▪ *2745 NE Broadway; 331-0722; map:FF5; every day.*

John Newbury Boot Shop A former police officer, John Newbury apprenticed eons ago as a bootmaker to a sheriff-moonlighting-as-a-shoemaker. Now, Newbury has been building boots in Sellwood for 20 years, sole to laces: line boots, cowboy boots, engineer boots. He'll measure your foot and finish your boots in his own good time—sometimes four months hence. ▪ *1655 SE Bybee Blvd; 235-7496; map:JJ5; Mon-Fri.*

Johnny Sole John Plummer's got sole. Even better, the 34-year-old entrepreneur keeps a close watch on the fashion trend-o-meter and stocks his once-tiny shoe boutique—now sprawling shoe mall—accordingly. Here you'll find everything from cocktail party heels to steel-toed work boots. Throw a cool collection of belts, purses, sunglasses, and jewelry into the mix, and the shop fills out two storefronts. ▪ *801 and 809 SW Alder St; 228-5844; map:I3; every day.*

Moda Now at a new Park Avenue address, Michael Jolley's Moda features cutting-edge footwear for women. With lines such as Paloma, Calvin Klein, Via Spiga, Robert Clergerie, and Kenneth Cole, the look is European, but the prices are affordable. There's also a notable selection of clothing by Bijou Bijou, Gautier, Annex, Tessuto, and Tehen. ▪ *6l5 SW Park Ave; 227-6522; map:H2; every day.*

Zelda's Shoe Bar Don't get confused by the name and order a mai-tai—this bar serves only fashion-forward shoes, to a well-heeled clientele thirsty for style. Sleek copper counters display a carefully chosen selection emphasizing designer looks in European leathers. Vans and a few sportier styles occasionally appear as blue-plate specials. ▪ *633 NW 23rd Ave; 226-0363; map:GG7; every day.*

SPECIALTY-SIZE CLOTHING

Generations This store carries a sizable selection of soft cotton clothing for both expecting mothers and children: Japanese Weekend is the hot label. One rack of resale clothing, too. *Portland Parent* has named Generations best local maternity shop for three years. Excellent occasional sales; ask to be placed on the mailing list. ▪ *4029 SE Hawthorne Blvd; 233-8130; map:GG4; Mon-Sat.*

Mimi Maternity Look here for upscale wear for moms-to-be—themselves upping the scales. This store, an outpost of the Philadelphia company, carries its own label's casual, career, and evening wear, plus Olga and Leading Lady lingerie. The entire collection is suited to fit women fashionably from their second month through delivery. Wednesdays, when markdowns occur, are good days to shop for bargains. ▪ *Pioneer Place; 241-1536; map:G3; every day.*

Sizes Unlimited/Big & Tall At this shop, clothing sizes stretch to the outer limits. There is nothing available for men 6'2" and under, but there is everything from suits to sportswear for the tall or heavyset man. Five stores offer free wardrobing and free delivery in the downtown Portland area. ▪ *909 SW Washington (and branches); 222-5270; map:I3; Tues-Sat.*

TOYS

Bridges Toy and Bookstore In addition to all the name-brand toys (Playmobil, Brio, Ambi, Breyer), this spacious Lake Oswego store also houses a great selection of children's books. Other noteworthy items: life-size Madeline dolls, wooden rocking horses, dress-up clothes, jazzy Hula Hoops, and a long aisle of things to make and do (beads, tie-dye, clay). Next door at **Baby Bridges Boutique** (699-0550), you'll find gorgeous layette sets, one-of-a-kind Moses baskets, and hand-painted furniture—nirvana for the indulgent grandparent. ▪ *218 A Ave, Lake Oswego; 699-1322; map:LL6; Mon-Sat.*

Child's Play You haven't lived until you've witnessed this shop's own band of stuffed primates singing "I'm a Bongo-Playing Monkey." Choose from a great selection of uncommon American and European toys for every stage of a child's development. While there is an immense selection of dolls (Ginny, Madame Alexander, and the hard-to-find American Girls Collection), we gravitate toward the strong art and science sections. Go often (and well before Christmas) to see Child's Play at its finest. ▪ *907 NW 23rd Ave; 224-5586; map:GG7; every day.*

▼

Toys

▲

Finnegan's Toys and Gifts The best toy store in town, Finnegan's can keep you and your child enthralled for the better part of an afternoon. A part of this spacious, always stimulating store is set aside for test drives of the windup cars, flip-over monkeys, and whatnot. Look for Ambi rattles, Playmobil gear, Brio trains, dollhouses, craft supplies, wooden and floor puzzles, and a great selection of puppets and stuffed animals. ▪ *922 SW Yamhill St; 221-0306; map:H2; every day.*

Kids at Heart A range of imaginative toys crowd this little shop on Hawthorne: dress-up helmets and fairy garlands, glow-in-the-dark soccer balls, MagiCloth paper dolls, and—surprise!—lots of Brio. A newer and roomier Kids at Heart, 20 blocks west, caters to those 8-and-up, with a focus on science and arts and crafts. ▪ *3435 SE Hawthorne; 231-2954; map:GG5; every day.* ▪ *1736 SE Hawthorne; 232-5927; map:GG5; every day.*

Paint the Sky Kites Enter this colorful store through the curtain of wind socks hanging on the front porch, and find yourself amid a friendly collection of kites and other stuff to fly in the great blue yonder: boomerangs, flying disks (aka Frisbees), banners, and bubbles. Kite-making supplies for do-it-yourself types. ▪ *828 NW 23rd Ave; 222-5096; map:GG7; every day.*

Tammie's Hobbies Tammie's is always abuzz with enthusiastic hobbyists. Now in a new location with ample parking, it's still one of the only Portland stores to carry German LGB electric train sets (and spare parts). Few outgrow the yearning for radio-controlled race cars, airplanes, and boats. You'll also find models of all sorts, a paint center, and the full range of paint-ball supplies. ▪ *12024 SW Canyon Rd, Beaverton; 644-4535; map:HH9; every day.*

Thinker Toys For years Multnomah neighborhood kids have been dragging their parents here to see what's new in Tye and Joan Steinbach's friendly shop. There's always plenty of stuff—dress-ups, puzzles, baby toys, Brio, and a nice selection of under-5 items, which the Multnomah neighborhood parents especially appreciate. Now there's a Moreland store, too. ▪ *7882 SW Capitol Hwy; 245-3936; map:JJ7; every day.* ▪ *1626 SE Bybee; 235-2970; map:JJ5; every day.*

Toy Bear Ltd. The upper-end inventory at this Gresham store has a bit of everything: science games, dolls, cars, puzzles, and stocking stuffers, all intelligently chosen. Clothing, too, including a large selection of Boy Scout, Girl Scout, and Camp Fire Girl particulars. ▪ *130 N Main St, Gresham; 661-5310; every day.*

VINTAGE

Ipnosi What a concept: Ipnosi carries all new vintage clothing—newly crafted men's and women's wear representing styles from the '30s to the '60s. (Think new fabric, new scent.) Don't want to buy 'em? Rent 'em. Prices are comparable to vintage resale. ▪ *616 NW 23rd Ave; 223-4373; map:FF6; every day.*

Keep 'Em Flying This vintage clothier is more austere than the rest. Perhaps that helps define the shop as one of the more elegant, too. Keep 'Em Flying (the name is from the WWII slogan) resells only the finest men's and women's garments from the 1900s to the 1970s. Jewelry, fine-quality shoes, and classic luggage can also be found here. ▪ *510 NW 21st Ave; 221-0601; map:FF6; Mon-Sat.*

Poker Face Partners Jason Brown and Andy Crawford opened this eclectic southeast Portland vintage shop two years ago with high standards and the ambition to make it Portland's best. Fast-forwarding to now, they've turned Poker Face into a hot spot for shoppers with a taste for first-rate vintage goods dating from the '40s to the '60s, as well as offering a contemporary line of rockabilly and street-style threads. ▪ *128 NE 28th Ave; 231-4366; map:GG5; every day.*

Ray's Ragtime Hundreds of gowns and glittery party dresses are arranged chronologically in this downtown shop. And more: groovy ties, collectible vases, and rhinestone baubles. Cool Hawaiian shirts are a favorite with bargain-hunting Californians and Japanese. Ray's collection of Victorian wedding dresses is accessible by appointment. ▪ *1021 SW Morrison St; 226-2616; map:I2; Tues-Sun.*

Torso In many vintage stores, you have to hunt for the great buys. At Torso, the vintage collection is so well displayed that you must first just stand and gawk. From Victorian black to '70s brights, all the pieces are in great shape; prices do reflect this. ▪ *2424 NE Broadway; 281-7230; map:GG5; Wed-Mon.* ▪ *64 SW 2nd Ave; 294-1493; map:I6; Wed-Mon.*

WINES, BEERS, AND SPIRITS

Burlingame Grocery If this market doesn't carry the bottled beer you're after, you're probably out of luck. Owner Tom Calkin and his staff strive to stock every beer that's available in the state (look for closeout specials: great beers that sold poorly in the Portland market are frequently available *en masse* at very attractive prices). The wine section is also very strong—from West Coast wines to Bordeaux to Italian reds, usually with once-a-month tastings. You can also pick up milk, eggs, and a loaf of bread here; it is a grocery, after all. ▪ *8502 SW Terwilliger Blvd; 246-0711; map:HH6; every day.*

Cheshire Cat Owner Ron Bronleewe scurries back and forth between the wine and a well-stocked cheese case to inform, sell, and chat. It's a tight squeeze between the shelves, wooden crates, and small counter; every possible square inch sports a bottle of wine. Wine samples to taste at the counter help consumers broaden their knowledge and make the right purchase. Interesting wines, high prices. ▪ *1409 NE Weidler (Irvington Market); 284-5226; map:FF5; every day.*

Clear Creek Distillery With fruit from his family's Hood River orchards, an absence of any additives whatsoever, and a large sparkling copper still, Stephen McCarthy creates a colorless, true pear brandy and an apple brandy lightly tinted with oak. Both digestifs smell of pure, beautiful fruit and smack a smooth 80 proof. A resourceful man, McCarthy also produces grappa—traditionally a peasant concoction made from the leftover fruit skins—with overwhelming success, as well as framboise (raspberry eau-de-vie), kirschwasser (cherry brandy), and blue plum brandy. The latest libation to join the stellar portfolio is a single-malt whiskey. Clear Creek is open daily during the week, but it's best to let them know you're coming. ▪ *1430 NW 23rd Ave; 248-9470; map:FF7; Mon-Fri.*

Fred Meyer Marketplaces Unfortunately, the wine-shop-within-a-grocery-store concept that took off so beautifully a few years ago has been pared back at Fred Meyer: only seven of the larger stores around town still have wine stewards on staff. Nevertheless, the selection is still above average (especially at the superstores), and if you keep your eyes peeled you're bound to find a deal. Make a point to peruse the beer selection—good choices, good prices. ▪ *3030 NE Weidler (and branches); 280-1300; map:FF4; every day.*

Great Wine Buys In the belief that her clientele responds best to personal recommendations, Rachel Starr has tasted thousands of wines and written tasting notes for them. The selection includes a number of moderately priced and high-end wines, all chosen with care. Retro furniture and wine racks are stacked with an international cache of good-value, good-tasting wines. Try Starr's own label of Oregon wines, and get samples at the tasting bar. ▪ *1515 NE Broadway; 287-2897; map:FF5; every day.*

Harris Wine Cellars Ltd. For years, this was one of only two places in Portland where the wine drinker could actually talk with a knowledgeable wine person. Art Thomas, the soft-spoken proprietor, is an educated oenophile. The shop in many ways seems a relic of the past, complete with cellar dust, old fixtures, labels from decades ago montaged for posterity, and rare fine wines found nowhere else in this market. If you're looking for the vigor displayed by newer wine tradespeople and more current selections, this is not the shop for you. Still, there is much to be seen and learned at this venerable wine "cellar." ▪ *2300 NW Thurman St; 223-2222; map:FF7; Mon-Sat.*

Liner & Elsen Ltd. Bob Liner and Matt Elsen have done a great job of raising the level of Portland's wine consciousness. Their shop is well stocked with wines—from dirt cheap to downright pricey—from many regions, and Matt or Bob is always available for educated, unpretentious advice. They also offer a number of unique services for the connoisseur and novice—regular tastings, a witty and informative monthly newsletter that previews special bottle and case prices, premium wine glasses, and temperature-controlled storage lockers. ▪ *202 NW 21st Ave; 241-9463; map:GG7; Mon-Sat.*

▼

Wines, Beers, and Spirits

▲

Martinotti's Cafe & Delicatessen See Markets and Delicatessens in this chapter. ▪ *404 SW 10th Ave; 224-9028; map:J2; Mon-Sat.*

Pastaworks See Markets and Delicatessens in this chapter. ▪ *3731 SE Hawthorne Blvd; 232-1010; map:GG5; every day.* ▪ *735 NW 21st (City Market NW); 221-3002; map:GG7; every day.*

Portland Wine Merchants Mediterranean yellow walls, antiques, and wooden cases filled with wine bottles make this one of Portland's more attractive wine shops. At the long bar you can order a taste or a glass from the blackboard selections; drink it while chatting with owner Rory Olson, or take it to a table up front. Informal drop-in tastings are held on Friday nights; Tuesday evenings are reserved for more serious types. ▪ *1430 SE 35th Ave; 234-4399; map:GG5; Tues-Sat.*

Wine Supply This beer- and wine-making supply shop also houses a small but excellent selection of wines. If your interests lie in French reds, German rieslings, and Northwest varietals, check out this well-chosen, reasonably priced collection. ■ *2758 NE Broadway; 287-2624; map:FF5; Mon-Sat.*

Wizer's Lake Oswego Foods Wizer's still offers one of the best selections of wine in southwest metropolitan Portland. Although not as robust as in past years, this wine department has a wide array of domestic and imported wines with a vast repertoire of sale items. And do explore the cellar—an inventory book should be available for perusal, and it's a treat to imagine owning some of the rare sweethearts (vintages back to 1934). Groceries, too. ■ *330 1st St, Lake Oswego; 636-1414; map:KK5; every day.*

Woodstock Wine and Deli Proprietor Gregg Fujino is one of Portland's most astute and friendly wine sellers. Together with Jim Clark, he takes seriously the tasks of tasting, cataloging, and researching wine. In 1995 the shop was expanded, which brought a lot of wine out of the closet and onto the highly organized (as in alphabetical) shelves. The recent addition of a restaurant kitchen and informal bistro fare makes the wine tastings last further into the evening. Located near Reed College, this shop is a good place to dine, browse, and learn. ■ *4030 SE Woodstock Blvd; 777-2208; map:HH4; Mon-Sat.*

LODGINGS

Lodgings

HOTELS

DOWNTOWN

The Benson Hotel ★★★   For decades, this was the only classy lodging in town, and it's still among the better places to stay. Owned by WestCoast Grand Hotels (the same group that operates the RiverPlace Hotel), the 286-room Benson distinguishes itself with its stunning architecture and opulent interior. Surrounded by a host of bank buildings and offices, and characterized by service that's competent but somewhat impersonal, the Benson is, literally and figuratively, really quite corporate. A brusqueness that may go unnoticed by the hurried business traveler can leave a more leisurely guest feeling chilled. Still, the Benson is often the choice of politicos and film stars, with names like Bill Clinton and Madonna in the guest book.

   Lumber tycoon Simon Benson built the hotel in 1912, giving orders to spare no expense. The resulting creation was a noble 13-story affair of brick and marble, with a palatial lobby featuring a stamped-tin ceiling, mammoth chandeliers, stately columns, a generous fireplace, and surrounding panels of carved Circassian walnut imported from Russia. Competition eventually brought an end to the hotel's reign as the grande dame of Portland hostelries, although the $20 million restoration in the early '90s was a gallant attempt to return it to its original stature. The marbled elegance of the lobby and lounge were restored, and the rooms slightly enlarged (bath and all) and updated with modern furnishings in shades of maroon and beige. There's also a weight room.

The hotel's two restaurants are the windowless and old-style elegant London Grill (see review in the Restaurants chapter) and the streetside casual restaurant Piatti, which serves pasta, pizza, and other Italian favorites. The lounge off the lobby is a lovely place for an after-dinner drink. ▪ *309 SW Broadway; 228-2000 or (800) 426-0670; www.holog.com/benson; map:I3; $$$; AE, DC, DIS, JCB, MC, V; checks OK.* &

Doubletree Red Lion Hotel This standard hotel in south downtown Portland sits close to an attractive urban renewal project: handsome apartment towers by Skidmore Owings & Merrill are set amid sensitive landscaping and fountains by Lawrence Halprin. You can stroll from the hotel through the towers and green space to the Civic Auditorium, as well as Portland State University. Doubles begin at $119, and the 235 rooms are unexciting, but some do look out onto a landscaped central courtyard with an outdoor pool. Business travelers appreciate the coffee-maker and ironing board in each room, and the weight room, which is open around the clock. ▪ *310 SW Lincoln St; 221-0450 or (800) 222-TREE; map:B2; $$$; AE, DC, MC, V; checks OK.*

Embassy Suites Portland Downtown [*unrated*] In its heyday, the Multnomah Hotel was a grand lodging. With its marble stairways and massive chandeliers, expansive lobby, and opulent style, this classic hotel was a home away from home for U.S. presidents, movie stars, and royalty. In 1965, however, the building was converted to office space for the federal government, and for more than a quarter century little attention was paid to it. Now Embassy Suites, a national hotel chain with a local outpost in Tigard, has lovingly restored the old Multnomah—touching up everything from the gold leaf in the lobby, to the swimming pool with its huge columns, to the molding along the upstairs hallways. Most suites include a separate sleeping area, a full made-to-order breakfast in the dining room, and amenities such as minikitchens and two telephones per room. This Embassy Suites is located a bit to the north of the downtown core, near Old Town, a moderate walk from the shops of Pioneer Place or the paths of Tom McCall Waterfront Park. The hotel opened at press time, in late 1997, and if the service, attention to detail, and amenities live up to the standard set by its location, the Embassy Suites will join the ranks of Portland's finer downtown luxury hotels. ▪ *319 SW Pine St; 279-9000; www.embassy-suites.com; map:I6; $$$; AE, DC, DIS, MC, V; no checks.*&

5th Avenue Suites Hotel ★★★ The Kimpton Group has done it again. This time it revamped the Lipman, Wolfe & Company department store (two blocks from the Hotel Vintage Plaza) and turned it into one of the most pleasant stays in the city—great for business travelers, yes, but excellent for well-to-do families, too.

Most of the 221 rooms are spacious suites, and they all have a sense of grandeur (and plenty of room for a crib, if requested). Each suite has three phones (with personalized voice mail and data ports) and a couple of televisions, and some even have their own fax machines. All rooms are equipped with such traveler's-choice details as pull-down ironing board and iron, plush cotton robes, and hair dryer. The staff is gracious and the bellhops extremely attentive (and, unlike any other Portland hotel of this caliber, they even welcome the occasional dog).

Kimpton has covered its bases: everything from indoor parking with an unloading area to protect you from the (high) chance of rain to the stunning but welcoming lobby with its large corner fireplace, where you'll find complimentary coffee and newspapers in the morning, and wine-tastings come evening. The Red Star Tavern and Roast House is an excellent open-spaced bistro (see review in the Restaurants chapter), and the indulgent Aveda Lifestyle Store and Spa is also located on the premises (see Body Care in the Shopping chapter). ■ *506 SW Washington St; (503)241-4100 or (800)551-0011; www.preferredhotels.com/preferred.html; map:H4; $$$; AE, DC, DIS, JCB, MC, V; checks OK.* &

The Governor Hotel ★★★ If the Heathman Hotel embraces art, and the Hotel Vintage Plaza celebrates wine, this hotel honors history. Nowhere is that more apparent than in the Governor's honey-hued lobby, which features a long and dramatic mural depicting scenes from the Lewis and Clark Expedition, heavy Arts and Crafts–style furniture, yards of mahogany, and a true wood-burning fireplace. Welcome to Wild West grandeur.

Some $15 million went into restoring the Governor Building and its neighbor, the Italian Renaissance Princeton Building, in 1993, and the two combine to make up the hotel. The rooms are a departure from the lobby: decorated in pale Northwest earth tones and a subtle oak leaf–patterned wallpaper, they feature standard hotel furnishings (although there is an irritating lack of places to set things). Some rooms have a whirlpool tub; suites feature fireplace, wet bar, and balcony. Almost all the rooms have big windows, but the upper-floor rooms on the northeast corner of the Princeton Building sport the best city views (we like room 5013). The list of amenities is long and includes access to the Princeton Athletic Club (adults only, for an $8 fee) and the business center, and 24-hour maid service. Jake's Grill, the restaurant downstairs (see review in the Restaurants chapter) also provides room service. ■ *611 SW 10th Ave; 224-3400 or (800)554-3456; governor@transport.com; www.teleport.com/~peekpa/governor.html; map:I2; $$$; AE, DC, JCB, MC, V; checks OK.*

The Heathman Hotel ★★★★ If you compare the larger, more fashionably attired guest rooms at Portland's ever-growing number of luxury hotels to the Heathman's rather small, conservatively furnished sleeping quarters, you might wonder at its four-star rating.

Wonder not. This 151-room landmark hotel retains its favored status because none of its competitors can match the quality of service or the scope of amenities offered at the historic Heathman. Built by hotelier George Heathman in 1927 and restored by local timber magnate Wallace Stevenson in 1982, the hotel has a meticulously courteous staff whose low-key, professional service is exceptional from checkin to checkout—and the longer your stay, the more apparent this attention.

The common rooms are handsomely appointed with Burmese teak paneling, and the elegant lobby lounge is a great place to enjoy afternoon tea (especially during the holiday season) or evening jazz and piano performances. Depending on your interests, you might be impressed by the video library (featuring more than 400 movies), the Mezzanine Library (with its collection of author-signed volumes), or the fitness suite (personal trainer upon request). Your only unfulfilled desire might be for a swimming pool.

A strong supporter of the arts, the hotel itself offers an impressive display of original artwork, from the spectacular Andy Warhol Endangered Species prints to the fanciful Henk Pander mural on the east wall of the Arlene Schnitzer Concert Hall, of which 80 guest rooms have an exclusive view.

Hotels

Downtown

Best of all, you're just steps (or room service) away from the Heathman Restaurant, where executive chef Philippe Boulot creates culinary masterpieces in the hotel's stellar kitchen (see review in the Restaurants chapter). ▪ *1001 SW Broadway; 241-4100 or (800)551-0011; www.holog.com/heathman; map:G2; $$$; AE, DC, MC, V; checks OK.*

Hotel Vintage Plaza ★★★★ This refined, smart hotel in the heart of the city is run by the Kimpton Group and, like many other Kimpton hotels, it is elegant but not opulent. We like the intimate scale of the hotel (107 rooms), the inviting lobby—which has recently been redone in lighter tones—and the gracious staff. Among the niceties standard to the Vintage Plaza are attentive bellhops (some of the best in town) who don't let you lift a thing, and the complimentary Oregon wines and classical piano in the early evening. The wine theme is apparent throughout the hotel; indeed, most rooms are named after an Oregon winery. (Others are named after NBA players, as this is their stomping ground when in town.)

In the early '90s Bill Kimpton saved this 1894 hotel from being converted into office space, and the refurbishment is quite lovely. Rooms are decorated either with cherry-wood furnishings and rich wine colors, or with wicker in beachy pastels. Attention shows in little touches, like hidden televisions, plush towels, and lots of convenient hideaways to stow your belongings. Among the handful of room possibilities are the stunning bi-level suites, with 1½ baths, an extra foldout bed, and plenty of seating; or the starlight rooms, with greenhouse-style windows (ask for one of the larger corner rooms), perfect for city stargazing or just watching the rain splash against the glass (truly worthy of the hotel's "Romance Package" designation). All rooms come with complimentary shoe shine, nightly turn-down service, morning coffee and baked goods in the lobby, and newspaper delivered to your door.

Pazzo Ristorante on the main floor serves excellent Northern Italian cuisine (see review in the Restaurants chapter). On Fridays and Saturdays, be sure to request a table in the intriguing wine cellar. Next door to the hotel, Pazzoria Cafe sells panini sandwiches, crusty Italian breads, and pastries to take out or eat in. ■ *422 SW Broadway; 228-1212 or (800)243-0555; www.holog. com/vintage; map:I3; $$$; AE, DC, DIS, JCB, MC, V; checks OK.*

Imperial Hotel ★ You won't feel like royalty by staying here, but if you don't have a king's booty at your disposal, the Imperial may fit the bill: a central location, clean, fairly quiet, friendly—and room rates that are about half those of the more luxurious hotels on SW Broadway. A 1995 remodel spiffed up the lobby and made some of the 136 rooms larger and more modern. You can request one of the new rooms, which tend to be larger and sport new linens and furniture, or one of the older rooms, which are usually smaller, less expensive, and less appealing. Each room's bathroom has retained its original charm, with tile floor and big porcelain tub. The folks here make you feel good: they'll park your car for you at all hours, and they'll even let you leave your baggage (locked) in the lobby for the afternoon after you've checked out. If you don't smoke, be sure to ask for a nonsmoking room (floors 2–6). ■ *400 SW Broadway; 228-7221 or (800)452-2323; www. hotel-imperial.com; map:I3; $$; AE, DC, DIS, MC, V; checks OK.*

Hotels

Downtown

Mallory Hotel ★★ It's difficult to say which Portland hotel has the greatest number of loyal patrons who return every time they're in town, but one good bet is the beloved Mallory. It's an older establishment in every sense—from the massive hunks of ornate wooden lobby furniture to the senior staff to the clientele, many of whom remember the Mallory from the '50s. It's also one of the best bargains in town, starting at $70 for a double and topping out at $110 for a suite—so it's a good idea to reserve a room far in advance. Several of the rooms have good views of the city or the West Hills. The Mallory sits in one of the few areas bordering downtown Portland that is genuinely quiet, and the new four-story parking garage makes parking a breeze. The dining room, with its chandeliers and gilded ceiling work, serves a splendid breakfast replete with simple, charming touches and almost motherly service. The only flaws of the Mallory are the Muzak and the lime green carpet you may be subjected to in unexpected places. ■ *729 SW 15th Ave; 223-6311 or (800)228-8657; map:I1; $$; AE, DC, DIS, MC, V; checks OK.*

Marriott Hotel ★ There's lots of glitter, bustle, and convention hustle at this behemoth hotel that would be a standard business lodging except for one important, redeeming quality: a terrific location, overlooking the Willamette River, that is convenient to downtown shopping and cultural centers. There are 503 rooms in the 14-story structure, and facilities include a 24-hour health club, an indoor pool, two restaurants, and two bars. Don't settle for the first price quoted—if you probe, you just might find that you qualify for more moderate prices (ask about weekend, seasonal, senior citizen, AAA, and other special rates). ■ *1401 SW Naito Pkwy; 226-7600; www.marriott.com; map:D4; $$$; AE, DC, MC, V; checks OK.*

Portland Hilton ★★ While a major remodeling job completed in 1997 did little to make the Hilton more attractive from the street, inside it looks like a new hotel. Alterations include smartened-up public areas that host an impressive collection of artwork from prominent Oregon artists, a full-service athletic club (complete with steam room, sauna, and massage therapist), a covered swimming pool, the 6,800-square-foot Pavilion Ballroom (popular for weddings), and a new street-side bistro with an open kitchen. The guest rooms are small, adequately furnished, and plainly decorated. A west-facing room on any of the floors above the 16th affords a lovely view of the city that stretches from the West Hills to St. Johns Bridge; in fair weather, an upper-floor room on the east side promises a view of Mount Hood. The Hilton boasts a prime location, between Broadway and the Portland Transit Mall, and near plenty of cultural attractions, shops, and businesses. ■ *921 SW Sixth Ave; 226-1611; www.hilton.com; map:G2; $$$; AE, DC, MC, V; checks OK.*

▼

Hotels

Downtown

▲

RiverPlace Hotel ★★★ Situated right on the city's showcase waterfront, with a twilight view of the twinkling lights in the marina, the pink-hued RiverPlace (run by the ubiquitous WestCoast Grand Hotels) is lovely to look at—and glorious to look out from. It's hard to believe, but true, that the RiverPlace is the only luxury hotel downtown that fronts the Willamette River. The better among the 84 rooms—doubles, suites, and condominiums—face the river or look north across park lawns to the downtown cityscape; others face a private courtyard. Inside each room are plush furnishings, a television concealed in an armoire, and a generously sized bathroom. Complimentary continental breakfast is brought to your room if you wish, along with a copy of the *New York Times*. Relax in the sauna or Jacuzzi of a private spa room, which can be rented by the hour; use of the adjacent RiverPlace Athletic Club is an extra $8.

There's also plenty of opportunity for exercise right outside the door: wide, paved paths lead from the hotel through the fountains and monuments of Tom McCall Waterfront Park and drop you at the foot of several east-west streets leading up through town (it's about 10 blocks to the shops at Pioneer Place). The hotel anchors the north end of the upscale RiverPlace complex, home to a tidy bank of condos, specialty shops, and a few bars and restaurants—including the hotel's Esplanade at RiverPlace (see review in the Restaurants chapter). During the summer there's a lively night scene to watch from the patio on the riverfront promenade; in winter, cozy up in the RiverPlace Lounge, with its equally good views and fireplace. ■ *1510 SW Harbor Way; 228-3233 or (800) 227-1333; www.riverplacehotel.com; map:D5; $$$; AE, DC, DIS, JCB, MC, V; checks OK.*

Silver Cloud Inn ★ Location alone would recommend this still-newish motor hotel on NW Vaughn Street; the Silver Cloud sits just a block off NW 23rd Avenue, a nice walk from some of the city's more intriguing boutiques and coffee stops. Plus, there are three or four highly recommended restaurants within a few blocks, and Forest Park is just up the hill. But this place has more than its address going for it: it's clean and well priced, and has easy freeway access and plenty of parking. No pool, unfortunately. ■ *2426 NW Vaughn St; 242-2400; map:GG7; $$; AE, DC, DIS, MC, V; checks OK.* ⴲ

EASTSIDE

Doubletree Portland Lloyd Center ★ Its new name has not visibly affected this corporate hotel, a good choice for eastside conventions or seminars. With 476 guest rooms, it's Oregon's second-largest hotel (the Portland Marriott is slightly bigger), with a number of well-organized meeting rooms, an exhibit hall, an outdoor pool, a workout room, and a courtesy airport van. A map in the lobby directs you to the three restaurants. Reserve an east-facing room above the fifth floor for a view of Mount Hood. The service at times seems as worn as the decor, which was at one time rather splendid, but the proximity to the Lloyd Center, the Rose Quarter, and the Convention Center makes it worth a stay. ■ *1000 NE Multnomah St; 281-6111 or (800) 222-TREE; www. doubletreehotels.com; map:FF5; $$$; AE, DC, MC, V; checks OK.* ⴲ

Marriott Residence Inn/Lloyd Center ★ This hotel near the Lloyd Center Cinema has 168 rooms that you might mistake, from the outside at least, for apartments. It's geared toward longer stays (four to seven days), and rates drop accordingly. Each room has a full kitchen and sitting area with couch and desk, and most have wood-burning fireplaces. Extra conveniences include dry-cleaning and grocery-shopping services. There isn't much of a view, and there's no restaurant, but a complimentary continental breakfast and afternoon hors d'oeuvres are served in the lobby. Three Jacuzzis and a heated outdoor pool are on premises for guest use, and an extra $4 a day gains you access to the Lloyd Center Athletic Club seven blocks away. ■ *1710 NE Multnomah St; 288-1400; map:FF5; $$$; AE, DC, MC, V; checks OK.* ⴲ

JANTZEN BEACH

Doubletree Hotel Columbia River ★ Considering that the Columbia River is one of the great waterways of the world and a mere 7 miles north of downtown Portland, you may wish to stay on its banks. This garish, rambling, 351-room motel is poised right at waterside. It offers a pool (seasonally) with a sun deck that virtually overhangs the river, and complimentary airport pickup. Nearby, there's the 27-hole Heron Lakes Golf Course (via a two-minute free shuttle), a jogging path, and a health club. Honeymooners are everywhere (the riverfront executive suites are in high demand; perks include 650 square feet, private deck, garden bathtub, and king-size bed). The dance floor at the informal Brickstones restaurant hops on Fridays and Saturdays. Next door is the Doubletree Hotel Jantzen Beach (909 N Hayden Island Dr, 283-4466); expect much the same. ■ *1401 N Hayden Island Dr; 283-2111 or (800)222-TREE; map:CC6; $$; AE, DC, MC, V; checks OK.*

AIRPORT

Sheraton Airport Hotel ★★ For the traveling businessperson, the airport's Sheraton tops the list. For one thing, it's located—literally—on the airport grounds (FedEx planes load up next door, and arrival and departure times are broadcast at the main entrance). Inside, amenities abound: everything from meeting rooms and a complete, complimentary business center (IBM computers, printer, fax machine, and secretarial services) and on-site travel agency to an indoor swimming pool, sauna, and work-out room. The executive suites consider the personal needs of the businessperson, with extra touches such as multiple phones, sitting area, jack for computer hookup, and pullout makeup mirror in the bathroom. We only wish they would give the hotel a quarter turn: Mount Hood stands tall to the east, but you'd never know it from the airport-facing rooms. ■ *8235 NE Airport Way; 281-2500 or (800)325-3535; sheraton@teleport.com; www.Sheraton. PDX.com; map:DD3; $$$; AE, DC, JCB, MC, V; checks OK.* &

GREATER PORTLAND: BEAVERTON

Greenwood Inn ★ Billed as a city hotel with resort-style comfort, the 251-room complex delivers, for the most part, on its promises. Located just off Highway 217, not far from Beaverton or Tigard, the Greenwood Inn is conveniently situated for those doing business in the Silicon Forest. A few of the suites have Jacuzzis, others have kitchens, and some rooms are set aside for guests with pets; the nicest rooms are those that were refurbished in the early '90s. The courtyard and trapezoidal pool are quite pretty. Inside the Pavillion Bar and Grill, the menu features fresh and local ingredients, lights are soft, and service treads the delicate line between chummy and concerned (see review in the Restaurants chapter). ■ *10700 SW Allen Blvd, Beaverton; 643-7444; $$; AE, DC, DIS, MC, V; checks OK.* &

▼
Hotels

Jantzen Beach

▲

Embassy Suites Hotel ★ The Embassy Suites is urban-moderno, right down to its location. It's adjacent to the sprawling Washington Square shopping complex in Tigard, about 15 minutes' driving time from downtown Portland. Hundreds of rooms (all with separate living room), an elaborate ballroom, and a swank conference center make this one of the Silicon Forest's biggest hotels. Complimentary services for guests include full breakfast, transportation to a nearby athletic club or the shopping mall, and the evening manager's reception—aka free drinks—from 5:30pm to 7:30pm in the atrium. Restaurant and lounge are the usual Denny's-gone-velvet found in all hotels of this genre. Double occupancy begins at $139, but ask about special rates. At press time, a new Embassy Suites Hotel just opened in downtown Portland (see review under Downtown). ▪ *9000 SW Washington Square Rd, Tigard; 644-4000; map:JJ9; $$$; AE, DC, MC, V; checks OK.* &

GREATER PORTLAND: LAKE OSWEGO

Holiday Inn Crowne Plaza ★ Definitely a business hotel, the Crowne Plaza sits right off I-5 near the Highway 217 intersection. Holiday Inn moved in about five years ago and spiffed the place up a bit, but the rooms are still fairly standard, unless you request one on the sixth floor—the concierge floor—where they were entirely redone. All guests receive a free pass to a nearby athletic club, complimentary van service within 5 miles, and plenty of business services. There are a lounge and restaurant, an indoor/outdoor pool, bicycles (there are trails behind the hotel), a sauna, and a whirlpool. Room rates plummet on the weekends. ▪ *14811 Kruse Oaks Blvd, Lake Oswego; 624-8400; www.crowneplaza.com; map:KK8; $$; AE, DC, DIS, MC, V; checks OK.* &

Hotels

Vancouver

Lakeshore Motor Hotel ★ From the street or parking lot, Lake Oswego's Lakeshore Motor Hotel looks like any another motel located on a main thoroughfare through town. From inside a lake-facing room, however, the view out the window is uncannily rural and picturesque. All of the rooms have a kitchenette and TV, and are clean and plainly decorated. Although the one- and two-bedroom suites offer more room, the studios allow you a view of the water without getting out of bed. Guests have year-round use of the heated pool, which is perched over the lake, and the lakeside rooms (be sure to request one) have private sun decks. ▪ *210 N State St, Lake Oswego; 636-9679 or (800)215-6431; map:LL6; $$; AE, DC, DIS, MC, V; checks OK.* &

GREATER PORTLAND: VANCOUVER, WA

Heathman Lodge [*unrated*] Vancouver's first luxury hotel—run by the pros who own Portland's venerable Heathman Hotel—gives a distinct first impression: it is simply stunning and totally out of place. The hotel looms like a National Park lodge as you approach it from busy SR500—but it's set squarely in a Clark County suburb, near a mini-mall and high-tech office space. Huge timbers support the porte cochère, and nearby a carved-cedar totem pole and a bronze sculpture of a Chinook chief enrich your first impressions, which only grow more positive as you step inside. There's a striking lobby with a basalt fireplace; bright pool- and exercise rooms; the top-drawer Hudson's Bar & Grill; a range of suites and guest rooms attractively furnished in Northwest style (complete with bedspreads created by Pendelton); and plenty of amenities for the business traveler. Perhaps best of all is that promise of excellent, understated service for which the Heathman Management Group has made itself known. The lodge is unlikely to itself become a destination because of the surrounding neighborhood, but for those travelers making Vancouver their destination, the Heathman Lodge should be at the top of their accommodations list. ▪ *7801 NE Greenwood Dr, Vancouver, WA; (360)254-3100 or (888)475-3100; www.holog.com/heathman; $$$; AE, DC, DIS, MC, V; checks OK.* &

INNS AND BED & BREAKFASTS

▼

SOUTHWEST

General Hooker's Many Portland bed-and-breakfast inns have a Rose Room (or some variation thereof), but at this conveniently located Victorian B&B, the Rose is *the* room. It's the only one of the four in the house with its own bath, and it also has a king-size bed and a private entrance to the sun deck. Like the other rooms, the Rose has its own VCR, but the best show is of the city lights twinkling outside the window. The General itself is a tad cluttered—it's not a huge house—but still clean and well kept. A night in one of the two rooms separated by a shared bath can be a bit awkward, and the refrigerator in the upstairs hall feels a bit out of place. Kids (over 10 only) might appreciate the bunk room downstairs. There is half-price use of the nearby Metro YMCA; also within walking distance are the Duniway Park track, Terwilliger Boulevard bike path, and Lair Hill public tennis court. Downtown is five minutes by car or an easy bus ride away. ▪ *125 SW Hooker St; 222-4435; www.teleport.com/~ghbandb; map:HH6; $$; AE, MC, V; checks OK.*

MacMaster House ★★ There are two kinds of B&Bs: one offers the amenities of a small hotel but is slightly more personable, and the other appeals to those who love these lodgings because they're nothing like hotels. The MacMaster House unquestionably falls into the second category. Everything here—from the florid furnishings and eclectic art to the mismatched, albeit lovely, china—reflects the personality of the amiable host, Cecilia Murphy. The massive portico flanked by Doric columns makes for an imposing entry, but the interior of this mansion feels more like Dr. Doolittle's library. Seven rooms range from small and bookish to large and fanciful; all house antiques, four boast fireplaces, two have private baths. Our favorite, the Artist's Studio on the third floor, has a claw-footed bathtub and the feel of a Parisian garret apartment. Lavish three-course breakfasts by chef Patrick Long might include pear and almond crisp, gingerbread, poached eggs over polenta, or salmon cakes. And the location couldn't be better, two blocks from the entrance of Washington Park (which incorporates the Rose Garden, the Japanese Garden, and Hoyt Arboretum) and a straight shot down to NW 23rd Avenue, renowned for its boutiques, galleries, and restaurants. ■ *1041 SW Vista Ave; 223-7362; www.macmaster.com; map:GG7; $$; AE, DC, DIS, MC, V; checks OK.*

NORTHWEST

Heron Haus B&B ★★½ Heron Haus is set in the exclusive West Hills overlooking the city—just blocks away from some of Portland's trendiest restaurants and hippest boutiques. The common areas in this luxurious 10,000-square-foot English Tudor home (built in 1904) include a bright living room with a cushy sectional sofa; a handsome, mahogany-paneled library with an inviting window seat; and a wicker-furnished sun room that overlooks the outdoor swimming pool. Six guest rooms, each with private bath (one with a turn-of-the-century seven-nozzle shower), are situated on the upper floors and comfortably furnished in pastels with sitting area, telephone, TV, and queen- or king-size bed. Four have fireplaces. The enormous (and extraordinary) bath in the Kulia Room could double as the set for a "Calgon, take me away!" commercial (in addition to a separate space with a stall shower and toilet, there's an elevated spa with a city view and all the deluxe bathing accoutrements one could want, including stacks of plush towels, his-and-her robes, expensive soaps, fragrant candles, and even a rubber ducky).

Don't expect a lot of gushy fussing-over from the innkeeper during your stay—guests are left to their own devices, and the owner (and various members of her family) tend to go about their business. A no-frills continental breakfast is served in the dining room at individual tables. And don't get your heart set on a particular room—requests are only sometimes honored. ■ *2545 NW Westover Rd; 274-1846; www.europa.com/~hhaus; map:FF7; $$$; MC, V; checks OK.*

NORTH

John Palmer House ★ This Victorian mansion is an impressively ornate place for a night's sleep: a canopied bed in one room, a fainting couch in another, and a gazebo with a Jacuzzi. Draw out the fantasy by having your hosts arrange a horse-drawn carriage to take you downtown in the evening. All in all, Mary (an elementary school guidance counselor) and Richard (a speech pathologist) Sauter run a tight ship and wisely let their professionally trained son, David, staff the kitchen. The Palmer House is also available for small corporate retreats and private functions. ■ *4314 N Mississippi Ave; 284-5893; map:EE6; $$; MC, V; checks OK.*

The Kennedy School [*unrated*] This unlikely spot is the latest in the McMenamin brothers' bid to outdo themselves yet again. Located in an abandoned Italian Renaissance–style public school building in the Concordia neighborhood of North Portland, this enterprise is part community center, part meeting facility, part fun house. The Kennedy School features 35 bed-and-breakfast guest rooms—two to a classroom!—each featuring a private bath, the McMenamins' signature commissioned artwork, Indonesian antiques—and, in some, chalkboards still in place. There's the requisite bar, brewery, and restaurant, with some not-so-common public areas as well: an excellent movie theater, a gymnasium, a wine bar/dessert room, a hot-water soaking pool for guests and community members, and a charming courtyard with a fireplace to warm you. When the place opened in October 1997, it was completely overrun with the curious; don't expect to call at the last minute for a room (although you might get lucky). ■ *5736 NE 33rd Ave; 249-3983; kennedy@mcmenamins.com; www.mcmenamins. com; map:EE5; $$; AE, DIS, MC, V; checks OK.*

NORTHEAST

The Clinkerbrick House Bed & Breakfast ★ While Bob and Peggie Irvine's clinkerbrick house in the Irvington neighborhood is open to guests, it's really the top floor that's yours, and privacy (for all parties involved) is encouraged with a separate entrance and key. Upstairs there's a small kitchen and dining area where you can procure a snack, make a cup of tea, or even cook if you so choose. Of the three rooms, the largest is the only one with a private bath; it also has a canopy bed and a private balcony. Our favorite room, oddly enough, is the smallest one, where the sun (when out) seems to shine brightest. Peggie prepares a full breakfast: perhaps a gingerbread waffle served out on the brick courtyard when the weather allows. ■ *2311 NE Schuyler St; 281-2533; map:FF4; $; MC, V; checks OK.*

The Georgian House Bed and Breakfast ★ On a summer day most of the guests can be found outside in the garden amid the fragrant lavender and roses, perhaps helping themselves to the berries that grow along the back fence. Given the lovely grounds and quiet neighborhood, this Irvington B&B combines the respite of a country getaway with a convenient location (downtown is but five minutes away by car). Antique furniture and collectibles blend with a contemporary country motif for a style that, depending on your tastes, is either charming or cluttered. Of the three upstairs rooms we like the East Lake for its private veranda and the Lovejoy Suite for its claw-footed bathtub. Willie Ackley, the likable host, has guests sign up for breakfast. One caveat: for anyone who likes to sleep in, the sign-up times are shamefully early. ■ *1828 NE Siskiyou St; 281-3301; map:FF5; $–$$; MC, V; checks OK.*

The Lion and the Rose ★★★ Located in an enormous 1906 Queen Anne home in the Irvington district, this elegant bed-and-breakfast inn, run by three hosts, leaves little to chance. There are candles and fine soaps in the baths, the refrigerator is fully stocked with beverages, cookies are baked daily, magazines are current, and extra fluffy blankets are brought in upon request. The seven rooms feature lavish drapery, antique furniture, and fine area rugs. Depending on your particular choice, the interior might seem rather masculine (the Starina, with its high-back bed and linens of rust and gold, exemplifies the Ralph Lauren look) or particularly feminine (the lavender and white Lavonna room, with window seats in the cupola, evokes Laura Ashley), but it all feels indisputably decorated. Most of the rooms have at least a shower; the Lavonna's bath is down the hall and is shared with another room. The rosy-hued Garden room has pretty four-poster twin beds.

A lavish breakfast is served in the inviting dining room—maybe a plate of fruit, a wedge of quiche, and hearty orange-currant muffins—and a lovely tea is offered from 4pm until 6pm (in fact, the proprietors will organize a tea party for you; you need provide only the guests). ■ *1810 NE 15th Ave; 287-9245; lionrose@ ix.netcom.com; www.lionrose.com; map:EE5; $$$; AE, MC, V; checks OK.*

Inns and B&Bs

Northeast

Portland Guest House ★½ You might expect a lot of clamor at this location, just a few steps from the restaurants and shops of busy NE Broadway, but owner Susan Gisvold has done an excellent job of soundproofing her little mauve-colored guest house, creating an urban retreat. Gisvold doesn't live here, but she might come around long enough to advise you on Portland doings and make sure the flowers in the window boxes are watered. Still, if you prefer to be fussed over on your visit, this may not be your place; it's more like a small inn than someone's home (although that doesn't forgive the complaints we've had of lax attention to detail). With seven rooms (five with baths), privacy is seldom a problem, and each room has its own phone and clock, items not standard in many B&Bs (making this a good place for business travelers as well). White carpets and antique linens provide a touch of class. When the weather's warm, the brick patio in the garden is a nice spot to read the paper or write a letter. ■ *1720 NE 15th Ave; 282-1402; pgh@teleport.com; www.teleport.com/~pgh/; map:FF5; $; AE, MC, V; checks OK.*

Portland's White House ★★½ New owners Steve Holden and Lanning Blanks have remodeled the carriage house, bringing the total number of guest rooms at the elegant White House to eight.

What hasn't changed are the fountains and circular driveway, and the place's imposing stature. Inside, the guest rooms have exquisite area rugs and other elegant appointments, as well as private baths. The Canopy Room is especially inviting, with its large canopied bed and bright bath. The Garden Room, with its private terrace, is a delightful room in the summertime (if you like, you can have your breakfast here). Evenings, wander down to the cozy parlor for a glass of sherry or a game of chess. ■ *1914 NE 22nd Ave; 287-7131 or (800)272-7131; map:FF5; $$$; DIS, MC, V; checks OK.*

AIRPORT

Edgefield ★ The McMenamin brothers of Portland microbrew fame did a terrific job of turning the former Multnomah County Poor Farm into a quirky but winning place to visit. There's the brewpub, of course, but there's also the movie theater, the winery, the respectable Black Rabbit Restaurant and Bar (see review in the Restaurants chapter), the amphitheater (which draws some big-name bands in the summer), the meeting and party sites, and 103 guest rooms spread throughout three buildings. All are furnished with antiques and cozy linens and embellished with custom artistry; most share a bath, although the three suites have private baths. Because the Edgefield is billed as a European-style bed and breakfast, the first meal of the day is included in the room rate, and there are glasses and pitchers readily available for fetching beer. There is also a men's and women's hostel, a great alternative for the budget traveler, as well as family rooms that sleep six. The proximity to (and location away from) airport property makes the Edgefield less conventional than the usual airport-area lodging alternatives. ■ *2126 SW Halsey St, Troutdale; 669-8610 or (800)669-8610; $$; AE, DIS, MC, V; checks OK.* ♿

HOSTELS

Portland International Hostel The Hawthorne district location for Portland's only official youth hostel couldn't be better for budget travelers; within blocks are great used bookstores, good eats, and plentiful coffee and microbrew hangouts. This hostel has the familiar rules: closed between 11am and 4pm, bring your own linens (or rent theirs), and an 11pm curfew (with a 24-hour security access code). Shared showers, bunk beds, blankets, a kitchen, and two small living areas are the amenities—plus all-you-can-eat pancakes come morning. The hostel encourages groups and has one private room, good for families. June through September admits Hosteling International members only, but you can buy an HI membership ($25 for the year) when you arrive. ■ *3031 SE Hawthorne Blvd; 236-3380; hip@teleport.com; map:GG4; $; MC, V; no checks.*

OUTINGS

Outings

CHAMPOEG–AURORA

The road to **Champoeg** (pronounced "shampooey"), off Interstate 5 south of Portland, winds through amber farm fields with green patches of fir and oak forests, past browsing cattle and horses, and leads to some of the state's most significant historic sites. Champoeg was the home of the Calapooya Indians before fur traders and settlers arrived in the early 1800s. In 1843, settlers here voted to form the first provisional government of the Oregon Country. Now the **Champoeg State Heritage Area** is a 568-acre park on the Willamette River. **[KIDS]** For a $3 fee, picnickers, kids on bikes, Frisbee throwers, and volleyball players enjoy the park on summer weekends. The excellent **Visitor Center** (8239 Champoeg Rd NE, St. Paul; 678-1251), tells of Champoeg's role in Oregon's history. The **Mother's Pioneer Cabin** (open Monday, Friday, and Saturday) is run by the Daughters of the American Revolution. There, visitors can admire an authentic log cabin and kids can knead bread dough, card wool, and make fires using flint and steel just as pioneer children did. Admission is $2 for adults, $1 for children.

Just west of the park entrance is the **Newell House**, 678-5537, a replica of the 1852 original, which serves as a museum of Native American and pioneer artifacts. On the grounds are the Butteville Jail (1850) and a pioneer schoolhouse. Call for hours (closed November through February). Admission is $2 for adults, $1 for children 11 and under.

The town of **Aurora**, midway between Portland and Salem on the east bank of the Willamette, is a well preserved turn-of-the-century village that's been put on the National Register of Historic Places. It's also a well-known antique center. Two dozen or so clapboard and Victorian houses line a mile-long stretch of Highway 99E, and more than half of them have been made into antique shops (most are closed Mondays). The town is fortunate to have as its only restaurant the popular Chez Moustache (21527 Hwy 99E, 678-1866), which changed ownership in 1997 but still serves French continental cuisine.

In 1856 a Prussian immigrant, Dr. William Keil, led a group of Pennsylvania Germans here to establish a **communal settlement** of Harmonites (Aurora is named for his daughter). Property, labor, and profits were shared, and the society prospered under his autocratic rule. Farming sustained the economy, but outsiders knew the colony for the excellence of its handicrafts: furniture, clothing, tools, embroidered goods, baskets, and clarinet reeds. After a smallpox epidemic in 1862 and the coming of the railroad in 1870, the colony gradually weakened.

The **Old Aurora Colony Museum**, at the corner of Second Avenue and Liberty Street, recounts the history of the town with five buildings: the ox barn, the Karus home, the Steinbach log cabin, the communal washhouse, and the farm equipment shed. Among the museum's annual events, Colony Days in August and the quilt show in October are standouts. (Open different days depending on the season; call ahead, 678-5754.) Admission is $3 for adults, $1.50 for children. Group tours are available by prior arrangement.

▼

Day Trips

Champoeg–Aurora

▲

FORTY-MILE LOOP TRAIL

The name **Forty-Mile Loop Trail** is misleading; the circuit actually stretches some 143 miles around Portland, and an estimated two-thirds of it is improved. The goal is to develop a hiking and biking path that will connect the parks along the Columbia, Sandy, and Willamette Rivers. With help from the city and county parks systems, a private citizens group known as the Forty-Mile Loop Land Trust has completed a healthy portion of the project.

The main section of the **Wildwood Trail** is the longest completed segment. Combined with the 10-mile-long **Marquam Nature Park**, a continuous path snakes 33 forested miles on the west side of the Willamette. A woodsy, unpaved path leads from the Sellwood Bridge through Willamette Park, gains elevation to Council Crest, Washington Park, Hoyt Arboretum, Pittock Acres, and Forest Park, and extends as far north as the St. Johns Bridge. Day hikers can park either at the zoo (look for the trailhead just north of the World Forestry Center) or at the Interpretive Center, on SW Sam Jackson Park Road just west of Duniway Park. Mountain bikers are allowed on the dirt trail but are not-so-quietly discouraged.

At the confluence of the Columbia and Willamette Rivers in north Portland is **Kelley Point Park**, where deciduous forests and meadows border the Columbia Slough, an excellent vantage point for watching river steamers, tankers, and barges. From here there's a connection to the **Marine Drive Trail**, a paved

12-mile segment that parallels the Columbia from I-205 through Blue Lake Park to Troutdale.

East of the Willamette, the **Springwater Corridor** is a stretch of abandoned rail line that extends from Boring to Sellwood, passing through Powell Butte Park, Leach Botanical Gardens, and Tideman-Johnson Park (where salmon spawn in Johnson Creek). The best access to the corridor is at Tideman-Johnson Park, at the south end of SE 37th Avenue. There is limited street parking.

Most recently, the **Peninsula Crossing Trail**, a 3-mile path that connects Willamette Boulevard to Marine Drive, was improved.

The Forty-Mile Loop Trail was the brainchild of the Olmsted brothers, who in 1904, at the time of the Lewis and Clark Exposition, suggested developing a park system around the city. The idea wasn't implemented until 1980, when a private, nonprofit group put together the land trust. Maps of the loop are available at REI (Jantzen Beach, 283-1300; Tualatin, 624-8600), Powell's Travel Bookstore (Pioneer Courthouse Square, 228-1108), and Portland Parks and Recreation (1120 SW Fifth Ave, Rm 1302; 823-5132).

MARYHILL MUSEUM OF ART

In the arid eastern reaches of the Columbia River Gorge, about 100 miles east of Portland and across the gorge in Washington state, the **Maryhill Museum of Art** (on Highway 14, 13 miles southwest of Goldendale, Washington; (509)773-3733), a massive neoclassical edifice, perches rather obtrusively upon the river's barren benchlands. Once the palatial residence of the eccentric Sam Hill (son-in-law of railroad tycoon James J. Hill), it is now a museum with a stunning collection of Rodin sculptures.

In 1907, Hill bought 7,000 acres here in Goldendale, Washington, with the intention of founding a Quaker agricultural community. When that failed to materialize, Hill lost interest in living in the "ranch house" named after his wife and daughter. It seems that the museum came about through a little help from his friends: famed dancer Loie Fuller (also a close friend of Rodin) encouraged Hill to turn his mansion into an art museum; art collector Alma Spreckels became Maryhill's principal benefactor; and Queen Marie of Romania (whom Hill met during their shared philanthropic work in Europe after World War I) offered Maryhill much of her royal and personal memorabilia and graced the dedication of the Maryhill Museum in 1926.

With one of the largest collections of **Rodin works** in the world (78 bronze and plaster sculptures and 28 watercolors), three floors of classic French and American paintings and glasswork, unique exhibitions such as chess sets and 19th-century royal Romanian furnishings, and splendid Native American art, the museum makes for quite an interesting visit. Along with its permanent collection, the museum also hosts a number of traveling collections, featuring Northwest artists as often as possible. A **cafe** serves espresso, pastries, and sandwiches; peacocks roam the lovely landscaped grounds. Maryhill is open daily from March 15 to November 15.

[FREE] Three miles east of the museum on Highway 14 is another of Sam Hill's eye-catching creations, a not-quite-life-size **replica of the inner third of Stonehenge**, built to honor the World War I veterans of Klickitat County. About 3 degrees off center, Hill's Stonehenge (not stones but poured concrete) actually functions as an observatory. It embodies Hill's personal vision: a pacifist, he considered his monument a statement on the human sacrifices made to the god of war.

Just 20 minutes north of Goldendale on Highway 97 is the **Goldendale Observatory**, a popular spot when comets drop by. High-powered telescopes offer incredible celestial views through unpolluted skies. Open Wednesday through Sunday year-round; (509) 773-3141.

See also Columbia River Gorge Scenic Area in the Excursions section of this chapter.

MCMINNVILLE (YAMHILL COUNTY)

To go exploring in Yamhill County is to partake in a banquet for all the senses. Hillsides are painted with the seasonal brights of deciduous trees, the local wineries are redolent with fermenting grapes, and fruit stands along Highway 99W beckon with perfectly ripened produce. For food lovers especially, this region is bliss.

There are cultural riches here as well. In the center of the county is the town of **McMinnville**, which—like the Oregon Trail that brought the early white settlers to this region—celebrated its 150-year anniversary in 1993. Best known as a farm center and the home of **Linfield College**—a liberal arts college that's been there almost as long as the town that surrounds it—McMinnville also has a historic hub, known as the **Downtown Historic District**. Pick up a walking-tour map at the Chamber of Commerce (417 N Adams, (503) 472-6196); it points out many late 19th- and early 20th-century buildings of interest up and down Third Street.

Reserve in advance a table at the popular **Nick's Italian Cafe** (521 E Third St, (503) 434-4471), where both à la carte meals and marvelous five-course dinners (which always start with minestrone and often include salt-grilled salmon) are served in a convivial atmosphere. Another possibility is the **Third Street Grill** (729 E Third St, (503) 435-1745), probably the most elegant setting for dinner in McMinnville. **The Golden Valley Brewery and Pub** (980 E Fourth St, (503) 472-1921) offers burgers, pizza, ribs, and homemade sausage with British-style brews.

Beyond McMinnville, about 10 minutes by car along Highway 18, is Bellevue, home of the thriving **Lawrence Gallery**, (503) 843-3633, with an outdoor garden where you are welcome to picnic among sculpture work (and buy it, if you'd like). Inside, prints, paintings, jewelry, and pottery are among the fine works by some 200 artists. The **Oregon Wine Tasting Room**, (503) 843-3787, is also here. This facility may be the only place in the state where you can sample under one roof wines from more than 50 different Oregon wineries—with an impressive and long roster of Oregon pinot noirs.

For those who yearn to see the Yamhill Valley from the air, Vista Balloon Adventures, (503) 625-7385, offers daily, dawn-departure **hot-air balloon rides**. The tickets ($175 per person; $150 per person with a group of four) include one hour of flying over wine country, from treetop level to 3,000 feet, and a fussy postflight fête that includes glasses of the local favorite, Argyle sparkling wine. (See also Wine Country later in the Day Trips section of this chapter.)

MOUNT HOOD

At 11,235 feet, Mount Hood is not the highest in the chain of volcanoes in the Cascade Range, but it is one of the most developed—in part due to the fact that it's an easy one-hour trip east from Portland. (Take I-84 east to the Wood Village exit, continue to Highway 26, turn left, and continue up the mountain). According to geologists, Mount Hood still conceals hot magma and is anxious to spew. For now, though, all's peaceful in the towns scattered on its flanks. On the way up, between Gresham and Government Camp, **Sandy** (named for the nearby river), with its white-steepled church, weekend country market, and fruit stands, makes a nice stop. Here you'll find **Oral Hull Park**, designed for the blind but a pleasure for the sighted as well, with splashing water and plants to smell and feel. You may walk through the garden only with permission if you aren't a guest at the lodge here; 668-6195. The knowledgeable staff at busy **Otto's Cross Country Ski Shop**, 668-5947, will outfit you with whatever ski gear you're lacking.

Farther uphill you'll pass through the aptly named town of **Rhododendron** (look for blooms in June). From Highway 26 at Government Camp, a 6-mile road twists its way to stunning **Timberline Lodge** (elevation 6,000 feet), with its impressive frontal views of Mount Hood's glaciers. Chairlifts take skiers and photographers up over the Palmer Snowfield (technically, the glacier has stopped moving) all year round. The massive timber-and-stone lodge was constructed by government workers in the 1930s, and throughout the building are structural and decorative pieces made by hand from native materials: the 100-foot-high chimney and enormous central fireplace were fashioned out of volcanic rocks from the mountain, the hand-wrought andirons were made from old railroad tracks, and the hardwood chairs and tables were hand-hewn from Oregon timber. The rooms with fireplaces get booked early. The lodge's **restaurant** serves an array of notable Northwest fare, but it too is popular, so reserve a table; 231-5400 or (800)547-1406 (reservations), or 231-7979 (information or the dining room).

The best deal is another 1,000 feet up the mountain. Organize a dozen or more of your best friends and head to **Silcox Hut**, which has been gutted and restored to its original stone-and-timber glory. Six cubicles off the large central room provide sleeping quarters for 24. In winter you can ride up on a snow-cat, have dinner, stay overnight, wake up to breakfast, then ski down to the lodge—all for $85 per person ($80 if you bring your own sleeping bag; 295-1827 (direct from Portland) or (800)547-1406 (out-of-state).

One of the best hiking trails, the **Timberline Trail**, leads 4½ miles west from Timberline Lodge to flower-studded **Paradise Park**. The Timberline Trail is a 40-mile circuit of the entire peak that traverses snowfields as well as ancient forests. The lower parts can blaze with rhododendrons (peaking in June) and wildflowers (peaking in July); all are easily reachable from trails that branch out from Timberline Lodge.

Mid-May to mid-July is the prime time for **climbing** Mount Hood, a peak that looks deceptively easy, although its last 1,500 feet involve very steep snow climbing. **Timberline Mountain Guides** in the Wy'east Day Lodge equips and conducts groups of climbers to the summit for a whopping $275 per person; (800)464-7704. The climb starts early in the morning; allow three to five hours to go up and one or two to come down.

[KIDS]Just east of the town of Government Camp on Highway 26, the meadows of **Trillium Lake** beckon picnickers. A scenic and accessible walking trail was recently built around the entire lake, passing through patches of trillium in the spring and columbine in the summer. In early August **huckleberry** pickers wander the trails from the Clark Creek Snow Park in search of their beloved berries. In winter you can take the kids sledding at the **Snow Bunny Lodge** on the north side of the highway. Mount Hood has a total of five ski areas: Mount Hood Meadows, Summit, Ski Bowl, Timberline, and Cooper Spur. The biggest, **Mount Hood Meadows** (off Highway 35; watch for signs), is also Portland's favorite for beginners and schussers alike. For information on any of the ski areas, or other Mount Hood activities, call the Mount Hood Information Center; 622-3360 (see also Skiing in the Recreation chapter). **Cooper Spur Ski Area** (on Cooper Spur Rd, off Hwy 35) has gentler slopes, and the year-round **Inn at Cooper Spur**, (541)352-6692, has rooms, cabins with fireplaces, and a restaurant renowned for its huge steaks and rough-hewn service. Another dozen or so miles down Cooper Spur Road is the 1889 Cloud Cap Inn, a log landmark at the timberline on the north flank of Mount Hood. No longer a hotel, it's anchored to the mountain by cables, and the view alone is worth the detour. The lodge is also an access point for the Timberline Trail. Call the Ranger Station in Hood River, (541)352-6002.

OPAL CREEK WILDERNESS

The old-growth controversy has probably drawn more visitors to the proposed Opal Creek Wilderness than to any other ancient stand. Its quiet beauty creates more converts than any self-righteous exhortation could. Two hours from Portland, Opal Creek is 36 miles east of Salem via progressively more primitive roads. A mountain bike is a great way to cover the 3 miles from the gate up to the quaint mining town of **Jawbone Flat**, where the trail begins (the way back is all downhill). Anyone there can point out the spot where a white water pipe marks the trailhead, across the Battle Ax Creek bridge and up a lane to the right. From there, it's about 3 miles on an unauthorized but well-traveled trail to the cedar grove, which has trees up to 250 feet high and 1,000 years old. Here the trail fades, requiring cross-country travel on steep terrain. The hiking is predictably rigorous in spots; practically the only old growth left is in places that are difficult to log. It's 13-plus miles for the round-trip hike; start early, bring a lunch, and dawdle in the forests.

The owners and managers of Shiny Rock Mining Company at Jawbone Flat have been working for decades to protect this gorgeous chunk of undesignated wilderness from still-pending timber sales. Meanwhile, the Oregon Natural Resources Council (238-6343) promotes legislative protection and public awareness of the area; every year they hold a picnic and conference, in fall and spring respectively. Call Friends of Opal Creek for **maps**, and they will remind you that the battle to preserve old-growth is ongoing and that tree-huggers need to stick close to their leafy stations; (503)897-2921.

Directions: From Portland, drive south on I-5, take the North Santiam Highway exit (Oregon Hwy 22), and drive east for about 25 miles. At a flashing yellow light between the state forestry department and the Swiss Village Restaurant (look for the Elkhorn Recreation Area sign), turn left and drive 21 miles due north up the Little North Fork Santiam River. When you cross the national forest boundary, the Little North Fork Road becomes Forest Service Road 2207. At the only major fork in the road, bear left on Forest Service Road 2209. Watch for deer as the road surface deteriorates into rutted dirt. Park at the gate; chances are good that you'll have lots of company.

SAUVIE ISLAND

Pastoral Sauvie Island, with its farms, orchards, produce stands, waterways, and wildlife—just 20 minutes from downtown Portland on Highway 30W—is a quick escape for bicyclists, birdwatchers, anglers, and boaters. The island is bounded on the east

Day Trips

Sauvie Island

by the Columbia River and on the west by the Multnomah Channel.

In summer, watch for "U-pick" signs, or buy **fresh produce** from one of the local markets, such as the Sauvie Island Farms Market (621-3988) or the Pumpkin Patch (621-3874). Be warned, though: on rainy days the broad, golden fields of the island turn into mud farms, so take your rubber boots if you're going to pick. If you're planning to bike around Sauvie, park your car at the east end of the bridge (you can't miss the lot), and from there take the 12-mile biking loop. At the halfway point, if you're feeling energetic, take the 5-mile side trip down to the Columbia. There are several bird-watching turnouts along the loop.

The northern half of the island is a game refuge of sorts. From October through January duck hunters show up, making it no place to hang around—for you or the ducks. At other times, bountiful **wildlife** can be seen in the marshes and open fields. Look for red foxes, black-tailed deer, great blue herons, geese, ducks, and migrating sandhill cranes. **Reeder Road** extends to the northern shore and to short sandy beaches that freighters and small pleasure craft pass by. The western branch of the road follows the dike of the Multnomah Channel, passing the historic Bybee-Howell House, humble houseboats, rickety marinas, and the old site of the Hudson's Bay Company's Fort William (abandoned in 1836; nothing remains), and then eventually dead-ends. You'll want to pick up a **parking permit** (daily or yearly) if you plan to venture to the refuge or beaches; permits are available at the grocery on your left immediately as you cross over the bridge onto the island.

The **Bybee-Howell House**, in Bybee-Howell Territorial Park, was built in 1858 by James F. Bybee on a donation land claim and was sold to neighbor Benjamin Howell in 1860. The Classic Revival–style two-story house has nine rooms and six fireplaces. [KIDS]The hands-on **Agricultural Museum** displays agricultural equipment used in cultivating and harvesting crops, a complete harness shop, dairy equipment, and hand tools for working wood, leather, and metal. In the adjacent **Pioneer Orchard**, there are more than 115 varieties of apple trees—many of them unknown to modern-day orchardists—brought here by pioneers. (House and museum open noon to 5pm weekends only, June 1 through Labor Day.) Admission is by donation. The park makes a lovely place for a summer picnic, and can be rented for special events. An especially nice fall tradition is the **Wintering In Festival** at Bybee-Howell House—complete with gallons of fresh apple cider. Call the Oregon History Center, 222-1741, for information.

SILVER FALLS STATE PARK
See Parks and Waterfront in the Exploring chapter.

You can drive to Vancouver, Washington, from downtown Port-land in about 15 minutes, but by most other measures the two cities seem light-years apart. While Vancouver residents regu-larly head to Portland for the sales tax–free shopping, Portland-ers, for their part, don't often venture north (the Clark County Fair seems to be one of the biggest draws). They should—espe-cially for the historical sites, but also for the restaurants. An added attraction: great bird-watching opportunities along the nature trails at the **Ridgefield National Wildlife Refuge**; (360)887-4106. Gradually expanding and improving, the refuge gets a boost from Ducks Unlimited, (916)852-2000, a private trust devoted to preserving wildlife habitats. Ridgefield is 3 miles west of I-5 (take exit 14) on the lowlands of the Columbia River.

[KIDS]Anyone with even a mild curiosity about what life was like here in the last century should head to **Fort Vancouver** ($2 per person, $4 per family, children free). First the headquarters of the Hudson's Bay Company (1825–1849) and then a U.S. military post until 1860, it has been reconstructed as the Fort Vancouver National Historic Site. Before you try to find your way to the fort, stop at the **Visitors Center** (1501 E Evergreen Blvd; take I-5 north to Vancouver, then take the Mill Plain Blvd exit; (360)696-7655) to gather maps and visit the museum, which presents a slide show of the fort's history. The old fort and officers' quarters are in different areas—a map will help.

The 1840s gardens of Fort Vancouver are flourishing. Some consider these early gardens the seedbeds of Northwest horti-culture and agriculture; this is the first known organized local planting of vegetables, herbs, and flowers in a formal plot (reflecting the garden's English origins as well as some exotic additions such as purple Peruvian potatoes and West Indian gherkins). The original master gardener was Scotsman Billy Bruce, who learned his craft from the Royal Horticultural Society on the Duke of Devonshire's estates. Now Rick Edwards plies his trade here, keeping a watchful eye on this historic green space.

The grand officers' quarters along **Officers' Row** have all been restored. The Marshall House, named for commanding officer George C. Marshall, is the fort's showpiece and is furnished in antiques. The rest are townhouses, offices, and a restaurant, **Sheldon's Cafe at the Grant House**, (360)699-1213, open for lunch and dinner Tuesday through Saturday (see review in the Restaurants chapter). The quarters of the Hudson's Bay Com-pany's chief agent, Dr. John McLoughlin, who later founded Oregon City, are also impressive.

The **Pearson Air Museum**, next to the fort (1105 E Fifth St, (360)694-7026), is one of the oldest operating airfields in the nation, with aviation artifacts and flyable vintage aircraft. The Air Museum holds a Freedom Day Dance in November, as well as an auction in the fall. Their **Fourth of July Fly-In** is a pre-fireworks celestial sparkler.

A 1½-mile promenade along the north bank of the Columbia makes for a pleasant walk; it's the first phase of a waterfront renewal plan under way. Afterward, there are plenty of places to sate your appetite. **City Grill** (at two locations: 916 SE 164th, (360)253-5399; and 605 NE 178th, (360)574-2270) features crab cakes, fresh seafood, pasta, and prime rib. For Mexican food there are several choices, but two good ones are **Mucho Gracias** (3300 Fourth Plain Blvd, (360)906-8481), with authentic and generous portions served in a hole-in-the-wall setting; and **Bernabe's Family Cafe** (9803 NE Hwy 99, (360)574-5993), where they make their own tortillas. Locals also rave about **Royal India** (316 SE 123rd Ave, (360)944-9883). And at **Tyrone's** (106 Evergreen, (360)699-1212) you can get a demitasse of espresso made from beans roasted by the proprietor—and a buttery croissant to go along with it. (See also the Location index in the Restaurants chapter for additional restaurants in Vancouver.)

WINE COUNTRY

As Portland continues to grow in size, so does its thirst for home-grown wine. While not too very long ago, the Oregon wine industry was considered sleepy and small, Oregon is now home to more than 100 bonded and licensed wineries. Winemakers are at work in Oregon as far south as Ashland, and as far east as Milton-Freewater, but the majority are clustered west and southwest of Portland in the northern Willamette Valley. This quiet agricultural area is being challenged by the migration of urbanites lured by its peaceful beauty. Once best known for its hazelnut and prune crops, it now boasts some of the finest vineyards on the West Coast and has a growing international reputation for **pinot noir** and **pinot gris**.

The topography is characterized by rolling hills whose verdant flanks—with good sunlight exposure, soil composition, and drainage—are choice locations for vineyards. The maritime climate, with frequent gentle precipitation, cooling breezes, and a long growing season, is suitable for such wine-grape varieties as chardonnay, pinot noir, riesling, and pinot gris.

The wineries themselves are delightful to visit for those with even a passing interest in wine. Foremost among the reasons must be the settings—some of Oregon's prettiest. In all seasons, there is much to take in, from misty hills reminiscent of a Japanese woodcut to flaming fall colors to the harvesting of the small, intensely flavored grapes. The individual wineries range from farmhouses with adjoining production facilities to efficient, modern plants. Almost all have tasting rooms staffed by either winery owners or workers with intimate knowledge of the wines and production methods. They usually welcome questions and take great pride in their products. Facility tours are often available—

to be sure, you may want to call ahead. And, of course, there are the wines to sample, which may include vintages not available elsewhere or small lots from grapes in scarce supply. Prices are close to standard retail, though bargains are occasionally found, especially for purchases by the case. Do take along bread, cheese, and other wine-friendly foods to enjoy. Many facilities have tables or grassy areas for picnicking.

To learn more about specific wineries and their specialties, call on the Oregon Wine Advisory Board (1200 NW Naito Pkwy, Suite 400, Portland; (800)242-2363), or the Portland/Oregon Visitors Association (26 SW Salmon, Portland; 275-9750) for **brochures, maps, and touring information**. Or visit a local Portland wine shop: the better ones have close ties to the Oregon wine industry and can help you set an itinerary. (See Wines, Beers, and Spirits in the Shopping chapter.) *NW Palate*, a locally published magazine that includes tasting notes and feature stories on Northwest wines, can be found in wineries and on the newsstand (or call 224-6039).

Below are some recommendations for wine touring. These places have tasting rooms open every day (unless otherwise noted); many have tables for picnicking, and some sell chilled wine. Calling in advance is always recommended; many are closed the month of January. Throughout the valley there are also a number of wineries open to the public only on Thanksgiving and Memorial Day weekends. The **Eyrie Vineyards** (472-6315), **Adelsheim Vineyard** (583-3652), **St. Innocent** (378-1526), **Ken Wright Cellars** (852-7070), and **Panther Creek Cellars** (472-5667) all make killer pinot noir, and most offer case discounts over the holiday weekends.

West of Portland There are several wineries due west of Portland worth visiting, so pack a picnic and head to the Tualatin Valley for a good day trip. **Ponzi Vineyards** (Vandermost Rd, Beaverton; 628-1227) was designed by Richard Ponzi with striking results. His bottlings (especially pinot noir, pinot gris, and dry riesling) are first-rate. Open every day; call ahead. **Oak Knoll Winery** (29700 SW Burkhalter Rd, Hillsboro; 648-8198) is one of Oregon's oldest and largest producers, famous for fruit and berry wines, plus award-winning pinot noir and riesling. Great picnic grounds; open daily. The beautifully reconstructed facilities at **Laurel Ridge Winery** (NW David Hill Rd, Forest Grove; 359-5436) are open daily (closed in January). Taste their excellent sparkling wine and good gewürztraminer and riesling on the site first chosen by a German winemaking family in the 1800s.

Yamhill County About 45 minutes southwest of Portland is Yamhill County. There are so many wineries in this area that several daylong tours can be made with no repeat visits to any one. In fact, Oregon has designated **Highway 99W** the state's official wine road. Local produce stands still dot the roadside in summer, but increasingly it's the wineries, antique shops, and B&Bs that draw visitors to these lush green hills. Start by making a dinner reservation at tiny **Tina's** (538-8880), along 99W in Dundee, or at **Red Hills Provincial Dining** (538-8224), also in Dundee—both excellent, creative restaurants (see reviews in the Restaurants chapter). In Lafayette, drop into the former **Lafayette Schoolhouse**, (503)864-2720, now a 100-dealer antique mall.

The **Yamhill County Wineries Association** offers a wealth of information about many of the area wineries (PO Box 871, McMinnville, OR 97128; (503)434-5814). Some good ones along 99W include **Rex Hill Vineyards** (30835 N Hwy 99W, Newberg; (503)538-0666), which has produced a number of vineyard-designated pinot noirs that received critical attention. Its location is splendid, with perennials in bloom even when the grapevines are not, making this one of the state's best visitor facilities. The tasting room is open daily from February through December. In Dundee, you can't miss the tasting room of **Argyle** (691 Hwy 99W, Dundee; (503)538-8520), which is producing some of the best sparkling wines in the region as well as fine dry riesling. **Erath Vineyards Winery** (9009 Worden Hill Rd, Dundee; (503)538-3318) is one of the pioneer Oregon wineries, noted for wonderful pinot noirs. Dick Erath doesn't look or act anything like a stereotypical winemaker, and his successful (and good-value) wines seem to prove that doesn't matter. His winery is in a beautiful setting, just up the hill from Crabtree Park (good for picnics). **Sokol Blosser** (5000 Sokol Blosser Lane, Dundee; (503)864-2282) is one of Oregon's most commercially successful wineries. High on a hill overlooking the Yamhill Valley, **Chateau Benoit Winery** (6580 NE Mineral Springs Rd, Carlton; (503)864-2991) is best known for its sparkling wines and sauvignon blanc. Open year-round, their facility has an astonishing view.

Salem Area   Salem, the state capital, lies just shy of an hour south of Portland. North and west of Salem are several of the newer vineyards and wineries. While a few are still developing their drop-in tasting trade, there are a couple that welcome visitors: **Bethel Heights Vineyards** (6060 Bethel Heights Rd NW, Salem; (503)581-2262) has a lovely location and a tasting room that commands an incredible view. Its wines have won several awards; try the pinot noir, chenin blanc, and riesling. Hours vary throughout the year; call ahead to confirm tasting hours. **Cristom** (6905 Spring Valley Rd NW, Salem; (503)375-3068), around the corner from Bethel Heights, also makes a noteworthy pinot noir, *and* keeps regular hours March through December. **Schwarzenberg Vineyards** (11975 Smithfield Rd, Dallas; (503)623-6420) is noted not only for its pinot noir and chardonnay but also for its setting near a wildlife preserve. Open weekends only.

EXCURSIONS

ASHLAND

The presence of the remarkable **Oregon Shakespeare Festival** helps make this charming southern Oregon town, five hours from Portland on I-5, one of the best tourist spots in the region. The play season draws an audience of nearly 350,000 over nine months, filling theaters to an extraordinary 97 percent of capacity. Visitors provide clientele for the fine shops, restaurants, and bed-and-breakfast inns. Amazingly, Ashland has not lost its soul: for the most part, it seems a happy little college town set in lovely ranch country—one that just happens to house the fifth-largest theater company in the United States.

The festival mounts plays in **three theaters**: two indoors, one out. Among the theater-related attractions are an exhibit center, where you can see costumes from plays past; lectures and concerts at noon; excellent backstage tours each morning; and Renaissance music and dance nightly in the courtyard. There are plenty of nearby daytime attractions on the **Rogue River**: rafting, picnicking, and historical touring. The best way to get information and tickets is through the comprehensive **Southern Oregon Reservation Center** (PO Box 477, Ashland, OR 97520; (541)488-1011, or (800)547-8052 outside Oregon), which offers ticket and accommodation packages. Last-minute tickets in the summer are rare; you can also try the box office, (541)482-4331.

Although you really should see a play while you're in town, there's more to Ashland than theater. At the **Pacific Northwest Museum of Natural History** (1500 E Main St, (541)488-1084) you can see dioramas, hands-on science labs, and interactive exhibits.

Lithia Park, designed by the creator of San Francisco's Golden Gate Park, extends 100 acres behind the outdoor theater and provides a lovely mix of duck ponds, Japanese gardens, grassy lawns, playgrounds, groomed or dirt trails for hiking and jogging, and the pungent mineral water that gave the park its name. Great for picnicking, especially after stocking up at nearby **Greenleaf Deli** (49 N Main St, (541)482-2808).

Weisinger's Vineyard and Winery is snuggled in a Bavarian-style building on Highway 99, just outside Ashland (3150 Siskiyou Blvd, (541)488-5989). The winery gift shop is the perfect spot to sample Oregon products. Jams, jellies, sauces, and, of course, wines are for sale.

Ashland is chock-full of good restaurants. Locals are fond of the charming **Chateaulin** (50 E Main St, (541)482-2264), with its traditional French cuisine, and the **Winchester Country Inn** (35 S Second St, (541)488-1113), in a century-old Queen Anne home. Two other exceptional restaurants, both with outdoor seating that is in high demand during the summer, are **Monet** (35 S Second St, (541)482-1339), a French restaurant in a gentrified old house, and **Primavera** (241 Hargadine, (541)488-1944), where you may want to order just from the wonderful list of appetizers. The 35-minute drive past red hills, jutting cliffs, and thick evergreens to **Green Springs Inn** (11470 Hwy 66, (541)482-0614) is a guaranteed escape from Ashland's tourist crowds; this unassuming restaurant with hearty soups and pastas doubles as a neighborhood store. And you can get breakfast through the lunch hour at **Geppetto's** (345 E Main St, (541)482-1138).

The Ashland area also is blessed with many terrific accommodations. **Country Willows** (1313 Clay St, (541)488-1590 or (800)945-5697) is about seven minutes out of town on 5 acres. For another out-of-town experience, wind your way up Mount Ashland Road through several miles of gargantuan evergreens to the huge, custom-made, log **Mount Ashland Inn** (550 Mount Ashland Rd, (541)482-8707 or (800)830-8707). One of Ashland's original bed-and-breakfast inns is the **Chanticleer** (120 Gresham St, (541)482-1919 or (800)898-1950); other notable B&Bs are the **Morical House Garden Inn** (668 N Main St, (541)482-2254 or (800)208-0960), **Cowslip's Belle** (159 N Main St, (541)488-2901 or (800)888-6819), and **Romeo Inn** (295 Idaho St, (541)488-0884 or (800)915-8899). A comfortable, though not posh, motel with a pool is the **Windmill's Ashland Hills Inn** (2525 Ashland St, (541)482-8310 or (800)547-4747).

CENTRAL OREGON: BEND AND SISTERS

By and large, Portlanders have great affection for central Oregon. Most people who visit are on vacation, getting physical in the great outdoors. Nighttimes are for soaking blissfully tired bones in a spa and gazing at the stars, breathing in the sage-scented air. **Bend** was a quiet, undiscovered high-desert paradise until the 1960s when a push to develop its recreation and tourism potential tamed nearby Bachelor Butte into an alpine playground. Then came the golf courses, the airstrip, the bike trails, the river-rafting companies, the hikers, the tennis players, the rock hounds, and the skiers. Now the place has achieved serious destination status.

With four express chairlifts and high-tech ticketing, **Mount Bachelor Ski Area** (22 miles southwest of Bend) is the most impressive ski area in the state. Thirteen lifts feed skiers onto 3,100 vertical feet of dry and groomed runs. Even if you don't ski, take the Pine Marten Express up to **The Skier's Palate** in the Pine Marten Lodge, where you can get a hot sandwich of Dungeness crab and bay shrimp (and a memorable margarita). High-season amenities include a ski school, racing, day care, rentals, an entire Nordic program with groomed trails, and better-than-average ski food at three day lodges; (800)829-2442.

Other attractions: **Pilot Butte** (just east of town off Hwy 20), a cinder cone with a road to the top, is a good first stop, offering a knockout panorama of Bend and the mountains beyond.

[KIDS] The excellent **High Desert Museum** (4 miles south of Bend on Hwy 97, (541)382-4754) is a nonprofit center for natural and cultural history that includes, among other things, a walk through 100 years of history, featuring excellent dioramas from the time when Native Americans were the main inhabitants of this area, and continuing through the 1890s. Twenty acres of natural trails and outdoor exhibits offer replicas of covered wagons, a sheepherders' camp, and a settlers' cabin. Three river otters and several porcupines inhabit the museum grounds. Open every day from 9am to 5pm.

Newberry National Volcanic Monument encompasses 56,000 acres of geologic attractions. **Lava Lands Visitor Center**, atop a high butte formed by a volcanic fissure, is a lookout point with accompanying geology lessons about the moonlike panorama created by central Oregon's volcanic activity; (541)593-2421. Here you can obtain more information about the **Newberry Crater** and other Newberry attractions. The **Pine Mountain Observatory** (30 miles southeast of Bend on Hwy 20, (541)382-8331) is the University of Oregon's astronomical research facility. One of its three telescopes is the largest in the Northwest.

Twenty-two miles north of Bend in Terrebonne lies **Smith Rock State Park**. Some of the finest rock climbers in the world gather there to test their skills on the red rock cliffs (see Climbing in the Recreation chapter for details). Year-round camping is available; (541)548-7501.

As for eats, Bend has plenty. Attached to an athletic club is **Scanlon's** (61615 Mount Bachelor Dr, off Century Dr, (541)382-8769), where you can get a rock shrimp pizza or a rack of lamb. The half-century-old **Pine Tavern Restaurant** (967 NW Brooks Ave, (541)382-5581) is everybody's perennial favorite for prime rib and other beefy entrees. At the **Broken Top Club** (61999 Broken Top Dr, (541)383-8210), diners are treated to magnificent views, elegant surroundings (in a golf course clubhouse), and stunning food; **Cafe Rosemary** (222 NW Irving, (541)317-0276) offers more urbane surroundings but also fabulous eats. Noteworthy too are the huevos rancheros and homemade muffins at the **Westside Bakery and Cafe** (1005 NW Galveston, (541)382-3426); Bend's own brewpub, the **Deschutes Brewery & Public House** (1044 NW Bond St, (541)382-9242); and, next door to the brewery, **Alpenglow Cafe** (1040 NW Bond St, (541)383-7676), which serves up sublime breakfasts and lunches.

Of the many places to stay, **Sunriver Lodge and Resort** (15 miles south of Bend, (541)593-1000 or (800)547-3922) is the biggest and best known. Sunriver is really more than a resort; it's an organized community with its own post office and 200 or so full-time residents. You can rent everything from rooms and condos to three-bedroom houses. The **Inn at the Seventh Mountain** (18575 S Century Dr, (541)382-8711 or (800)452-6810) is the resort closest to Mount Bachelor, and there's a long roster of activities at the multi-condominium facility, including an 18-hole golf course. At the intimate **Pine Ridge Inn** (1200 SW Century Dr, (541)389-6137 or (800)600-4095), the emphasis is on luxury and privacy. More reasonably priced is Best Western's **Entrada Lodge** (19221 Century Dr, (541)382-4080 or (800)528-1234) if all you need is a sleep and, okay, maybe a soak in a hot tub. The **Lara House Bed and Breakfast** (640 NW Congress St, (541)388-4064), once a run-down boardinghouse in one of Bend's largest and oldest homes (1910), is now a bright and homey six-bedroom inn.

Twenty-two miles northwest of Bend on Highway 20 is **Sisters**, a charming pseudo-cowboy town named after the three mountain peaks that dominate the horizon (Faith, Hope, and Charity). On a clear day (and there are about 250 of them a year), Sisters is exquisitely beautiful, surrounded by mountains, trout streams, and pine and cedar forests. **Santiam Pass**, wedged between two national forests, and the alpine lakes on the west side of **Three Fingered Jack** are two favorite outdoor playgrounds. Several **mountain-biking trails** begin right in town and continue south into Forest Service land; stop by the Sisters Ranger Station for a map or call (541)549-2111. In June, Sisters hosts thousands of visitors for its annual rodeo; the rest of the year, you can check out the very good art galleries and a host of shops that sell mountain gear, fly-fishing equipment, and freshly roasted coffee beans.

▼

Excursions

Central Oregon

▲

The social centerpiece of Sisters is **Hotel Sisters and Bronco Billy's Saloon** (corner of Fir and Cascade Sts, (541)549-RIBS), dishing up Western-style ranch cooking. Pizza fiends opt for utterly fresh from-scratch pizzas at **Papandrea's Pizza** (east of town on the Cascade Hwy, (541)549-6081), the original link in a small chain.

Eight miles west of Sisters, the 1,800-acre, unassumingly spectacular **Black Butte Ranch** (Hwy 20, (541)595-6211) is rimmed by the Three Sisters mountains and scented by a plain of ponderosa pines. The area has limitless, year-round recreation. Nearby, the tiny town known as **Camp Sherman** is one of our favorite spots. Stay in one of the 11 wood-shake cabins with river-facing decks and river-rock fireplaces at the **Metolius River Resort**, (541)595-6281, or at the more private **House on the Metolius**, (541)595-6620, a favorite with fly fishermen.

COLUMBIA RIVER GORGE SCENIC AREA

In 1792 Boston trader Robert Gray and his crew became the first white people to sail on a strip of then-wild water that flowed into the Pacific Ocean. They named it the Columbia, after their ship, and proclaimed it a "noble river." Then, after a week or so, they sailed out to sea without much of a second thought; Gray barely acknowledged his find when he returned to Massachusetts. Historians note that Gray sailed on rather hastily because he didn't find any sea-otter pelts to buy from the native people on the banks of the river. Would he have lingered a bit if he'd sailed the *Columbia Rediviva* as far east as the majestic Columbia River Gorge? This landscape, with its magnificent waterfalls, dramatic cliffs, and rock formations cut by the river, is enough to make anyone stop and stare.

Driving in the gorge (just east of Portland) was at one time not for the queasy, because of the narrow, winding highway. But now most of the traffic is out on I-84, leaving the beautiful old **Historic Columbia River Highway** (aka Highway 30)—an engineering marvel that originally went from Portland to Moser—for the take-your-time wanderers. Portions of the old highway near Bonneville Dam have recently been restored for **hikers and cyclists**; call Friends of the Columbia Gorge, 241-3762, for specifics.

From Portland, taking a drive on the scenic highway is an easy 20-mile trip from Troutdale east (from I-84 take exit 14). If it's after 2pm on Sunday (or dinnertime any other day of the week), you can stop off at **Tad's Chicken 'n' Dumplings** (a mile east of Troutdale on Hwy 30, 666-5337), or visit the McMenamins establishment **Edgefield**, with its multitude of options for eating and drinking (2126 NE Halsey, Troutdale; 669-8610).

Once you're on the scenic highway, popular viewpoints and attractions are numerous: **Crown Point**, 725 feet above the river, features a Cascadian vista house. **Larch Mountain**, 14 miles upriver from Crown Point, is one of the best sunset-watching spots in western Oregon, excluding the summit of Mount Hood. A short trail leads to Sherrard's Point—the summit—a rocky promontory jutting out from the mountaintop. From here there are spectacular 360-degree views of Mount Hood, Mount Adams, Mount St. Helens, Mount Jefferson, the Columbia River Gorge, and all of Portland.

Multnomah Falls ranks second-highest in the country at 620 feet (in two steps). The wood and stone Multnomah Falls Lodge, at the foot of the falls, was designed in 1925 by the notable architect Albert E. Doyle (of Portland's Benson Hotel fame). Now a National Historic Landmark, the lodge houses a naturalists' and visitors center. The large restaurant serves good breakfasts (brunch on Sundays), lunch, and dinner but does not have overnight facilities; 695-2376. **Oneonta Gorge** is a narrow, dramatic cleft through which a slippery half-mile trail winds to secluded Oneonta Falls; this rugged trail, mostly through the actual streambed, is suitable only for the adventurous.

Bonneville Dam, the first federal dam on the Columbia, offers tours of the dam itself, the fish ladders (seen through underwater viewing windows), and the locks; (541)374-8820. You can tour the **Bonneville Fish Hatchery** (next to the dam) all year round, but the best time is September through November, when the chinook are spawning. Be sure also to visit the outdoor pond where the huge sturgeon reside; (541)374-8393. The **Bridge of the Gods**, in the old river town of Cascade Locks, is now steel, but at the site is a fine little museum that recounts the Indian myth about the original, legendary arching-rock bridge that collapsed into the Columbia River long ago. The locks themselves are a site worth seeing; the stonework is beautiful and the scale awesome, accentuated by the small figures of the people who fish off the walls. The **stern-wheeler** *Columbia Gorge* departs three times daily in the summer from the locks marina, stopping at Bonneville Dam and Stevenson Landing; (541)374-8427. (See River Cruises in the Major Attractions section of the Exploring chapter.)

Near the bustling town of **Hood River**, fruit orchards are everywhere. Sunny weather combines with substantial moisture (about 31 inches of rain annually)—perfect for cultivating pears, apples, and plums. It's pastoral indeed, but there's drama, too: 30 miles to the south, 11,235-foot Mount Hood looms, but from the town itself the stunning views are of Washington's 12,326-foot Mount Adams. And then there's the **windsurfing**, which has transformed this once-sleepy town into a kaleidoscope of color.

In summer you can't miss the board sailors dotting the river with their brilliant sails and lending the town a distinctly touristy feel. They've come since the 1980s because of the roaring winds that blow opposite the Columbia River current, making Hood River one of the world's top three windsurfing destinations (Hawaii and Australia are the other two). While Hood River reaps all the sailboard mythology, in fact the waters on the Oregon side of the Columbia are reportedly tame compared to those off the Washington banks, where boardheads claim the wind "really pulls." Hence, the hottest sailors circumvent rocky shores and industrial areas to surf off points on the river's north bank such as Swell City and Doug's Beach. To find them, follow the streams of vans and wagons piled high with boards and masts, tune in to radio station KMCQ-104 for the local wind report, or call (541)386-3300 for a recorded message.

Two fine spectator spots are located right in Hood River. The **Hood River Waterfront Centre Event Site** is a grassy park with a small sandy beach and unrestricted access to the Columbia (from I-84 follow signs). Sailing is somewhat easier at the **Columbia Gorge Sailpark/Port Marina Park**, which features a marina, rental shop, and cafe with enclosed porch. (After all, who wants to *dine* in the wind?) For lessons or for information on wind conditions, sailboard rentals, or launching spots, investigate the multitude of sailboard equipment shops, including **Hood River Windsurfing** (4 Fourth St, (541)386-5787 or (541)386-1423 to set up lessons) and **Big Winds** (505 Cascade, (541)386-6086). **Kerrits** (316 Oak St, (541)386-4187) makes colorful and practical activewear for women (that is, the suit remains on your body when you fall off your board); Kerrits recently added a line of kids' clothing that includes knock-your-socks-off polar fleece. Down the street, **Windwear** (504 Oak St, (541)386-6209), sells probably the most stylish onshore clothing in town, at boutique prices.

As locals strongly attest, there was life in Hood River before the windsurfers arrived. The **Hood River County Museum**, located at Port Marina Park, (541)386-6772, is open April through late October, every day 10am–4pm. The museum exhibits, among other things, Native American artifacts of the region. It adjoins the local **Visitor Information Center**, (800)366-3530 (sometimes closed on winter weekends). In town, you'll find **Waucoma Bookstore** (212 Oak St, (541)386-5353); the **Columbia Art Gallery** (207 Second St, (541)386-4512), which exhibits the work of contemporary local artists; and **Wy'East Natural Foods** (at Fifth and Oak, (541)386-6181), where locals and passers-through alike shop for organic produce and Nancy's yogurt. **Public rest rooms** are located at Second and State Streets, on the ground floor of the city hall. The library park, just up from where Oak intersects with Fifth, sports a great view of both the town and river.

The region's bountiful orchards and beautiful landscape are celebrated during the wonderful small-town **Blossom Festival**, held annually in mid-April (see the Calendar chapter). The **Mount Hood Railroad**, (541)386-3556 or (800)872-4661, makes two- or four-hour round trips—and dinner-train excursions—from the quaint Hood River Depot into the heart of orchard country; call for the schedule. You can buy the fruit of the orchards at **The Fruit Tree** (4140 Westcliff Dr, (541)386-6688), near the Columbia Gorge Hotel; at **River Bend Country Store** (2363 Tucker Rd, (541)386-8766); or at one of the many fruit stands that dot the valley. **Rasmussen Farms** (3020 Thomsen Rd, 1 mile off Hwy 35, (541)386-4622), in addition to selling seasonal fruit, also has a pumpkin patch and U-pick flower fields. For wine tasting, visit **Hood River Vineyards** (4693 Westwood Dr, (541)386-3772), known for its pear and raspberry dessert wines. Beer aficionados head for the **WhiteCap BrewPub** (506 Columbia St, (541)386-2247) for handcrafted Full Sail ales and light meals. The outdoor deck (with live music on weekends) is an apt place for tired board sailors to unwind while keeping the river in sight.

Panorama Point, a half-mile south of Hood River on Highway 35, has the best view of the valley leading to Mount Hood. For another breathtaker, go east on I-84, exit at Mosier, and climb to the **Rowena Crest Viewpoint**, on old Highway 30; the grandstand Columbia River view is complemented by a wildflower show in the **Tom McCall Preserve**, maintained by The Nature Conservancy.

A mile up a gravel road, **Stonehedge Inn** (3405 Cascade Dr, (541)386-3940) is a remote dining hideaway with one dressy,

▼

Excursions

Columbia River Gorge

▲

dark-paneled room, a homey library, a long, enclosed porch with a view, an intimate bar, and superb food. Locals like **The Mesquitery** (1219 12th St, (541)386-2002) for substantial barbecue, and **Chili's Cantina** (113 Third St, (541)387-2457). At **Big City Chicks** (1302 13th St, (541)387-3811), the menu incorporates satays from Thailand, curries from India, Mexican moles, and more. Breakfasting boardheads scarf down the best multigrain pancakes in town at **Purple Rocks Art Bar and Cafe** (606 Oak St, (541)386-6061). **Bette's Place** (416 Oak St, (541)386-1880), a diner-type cafe that's been serving practically the same menu for more than 20 years—bear-claw pastries, patty melts, and banana splits—has been discovered by the out-of-town crowd. Outside the city limits, on the way up to Mount Hood, is **Santacroces' Italian Restaurant** (4780 Hwy 35, (541)354-2511), where the Santacroces bake their own bread, make their own Italian sausage, and serve the best pizza in the valley—all with good humor.

The **Historic Columbia River Highway**, completed in 1920, was crowned a year later by lumber baron Simon Benson's luxury lodging, the **Columbia Gorge Hotel** (4000 Westcliff Dr, (541)386-5566 or (800)345-1921 in Oregon only). It is Hood River's most grand structure, and its dining room is the town's fanciest restaurant. In 1990 the turn-of-the-century **Hood River Hotel** (102 Oak St, (541)386-1900) was restored to its former role as a simple but comfortable country hotel. Eight kitchen suites are available, but for those who don't want to cook, the small dining room serves up reasonably priced meals that are strong on local fruit and fish. The impressive **Lakecliff Estate** (3820 Westcliff Dr, (541)386-7000) is everyone's favorite bed and breakfast, with the same stunning view of the river as the Columbia Gorge Hotel. An inexpensive alternative is the modest **Vagabond Lodge** (4070 Westcliff Dr, (541)386-2992), located next door to the Columbia River Gorge Hotel—ask for a cliffside room.

Twenty minutes east of Hood River is **The Dalles**, a particularly historical stop along this stretch. In the 1840s, the Oregon Trail ended here; goods from wagons were loaded onto barges for the final float to Portland. Later, Fort Dalles was here; an 1850 surgeon's house at the fort is now a museum (15th and Garrison Sts), with exceptional relics from the pioneer trails. Architecturally, the town is much more interesting than others nearby, with nicely maintained examples of colonial, Gothic Revival, Italianate, and American Renaissance styles.

The best way to cap an afternoon of contemplating the past is to picnic at **Sorosis Park**, a large, shady park that is the highest overlook on the scenic drive through the gorge. Or visit **River Front Park**, adjacent to I-84, for river access and tamer sailboarding winds. A stay in the circa-1899 **Williams House Inn** (608 W Sixth St, (541)296-2889), surrounded by a 3-acre arboretum, is a history lesson in itself. The **Baldwin Saloon** (First and

Court Sts, (541)296-5666), built in 1876, has been a steamboat navigational office, warehouse, coffin storage site, and saddle shop; today it's been restored to its original use as a restaurant and bar. It's gorgeous, and the food is great too. The humble-looking **Ole's Supper Club** (2620 W Second St, (541)296-6708), in the industrial west end of The Dalles, prepares an excellent slab of prime rib and has a notable wine list (the bar doubles as a wine shop).

The **Columbia Gorge Discovery Center/Wasco County Historical Society** at Crates Point (5000 Discovery Dr, (541)296-8600) opened in the spring of 1997. Exhibits focus on the life and use, past and present, of this stretch of the Columbia, from how the Native Americans used the river to its current popularity as a windsurfing spot (there's even a board you can ride that simulates surfing the river). The location is stunning and the architecture noteworthy.

LONG BEACH PENINSULA

From Astoria, journey across the Columbia on the 4-mile Astoria-Megler Bridge, the longest continuous truss span in the world, to Washington State. Long Beach Peninsula, with its 28 uninterrupted miles of beach, draws clam diggers by the hundreds. Take note: Oregonians are sometimes put off by the curious driving-on-the-beach sport that is still enjoyed here.

Ilwaco is famed among sport-fishermen for its plentiful **charter fishing** businesses and its treacherous sandbar. Two popular operators, both located at the port docks, are Sea Breeze Charters, (360)642-2300, and Coho Charters, (360)642-3333. Because of intermittent ocean closures for sport-fishing, many charter operators are now offering eco-tours. Phone ahead for information.

The 2,000-acre **Fort Canby State Park** stretches from North Head south to Cape Disappointment at the mouth of the Columbia. Hiking and biking trails thread the park, and there is year-round camping on 250 sites; (360)642-3078 or (800)233-0321. For outrageous views, hike the trail to the North Head lighthouse or the Lewis and Clark Interpretive Center, (360)642-3029, an old gun emplacement clinging to Cape Disappointment, 200 feet above the crashing surf.

In **Seaview**, stop for lunch or dinner at the excellent **Shoalwater**, in the historic Shelburne Inn (Pacific Hwy 103 and N 45th, (360)642-4142), a lovely place for an overnight stay. The Shoalwater's forte is fresh, skillfully prepared seafood, and the menu changes seasonally, following the local catch. Those with time to travel might want to drive the peninsula north to **Oysterville**, now a National Historic District but at one time a thriving boomtown following the discovery of the rich oyster beds of Willapa Bay (follow Sandridge Rd north to the Oysterville sign). Plaques mark the tidy historic homes and the restored Oysterville

Church. Beyond is **Leadbetter Point Natural Area**, where the beaches, woods, and marshes draw hikers and bird-watchers. **The Ark**, on the old Nahcotta Dock, serves fresh oysters and other local seafood (273 Sandridge Rd, (360)665-4133). **Long Island**, a wildlife refuge in Willapa Bay, harbors one of the last old-growth cedar forests in the state. There are oysters to pick and a few superb camping sites on the island, though it can be reached only by boat. Information about the island and a boat ramp are found near the southeastern corner of the island, just off Highway 101.

MOUNT ADAMS AND STEVENSON, WASHINGTON

Mount Adams and the surrounding area are a natural splendor largely overlooked by visitors in favor of the mountain's "big brother," Mount Rainier, to the north and the show-stealing wind-surfers on the Columbia to the south. Similar to Mount Rainier in terrain but smaller (12,276 feet) and much safer, Mount Adams offers good technical (requiring ropes and experience) and non-technical climbs. [KIDS] As long as they are limber and game for whatever weather comes their way, even children should be okay on the easier ascents. Besides climbing to the summit of this massive volcano, hikers and skiers can explore miles of wilderness trails in the **Mount Adams Wilderness Area** and the **Gifford Pinchot National Forest**.

Directions: Take I-84 east from Portland, cross the Columbia River at Hood River, and double back west on Highway 14 just to Highway 141. Turn right and head north to Mount Adams. It's about a two-hour drive from Portland.

Volcanic activity long ago left the area around the mountain honeycombed with caves and lava tubes, including the **Ice Caves** near Trout Lake, with stalactites and stalagmites formed by dripping ice. To the southwest of Trout Lake is the Big Lava Bed, a 12,500-acre lava field filled with cracks, crevasses, rock piles, and unusual formations. Contact the **Mount Adams Ranger Station** in Trout Lake, (509)395-2501, to register for ascents up the mountain and for information on area activities.

In the warm months, this area is a land of abundance: morel mushrooms in the Simcoe Mountains (April through June), wild-flowers in the Bird Creek Meadows (part of the only area of the Yakama Indian Reservation open to the public) in late July, and wild huckleberries—reputedly the best in the state—in and around the Indian Heaven Wilderness (mid-August to mid-September). Guides to flora and fauna—edible and otherwise—as well as free trail guides are for sale at the Mount Adams Ranger Station.

Most people come here to camp, but the cabins and lodge at the **Flying L Ranch** (a half-mile off the Glenwood-Goldendale Road on Flying L Lane, (509)364-3488) make a pleasant place for an overnight stay if you're not up for roughing it. Owners Jeff Berend and Jacqui Perry are as committed to huckleberry pancakes and the ranch newsletter as the previous owners were. From this base you can bicycle the backroads around Glenwood, bird-watch at the **Conboy Lake National Wildlife Refuge**, or ski the 3 miles of groomed trails on the ranch property. When returning, don't take the quickest route back to Portland. Instead, consider driving Highway 14 east to Goldendale, and returning by I-84 west. It's a spectacular loop.

Another gorge attraction on the Washington side of the Columbia River is the impressive **Skamania Lodge** (1131 Skamania Lodge Way, Stevenson; (509)427-7700), about 45 minutes east of Portland. (Take I-84 east to Cascade Locks and cross the Columbia at the Bridge of the Gods.) Skamania was constructed in the early 1990s with the help of a $5 million grant to spur economic development on the Washington side of the river. Built in the style of the old Cascade lodges with big timbers and river rock, it's not meant to be a four-star resort (there's no valet parking, turn-down service, or private decks, and only one pressed log in the fireplace). But the common rooms are grand, the conference center works well, and the setting in the woods overlooking the river is pleasant indeed.

Skamania is a huge hostelry—195 rooms—and the amenities are numerous: bar, restaurant, lap pool, saunas, outdoor hot tub, 18-hole public golf course. The Forest Service's small room in the massive lobby offers maps and info on area recreation, wildflower and geology books, and so on. A day pass ($8.50 for adults, $4.50 for kids) buys you entrance to the pool, hot tub, and workout center without being a hotel guest; anyone can hike the trails. Sunday brunch in the restaurant draws folks from a one-hour radius for a spread that includes fresh crab, smoked salmon, omelets made to order while you watch, and miles of pastries and desserts.

The **Columbia Gorge Interpretive Center**, (509)427-8211, located just below the lodge on Highway 14, displays the history of the gorge via a nine-projector slide show that re-creates the gorge's cataclysmic formation, and includes Native American fishing platforms and a 37-foot-high replica of a 19th-century fishing wheel.

At **Carson Hot Springs**, (509)427-8292, about 15 minutes east of Stevenson, people come to take the waters—mineral baths and massages. The women's side is much more crowded than the men's side, so if your flock is mixed, the men will finish sooner. To avoid this problem, reserve a massage in advance ($40 an hour), and a bath time will be reserved for you as well. There are also rooms at the lodge and cabins to rent—nothing fancy—for inexpensive rates ($30–$50).

The flat-topped Mount St. Helens, about an hour north of Portland and east of I-5, enthralls visitors. On a clear day it is well worth the trip to see the 8,365-foot remains of the volcano, as well as the vegetation that's sprouted since St. Helens' incredible eruption of May 18, 1980 (it's 1,300 feet shorter than before the blast). There are two areas to explore, and each is reached by a different highway. One area is the south and east sides of the volcano, where climbers ascend and where there are caves to brave; and the other is the west side, where a string of visitors centers educate about the blast and the area's regrowth. All visitors must display a **Monument Pass** at developed recreation sites; these passes are $8 per person for three days ($4 for seniors, free for children under 15) and can be purchased at visitors centers and information stations throughout the area.

Mount St. Helens: South and East Sides   Take I-5 north about 25 minutes from Portland and take the Woodland exit. Travel east on Highway 503, but before leaving Woodland, check out the map at the visitors center; the St. Helens area has a confusing range of attractions, and it may help to orient yourself at the beginning of your trip. There are two possibilities for spelunking at the **Ape Caves** on Forest Service Road 8303, an hour from Woodland: the moderately difficult lower cave, which is three-quarters of a mile long, and the more challenging 1½-mile-long upper cave. This lava tube, the longest in the continental United States, was formed 1,900 years ago in a St. Helens blast. Rent lanterns and gather more information at the **Apes Headquarters**, open daily from mid-May until the end of September. For a dramatic view of a vast pumice plain, travel east another hour and 45 minutes to the **Windy Ridge viewpoint**, situated within 4 miles of the volcano.

For information on climbing St. Helens, call the **Climbing Information Line**, (360)247-3961. You'll need a permit (a few are available on a daily basis, but it's best to reserve in advance), and most climbers take one of two trails (Butte Camp or Monitor Ridge) up the south face—more of a rugged hike than real alpine climbing, but an ice ax is still recommended. The all-day climb (8 miles round trip) is ideal for novice alpinists; the only big dangers are some loose-rock cliffs and the unstable edge around the crater. In winter you can ski down.

Mount St. Helens: West Side   Take I-5 north about 40 minutes from Portland, take the Castle Rock exit, and turn east on the recently completed **Spirit Lake Memorial Highway** (Highway 504). Just off the freeway, before you begin the ascent to the ridge, you can see the 25-minute Academy Award–nominated *The Eruption of Mount Saint Helens* projected on the **Cinedome's** three-story-high, 55-foot-wide screen. The rumble alone, which rattles your theater seat, is worth the $5 admission; (360)274-8000. On your way up to the volcano, about 5 miles east

▼

Excursions

Mount St. Helens

▲

of I-5, sits the oldest of the visitors centers in the Mount St. Helens area, the wood-and-glass center at **Silver Lake**; (360)274-2100. Built shortly after the eruption, this center commemorates the blast with excellent exhibits, a walk-through volcano, hundreds of historical and modern photos, geological and anthropological surveys, and a film documenting the area's destruction and rebirth.

The second visitors center, complete with cafe, gift shop, and bookstore, sits atop the windswept **Coldwater Ridge**, 43 miles east of I-5; (360)274-2131. It's a multimillion-dollar facility with a million-dollar view—of the crater just to the west, the debris-filled valley of the Toutle River's North Fork, and new lakes formed by massive mudslides. The speed and heat of the blast, estimated at 600 miles an hour and up to 500 degrees in temperature, scalped at least 150,000 acres surrounding the mountain. The Coldwater Ridge center focuses on the astounding biological recovery of the landscape. From the visitors center, you can descend the short distance to Coldwater Lake—where there is a picnic area and boat launch—or take a guided interpretive walk.

The new **Johnston Ridge Observatory** opened to the public in May 1997 and is located at the end of Spirit Lake Memorial Highway, about 51 miles east of I-5; (360)274-2140 (call in winter to be sure the facility is open). This futuristic-looking structure, within 5 miles of the crater, offers the best views yet of the steaming lava dome inside the crater—unless, of course, you climb the volcano (see Mount St. Helens: South and East Sides for climbing details).

Excursions

Mount St. Helens

Two visitors centers can be visited without the Monument Pass: Cowlitz County's **Hoffstadt Bluff** center (milepost 27 on Spirit Lake Memorial Highway; (360)274-7750), which explores the lives and deaths of those most directly affected by the blast, and Weyerhaeuser's **Forest Learning Center** (at milepost 33.5; (360)414-3429), which focuses on the land's recovery in the wake of the eruption.

Every gift store along the way offers something of interest besides tourist trinkets: the family who owns **19 Mile House** in Kid Valley, (360)274-8779, serves some of the best fruit cobblers you'll ever eat. Around the corner you'll get a look at Blair Barner's **mud-filled A-frame**; he calls his business—a souvenir shop and helicopter rides—North Fork Survivors, (360)274-6789. No fancy hotels yet, but Mark Smith's **"tent and breakfast"** in the blowdown area is a real kick, and we give it four stars—as will families looking for fun lodgings. You sleep in roomy Beckel wall tents, with a chuck-wagon dinner and breakfast beside the lake ($125 per person; Mount St. Helens Adventure Tours, (360)274-6542). Smith provides fishing gear, cedar-strip canoes, fishing permits, van tours, cross-country ski trips, and guided hunting trips. The friendly proprietors at **Volcano View Mountain Bike Tours**, (360)274-4341, will outfit you with a bike and take you on a tour of some of the lesser-traveled areas around St. Helens—lunch included.

NATIVE AMERICAN HISTORY

When explorers Meriwether Lewis and William Clark pushed through to the mouth of the Columbia River at present-day Astoria in 1805, the greater Willamette Valley and the Columbia Gorge area were home to dozens of Native American tribes. These days it might seem easier to find the location of a particular tribe's gambling casino than to locate a place to learn about its cultural heritage, but there actually are a number of excellent museums and cultural sites focusing on Native American history within a day's trip from Portland.

About a two-hour drive from Portland over the scenic Mount Hood Highway, the award-winning **Museum at Warm Springs** (Hwy 26 at Warm Springs, (541)553-3331) was built by three tribes (Wasco, Paiute, and Warm Springs) and is located on the Warm Springs Reservation. The museum introduces visitors to the tribes of the Columbia River Gorge through stunning beadwork, songs, stories, and historical and contemporary exhibits. Stay overnight at **Kah-Nee-Ta Resort**, (541)553-1112, which is owned by the Confederated Tribes of Warm Springs and sits on Highway 3, off Highway 26 in the Warm Springs River canyon. Among Kah-Nee-Ta's charms are its spring-fed swimming pools, fine restaurant, spa, and golf course.

Head north the next day to the Columbia River on Highway 97. Cross the Columbia at Bigg's Junction and travel up the hill to the **Maryhill Museum of Art** (35 Maryhill Museum Dr, Goldendale, WA; (509)773-3733) to see the fine collection of Klickitat and Wasco baskets. (See Maryhill Museum of Art in the Day Trips section of this chapter.) You might continue on Highway 97 an hour north, past Mount Adams (the Yakama tribe's sacred mountain, Pahto, returned to them by President Nixon), to the **Yakama Nation Cultural Heritage Center** (280 Buster Rd, Toppenish, WA; (509)865-2800). Another option is to head two hours east to the spectacular **Tamustalik Cultural Institute** (on the Umatilla Indian Reservation, just east of Pendleton, off I-84 on Hwy 331; (541)966-9748). This museum tells the story of the Oregon Trail migrations from the perspective of the resident Cayuse, Nez Perce, and Walla Walla Indians. A popular "trail trash" exhibit shows belongings dumped off the wagons by weary pioneers.

On the return to Portland via I-84, you'll want to stop at the **Columbia Gorge Discovery Center at Crate's Point** (just west of The Dalles—watch for signs; (541)296-8600). For centuries, the area around The Dalles was a major Native American trade center. In the early 1800s, it was home to Hudson's Bay Company trappers, and later the area served as a pioneer staging ground for the last leg of the Oregon Trail. The best exhibit is a

33-foot working model of the Columbia River that removes the current dams to expose Celilo Falls, an immense basalt chasm of roaring waterfalls and the traditional fishing grounds of the Columbia River tribes.

Indian commerce and wealth were already well established when the Hudson's Bay Company built its Northwest trading headquarters on the Columbia River at **Fort Vancouver**. At the **Fort Vancouver National Historic Site** (10 minutes north of Portland off I-5; 1501 E Evergreen Blvd, Vancouver, WA; (360)696-7655), visitors can see the stockade and tour five major restored buildings: an Indian trade shop stocked with replicas of trade goods, the chief factor's residence and kitchen, a blacksmith shop, a bakery, and a shipping warehouse filled with furs. There's also a period vegetable and flower garden. (See also Vancouver, Washington, in the Day Trips section of this chapter.)

Multnomah County is named for the tribe that once occupied this area; explorers Lewis and Clark reported sighting Chinook villages all along the Columbia River from the gorge to the Pacific Ocean. You won't find much information about the Chinooks in Portland, although **Powell's City of Books** (1005 W Burnside, 228-4651) offers more than 5,000 new and used books by and about Native Americans, and the **Oregon History Center** (1200 SW Park Ave, 222-1741) has collections of basketry, beadwork, leatherwork, and stone representing Northwest tribes, as well as more than 1,000 photographic images of Indians in its library.

Farther afield, near the mouth of the Columbia River outside Astoria, is **Fort Clatsop National Memorial** (follow the well-marked signs from Hwy 101 at Warrenton; (503)861-2471), where Lewis and Clark's bacon was saved one cold winter by the Clatsop band of Chinooks.

Most Northwest tribes lost their land and economic strength to the newcomers. Today they're gaining it back through casinos, whose revenues help fund interpretive centers, traditional and contemporary art, and other tribal enterprises. Two of the largest casinos are near the Oregon Coast—**Spirit Mountain** at Grand Ronde, (800)760-7977, and **Chinook Winds** at Lincoln City, (800)863-3314—and both offer big-name entertainment. For information on current Native American tours, powwows, rodeos, and other events, or for maps and brochures, contact the Portland office of the **Affiliated Tribes of Northwest Indians** (222 NW Davis St, Suite 403, (503)241-0070).

OREGON COAST: ASTORIA

The oldest U.S. settlement west of the Rockies, **Astoria** today is an unpretentious coastal town of about 10,000 people—a stop for oceangoing freighters and a home port for commercial fishing boats. The town has come into its own as a tourist destination that boasts a wealth of history, Victorian architecture, and natural beauty. **Sixth Street River Park**, with its always-open, covered observation tower, provides the best vantage point for viewing river commerce, observing bar and river pilots as they board tankers and freighters, and watching seals and sea lions search for a free lunch. Downtown, there are art galleries tucked in next to the fishermen's bars and mom-and-pop cafes, and a few notable restaurants as well. Bed and breakfasts have proliferated, particularly in the lovely Victorian homes on the steep hillsides overlooking the river. Other Victorian houses are, one by one, undergoing restoration.

The history of U.S. exploration and settlement here begins with Captain Robert Gray, who sailed up the river in 1792, naming it after his ship, the *Columbia Rediviva*. In 1805–06, Lewis and Clark spent a miserably rainy winter at the now-restored **Fort Clatsop National Memorial** (6 miles southwest of Astoria, (503)861-2471). Besides audiovisuals and exhibits in the visitors center, there are living history demonstrations (musket firing, candle-making) during the summer.

[FREE] Five years later, in 1910, New York fur trader John Jacob Astor, one of America's wealthiest individuals, sent to the Northwest the fur-trading company that founded **Fort Astoria**. The fort had all but disappeared by the mid-19th century but now has been partially reconstructed (at 15th and Exchange Sts).

The city of Astoria really dates back to the late 1840s, when it began to thrive as a customhouse town and shipping center. The well-maintained Victorians lining the harbor hillside at Franklin and Grand Avenues provide glimpses of that era. Now Astoria is a museum without walls, an unstirred mix of the old and new that finds common ground along the busy waterfront—once the site of canneries and river steamers, now an active port for ocean-going vessels and Russian fish-processing ships. Salmon and bottom-fishing trips leave from here.

[FREE] The first stop for most visitors is the **Astoria Column**, atop Coxcomb Hill, Astoria's highest point. The climb to the top is 164 steps but is well worth it: from there you have an endless view of the harbor, the Columbia estuary, and the distant head-lands of the Pacific. Spiral murals of the region's history wrap around the column. To get there, drive up to the top of 16th Street and follow the signs.

[KIDS] **The Columbia River Maritime Museum** (on the waterfront at the foot of 17th St, (503)325-2323) is the finest museum of its type in the Northwest. The 1951 Coast Guard *Lightship Columbia* is moored outside, and inside are restored small craft and thematic galleries depicting the Northwest's mar-itime heritage: fishing and whaling, fur trading, navigation, and shipwrecks. Admission is $5 for adults, $2 for children.

Two other museums devoted to Astoria's history are operated by the Clatsop County Historical Society. One is the **Clatsop County Heritage Museum** (16th and Exchange Sts, (503)325-

2203) in the 1904 city hall building. The **Flavel House** (Eighth and Duane Sts, (503)325-2563) is the city's best example of ornate Queen Anne architecture, built by the Columbia River's first steamship pilot, Captain George Flavel.

Astoria's intelligentsia frequent **Ricciardi Gallery** (108 10th St, (503)325-5450), which offers pleasing regional art and espresso. **Parnassus Books** (234 10th St, (503)325-1363) is a good browse, and **Persona Vintage Clothing** (100 10th St, (503)325-3837), with its high-quality merchandise, is a special treat. **Josephson's Smokehouse** (106 Marine Dr, (503)325-2190) prepares superb alder-smoked salmon, tuna, and sturgeon. Buy fresh seafood at **Fergus-McBarendse** (at the foot of 11th St, (503)325-0688). **Lagniappe Cafe** (817 Exchange St, (503)325-5181) affords a lovely garden setting for sipping espresso or munching baked goods. Doughy, chewy orbs rivaling the big-city's best can be had at **Ben's Blest Bagels** (1448 Commercial St, (503)325-9144).

The best meals in town—fresh and vegetarian-oriented, but with plenty of seafood—can be found at the **Columbian Cafe** (11th St and Marine Dr, (503)325-2233), which feels less cramped since its renovation. At **Ira's** (on Commercial St between 9th and 10th, (503)338-6192), bagel sandwiches, salmon-and-pepper pastas, and 10-green salads dressed with feta, walnuts, and sun-dried tomato vinaigrette are excellent noon options. The place to go for Sunday brunch is the **Cannery Cafe** (at the foot of Sixth St, (503)325-8642), which sits on pilings right over the water. **The Rio Cafe** offers inspired south-of-the-border cuisine (125 Ninth St, (503)325-2409).

Bed-and-breakfast inns are plentiful in Astoria. Two blocks from downtown is the stylish **Franklin Street Station** (1140 Franklin Ave, (503)325-4314), but better situated and with its own terraced garden is the elegant **Columbia River Inn** (1681 Franklin Ave, (503)325-5044). The reasonably priced and rambling **Rosebriar Inn** (636 14th St; (503)325-7427) has 11 rooms, each with a private bath.

Astoria is a natural starting point for excursions to the Oregon and Washington coasts. Panoramic ocean views can be had from the **South Jetty lookout tower**, Oregon's northwesternmost point. **Fort Stevens State Park**, 20 minutes southwest of Astoria on Highway 101, is a 3,500-acre park offering 604 campsites, 7 miles of bike paths, uncrowded beaches, and **yurts** (rigid-walled, domed tents) for rent. (The yurts in Oregon state parks have light, heat, and sleep space for eight people. For reservations and information, call Reservations Northwest; (800)452-5687). Walk the beach to see the rusted hulk of the British schooner *Peter Iredale*, wrecked in 1906. Fort Stevens, built at the mouth of the Columbia during the Civil War as part of Oregon's coastal defense, was fired upon in June 1942 by a

Japanese submarine. It was the only military fort in the continental United States to see action during the war.

OREGON COAST: GEARHART AND SEASIDE

To many Portlanders, the Oregon Coast in summertime connotes two things: majestic beauty and throngs of tourists. Older beachgoers may still remember when you could leave the city on the spur of the moment on Friday afternoon, drive to the coast, and rent an oceanfront cabin for the weekend. Those times are history. Campgrounds are often full in the summer, and many lodgings are booked weeks (sometimes months) in advance. But that's not the case everywhere, and determined city dwellers don't forgo the beach just because parts of it are jammed. Although many towns along the coastline are mobbed at least part of the year, some of the shoreline—known for its foggy, wild beaches (virtually all are public), jagged promontories, and abundant marine life—remains essentially untouched; it just takes a little exploring to find the less traveled spots. And the true Northwesterner knows just how spectacular the beach is on a stormy winter day.

One hundred years ago, affluent Portland beachgoers rode Columbia River steamers to Astoria and then hopped a stagecoach to Seaside, the Oregon Coast's first resort town. As the place became more crowded, fashionable Portlanders began to build their summer cottages (some of them substantial dwellings) a bit to the north, in **Gearhart**, which to this day is mostly residential. The wide beach is backed by lovely dunes, and razor-clam digging is popular here—the gas stations along Highway 101 even rent shovels. **Gearhart Golf Course**, which opened in 1892, is the second-oldest course in the West—a 6,089-yard layout with sandy soil that dries quickly; open to the public, (503)738-3538. The **Gearhart Ocean Inn** (67 N Cottage, (503)738-7373) evokes the charm of yesteryear—and has some good off-season lodging deals besides. Stop for a sandwich or a slice of out-of-this-world cheesecake at the airy **Pacific Way Bakery and Cafe** (601 Pacific Way, (503)738-0245).

In **Seaside**, resort hotels, shops, and tourist amenities of all sorts abound. Visitors mill along Broadway, eyeing the entertainment parlors, the taffy concession, and the bumper cars, and then emerge at the **Prom**, the 2-mile-long cement "boardwalk" that's ideal for strolling. There's something about the beach that gives visitors a hankering for clam chowder or a quick seafood dinner. Many quell their hunger at **Dooger's Seafood and Grill** (505 Broadway, (503)738-3773) or **Breakers** (414 N Prom, (503)738-3334), half hidden inside the Ocean View Resort.

Surf fishing is popular here, particularly at the south end of town in the cove area (also frequented by surfers). Steelhead and salmon are taken only from the Necanicum River, which flows through town. The trailhead for the **6-mile hike** over Tillamook

Head is at the end of Sunset Boulevard, at the town's south end. The spectacular and rugged trail ends at Indian Beach in Ecola State Park, just to the north of Cannon Beach (see next listing).

As for a place to rest your head, here are a few of the many options: **Anderson's Boarding House** (208 N Holladay Dr, (503)738-9055), a bed and breakfast that, with its fir tongue-and-groove walls and beamed ceilings, retains a very beachy feel; **Beachwood Bed and Breakfast** (671 Beach Dr, (503)738-9585), an adults-only lodging one block from the beach; and the upbeat and stylish—if exorbitantly priced—**Shilo Inn** (30 N Prom, (503)738-9571).

OREGON COAST: CANNON BEACH TO GARIBALDI

Cannon Beach relishes its reputation as the Carmel of the Northwest. This artsy community with a hip ambience has strict building codes that prohibit neon and ensure that only aesthetically pleasing structures of weathered cedar and other woods are built. During the summer the town explodes with visitors who come to browse local galleries and crafts shops or rub shoulders with the coastal intelligentsia on crowded Hemlock Street. Its main draw is the spectacular beach—wide, inviting, and among the prettiest anywhere. Dominating the long, sandy stretch is **Haystack Rock**, one of the world's largest coastal monoliths. It's impressive enough just to gaze at, but check it out at low tide to observe the rich marine life in the tidal pools.

Ecola State Park (on the town's north side) has fine overlooks, picnic tables, and good hiking trails. If you climb to Tillamook Head, you can see the Tillamook Rock Light Station, a lighthouse built offshore under difficult conditions more than 100 years ago and abandoned in 1957. Today it is a columbarium (a facility for storing cremated remains) called "Eternity at Sea." No camping along the trail, except for summer campsites atop the Head.

Shopping is a favorite pastime in Cannon Beach, and there are enough stores along Hemlock Street, the main drag, to keep you busy until the tide goes out. **Galleries** are also numerous on N Hemlock: especially good ones are **White Bird**, featuring a variety of arts and crafts, (503)436-2681; **Haystack Gallery**, with prints and photographs, (503)436-2547; and **Jeffrey Hull Watercolors**, in Sandpiper Square, (503)436-2600. **Greaver Gallery** (on S Hemlock, (503)436-1185) has beachy paintings and prints.

The **Coaster Theater** (108 N Hemlock St, (503)436-1242) presents good summer plays, as well as local and out-of-town shows in the winter. Also, the **Haystack Program in the Arts** (in Portland, 725-8500), offered through Portland State University, conducts arts workshops for adult students at the Cannon Beach grade school.

There are several good restaurants in town. Reserve for dinner at the **Cafe de la Mer** (1287 S Hemlock St, (503)436-1179),

Excursions

Oregon Coast: Cannon Beach to Garibaldi

a longtime favorite. Another chic dinner spot is **The Bistro** (263 N Hemlock St, (503)436-2661). Everyone in town seems to gather for breakfast at the **Lazy Susan Cafe** (126 N Hemlock St, (503)436-2816)—unless they've stopped in for a frittata at our favorite, the **Midtown Cafe** (1235 S Hemlock, (503)436-1016).

There is a confusing array of lodging options in Cannon Beach, but two can't-miss choices are the **Argonauta Inn** (188 W Second, (503)436-2601) and the **Cannon Beach Hotel** (116 S Hemlock, (503)436-1392).

Tolovana Park, nestled on Cannon Beach's south side, is more laid-back and less crowded than its neighbor. Leave your vehicle at the Tolovana Park Wayside (with parking and rest rooms) and stroll the uncluttered beach. At low tide you can walk all the way to Arch Cape, some 5 miles south, but take care: the incoming tide might block your return. Eat a breakfast burrito at the **Homegrown Cafe** (3301 S Hemlock St; (503)436-1803). The tidy and cute oceanfront **Sea Sprite Guest Lodging** (280 Nebesna St, (503)436-2266) has five units. More extravagant is the **Stephanie Inn** (2740 S Pacific, (503)436-2221), a gorgeous, elegant 46-room hotel.

▼

Excursions

━━━━━━━━━━

*Oregon
Coast:
Cannon
Beach to
Garibaldi*

▲

Just south of here is **Oswald West State Park**, with one of the finest campgrounds on any coast in the world. You walk a half-mile from the parking lot (where wheelbarrows are available to carry your gear) to tent sites among old-growth trees; the ocean, with a massive cove and tide pools, is just beyond. No reservations, but the walk deters some of the crowds who might otherwise come.

Low-key **Manzanita** is gaining popularity as a second home for in-the-know Portlanders. The attractions are obvious: the adjacent Nehalem Bay area is a windsurfing mecca; **Nehalem Bay State Park**, just south of town, offers hiking and bike trails as well as miles of little-used beaches; and overlooking it all is nearby **Neahkahnie Mountain**, with a steep, switchbacked trail leading to the 1,600-foot summit, boasting the best viewpoints on Oregon's north coast. Hundreds of miles of Coast Range logging roads offer unlimited mountain-biking thrills. Yurts are available for rent in the park (see the Oregon Coast: Astoria section, above, for information on this lodging option).

A block and a half off the beach, the **Blue Sky Cafe** (154 Laneda Ave, (503)368-5712) has a menu that is far-flung and ambitious—and lacks any pretention. A tad more formal but equally intriguing is **Jarboe's** (137 Laneda Ave, (503)368-5113). The best pizza on the north coast can be had at **Cassandra's** (60 Laneda Ave, (503)368-5593). For a pampered, adults-only retreat, try the **Inn at Manzanita** (67 Laneda Ave, (503)368-6754).

Rockaway Beach offers little in the way of quaintness, but the beach is splendid, especially at the **Twin Rocks** area south of town.

Several establishments in **Garibaldi** sell the area's freshest seafood. **Miller Seafood**, (503)322-0355, on Highway 101, is the easiest to find; salmon, lingcod, and bottom fish are featured. **Smith's Pacific Shrimp Co.**, (503)322-3316, sells fine shrimp and has viewing rooms at 608 Commercial Drive. And in nearby **Bay City**, **ArtSpace** (Hwy 101 and Fifth, (503)377-2782) is a gallery and bistro where oysters are always artistically rendered; or you can make a quick stop at **Downie's Cafe** (9320 Fifth St, (503)377-2220) for a rich, chunks-o'-clam chowder.

OREGON COAST: TILLAMOOK TO NESKOWIN

Tillamook is dairy country par excellence. On the north end of town along Highway 101 sits the home of Tillamook cheese, the **Tillamook County Creamery Association**; (503)842-4481. Loads of tourists come for the self-guided tour, but frankly, there's not that much to see. Instead, go about 1 mile south on 101 to the **Blue Heron French Cheese Company** (2001 Blue Heron Dr, (503)842-8281)—it's less kitschy and better stocked. Blue Heron offers a variety of cheeses and other Oregon-made specialty foods that visitors can sample, as well as a wine-tasting room.

The **Pioneer Museum** (Second St and Pacific Ave, (503)842-4553) occupies three floors of the 1905 county courthouse in Tillamook. Shipwreck buffs will be particularly interested in the artifacts (including huge chunks of beeswax with Spanish markings) from an unnamed 18th-century Spanish galleon that wrecked near the base of Neahkahnie Mountain. Adult admission is $2.

Traveling south from Tillamook, you have a choice. One option is to stick close to the water, following the 22-mile **Three Capes Scenic Drive**, arguably Oregon's most beautiful stretch of coastline. The narrow, winding road skirts Tillamook Bay, climbs over **Cape Meares**, traverses the shores of Netarts Bay, and runs over **Cape Lookout**, the westernmost headland on the north Oregon coast. The trail from the parking lot at the cape's summit meanders through primeval forests of stately cedar and Sitka spruce. The lower side of the drive provides spectacular ocean vistas. Down at sea level, the desertlike dune landscape presents a stark contrast to Cape Lookout's densely forested slopes. The road to **Pacific City** and the route's third cape, **Cape Kiwanda**, runs through lush, green dairy country. All have excellent camping facilities, and Cape Lookout has yurts as well (see the Oregon Coast: Astoria section, above, for information).

You'll pass through two towns on this route: the first is **Oceanside**. In the evening, slip into **Roseanna's Oceanside Cafe** (1490 Pacific St, (503)842-7351) for an outstanding wedge of Toll House pie topped with Tillamook ice cream, then roll into one of the 17 rooms at the **House on the Hill** (1816 Maxwell Mountain Rd, on Maxwell Point, (503)842-6030).

About 20 miles south of Oceanside, the dory fleet comes home to **Pacific City**, where salmon-fishing boats are launched from trailers in the south lee of Cape Kiwanda. This town is also known for another kind of fleet: hang gliders that swoop off the slopes of the cape and land on the sandy expanses below. The region's second Haystack Rock (Cannon Beach has the other) sits a half-mile offshore. Even if you've never visited before, this area may look familiar: the late Ray Atkeson, a nationally acclaimed Oregon photographer, made Cape Kiwanda the most photographed spot on the Oregon Coast. **Robert Straub State Park**, worth visiting, sits at the south end of town and occupies most of the Nestucca Beach sand spit. The Nestucca River flows idly to the sea right outside the **Riverhouse Restaurant** (34450 Brooten Rd, (503)965-6722), a calming, apple-pie sort of place. Gargantuan cinnamon rolls and loaves of crusty bread can be had nearby at the **Grateful Bread Bakery** (34805 Brooten Rd, (503)965-7337). At the secluded **Eagle's View Bed and Breakfast** (37975 Brooten Rd, (503)965-7600), all five guest rooms have private baths. As you might guess, the panoramas are grand.

If you decide to forgo the Three Capes Scenic Drive, Highway 101 will steer you from Tillamook through Nestucca dairy land, some of the most fertile in the state. Nestled in the heart of the Nestucca River valley is **Cloverdale**, the town that became famous for a 1986–87 battle with state officials over two roadside signs (featuring Clover the Cow) that violated a state signage law. Outside Cloverdale, in the middle of nowhere, is the historic 1906 **Hudson House Bed & Breakfast** (37700 Hwy 101 S, (503)392-3533). Just south, in the diminutive town of **Neskowin** (the final port of refuge before the touristy 20-mile stretch from Lincoln City to Newport), stands **The Chelan**, (503)392-3270, attractive, substantial, cream-colored adobe condominiums right on the beach.

Otis is barely more than a junction, but the busy **Otis Cafe**, (503)994-2813, and its down-home breakfasts, shakes, and house-made pies—good enough to have been touted in the *New York Times*—have put this tiny town on the map.

OREGON COAST: LINCOLN CITY TO CAPE FOULWEATHER

Hordes from the Willamette Valley converge in **Lincoln City** year-round—for a lot of different reasons. Whale watchers appreciate the nearby viewpoints, shoppers hunt for bargains at the huge outlet mall on the east side of 101, and others simply pass through before dispersing to quieter points north and south (though these days they have a bit of driving to do; there's congestion all the way south to Newport, especially during the summer).

Unfortunately, this strip town offers little in the way of outstanding lodgings, although the restaurant scene is ever-improving. Consistently the finest place to dine is **Bay House**

(5911 SW Hwy 101, (541)996-3222), where the food, like the view, is worth savoring. Locals stand in line rain or shine for half-pound burgers from **Dory Cove** (5819 Logan Rd, 1 mile off Hwy 101, (541)994-5180), and at the hip **Chameleon Cafe** (2145 NW Hwy 101, (541)994-8422), where you can go Mexican or Mediterranean—depending on your mood. Part deli, part bistro, the **Salmon River Cafe** (40798 NW Logan Rd, (541)996-3663) features three inspired meals a day. At the **Lighthouse Brew Pub** (4157 N Hwy 101, (541)994-7238), expect the same pub grub as at any McMenamins establishment—and beer made on the premises. Two good stops are **Barnacle Bill's Seafood Market** (2174 NE Hwy 101, (541)994-3022), famous for smoked fish—salmon, sturgeon, albacore, and black cod—and fresh seafood, and **Catch the Wind Kite Shop** (266 SE Hwy 101, (541)994-9500), the headquarters for a coastal chain of excellent kite stores. **Inlet Garden Oceanview Bed and Breakfast** (646 NW Inlet, (541)994-7932) is a good alternative to the glitzy motel scene prevalent in Lincoln City.

Gleneden Beach is home to the innovative restaurant **Chez Jeannette** (7150 Old Hwy 101, (541)764-3434), where flower boxes decorate the windows and whitewashed brick walls lend a French country inn ambience. The buildings at **Salishan Lodge** (Hwy 101, (800)452-2300)—perhaps the coast's best-known resort—blend well with natural landscaping that lessens the visual impact on the hillside. The beach, a half-mile away, is a splendid strand of driftwood and gulls. A standard of excellence is adhered to throughout the resort.

Excursions

*Oregon
Coast:
Lincoln City
to Cape
Foulweather*

Once a charming coastal community, **Depoe Bay** today is mostly an extension of Lincoln City's strip development. Driving south down Highway 101, it's hard to tell where one community ends and the other begins. Fortunately, some of the original Depoe Bay, including its tiny harbor, remains intact. During the **gray-whale migratory season** (December through April), the leviathans cruise within hailing distance of the headlands. In the week between Christmas and New Year's, and then again during Oregon schools' spring break, knowledgeable volunteers from the Hatfield Marine Science Center in Newport (see next listing) staff 23 **viewing sites** along the coast, answering whale-related questions and sharing binoculars. To get closer to the action, consider a **whale-watching cruise**; Deep Sea Trollers, (541)765-2248, is one of several operations offering trips each day. Another place to watch whales is from your nicely appointed room at the **Channel House** (35 Ellingson St, (800)447-2140), a small, neat inn perched right on the rocks. Breakfast is included with your room, but for lunch or dinner, you'll want to check out **Tidal Raves** (279 NW Hwy 101, (541)765-2995), a cliffside restaurant that serves imaginatively prepared seafood.

Cape Foulweather, christened by famed British explorer Captain James Cook when he sailed by in 1778, is aptly named:

fog often enshrouds it, even though sunny skies may appear just to the north and south. Reach the cape by the Otter Crest Loop, 2 miles south of Depoe Bay. It has an inspiring viewpoint for watching birds, sea lions, and surf. Adjoining it is the **Lookout Gift Shop and Observatory**, a rarity: its gifts are carefully selected items from craftspeople around the world; (541)765-2270. On the Otter Crest Loop, in a 100-acre parklike setting, is the **Inn at Otter Crest**, (541)765-2111, with exquisite, lush landscaping (including marine tidal gardens) and adequate condominium resort facilities.

OREGON COAST: NEWPORT TO WALDPORT

[KIDS] The most popular tourist destination on the Oregon Coast, **Newport**, has Keiko fever—and it's a year-round malady. And it's catching. You'll want to see the beloved orca (star of the *Free Willy* movies) and the other treasures at the **Oregon Coast Aquarium** (2820 SE Ferry Slip Rd, (503)867-3474), a world-class facility that showcases plants and animals of the Oregon Coast. The 29-acre site boasts a walk-through aviary, a sea-otter pool, a wetlands area, and a continuously playing whale film.

[FREE] Nearby, the newly refurbished **Hatfield Marine Science Center** (2030 S Marine Science Dr, (541)867-0100) features a replica of a tide pool, educational programs, and a full range of free nature walks, field trips, and films, especially during the summer Seatauqua program.

Newport itself tends to sprawl. Veer off Highway 101's commercial strip and seek out **the bay front**, where fishing boats of all types—trollers, trawlers, shrimpers, and crabbers—berth year-round. Nearby, take a drive out on the **South Jetty Road** for sea-level views of harbor traffic. A walk through the congenial Nye Beach area offers glimpses of the old and new in Newport, a potpourri of Newport's professionals, tourists, writers, and fishermen.

The **Newport Performing Arts Center** (777 S Olive, (541)265-ARTS) is an attractive wooden structure that hosts music, theater, and other events, some of national caliber. The **Visual Arts Center** (839 NW Beach, (541)265-5133) offers an oceanfront setting for exhibits and classes. For a bird's-eye perspective of boats, bay, and ocean, take a drive through **Yaquina Bay State Park**, which wraps around the south end of town. Marine Discovery Tours, (541)265-6200, has a privately owned 48-passenger vessel that operates as a floating classroom. You can sign up for **eco-tours** that vary from scouting oyster beds to marine bird-watching and ocean exploration.

Newport offers two very different options for entertainment: **art galleries** and **fishing charters**. Worthwhile galleries on SW Bay Boulevard along the waterfront include the **Oceanic Arts Center** (444 SW Bay Blvd, (541)265-5963) and the **Wood Gallery** (818 SW Bay Blvd, (541)265-6843). The former offers mostly jewelry, paintings, pottery, and sculpture; the latter, functional sculpture, woodwork, pottery, and weaving. Most fishing charters provide bait and tackle, clean and fillet your catch, and even smoke or can it for you. Many operators have initiated **whale-watching excursions** as well as half- and full-day fishing trips. Sea Gull Charters (343 SW Bay Blvd, (541)265-7441) and Newport Sport Fishing (1000 SE Bay Blvd, (541)265-7558 or (800)828-8777) are two popular operators.

On a sunny day in town, request an outdoor table overlooking the bay at the **Canyon Way Bookstore and Restaurant** (1216 SW Canyon Way, (541)265-8319). Another longtime favorite is **The Whale's Tale** (452 SW Bay Blvd, (541)265-8660), where you can try a fresh jalapeño omelet or a plate of Jaquina oysters.

Even though there are a number of places to stay in Newport, you won't want to drop into town without a reservation. The first bed and breakfast in Lincoln County was the comfortable **Ocean House** (4920 NW Woody Way, (541)265-6158) at Agate Beach; its recent remodel made it roomier but less quaint. For maximum quaintness, check out the **Sylvia Beach Hotel** (267 NW Cliff St, (541)265-5428), an 85-year-old hotel that currently enjoys what must be its happiest and most imaginative incarnation: each room is decorated to commemorate a different author. Book lovers also appreciate the Sylvia Beach's bluff-top location and delicious breakfast. Next door, the newer **Nye Beach Hotel & Cafe** (219 NW Cliff St; (541)265-3334) has 18 tidy guest rooms that each feature private bath, fireplace, willow loveseat, balcony, and ocean view.

South of Newport is **Seal Rock**, not much more than a patch of strip development along Highway 101. Within that patch though, is **Yuzen** (8 miles south of Newport on Hwy 101; (541)563-4766), a Japanese restaurant residing in a Bavarian-style building, which offers the Oregon Coast's finest Japanese cuisine.

Farther south yet, at the estuary of the Alsea River, sits **Waldport**, a small, untrammeled town that offers visitors one small museum and one expansive, beautiful bridge. At the south end of the Alsea Bay Bridge (rebuilt in 1991) is an interpretive center with historic transportation displays. Waldport's bay is a good place for clamming and crabbing; equipment (including boats) can be rented at the **Dock of the Bay Marina** (1245 Mill, (541)563-2003) in the Old Town section, on the water just east of the highway. The remote, pocket-size **Drift Creek Wilderness** is tucked into the Coast Range halfway between Seal Rock and Waldport. Visit the Waldport Ranger District office (south of town off Hwy 101, (541)563-3211) for maps and information.

The three lodging options we like best in the Waldport area seem to offer something for every guest. South of town, the **Cape Cod Cottages** (4150 SW Pacific Coast Hwy, (541)563-2106) occupy 300 feet of ocean frontage with easy beach access. The larger units sleep as many as eight; kids love it here. At the

Cliff House Bed and Breakfast (1450 Adahi Rd, (541)563-2506) are four ultra-posh (and expensive) rooms that feature antique furnishings, chandeliers, color TVs, water views, and balcony overlooks. Finally, the owners of the **Edgewater Cottages** (3978 SW Pacific Coast Hwy, (541)563-2240) live there, maintaining a homey feeling among their nine units, which are a favorite of honeymooners.

RECREATION

Recreation

ACTIVE SPORTS

Metropolitan U-Haul companies are a good measure of a city's quality of life. It isn't surprising that the cost of renting a one-way U-Haul to Portland is a lot higher than the cost of renting one to leave. The lines at the grocery stores, banks, traffic signals, and hip clubs hint at the city's bulging seams. Thankfully, most people still smile as they wait—and even yield the right of way at stop signs. Perhaps it's the melding of alpine and ocean wind currents with a bit of wine country air blowing in that keeps us happy to be here; more likely, it's because the growth in population has not led to a compromise in recreation. Who cares if you have to wait in a post office line, when you can still set out for a day of hiking, birding, kayaking, golfing, fishing, or bicycling and not see another soul for hours?

Outdoor Recreation, published three times a year by Portland Parks and Recreation (1120 SW Fifth Ave, Rm 1302; 823-5132), is a comprehensive guide to seasonal recreation programs. There is something in it for everyone: from cross-country ski trips, fly-fishing, and whale watching in winter, to hiking, paddling, biking, tot walks, and historic bridge tours in summer. Pick it up free at libraries and outdoor stores. *Metro GreenScene,* another triannual guide to the great outdoors, focuses on wildlife habitats (see Bird-Watching/Wildlife Viewing for more information).

BICYCLING

In recent years, *Bicycling* magazine has rated the City of Roses the most bike-friendly city in the country. Why? Portland's diverse topography—flat and breezy stretches on the east side, steep and breathless hills on the west—has something for every cyclist. In fact, many people bike to work, and some of the

Portland Police neighborhood patrols and the urban messengers work on bikes. Want to know the quickest and safest bike route to your destination? Grab a copy of the Metro map **Bike There**, available at area cycle shops ($3.95) and at Powell's Travel Store (SW Sixth Ave and Yamhill St; 228-1108).

You can take your bike on any **Tri-Met bus or light-rail train** if you purchase a permanent $5 pass, available at the Tri-Met office in Pioneer Courthouse Square (238-7433). Buses and trains are outfitted with racks to make the going easy.

Cyclists looking for organized 30- to 100-mile rides at a touring pace should call the **Portland Wheelmen Touring Club** hotline (257-7982). As many as 120 people show up for group and nongroup rides—several each week—and you don't have to be a member to pedal along. The oldest club in town, **Rose City Wheelmen**, has evolved into a masters racing club primarily for those age 30 and older. RCW, known for its annual race at Mount Tabor, holds training rides every Saturday.

Serious about your cycling? So is **Raindance Velo Club** (231-4672). About half of the 55 members constitute a core of racers that recently won the state best all-around rider and team competition. The rest of the members are sport riders with a need for speed. In addition to balancing the desires of competitive racers and fitness riders, the club promotes races, sponsors training rides, and is active in community outreach and safety education. All ages are welcome. The **Beaverton Bicycle Club** (649-4632), which sponsors road, track, and criterium events, has a strong group of junior riders but no age limit.

▼

Active Sports

Bicycling

▲

The **Oregon Bicycle Racing Association** acts as a clearinghouse for race information for the 23 competitive clubs in Oregon. Call the OBRA hotline for event information (661-0686). From May to mid-September, races are held at Portland International Raceway on Tuesday nights—women and masters on alternate Mondays—and at the Alpenrose Dairy Velodrome on Thursday nights (6149 SW Shattuck Rd, 244-1133). The velodrome is the second shortest in the country (hence heroically steep) and is situated next to a working dairy farm. Admission is free for spectators. Classes are offered on Wednesdays, and fixed-gear bikes are available to rent for $5.

In the interest of protecting environmentally sensitive areas, **mountain biking** is restricted to a handful of marked trails in the metropolitan region, but the available choices are well managed and rewarding. Mountain bike **trail maps** are available from Portland Parks and Recreation (1120 SW Fifth Ave, Rm 1302; 823-5132) for Forest Park, Powell Butte, and the Springwater Corridor. Fat-tire cyclists looking for like minds can call **PUMP** (Portland United Mountain Pedalers, 223-4471 or 223-3954), whose motto is "Mountain biking is not a crime," for information on organized year-round weekend rides or to be put on a mailing list for their newsletter (see also Leif Erickson Drive listing).

Though one avid **cyclocross** racer has described that sport as "ballet on wheels," a less biased observer might see it as a mud festival for people who just can't get off their bikes—even for a few months each year. (Cylocross first gained popularity in Europe, as a means of breaking up the winter doldrums between racing seasons.) There are six races in the annual **Fat Tire Farm Cross Crusade**, which runs mid-October through December. A typical cyclocross course includes paved roads, gravel, and single-track trail and takes riders through mud bogs, over barriers, down sharp slopes, and up steep, short hills. Racers spend about 30 percent of the race running with their bikes slung by their sides or over their shoulders. Interest in the sport has grown remarkably over the past five years; over 200 racers, and an equal number of spectators, show up, rain or shine. For race information, contact Fat Tire Farm Mountain Bike Company (2714 NW Thurman St, 222-3276).

Following are a few favorite mountain and road bike routes in the area. For more rides and details, ask the resident experts at a local bike shop or hunt for a used copy of the out-of-print *Best Bike Rides Around Portland,* by Anndy Wiselogle and Virginia Church.

Hagg Lake [KIDS] From early spring to October, cyclists swarm the well-marked bike lane around man-made Henry Hagg Lake in Scoggins Valley Park. The loop follows gentle hills and fields for 10½ miles, passing numerous picnic and swimming spots. Ambitious cyclists can start in Forest Grove and take the Old TV Highway to Scoggins Valley Road. ■ *7 miles southwest of Forest Grove; open sunrise to sunset; 359-5732.*

Active Sports

Bicycling

▲

Leif Erickson Drive Fat-tire affinity? Forest Park is your kind of place. This 11-mile gravel road twists along the park's north side. For the first 6 miles, the road threads in and out of the gullies, offering occasional spectacular views of the Willamette River and northeast Portland. The last 5 miles are the most isolated and peaceful. Leif Erickson is rough going, but possible, on touring bikes. Although the fragile Wildwood Trail is off-limits, four other areas are open for mountain biking. Take the cutoff to NW Skyline Boulevard via Fire Lane 3 (just past the 3½-mile marker), NW Saltzman Road (6 miles), Springville Road (9¼ miles), or NW Germantown Road (11 miles). Then loop back on the precariously busy Highway 30, or continue to Bonneville Road and Fire Lanes 12 and 15. If you yearn to tread the terrain but don't own gear, Fat Tire Farm Mountain Bike Company (2714 NW Thurman St, 222-3276), located about a mile from the Leif Erickson gate into Forest Park, will rent you everything you need. PUMP organizes year-round, after-work rides (see Bicycling introduction for more information). Meet at the gate to Leif Erickson Drive at 6pm Wednesdays. ■ *NW Thurman St to NW Germantown Rd; map:DD9–GG7.*

Marine Drive Just across the Willamette from Sauvie Island, Kelley Point Park anchors a favorite ride that follows the Columbia east along the airplane-swept flats of N Marine Drive. Most riders take the river road, but you can also cross over I-205 (there is a bike lane) into Washington and back to the bike path alongside the roaring I-5 via Evergreen Highway and Columbia Way. ▪ *Kelley Point Park at confluence of Willamette and Columbia Rivers to east end of N Marine Dr; map:AA9–BB6.*

Sauvie Island On this ride, the ends justify the means. Endure 10 miles of pedaling alongside 18-wheelers through the mostly industrial section of Highway 30 from northwest Portland to Sauvie Island (or opt to take Tri-Met bus 17 or a car), and you'll be rewarded. The island offers a bicycle-friendly—as long as you ride single-file—12-mile loop with many scenic offshoots. Forgo the head-down hammer for a chin-up view of farm animals, U-cut flower and U-pick vegetable farms, blue herons, and more. ▪ *Sauvie Island, 10 miles northwest of Portland via Hwy 30; map:CC9.*

Skyline Boulevard This 17-mile loop requires pedaling an elevation gain of 1,400 feet, but Skyline Boulevard is truly the most scenic ridge-top road around, offering broad views of the Willamette Valley. Begin in Portland or in Beaverton (the climb is about the same either way). Turn off NW Cornell onto 53rd Avenue or Thompson Road for a peaceful (albeit steep and winding) climb to Skyline. Pack a few dollars and plan to stop for microbrews and a view at the Skyline Tavern or burgers, fries, and malts at the Skyline Restaurant. ▪ *Skyline Blvd between NW Cornell and Rocky Point Rds; map:DD9–GG7.*

Springwater Corridor Since 1990 when the City of Portland acquired the land, nearly 20 miles of abandoned rail line between Milwaukie and Boring have been open to mountain bikers, hikers, and horseback riders. The wild and weathered rail bed was replaced by a tamer, smooth surface called "sandseal." While mountain bikes are still the best two-wheel bet in the corridor, narrow road-bike tires can also negotiate the trail. The paved surface runs from Westmoreland (map:JJ5) east to Gresham (map:JJ1). Signals, crosswalks, and warning signs add a modicum of safety. Trailheads and toilets are located at SE Johnson Creek Boulevard, SE Hogan Road, and SE 136th Avenue. ▪ *Portland Parks and Recreation, 823-2223.*

BIRD-WATCHING/WILDLIFE VIEWING

Water makes Portland a wildlife haven. The infamous rainfall results in lush vegetation, and the confluence of the Columbia and Willamette Rivers lures myriad waterfowl. Streams, lakes, and wetlands form an emerald necklace around the metropolitan area. A 1994 merger between the Multnomah County Park Services Division and Metro's Greenspaces program resulted in a regional effort to protect wildlife habitats and promote respon-

sible use of natural areas. Three times a year, Metro's Regional
Parks and Greenspaces Department publishes *Metro Green-
Scene,* a guide to hikes, benefit concerts, history tours, biking,
river trips, and other organized activities that increase awareness
of local wildlife habitats. To receive a copy, call Metro (797-1850).

From blue herons to beavers, minks to muskrats, an impressive array of wildlife calls Portland home. Every glove compart-
ment should include a copy of the *Oregon Wildlife Viewing Guide*
(available from Defenders of Wildlife in Lake Oswego, 697-3222;
or Falcon Press, (800)582-2665). Many **viewing sites** are marked
with state highway signs depicting binoculars. For nature
unleashed, venture to **Powell Butte**, **Sauvie Island Wildlife
Management Area**, or **Kelley Point Park** (see Parks and Waterfront in the Exploring chapter). Here are a few other notable natural areas.

Beggars-tick Wildlife Refuge   Named after a native sunflower, the
Beggars-tick Wildlife Refuge serves as a wintering habitat for a
diversity of waterfowl: wood duck, green-winged teal, and
hooded merganser, to name a few. The refuge provides a permanent residence for muskrats, raccoons, and other species. ▪ *SE
11th Ave and Foster Rd; map:II5.*

Heron Lakes Golf Course   Built around wetlands, the course is
home to blue herons as well as other waterfowl. Ask for permission and directions at the pro shop, and once on the course, be
sure to keep your eyes open for birdies of the round, white, dim-
pled sort. ▪ *3500 N Victory Blvd; 289-1818; map:CC7.*

Oaks Bottom Wildlife Refuge   These 160 acres of woods and wetlands form the first officially designated wildlife refuge in Portland. The walk, just short of 3 miles, begins in Sellwood Park.
More than 140 species of birds have been spotted here, among
them the great blue heron, which feeds on carp in the Bottom.
Others include pileated woodpeckers and warblers (spring) and
green-backed herons (spring and summer). ▪ *Trailheads: SE Seventh Ave and Sellwood Blvd (Sellwood Park); SE Milwaukie Blvd
and Mitchell St; map:HH5.*

Portland Audubon Society Sanctuary   [KIDS]Every birder in the
state ends up here eventually—in part for the winged species
that flock here and in part for the selection of excellent naturalists' books. This 160-acre sanctuary is surrounded by the vast
wilderness of Forest Park and connects to the Wildwood and
Macleay Park Trails. The trails wrap around a pond and follow
the creek. At the Wildlife Care Center, visitors can view barn and
screech owls, red-tailed hawks, and injured fowl on the mend.
The Audubon House features a nature-oriented store, an interpretive area, and a viewing window overlooking the feeding platforms for local songbirds. Year-round, the Audubon Society
sponsors free field trips as a way of fulfilling its mission to teach

people about how special nature is. During winter, spring, and summer vacations, the sanctuary offers educational nature classes for kids. To listen to the weekly updated Rare Bird Alert message, ask for extension 200. ▪ *5151 NW Cornell Rd; 292-6855; map:FF7.*

Ross Island Ross Island actually includes the complex of Ross, Hardtack, East, and Toe Islands. All but one are owned by Ross Island Sand and Gravel and are slowly being devoured by the company's backhoes. On the northwest side of privately owned Toe Island is a 50-nest great blue heron rookery in a black cottonwood grove. The rookery can be viewed only by boat or with binoculars from the mainland. Best shoreside views (try for winter, when the trees are leafless) are from the Willamette Greenway, just north of Willamette Park. Look for belted kingfishers nesting on the island's steep banks, as well as beavers and red foxes. The nearest boat ramp is in Willamette Park, but please don't land on the island. ▪ *Willamette River, just south of Ross Island Bridge; map:HH5.*

Wallace Park If you loved Alfred Hitchcock's classic *The Birds*, you won't want to miss Wallace Park in September. For about a two-week period during their migratory route south, vaux's swifts roost in the several-story-tall chimney of Chapman School on the west side of the park. Each evening thousands of birds circle the chimney and then drop down inside, one by one, for the night; at sunrise they fly out just as dramatically. Spectator conversation usually revolves around the swifts that flew in first: can they actually sleep at the bottom of the pile, and what happens if one bird becomes claustrophobic? ▪ *NW 26th Ave between Pettygrove and Quimby Sts; map:GG7.*

CANOEING/KAYAKING
(See also River Rafting in this chapter)

Four rivers converge in the Portland area. Boaters leisurely paddle kayaks and canoes along the shores of the **Willamette and Columbia Rivers**, watching for blue herons, which nest along the banks. Whitewater kayakers surf the rapids of the **Sandy and Clackamas Rivers**. Pick up a copy of *Oregon's Quiet Waters: A Guide to Lakes for Canoeists and Other Paddlers*, by Cheryl McLean and Clint Brown. It includes more than a dozen lakes within two hours of Portland. Another must-read for Portland paddlers is the recently published second edition of *Canoe and Kayak Routes of Northwest Oregon*, by Phil N. Jones. The Oregon Ocean Paddling Society (OOPS) fills a niche, too; the club has 300 active members (PO Box 69641, Portland, OR 97201).

South of the city, canoe and kayak rentals are available from either of two shops on opposite sides of the Willamette. On the west side, across SW Macadam Avenue from Willamette Park, **Ebb & Flow Paddlesports** (0604 SW Nebraska St, 245-1756;

map:JJ6) rents canoes, sea kayaks, and accessories for $15 to $35 a day. The store, owned by Donna and Peter Holman, two OOPS founders, also offers sea kayaking classes and family and private lessons. On the east side, there's the 36-year-old floating **Sportcraft Marina** (1701 Clackamette Dr, Oregon City, 656-6484; map:OO4), which rents flatwater kayaks, canoes, and motorboats. The marina's history actually dates back to the 1920s when it was just a floating moorage; enterprising high school students augmented their allowances by offering rowboat rides. And, though it started as a specialty store for whitewater enthusiasts, **Alder Creek Kayak Supply** (250 NE Tomahawk Island Dr, 285-0464; map:CC6) now rents and sells a variety of inflatable kayaks, touring canoes, and flatwater kayaks and offers trips, tours, and classes.

CLIMBING

On July 19, 1894, aided by the complex carbohydrates of an old-fashioned bean bake, 193 persons climbed Mount Hood and initiated themselves as members in the **Mazamas** (909 NW 19th Ave, 227-2345; map:FF6). Now 3,000 members strong, the Mazamas is Oregon's biggest climbing group and the standard local means of acquiring mountain- and rock-climbing skills. This safety-conscious organization is a superb resource, offering seasonal group climbs, weekly lectures at its clubhouse, midweek rock climbs, day hikes, and other adventurous activities both in and outside of the Northwest.

Throughout the year, avid rock climbers—as well as those just starting out—hone their skills at local indoor climbing facilities: the **Portland Rock Gym** (2034 SE Sixth Ave, 232-8310; map:GG5) and **Stoneworks Climbing Gym** (6775 SW 111th Ave, Beaverton; 644-3517). Portland Rock Gym accommodates a 40-foot lead wall; there's 8,000 square feet of climbing, 25 top ropes, and 12 lead routes. The newer Stoneworks features 13 roped sections of wall and a large bouldering area. On Sunday mornings, kids are encouraged to climb the walls during Stoneworks' junior program. **Costco's SportsNation**—a sports megastore that includes basketball and volleyball courts, and a soccer/hockey rink—also boasts the highest indoor rock-climbing wall (45 feet) in the Portland area (18120 SW Lower Boones Ferry Rd, Tigard, 968-4500; map:MM9. See complete listing in the Shopping chapter under Outdoor Gear.).

Oregon Mountain Community—**OMC**—rents and sells ice and alpine climbing gear as well as rock shoes. Check out the piles of adventure literature lining the entrance for info on classes and trips, and the For Sale bulletin board for gear. **Recreational Equipment Inc.**—better known as **REI**—has teamed up with Adventure Smith Guides to offer a full line of indoor rock-climbing classes for ages 8 and up. Call REI's customer service for information (624-8600). The store also rents and sells climbing equipment. The **Portland Parks and Recreation** (823-5132) spring/summer schedule of events includes rock-climbing classes in Portland and at Smith Rock State Park, and mountaineering ascents of Mount Hood and Mount St. Helens.

The following are a few of the major climbs (alpine and rock) within three hours of Portland. For a more complete list, talk to the experts at one of the local rock gyms or outdoor stores. Both of the definitive sources for climbing around Portland—*Portland Rock Climbs: A Climber's Guide to Northwest Oregon,* by Tim Olson, and *Oregon High: A Climbing Guide,* by Jeff Thomas—are out of print. Rumor has it that there may be a few precious copies hidden away; if you're lucky, you may find one at a used book store.

Broughton's Bluff   While it pales in comparison to the beauty and quality of Smith Rock, Broughton's Bluff is just 30 minutes from Portland and offers about 200 midrange to difficult climbs. A new trail was cut in 1990, and the rock is relatively clean. The south-western exposure protects climbers from the cold winds of the Columbia River Gorge. ▪ *Lewis and Clark State Park, above east bank of Sandy River.*

Horsethief Butte   Here's a good practice spot, a basaltic rock mesa offering corridors of short climbs and top-rope challenges. ▪ *2 miles east of The Dalles bridge, on Hwy 14.*

Mount Adams   See Excursions in the Outings chapter; call the ranger station to register for ascents. ▪ *95 miles northeast of Portland; Mt Adams Ranger Station, (509)395-2501.*

Mount Hood   When British navigator Captain George Vancouver first spied Mount Hood from the mouth of the Columbia River in 1792, he thought it must have been the highest mountain in the world. At just over 11,235 feet, Mount Hood is not even the highest in the Cascades, but its beautiful asymmetry and relative ease of ascent make it one of the busiest peaks in the country. Still, unpredictable weather and very steep snow climbing (the last 1,500 feet) require either a skilled guide or solid moun-taineering skills. In summer, smart climbers start early, finishing before the heat of the day turns the snow to mush. **Timberline Mountain Guides**, (800)464-7704, are based, in summer, at the Wy'east Day Lodge at Timberline. The primary guide service on Mount Hood, this group teaches mountaineering, mountain-climbing, and ice-climbing courses; rock climbing is taught at Smith Rock State Park and Broughton's Bluff, and in the Columbia Gorge. For more information, see Day Trips in the Outings chapter. ▪ *50 miles east of Portland; Mt Hood National Forest, 668-1700.*

Mount St. Helens   See Excursions in the Outings chapter. ▪ *55 miles northeast of Portland; Mt St. Helens National Volcanic Mon-ument Headquarters, (360)247-5473.*

Smith Rock State Park   Its extreme difficulty (the welded tuff
surfaces are sometimes soft enough to tear off in your hand),
stunning scenery, and arid climate have helped make Smith Rock
a mecca for world-class climbers. The park is open year-round,
but rock climbers are busiest February through November,
before and after the rainy season. There are more than 1,000
routes in the park (as well as a few great hiking trails and scenic
vistas), something for all abilities. The nationwide climbing con-
sensus is that "Just Do It" is one of the hardest in the country.
Bivouac camping only—no trailers—in the state park along
Crooked River. ■ *9 miles northeast of Redmond on Hwy 97, 3 hours*
southeast of Portland; Smith Rock State Park, (541)548-7501.

FISHING

To maintain a minimum number of spawning chinook salmon,
the Oregon Department of Fish and Wildlife has issued **quotas**
on Portland-area waters. It used to be that from February
through June, fanatical anglers would line their boats from bank
to bank across the Willamette, wait for the river's monsters to
bite, and be rewarded with 10- to 30-pound salmon. In recent
years, quotas of 3,000 or 6,000 fish caught after April 1 have
brought the season to a close by mid-May. Plus, the fishing week
has been limited to two days in some instances. Even so, there is
a lot of fun to be had—industrious fishermen will take to other,
legal waters or spend the off days roaming through the gear at
GI Joe's (1140 N Hayden Meadows Dr, 283-0318, and additional
stores throughout the Portland area).
Fishing in Portland is a year-round sport. The Clackamas and
Sandy Rivers lure a steady stream of fishermen to their banks
and wading pools for spring chinook salmon and summer and
winter steelhead. The Willamette River right in Portland is a
good place to catch warm-water species such as bass and crap-
pies; Blue Lake Park and Cedar Island are also good bets. For
more info on the best bets for local fishing, pick up copy of the
eighth edition of *Fishing in Oregon,* by Madelynne Sheehan and
Dan Casali, at a local outdoor store. Hogliners and other anglers
can find salmon and steelhead tag information at the **Oregon
Department of Fish and Wildlife** (PO Box 59, Portland, OR
97207; 872-5268). A 24-hour automated number provides answers
to often-asked questions (872-5263); also, pick up the annual reg-
ulations at fishing goods stores or get them by writing the department. **Out-of-state fishermen** can call (800)ASK-FISH for
information. The state sponsors a **free day of fishing** on an early
Saturday in June. The Oregon State Marine Board (435 Commercial St NE, Salem, OR 97310; (503)378-8587) publishes a guide to
the lower Columbia and Willamette Rivers, as well as a statewide
facilities guide that includes information on boat ramps, parking,
and types of fishing available.

Two reputable **charter companies** are Reel Adventures (622-5372) and Red Dog Outdoors (based in Salem; (503)391-9004). They'll take you where the fish are—in both local and coastal rivers.

Two local sport-fishing groups have been especially active in watching over area fish populations. The **Association of Northwest Steelheaders** (PO Box 22065, Milwaukie, OR 97269; 653-4176) promotes fishery enhancement and protection programs, river access, and improved sport-fishing. Since 1958, the **Oregon Bass and Panfish Club** (282-2852) has promoted preservation of, improvement of, and education about warm-water fishery in Oregon. Thanks to the club's efforts, access to warm-water fishing—which has been diminishing due to the amount of shoreline that is privately owned—may be stabilizing.

GOLFING

Portland has more golfers than greens. A 1990 study by Portland Parks concluded that Portland could easily support another 20 courses. Currently, there are about two dozen 18-hole golf courses within 20 miles of the city center, though half are private, including the most spectacular courses: the Columbia-Edgewater Country Club (2138 NE Marine Dr, 285-8354), Portland Golf Club (5900 SW Scholls Ferry Rd, 292-2778), Riverside Golf & Country Club (8105 NE 33rd Dr, 282-7265), and Waverly Country Club (1100 SE Waverly Dr, 654-9509).

The following are the best of the public courses in the Portland area.

Cedars Golf Club   Just north of Vancouver, the Cedars offers a long, rolling challenge with a lot of water hazards. Nice clubhouse facilities. ▪ *15001 NE 181st St, Brush Prairie, WA; (360)687-4233 or (503)285-7548.*

Eastmoreland Golf Course and Driving Range   Bordered by the Crystal Springs Rhododendron Garden and blessed with venerable trees and lovely landscaping, the second-oldest golf course in the state is a technically challenging championship course. Eastmoreland was named one of the top 25 public golf courses in the nation in 1991 by *Golf Digest*. ▪ *2425 SE Bybee Blvd; 775-2900 (for tee times call 292-8570 and ask about the free online reservation service at www.golf-network.com); map:II5.*

Heron Lakes Golf Course   Designed by renowned golf course architect Robert Trent Jones Jr., Heron Lakes is a championship-quality public golf facility with two 18-hole courses. Great Blue has been described as one of the hardest courses in the Northwest—thanks to water and sand on every hole. The Green Back is a bit less challenging and retains the old, economical rates. Located just 15 minutes from downtown, Heron Lakes is one of the busiest in the city. ▪ *3500 N Victory Blvd; 289-1818; map:CC7.*

Pumpkin Ridge: Ghost Creek Course   Pumpkin Ridge's recent
claim to fame was hosting the 1997 U.S. Women's Open and 1996
U.S. Men's Amateur Championship golf tournaments. Back in
1993, *Business Journal* ranked it as the toughest in the Portland
area. And in 1996, *Golf* magazine rated it the fifth-best golf course
in America. Designed by Robert E. Cupp, it features natural areas
and views of both the Cascades and the Coast Range. A second
course at Pumpkin Ridge—Witch Hollow—is private. ■ *12930
NW Old Pumpkin Ridge Rd, Cornelius; 647-4747.*

The Reserve Vineyards and Golf Club   Spanking new in 1997, the
Reserve is a 36-hole, semiprivate golf facility with two courses,
one designed by John Fought and the other by Robert Cupp.
Fought's is a championship, traditional, 7,300-yard course with
114 bunkers; Cupp's is a slightly less difficult, open-design course
with lots of water and trees. ■ *4747 SW 229th, Aloha; 649-2345.*

HIKING

Oregon offers superlative hiking. The cascading waterfalls of the
Columbia River Gorge, the alpine lakes of the Cascades, the des-
olate peaks of the Wallowas, majestic Mount Hood, and the
rugged Oregon Coast—all (except perhaps the Wallowas) are
within easy access of Portland. To really get away, however, you
barely need to leave the city limits. A 24-mile hike, the Wildwood
Trail, begins in northwest Portland (see listing below). The Wild-   **Active Sports**
wood Trail in Forest Park is part of a 140-mile hiking/biking/   *Hiking*
running loop around the city (see Forty-Mile Loop Trail in the
Outings chapter).

Looking for company? Metro's Regional Parks and Greenspaces Department publishes a seasonal guide to organized outdoor activities, including hikes. To request a copy of *Metro
GreenScene,* call 797-1850.

For tramping farther afield, good maps of hikes in the gorge
and around Mount Hood can be found at the U.S. Forest Service
office (800 NE Oregon St, 872-2750) and at local outdoor stores.
Parking lots at some trailheads are notorious for car break-ins—
don't leave anything valuable behind.

The following are a few of the better close-in hikes.

Kelley Point Park   See Parks and Waterfront in the Exploring
chapter. ■ *N Suttle Rd off west end of N Marine Dr; map:AA9–BB6.*

Lower Macleay Park   Balch Creek is one of the few creeks that
still flows unfettered down the heavily developed West Hills.
Lower Macleay Trail connects NW Upshur Street to Forest
Park's long Wildwood Trail, but hikers can make a 2-mile loop up
Balch Canyon by taking a right at the first trail intersection at the
stone hut, then right again at the second, ending up on NW
Raleigh Street. A short northeasterly walk through the neighborhood takes you to the Thurman Bridge above the park; take the
stairs on the east side of the bridge back down to the starting

point. At the park, the creek disappears unceremoniously into a drainpipe. ▪ *NW 29th Ave and NW Upshur St; map:FF7.*

Marquam Nature Park A series of trails makes this one of the best hilly hiking areas in the city. From the parking lot and shelter off SW Sam Jackson Park Road (just west of the Carnival Restaurant), the **trail to the right** climbs 900 feet to Council Crest. To walk to the Washington Park Zoo, continue over the top to the intersection of SW Talbot and SW Patton Roads. A short downhill trail leads to a Highway 26 overpass. The **trail to the left** of the shelter follows an old roadbed up and around Oregon Health Sciences University, crosses Marquam Hill Road, and comes out on Terwilliger Boulevard. At Terwilliger and Nebraska, the trail departs from the bike path and goes under Barbur Boulevard and I-5, coming out in John's Landing, four blocks from Willamette Park. **A third trail**, a 1½-mile nature loop, also begins at the shelter; follow the signs. The trails are all remarkably quiet and peaceful; however, be forewarned: it's becoming more common to round a corner on a trail and stumble upon folks making their home in the woods. ▪ *Trailheads: Council Crest Park, SW Sam Jackson Park Rd (just west of the Carnival Restaurant); SW Terwilliger Blvd, near the OHSU School of Dentistry; map:GG7.*

Oaks Bottom Wildlife Refuge See Bird-Watching/Wildlife Viewing in this chapter. ▪ *Trailheads: SE Seventh Ave and SE Sellwood Blvd (Sellwood Park); SE Milwaukie Blvd and SE Mitchell St; map:HH5.*

Sauvie Island See Day Trips in the Outings chapter. ▪ *10 miles northwest of Portland via Hwy 30; map:CC9.*

Springwater Corridor One of the region's best rails-to-trails hikes. See Bicycling in this chapter. ▪ *Portland Parks and Recreation, 823-2223.*

Wildwood Trail (Forest Park) One of the country's longer natural woodland trails winding through a city park, the Wildwood Trail is Portland's cherished refuge for hikers and runners. The shady route through groves of fir and aspen officially begins at the World Forestry Center and travels north, linking such attractions as the Hoyt Arboretum, Pittock Mansion, and the Portland Audubon Society Sanctuary before it plunges into the less-trod territories of Forest Park. It ends 24½ miles later, at NW Germantown Road. Many spurs cross the trail, joining it to various neighborhoods and parks. The first 10 miles are well used; the last are good for solitude. Large, glass-encased maps of the entire trail are situated at convenient locations along the way. The Hoyt Arboretum Tree House has brochures and maps. Many of the trail-marked trees—bearing a green diamond—have a mileage marker posted higher up on the trunk.

The best place to pick up the southern end of the Wildwood Trail is at its origin, at the World Forestry Center near the

Washington Park Zoo. The trail travels north and crosses W
Burnside, then climbs up to Pittock Mansion or farther north to
NW Cornell Road (and the Audubon sanctuary). Another option
is to explore the branching trails of the Hoyt Arboretum in Washington Park. Beware: These are the most used parts of the trails, and they are also very hilly. Another trail begins across the Highway 26 overpass and continues south, connecting the Wildwood Trail to panoramic Council Crest. A walk on this uncrowded mile-long trail is best when timed with the setting sun.

The northern 10 miles of the trail (from NW Cornell to NW Germantown Rd) is a departure from the comforting rest stops of zoo, arboretum, mansion, and gardens. This part—a favorite for runners and walkers training for marathons—is composed of long, solitary stretches of rolling hills with just a few brutally steep sections. Bring plenty of water, as there are no drinking fountains. Get to the northern section via NW Cornell, 53rd Avenue, or the Leif Erickson gate at the end of NW Thurman Street (hike Leif Erickson Road up to the Wild Cherry Trail, which climbs to Wildwood). While the weather in recent winters has wiped out many sections of Wildwood (especially its access trails), thanks to an amazing trail crew, repairs are fast and thorough. ■ *Main trailheads: W Burnside gravel parking area, map:GG7; Washington Park, map:GG7; NW Cornell Rd, map:FF7; NW Thurman St, map:EE7.*

HORSEBACK RIDING

Flying M Ranch [KIDS] Known for its Old West down-hominess, the Flying M is a great place to take the kids (over age 10) riding. The fee is $17 per hour, including a guide. Pony rides for the younger set are $4.25 for 15 minutes. For more adventuresome travel, a handful of two-day overnight rides up Trask Mountain are scheduled each summer, including all meals, lodging, and Joe Justin's campfire songs at the top of the mountain. Flying M also takes private groups on overnight trail rides. Call for information. ■ *10 miles west of Yamhill, watch for signs; 662-3222.*

Lakeside Horse Rentals You have 70 acres of meadowlike property to explore without a guide, but you'll have to keep your steed to a walk or a trot ($13 per hour). Inquire about the Lakeside location at McIver State Park, where you can go a lot farther afield, albeit led by a guide. ■ *22551 S Eaden Rd, Oregon City; 631-4502; map:II1.*

ICE-SKATING

Ice Chalet Clackamas [KIDS] Yes, Tonya Harding practiced here. That was when her triple axel was more famous than her dubious dealings and when the rink was still owned by Ice Capades Chalet. After three owners in three years, the rink is now back in the hands of the people who ran it from 1981 to 1993. They offer 6- and 10-week figure skating and hockey lessons. Public skate admission (including rentals) is $7.50 for kids 17 and younger, and $8.50 for adults. The rink sits on the lower level of the mall's food court, thrilling the munch-time crowd. ■ *Clackamas Town Center; 786-6000; map:KK3.*

Lloyd Center Ice Chalet [KIDS] For 30 years, only the Portland sky covered the ice rink at Lloyd Center, but in 1990, the rink and the mall went undercover. The renovated facility includes a pro skate shop, and group and private lessons are available. Public skate admission (including skate rentals) is $7.50 for kids 17 and younger, and $8.50 for adults. ■ *960 Lloyd Center; 288-6073; map:FF5.*

Valley Ice Arena [KIDS] This rink is the largest around and has been a fixture at the Valley Plaza Shopping Center for almost 30 years. Lessons are available, and skate rentals are free with a $6 admission. Public skating most weekday mornings, afternoons, and weekends. The Portland Winter Hawks hockey team regularly scrimmages here. ■ *9250 SW Beaverton-Hillsdale Hwy (Valley Plaza Shopping Center), Beaverton; 297-2521; map:HH9.*

LASER TAG

Remember "freezetag"? You ran around avoiding IT until IT tagged you, and then you had to freeze until you were freed. Well, laser tag is freezetag for the 21st century. Players are equipped with red-, yellow-, or green-beamed laser guns and laser-sensitive vests. They run around in "fully fogged" arenas and gain points deactivating their opponents and their opponents' bases. Games cost around $6 and last about 15 minutes (plus extra time for instructions and suiting up). Techno music and strobe lights add to the drama. [KIDS] Though laser tag is most popular with the 10-year-old set, it's been known to bring out the kid in a lot of adults as well. **Laserport** (10975 SW Canyon Rd, Beaverton, 526-9501; map:II9) has been around since 1994. **Ultrazone** (16074 SE McLoughlin Blvd, Milwaukie; 652-1122) is a newer 5,000-square-foot arena on two levels. **Wilsonville Family Fun Center** (29111 SW Town Center Loop West, Wilsonville; 685-5000) offers go-carts, bumper boats, batting cages, miniature golf, and game rooms. Laser tag—called LaserXtreme—was added in the spring of 1997. Anyone over 44 inches tall can join the forces of a red or green team for a 12-minute game. If you work up an appetite, you can take your chances at Bulwinkle's Family Restaurant.

RIVER RAFTING
(See also Canoeing/Kayaking in this chapter)

The local rafting season generally runs from May to October. Outfitters rent the necessary equipment to run the four closest whitewater rivers—Clackamas, Sandy, White Salmon, and Klickitat. Since river conditions can change rapidly, inexperienced rafters should stick to guided trips.

One of the most reputable rental outfitters is **River Trails**
Canoe and Raft Rentals (336 E Columbia River Hwy, Troutdale; 667-1964), through which, for $55 per raft, up to four people
can float the relatively calm section of the Sandy from Oxbow
Park 9 miles to Lewis and Clark Park. In May and June, more
confident rafters can run the longer section that starts 16 miles
upriver, which is designated an Oregon Scenic Waterway and
includes Class III rapids.

Less than two hours from Portland, **Phil's White Water
Adventure** (38 Northwestern Lake Resort, White Salmon, WA;
(800)366-2004) offers guided day trips on the White Salmon.
White Water runs three trips a day down the White Salmon,
recently designated a Wild and Scenic river. From April to
October, spend 2½ hours floating through inspiring scenery. Fed
by springs, the White Salmon has rapids in Classes II, III, and IV.
Prices start at $50 per person; call for reservations.

For those on their own, a good place to start gathering equipment and information is **Andy & Bax Sporting Goods** (324 SE
Grand Ave, 234-7538), Portland's premier rafting store. **Wild
West Whitewater** rents rafts and sells whitewater raft frames
(6411 SE 97th, 788-2961). Or take the **Mazamas** class in April—
see Climbing in this chapter for information about the organiza-   ▼
tion (227-2345).

ROLLER AND IN-LINE SKATING/ROLLER HOCKEY/
SKATEBOARDING

[KIDS] Remember when skates buckled over your shoes and off
you went down the road? Things have changed. Roller skating   ▲
has been joined by roller hockey, in-line skating, and **"aggressive skating"**—the name for what those amazing kids who
skateboard down railings, catching some serious air, and (mirac-
ulously) land back on their boards are doing. In Portland, most
action of this sort takes place on the east side of the Burnside
Bridge. Aggressive skaters farther afield also have a **skate park**
facility in Forest Grove. For **roller hockey** players, the best bets
can be found at **Costco SportsNation** and **Skate World**. For up-
to-date information on the best half-pipes, skate parks, and roller
hockey leagues, try **Sportworks** (421 SW Second Ave, 227-5323;
map:H6). **In-line skaters** who long for open skies have a few
options to choose from in Portland: Tom McCall Waterfront Park
(see Major Attractions in the Exploring chapter), Springwater
Corridor (the paved section in Gresham; see the Bicycling section in this chapter), and the bike pathway along I-205.

Costco SportsNation This sports megastore (see the Climbing
section in this chapter) has a year-round, weekend roller hockey
league. To play in a league game—open to members of Sports-
Nation and "free agents" (nonmembers)—players must have all
hockey equipment as well as in-line skates. For indoor in-line

skating practice, check out the "No Stick Time" free skate on Friday, Saturday, and Sunday mornings. Skating is available only on the weekends, as a soccer turf is rolled out for use Monday though Thursday. ▪ *18120 SW Lower Boones Ferry Rd, Tualatin; 968-4500; map:MM8.*

Oaks Amusement Park   Though the Northwest's largest roller-skating rink normally stays open year-round (even though the park closes in winter), horrible floods during the winter of 1996 necessitated a temporary closure. Damage was kept to a minimum, however, thanks to the rink's floating floor, which is designed so that it can be cut away from the wall to float atop rainwater. A live DJ rocks the rollers Friday and Saturday nights, and a giant Wurlitzer pipe organ plays Tuesday through Thursday nights and Sundays. The rink's available for private parties; call ahead. ▪ *Foot of SE Spokane St, north of Sellwood Bridge on the east riverbank; 236-5722; map:II5.*

Skate World   Though Skate World describes itself as a "clean, family-oriented, modern skate center," this decades-old rink welcomes all sorts of patrons and parties—recently a local dentist threw a skating party for all his patients. There's a roller hockey league for both kids and adults at the Hillsboro branch. Prices range from $2.50 to $6 including rentals. ▪ *1220 NE Kelly, Gresham; 667-6543.* ▪ *4395 SE Witch Hazel Rd, Hillsboro; 640-1333.*

▼

Active Sports

Skating

▲

Sportworks   Pretty much anything you ever wanted to know, buy, or rent involving in-line skates, snowboards, skateboards, and related stuff can be found here. At various times throughout the year, from approximately October through March, Sportworks turns the concourse level of the Memorial Coliseum into an in-line roller rink and offers free lessons. Admission is $7 at the Coliseum, $5 in advance at Sportworks, not including rentals. ▪ *421 SW Second Ave; 227-5323; map:H6.*

ROWING

The Willamette is to Portland what the Charles is to Boston. When the weather is good, it's best to get on the water at sunrise—later, barges and motorboats turn smooth water to chop. Most rowing takes place between the Sellwood and Fremont Bridges, and boathouses on this stretch of water are at a premium. **Oregon Rowing Unlimited** (233-9426) offers youth programs, coaching, and moorage at RiverPlace Marina and Oaks Park. Farther downriver, **Station L Rowing Club** (just north of the River Queen restaurant, 1466 NW Front, 222-3248) focuses on open and masters sweep rowing. An all-volunteer club, Station L shares its boathouse with the crew from Lewis and Clark College. Dues are $25 per month; members are entitled to the use of equipment and coaching. Novice sweep classes are also offered. The club is on the water March through November.

Regardless of the weather, Portlanders like to run—a lot. And those who don't run, walk. The **Oregon Roadrunners Club** (4840 SW Western Ave, Beaverton; 646-7867) is the fourth-largest running/walking club in the country, with 2,400 active members at $25 a year, or $35 a family. The club coordinates two track clubs for kids, sponsors running clinics, and publishes a magazine and newsletter. ORRC puts on more than 25 local races—including one of the country's best 26-milers, the Portland Marathon, held the last Sunday of September or the first weekend in October. For race information (updated monthly), call the ORRC/Nike Runners Hotline (223-7867). **Team Oregon** (244-0902; www.teamoregon.com), a 14-year-old running club run by Patti and Warren Finke, organizes the Portland Marathon Training Clinics from March until the September race. The clinics ($75 for five running clinics or four walking clinics) cover topics essential to successful completion of the marathon. They also hold very popular, free training runs (every other Saturday and Sunday) and walks (once a month) in the months leading up to the race.

Portland's Little Red Book of Stairs: The City's Ultimate Guide to More Than 150 Curious and Colorful Outdoor Stairways, by Stefana Young ($12.95), is a must-have book published in 1997 for those who love the burn of the stairs or the view from the top. Young and her dog logged many miles researching this user-friendly spiral-bound book. Descriptions include location, year built, number of stairs, and information on the degree of difficulty and scenery. Pick one up from Powell's Travel Store (228-1108).

Active Sports

Running and Walking

▼

▲

Council Crest Park Hewett, Humphrey, and SW Fairmount Boulevards form a figure eight, creating one of the more popular recreation paths in the city. People walk, run, cycle, even roller-ski here. The most heavily used portion is 3½-mile Fairmount Boulevard, which circles the park, a moderately hilly course that on a clear day overlooks virtually everything from the Willamette Valley to Mount St. Helens. Take SW Hewett Boulevard to avoid the busier Humphrey Boulevard during rush hour—making, in fact, a figure *nine*. ▪ *Top of Marquam Hill; map:HH7.*

Duniway Park and Terwilliger Boulevard Runners have worn grooves into the lanes of the Duniway track, which now holds water like a drainage ditch. Up one terrace, however, is the quarter-mile sawdust track. The track has certain conveniences—the adjacent YMCA, an exercise and stretching area, public toilets—but parking is not one of them. At 5pm you won't find a space, legal or illegal, for your car in the tiny lot. Terwilliger continues all the way to Lake Oswego, although few trot that far, due to the hills and hard asphalt surface. ▪ *North end of SW Terwilliger Blvd to Barbur Blvd and I-5; map:GG6–II6.*

Glendoveer Golf Course   The sawdust trail around the circumference measures 2 miles 95 feet, according to one coach who measured it for his team's workouts. The north and south sides border sometimes busy streets, but the east-end trail curves through a miniature wildlife refuge in woods overrun with well-fed (and fearless) rabbits. ▪ *14015 NE Glisan St; 253-7507; map:FF1.*

Greenway Park   A suburban common, Greenway is surrounded by fairly new commercial and residential developments. The 2½-mile trail follows Fanno Creek to SW Scholls Ferry Road, where the asphalt ribbon doubles back. ▪ *SW Hall Blvd and Greenway St, Beaverton; map:HH9.*

Laurelhurst Park   Once a gully and swamp, Laurelhurst is now a lovely 25-acre parkland where paved and gravel trails crisscross under elegant shade trees, and a pond set amid manicured lawns holds ducks. The 1⅓-mile path rings the park, but pay attention to the kids on bikes and roller skates. ▪ *SE 39th Ave between SE Ankeny and SE Oak Sts; map:FF4.*

Leif Erickson Drive/Forest Park   See Bicycling or Hiking (Wildwood Trail) in this chapter. ▪ *NW Thurman St to Germantown Rd; map:DD9–FF7.*

Mount Tabor Park   The only volcano within city limits in the Lower 48 has one of the better eastside views of Portland's West Hills. Tabor was named in honor of a faraway twin peak in the Biblical Palestine. Asphalt roads loop up the hill. Dirt trails stretch for 1 to 5 miles. ▪ *SE 60th Ave and Salmon St; map:GG3.*

Powell Butte   See Parks and Waterfront in the Exploring chapter. ▪ *SE Powell Blvd and 162nd Ave (unmarked street); map:HH1.*

Tom McCall Waterfront Park and Willamette Park   Noontime runners flock to the promenade in what's considered by many to be the city's front yard. It runs only 1¾ miles north to the Broadway Bridge; however, south of RiverPlace (after a brief interruption) the path reappears along the river to Willamette Park, making a round trip of 6½ miles. ▪ *West bank of Willamette River, stretching 3¼ miles south from downtown Portland; map:A6–K6.*

Tryon Creek State Park   See Parks and Waterfront in the Exploring chapter. ▪ *11321 SW Terwilliger Blvd, 1 mile off Hwy 43 in Lake Oswego; 636-4398; map:II5–JJ5.*

Tualatin Hills Nature Park   Fortunately, the Tualatin Hills Park and Recreation District has left St. Mary's Woods virtually untouched since it purchased the 180 acres from the Catholic archdiocese of Portland in the mid-1980s. Deer trails work their way through the woods, but the path (clearly marked) makes a 1-mile loop on the west bank of Beaverton Creek. If it's wet out, the dirt trail is likely to be quite muddy. ▪ *SW 170th Ave, Beaverton; 645-6433.*

Scores of speedboats chop up the water on the Willamette River, making a simple Sunday sail a fight for survival. And while sailing on the Columbia is certainly pleasant, board-sailing gets more attention on that river these days. Nevertheless, sailing is a business for the following organizations, which specialize in rentals and instructions. Beginners may also want to contact the Lake Oswego Recreation Department (636-9673) for sailing lessons through Lewis and Clark College.

Island Sailing Club   This members-only Columbia River club, located east of Jantzen Beach, offers instruction for American Sailing Association certification and rentals (20- to 30-foot crafts). Members are welcome at the club's two Washington locations. Charters are available; open year-round. ▪ *515 NE Tomahawk Island Dr; 285-7765; map:CC6.*

Portland Sailing Center   Primarily a sailing school, the center allows students at all skill levels to practice the particulars of tacking and jibing on a range of boats. The center also rents to certified parties and offers brokered charters far beyond the banks of the Columbia—to Baja or the San Juans, for example. The staff is terrific. Hours are 10am to 6pm, seven days a week, all year round. ▪ *3315 NE Marine Dr; 281-6529; map:CC4.*

SKIING: CROSS-COUNTRY

The growing popularity of cross-country, or Nordic, skiing has outpaced the availability of new snowparks and trail information. Many maps list the popular or marked trail systems, but Klindt Vielbig's guide, *Cross-Country Ski Routes of Oregon's Cascades,* offers a more comprehensive listing.

Mount Hood   It takes more than looking out the window to assess weather conditions at Mount Hood. Miserable weather in Portland sometimes shrouds excellent Nordic conditions on the mountain. Snow reports can be dialed at the summit ski areas (the snow's rarely the same at all three): Timberline (222-2211), Mount Hood Meadows (227-SNOW), and SkiBowl (222-BOWL). In Portland, call 222-2211 for road conditions. Each area on the mountain has some form of Nordic program (see Skiing: Downhill in this chapter).

The Portland chapter of the **Oregon Nordic Club** (PO Box 3906, Portland, OR 97208; 255-0823) operates the popular weekend Nordic center at Teacup Lake, on the east side of Highway 35, across from the Mount Hood Meadows parking lot. The 20 kilometers of groomed trails are open to the public for a small donation. The Nordic Club schedules year-round weekend activities, including hiking, backpacking, and cycling.

South of Highway 26 on Forest Service Road 2656, just past the Timberline Lodge turnoff, the Trillium Lake Basin is especially popular. Local resident David Butt voluntarily grooms the two main areas, Trillium Lake Road and Still Creek Campground Loop, as well as six other trails. For trail information and other snowpark areas, call the Zig Zag Ranger Station. ■ *About 60 miles east of Portland; Zig Zag Ranger Station; 668-1704.*

Santiam Pass The U.S. Forest Service trail system at Ray Benson Snopark near the Hoodoo ski area is one of the most extensive in the state, with warming huts (and wood stoves) at the trailhead and beyond. ■ *86 miles southeast of Salem at Santiam Pass; McKenzie Ranger District, (541)822-3381; Sisters Ranger District, (541)549-2111.*

Southwest Washington Oregon permits are valid for seven snowparks in Washington. Along the Upper Wind River the terrain is generally rolling, through heavy clear-cuts and forested areas (20 miles of groomed, well-marked trails). Two areas south of Mount St. Helens are both accessible from Road 83. Recommended are the Marble Mountain–Muddy River area and the Ape Cave–McBride Lake–Goat Marsh area. Unmarked roads through gentle wide-open areas offer extensive views of the mountain itself. (See also Excursions in the Outings chapter.) ■ *76 miles east of Portland, 26 miles north of Carson, WA; Wind River Ranger District, (509) 427-3200; St. Helens Ranger District, (360)247-3900.*

Three Sisters Wilderness Fifteen miles west of Bend on the road to Mount Bachelor, the U.S. Forest Service's Swampy Lakes trail system has warming huts and exquisitely beautiful (if hilly) terrain. Six more miles up Century Drive is the snowpark for Dutchman Flat, a trail system that connects to Swampy Lakes. Together, the systems are the best-planned web of trails in Oregon. ■ *180 miles southeast of Portland; Bend Ranger District, (541)388-5664.*

SKIING: DOWNHILL

Mount Bachelor See Central Oregon: Bend and Sisters in the Excursions section of the Outings chapter. ■ *PO Box 1031, Bend, OR 97709; 183 miles southeast of Portland (22 miles outside of Bend); (541)382-2607.*

Mount Hood Meadows The Meadows offer the most varied terrain of all Mount Hood ski areas—from wide-open slopes for beginners and novices to plenty of moguls and steep, narrow chutes for the experts. This ski area is big; there are 82 runs, including one that goes on for 3 miles. Lift lines can be long, too, but express lifts, such as Jacob's Ladder and the Mount Hood Express, get skiers on the mountain in a hurry. The rope tow is free. There are two day lodges, and night skiing is offered Wednesday through Saturday. Nordic skiers come for the 15 kilometers of cross-country trails; when they're groomed, the fee is $7. ▪ *PO Box 470, Mount Hood, OR 97042; 68 miles east of Portland; 227-7669 (from Portland) or (503)337-2222.*

Mount Hood Skibowl With 210 acres under lights, Skibowl is America's largest night ski area. It's also the state's lowest-elevation ski area, which means it suffers during seasons with light or late snowfall, but snowmaking in the lower bowl has added some consistency. And if you're not satisfied with the ski conditions in the first hour out, you can turn in your lift ticket for a pass to be used another day. The lower bowl suits beginners and intermediates, while the upper bowl is challenging enough to host ski races. Also, a snow-board park includes an in-ground half-pipe for the above-ground hard-core. Five rope tows, four double chairs. ▪ *PO Box 280, Government Camp, OR 97028; 53 miles east of Portland on Hwy 26; 222-2695.*

Timberline See Mount Hood in the Outings chapter. ▪ *Government Camp, OR 97028; 60 miles east of Portland (6 miles north of Government Camp); 231-7979 (from Portland) or (503)272-3311.*

SWIMMING

Water, water everywhere—but the Portland Parks and Recreation Department discourages swimmers from plunging into the Willamette River. Although cleaner than it was in the early half of this century, the Willamette contends with occasional sewage spills and barge traffic. The Columbia River, however, has two popular wading areas, at Rooster Rock State Park and Sauvie Island (see Parks and Waterfront in the Exploring chapter).

The few indoor public pools in the city are busy during the winter. [KIDS]Every year, thousands of children take swimming lessons through **Portland Parks** (823-SWIM); Wilson High School's pool in southwest Portland and the Sellwood Pool in Southeast—both outdoor pools—are two of the more popular. The city charges $2 for adult general admission; youth, $1.25; 2 years and under, free with parent.

The largest indoor swim spot is **North Clackamas Aquatic Park** (7300 SE Harmony Rd, Milwaukie; 650-3483 (hotline) or 557-7873), where there are attractions for all ages. Four-foot waves roll into one pool, and older kids can dare the twister and drop slides. There's a heart-shaped whirlpool for adults, and an outdoor sand volleyball court. Admission isn't cheap: $9.50 for adults; $6.50 for ages 9 to 17; $4.50 for ages 3 to 8; under age 3 free (less for the lap pool only; all prices discounted two hours before closing). Lessons and aquatic exercise programs are available.

Most high schools have pools, but public access is usually limited to the summer months. Both the Mount Hood Community College and Tualatin Hills aquatic centers can handle many swimmers (see listings). The following are the better public pools in the area.

Columbia Pool   One of Portland's largest indoor pools is actually two 25-yard pools side by side. The shallow one ranges from 2 to 3 feet deep; the deep pool slopes to 8 feet. ■ *7701 N Chautauqua Blvd; 823-3669; map:DD7.*

Dishman Pool   This indoor public pool's best feature is its 10-person whirlpool. ■ *77 NE Knott; 823-3673; map:FF6.*

Harman Swim Center   A hot spot in the Tualatin Hills Parks and Recreation Department's award-winning swim program—literally. At 88 degrees, the water's extra 4 degrees make it noticeably warmer than the other pools in the district. Swimming instruction for all ages. The pool runs the area's largest water therapy program for disabled or physically limited individuals. ■ *7300 SW Scholls Ferry Rd, Beaverton; 643-6681; map:HH9.*

Metro Family YMCA   Its location next to the Duniway Park track and running trail makes the Barbur YMCA extremely popular (avoid parking headaches and take one of the many buses that stop here). The pool is available for lap swimming whenever the YMCA is open (except for a brief period on Saturdays). A $10 day pass entitles visitors to the use of the entire facility. Members of the Southeast and Northeast YMCAs are welcome free anytime; members of other YMCAs are entitled to 21 free visits, and after that it's $10 a day. Water step-aerobics and swim lessons available to members. ■ *2831 SW Barbur Blvd; 294-3366; map:A1.*

Mount Hood Community College (Aquatics Center)   The Aquatics Center runs four pools: an outdoor 50-meter pool (June to early October) with morning, noon, and evening lap swims; an indoor 25-yard six-lane pool; a very warm (90 to 92 degrees) 4-foot-deep pool for the physically impaired; and an oft-used hydrotherapy pool. Fee is $1.50 per visit; annual memberships are available for families ($120) and individuals ($90). Summer passes cost $80 for families, $60 for individuals. ■ *26000 SE Stark St, Gresham; 667-7243.*

Oregon City Municipal Swimming Pool   Lap swimming, swimming lessons, and water exercise classes are all available in this 25-meter, six-lane indoor pool. Open year-round. ■ *12th Ave and Jackson St, Oregon City; 657-8273; map:OO4.*

Tualatin Hills Parks and Recreation Swim Center   This is Portland's largest enclosed public swimming pool (50 meters). It's part of a large recreation complex in the Sunset Corridor, where the facilities include covered tennis courts, playing fields, and a running trail. $1.75 per swim; $1.25 for children. Memberships and lessons available. ■ *15707 SW Walker Rd, Beaverton; 645-7454.*

Portland is well supplied with **public tennis courts**. Portland Parks and Recreation has 112 outdoor courts at 40 sites. Washington Park, which has six lit courts above the Rose Garden—and a waiting line on warm weekends—is a favorite. For a nominal fee, one-hour court reservations can be made May through September for individual outdoor courts at Grant, Portland Tennis Center, and Washington Park. Otherwise it's first come, first served—and free.

In addition, the city owns two **indoor tennis centers**. The excellent Portland Tennis Center (324 NE 12th Ave, 823-3189 or 823-3190; map:GG5) was the first municipal indoor court in the Western states financed by revenue bonds. It has eight outdoor and four indoor courts ($5–$5.25 each for singles on weekends and after 4pm; early weekday play is $5.25). At St. Johns Racquet Center (7519 N Burlington St, 823-3629; map:DD8), everything is undercover—three indoor tennis courts ($15 per court for adults, $10 for juniors) and Portland's only public racquetball courts (there are four; $9 per court).

Other area **indoor courts** that are open to the public, though some require more than a full day's advance notice, include Glendoveer Tennis Center (NE 140th Ave and NE Glisan St, 253-7507; map:FF7); Lake Oswego Indoor Tennis Center (2900 SW Diane Dr, Lake Oswego; 635-5550, 636-9673 in summer; map:KK6); Tualatin Hills Parks and Recreation District Tennis Center (15707 SW Walker Rd, Beaverton; 645-7457); Vancouver Tennis and Racquetball Center (5300 E 18th St, Vancouver, WA; (360)696-8123; map:BB5); and Nautilus Plus Sportcenter (8785 SW Beaverton-Hillsdale Hwy, 297-3723; map:HH8). Weekdays are a better deal.

Active Sports

Tennis

Here are a few of the better courts in the area (call Portland Parks and Recreation for others; 823-2223).

West Side
Gabriel Park.......................SW 45th Ave and Vermont St; map:II7
Hillside................................653 NW Culpepper Terrace; map:FF7

Southeast
Col. Summers ....SE 20th Ave and Belmont St; map:GG5
Kenilworth....................SE 34th Ave and Holgate Blvd; map:HH4

Northeast
Argay....................................NE 141st Ave and Failing St; map:FF1
U. S. Grant....................NE 33rd Ave and Thompson St; map:FF4

WINDSURFING
See Columbia River Gorge Scenic Area
in the Outings chapter.

SPECTATOR SPORTS

See the Calendar chapter for information on specific events.

Multnomah Greyhound Park   You've seen the Kentucky Derby, right? Well, here dogs run instead of horses, the track is smaller (no more than 770 yards), and instead of a jockey urging the animals on, the greyhounds chase a little mechanical rabbit. The season runs from May to October. Admission is $1.50. No children under 12 are allowed during evening races. ■ *NE 223rd Ave and NE Glisan St, Fairview; 667-7700.*

Portland Forest Dragons If ever there were a time when the Forest Dragons football team needed their fans, this is it. The 1997 inaugural football season started with a five-game losing streak, despite the 10,000 fans who regularly descend upon the Rose Garden to cheer for the newly formed team. ■ *Rose Garden; 297-2255; www.arenafootball.com/portland.html; map:N8.*

Portland Meadows   On Friday, Saturday, and Sunday from October through April you can catch live horse racing at the Meadows, but from Monday through Thursday you have to settle for simulcasts of greyhound and horse racing. Greyhound simulcast only on Monday and Tuesday; both greyhound and horse simulcasts Wednesday through Sunday. ■ *1001 N Schmeer Rd; 285-9144; map:BB6.*

Portland Power   With a 14–26 record for its 1997 inaugural season, the Portland Power women's basketball team has room to improve—but nothing to be ashamed of. Fan support—something everyone wondered about—was enthusiastic throughout the season. It's part of the American Basketball League, which, at press time, includes an eager nine teams in midsize cities across the nation. ■ *Memorial Coliseum; 236-HOOP; map:O7.*

Portland Pride Soccer   For fast-action, rock 'n' roll, professional indoor soccer, the Portland Pride delivers. The season runs through the summer months at Memorial Coliseum, with the best soccer players in the state participating. Win or lose, the kids love it, and affordable ticket prices—some under $10— make it possible to take the whole family. ■ *Memorial Coliseum; 684-KICK; map:O7.*

Portland Rockies Baseball   Believe it or not, Portland was without a baseball team for a brief time after the Portland Beavers departed to Salt Lake City in the early '90s—but with the arrival of the Bend Rockies, all that changed. The 1995 season—mid-June through Labor Day—was the first for this team in Portland, and by 1997, the Rockies were the Northwest League Champions.

The 38 home games at Civic Stadium provide baseball lovers with plenty of wins, not to mention a good excuse to munch hot dogs and do the Wave. ▪ *Civic Stadium, SW 20th Ave and Morrison St; 223-2837; www.portlandrockies.com; map:GG7.*

Portland Trail Blazers Basketball Will the Trail Blazers have a new coach with each edition of *Portland Best Places*? Last time, we welcomed new head coach P. J. Carlesimo. Now Carlesimo is history after just three seasons (totaling 140 wins and 118 losses), and Mike Dunleavy has arrived to take over. One thing is for sure, the Blazers' new, spacious, state-of-the-art arena—the Rose Garden—isn't going anywhere. ▪ *Memorial Coliseum; 231-8000 (tickets) or 321-3211 (events hotline); map:O7.*

Portland Winter Hawks Ice Hockey See tomorrow's NHL players today in the WHL (Western Hockey League). This developmental league grooms young hockey players for the big time. The 72-match season runs from October through March, with admission prices ranging from $10 to $14. Tickets are available at all Ticket-master locations and at the box office. ▪ *Memorial Coliseum; 238-6366; map:O7.*

ESSENTIALS

Essentials

TRANSPORTATION

AIRPLANES: PORTLAND INTERNATIONAL AIRPORT (PDX)

If airport size serves as any measure of a city's growth and stature, then judging by the continuous construction at **Portland International Airport**, or **PDX** (map:DD3), this town must surely be joining the ranks of the country's major metropolises. The latest in an ongoing series of construction projects is the $141 million "PDX2000," initiated in May 1996. When this phase is complete—sometime in 1999—there will be an additional four levels in the parking garage, along with more lanes and curb space to the roadway in front of the terminal and improved pedestrian passageways in the ticket lobby and baggage claim area. Also, a new canopy over the roadway in front of PDX will protect travelers from the unpredictable Portland weather. Meanwhile, though, finding a parking spot is like finding the proverbial needle in a haystack; so, to be safe, call ahead (288-PARK) before your next trip to PDX.

Otherwise, it's business as usual. The airport is about 20 minutes northeast of downtown, with uncomplicated freeway access via I-84 and I-205 (allow extra time during rush hour). Eighteen passenger airlines service PDX, with direct flights or easy connections to most large U.S. cities and even some small Oregon ones (such as Astoria). Overall, the airport provides service to 120 cities worldwide, including many Pacific Rim destinations.

Public information centers are located on the upper and lower levels of the terminal. They are staffed from 6am to 11:30pm every day. For **airport information**, call 460-4234.

The **airport's paging service** (460-4040) is provided through white courtesy telephones located throughout the terminal. To page from within the terminal, simply pick up one of these phones and place your request. The **Lost and Found** (460-4272) is located on the airport's lower level. It is open Monday through Friday; call ahead for hours.

The main concession area, known as the **Oregon Market**, is an attractive midterminal mall. Among the shops are a host of quintessential Oregon businesses: Powell's Books, the Nike Store, the Real Mother Goose, Norm Thompson Outfitters, Made in Oregon, and the Oregon Pendleton Shop (see the Shopping chapter). Airport contracts stipulate that prices in the Oregon Market shops must match those in the stores' other Portland outlets—so shopping at PDX is actually an affordable pleasure, not just a costly diversion.

Restaurants holding court in the main terminal include Wendy's, Macheezmo Mouse, Cool Temptations, Coffee People, Marsee Baking, Panda Express, and Creative Croissants Deli. Thirsty travelers can check out the new passel of theme bars, where those famous Oregon microbrews flow freely.

[KIDS] [FREE] Off the Oregon Market is a **nursery** with a changing table, a crib, chairs, and a private rest room, all of which may be used free of charge.

The **PDX Conference Center** (460-4050), located on the mezzanine overlooking the Oregon Market, is a popular stopover for business travelers. The center is open from 7am to 6pm weekdays. (See Meetings, Conferences, and Receptions under Business Services in this chapter.) Services include a fax machine, photocopying, computer rental, overnight shipping, and credit card telephones. There's also a lounge where you can unwind with a copy of the *Wall Street Journal*. Limited clerical help is available in the Conference Center.

Drivers have three choices for **parking** (288-PARK) at PDX. Rates range from $2 an hour in the temporary short-term lot (previously the long-term lot; maximum $22 per day) and $2 an hour in the parking garage ($48 maximum per day) to $6 per day or $36 maximum per week in economy. Free shuttle buses run from the economy lot every five minutes. All lots are open 24 hours. Tune your radio to 530AM a few miles from the airport for current traffic information and construction updates.

Perhaps the easiest way to get from the airport to downtown Portland (and vice versa) is on the **DASH (Downtown/Airport Shuttle Service)** operated by Raz Transportation (246-4676). Vans depart from PDX every 15 minutes, from 5:30am to 12:30am. One-way cost is $9 for adults, $2 for children ages 6 to 12 (younger children ride free). Stops include the Greyhound terminal, Benson Hotel, Hotel Vintage Plaza, Hilton Hotel, Heathman Hotel, Portland Inn, Riverside Inn, and Marriott Hotel. Allow at least 35 minutes for the trip.

The east side of the city is served by the "Blue Star," or **Eastside Airporter** (249-1837), whose vans are at the airport every half hour from 4:30am to midnight; rates for door-to-door service in northeast Portland start at $6.50 and increase according to mileage. The Airporter vans also service Hood River/The Dalles; Vancouver and Longview, Washington; the Troutdale and greater

Gresham area; and Milwaukie and Oregon City; call for routes and prices.

The **Beaverton Airporter** (649-2213) leaves the airport at a quarter past the hour, every hour, from 9:15am until noon. Between noon and 10:15pm (every day except Saturday) the vans go twice each hour, at a quarter past and a quarter till the hour. Rates are $15 one-way to most major Beaverton hotels. Door-to-door service is available too. The Beaverton Airporters also go to Hillsboro; call for fare information. The **Lake Oswego Airporter** (639-1332), which will pick you up from your home or hotel as early as 4am from as far away as Tigard, Tualatin, or Wilsonville, is available by reservation only; prices vary depending on the number of people traveling.

The most economical trip ($1.05) into the city is via **Tri-Met** (238-7433). Catch bus 12 from just outside the baggage claim area; the trip to the downtown mall takes approximately 40 minutes, traveling via Sandy Boulevard.

AIRPLANES: CHARTER

From Portland International Airport, **Flightcraft** (331-4200) offers 24-hour service, seven days a week. You can charter a plane to anywhere in the United States or Canada; call for information.

Also offering 24-hour service seven days a week, **Aero Air** (640-3711) charters planes from the Portland-Hillsboro Airport, 18 minutes west of downtown Portland off Hwy 26, and features a full-service maintenance center.

Aurora Aviation (678-1217), at the Aurora Airport, 20 minutes south of Portland on I-5, provides scenic flights and 24-hour, seven-day-a-week charter/air taxi service, as well as flight training, aircraft rental, and pilot supplies.

Fifteen minutes east of the city, **Aero West** (661-4940) in Troutdale offers scenic and charter flights throughout the Pacific Northwest, including the Columbia River Gorge and Mount St. Helens.

BUSES AND LIGHT RAIL: TRI-MET/MAX

Tri-Met (238-RIDE): More than 80 bus lines and the sleek light-rail train **MAX** (Metropolitan Area Express) make it exceptionally easy to get around the city without a car. You'll find bus stops throughout the city proper—just look for the blue and white signs. Most buses run at 15- or 30-minute intervals throughout the week, with express service during rush hours on some routes. (There are exceptions; for instance, the bus to Tualatin goes only once every two hours during midday. Call Tri-Met for schedules on specific routes.) Ninety percent of the buses are **wheelchair accessible**.

Almost all of the bus lines run through the Portland Transit Mall (on SW Fifth and SW Sixth Aves) along Pioneer Courthouse

Square. Buses run north across Burnside all the way to the new Tri-Met North Terminal, just past the Greyhound station and just across the street from Union Station. The terminal is now the first stop on the transit mall and serves as a pit stop for bus drivers, providing a place to park their buses while they take a break and wait to complete their schedule.

On its 15-mile light-rail course from the downtown area, MAX begins in the Goose Hollow neighborhood at SW Salmon Street and SW 18th Avenue, passes through downtown and Old Town, crosses the Steel Bridge, and continues on the east side, swinging by the Oregon Convention Center and the Lloyd Center before making its way to Gresham. Glass-covered stations along the way maintain schedule information and ticket machines. The comfortable trains run every 15 minutes most hours of the day—more frequently during rush hour—every day of the week. The fares are the same as those for Tri-Met buses, and **the tickets are interchangeable**.

The westside expansion of MAX is under way and, if the schedule stays on track, you should be able to hop a train in Gresham and ride 33 miles to Hillsboro by September 1998. Of the 20 stops between downtown and Hillsboro, 9 will accommodate a total of 3,700 parked vehicles. The Washington County bus system will be rerouted to feed the MAX stations, all of which, in true Portland fashion, are to be liberally embellished with public art. Nine artists have collaborated with architects and engineers to create individual identities for each station.

[FREE] Travelers in the downtown area can **ride for free** (buses or MAX) anywhere in the 300-block "Fareless Square." The square extends from I-405 on the south and west to NW Hoyt Street on the north and the Willamette River on the east. **Fares** outside the square are $1.05 for travel in two zones (from downtown to residential areas within the metropolitan area) and $1.35 for three zones (necessary for travel from downtown to most parts of Tigard, Beaverton, Gresham, Milwaukie, and Lake Oswego). Youth tickets are 80 cents per ride, and as many as three children age 6 and younger can ride free with a fare-paying customer. All-day tickets are $3.25. Honored citizens—those 65 and older or disabled—can catch a bus for 50 cents per ride or pay $10 for a monthly pass.

You can purchase tickets and obtain scheduling information at **Tri-Met's Customer Assistance Office** in the middle of Pioneer Courthouse Square (map:H3). It's open from 9am to 5pm weekdays. You can also purchase tickets aboard buses (bring exact change, as drivers won't make change for you) or from the ticket machines at each stop along the MAX line. Tri-Met runs on the **honor system**; that is, bus drivers only sometimes check fares from downtown, and MAX drivers never check fares. How- ever, Tri-Met inspectors randomly request proof of fare payment on buses and MAX, and passengers who haven't paid are fined or cited in district court.

You can take your **bike on the bus** (or on the train). All Tri-Met buses are outfitted with bike racks, as is MAX; purchase a one-time bike pass for $5.

BUSES: OUT-OF-TOWN AND CHARTER

Greyhound-Trailways Bus Lines (550 NW Sixth Ave, 243-2357 for local arrival and departure information or (800)231-2222; map:L4) has a full schedule to and from Portland. The terminal is about six blocks north of W Burnside, within walking distance of the downtown hub. For package service, call 243-2333. You can charter a bus from **Evergreen–Gray Line of Portland**, which also conducts local tours and specialty tours to destinations throughout Oregon (285-9845; see Motor Tours in the Exploring chapter).

TAXICABS

Portland is not New York City, and cabbies are sometimes hard to flag down on the street. You'll have better luck finding a phone and calling for one. Your options? **Portland Taxi** (256-5400), **Broadway Cab, Inc.** (227-1234), and **Radio Cab** (227-1212).

TRAINS

Eight blocks north of W Burnside, near the Greyhound bus terminal, stands **Union Station** (800 NW Sixth Ave, map:M4). A Portland Historic Landmark that's also on the National Register of Historic Places, this grand old building serves as the city's **Amtrak** passenger station; (800)872-7245 for 24-hour reservations and information or 273-4866 for local information. With its prominent tower, great curving entrance, and muscular features, this romantic structure memorializes the bygone era of the great railways. Worth a visit in itself, the more-than-100-year-old station serves as a fitting terminus to the recent northern extension of the transit mall. Amtrak trains run north, south, and east daily. To reach the baggage room or package express service, call 273-4871.

TROLLEY

[FREE] The oak-paneled and brass-belled **Vintage Trolley** (323-7363) follows the MAX route from the Lloyd Center to the downtown turnaround at SW 11th Avenue and back. Top speed is 35 miles an hour, and rides are free. The ride takes about 40 minutes and trolleys run about a half hour apart, 9:30am to 3pm weekdays, 10am to 6pm weekends.

CATERERS

Ron Paul Catering & Charcuterie (1441 NE Broadway, 284-5439, map:FF5) is one of the better caterers in town, and its chic eatery in northeast Portland is the perfect place for discussing party arrangements. Ron Paul has two other outlets—one on SW Macadam and one downtown. Up in northwest Portland is **Briggs & Crampton, Inc.** (1902 NW 24th Ave, 223-8690, map:FF6), another excellent catering service, run solely by Nancy Briggs, who has garnered a national reputation for her two-person lunch feasts. **Food in Bloom** (2701 NW Vaughn St, Suite 421, 223-6819, map:FF7) in Montgomery Park is also a good bet. (For other recommendations, see the index at the beginning of the Restaurants chapter.)

CHILD CARE

Most major hotels can arrange for baby-sitters if notified in advance. The **Northwest Nannies Institute** (245-5288) places course graduates for live-in or daily care throughout the metro area. **Metro Child Care Resource & Referral** (253-5000) offers free information on day-care services in the tri-county area.

COMPLAINTS

To register a complaint about an abandoned automobile or a large truck parked in a residential area, call the **Abandoned Auto Hotline** (823-7309) and select from a menu of options, or call 823-6814 to reach an operator. To report residential nuisance properties, call 823-7306. For barking dogs or stray, biting, injured, or loose animals, call **Multnomah County Animal Control** (248-3066). Help for rodent and mosquito problems is available through **Multnomah County Vector and Nuisance Control** (248-3464). Anything else to gripe about? Whatever your complaint, you can probably find help by calling the **City of Portland's information** number, 823-4000, or **Multnomah County's general information** number, 248-3511.

DISABILITY AID

Independent Living Resources offers a wide range of services to promote independent living (232-7411). **Portland Parks and Recreation** (426 NE 12th Ave, 823-4328) offers recreation for persons age 5 or older with disabilities, with a focus on integration into other Parks and Recreation programs. Programs meet in various locations throughout the city and include community outings, monthly dances, special-interest classes such as music and art, weekly bowling, and an integrated summer day camp for children of all abilities.

DISCRIMINATION

You can call the **Metropolitan Human Rights Commission** (1120 SW Fifth Ave, 823-5136, map:G3) with any kind of discrimination complaint. As an information and referral service, the agency has no enforcement power, but can steer you in the right direction by mapping out available avenues for recourse.

DRINKING FOUNTAINS

No one will ever go thirsty in Portland. Tapped into the city's well are a number of four-petaled drinking fountains (located in many downtown public areas), given to the city by lumberman and philanthropist Simon Benson in 1912. Once continuously flowing, the fountains are now fitted to turn on and off.

DRY CLEANERS AND TAILORS

One of the most convenient dry cleaners in the downtown area is **Bee Tailors and Cleaners** (939 SW 10th Ave, 227-1144, map:G2), open weekdays and Saturday mornings. Bee offers curbside service; just honk. Or try **Levine's**, with several branches downtown and the main location at 2086 W Burnside (223-7221, map:GG6).

FOREIGN EXCHANGE

Exchange currency at any main bank branch, at the **American Express Travel Agency** (1100 SW Sixth Ave, 226-2961, map:H4), or at **Travelex America** (281-3045), located at Portland International Airport across from the United Airlines ticket counter.

FOREIGN VISITORS: LANGUAGE

The **World Trade Center**'s Language Services (121 SW Salmon St, Suite 250, 464-8888, map:F5) offers written translation, interpretation, cultural training, and language instruction services to businesses and private individuals. The Language Service's private English programs are tailored to the client's needs and involve total immersion for as long as desired. Many take lessons in the classroom and then go on field trips in the afternoon, accompanied by a guide and speaking nothing but English on the way.

LEGAL SERVICES

The **Oregon State Bar Lawyer Referral Service** (5200 SW Meadows Rd, Lake Oswego, 684-3763, map:KK8) has offered referrals since 1971. Expect to pay $35 for an initial office consultation, after which you will be charged the firm's normal hourly rates. A reduced-fee program is available. **Multnomah County Legal Aid** (700 SW Taylor, Suite 300, 224-4086, map:G3) offers limited legal services to qualified low-income Multnomah County residents, based on client income and case.

LIBRARIES

[KIDS]The **Multnomah County Library** has 15 branches throughout the city, with film-, tape-, and book-borrowing plus other services. The library sponsors a variety of films, lectures, and programs for children. Portlanders were delighted when the **Central Library** (801 SW 10th Ave, 248-5123, map:H1) reopened in April 1997 after being closed for three years of remodeling.

The **Clackamas County Public Library System** has 13 branches. Call individual branches for hours and events. The **Beaverton City Library** (12500 SW Allen Blvd, Beaverton, 644-2197, map:II9), Washington County's biggest, is available for use by citizens in Washington, Multnomah, or Clackamas Counties and is open seven days. Although Washington County's 11 libraries are individual, nonbranch entities, they all share databases.

LIMOUSINE SERVICE

For more than 20 years the **Oregon Limousine Service** (1424 NE 80th Ave, 252-5993) has supplied extraordinary cars and drivers for celebs, newlyweds, executives, and others.

LOST CAR

If you suspect your car has been towed, call the **Police Bureau**'s Auto Records/Impounds line (823-0044). If there's no mention of it in their records, call 230-2121—it's probably been stolen.

MEDICAL AND DENTAL SERVICES

Several hospitals provide physician referrals: **Adventist Medical Center** (10123 SE Market St, 256-4000, map:GG2); **Eastmoreland Hospital** (2900 SE Steele St, (800)700-3956, map:HH4); **Providence Portland Medical Center** (4805 NE Glisan St, 215-6595, map:GG4); and **St. Vincent Hospital** (9205 SW Barnes Rd, 291-2188, map:GG8). **Legacy Health System**, which locally comprises both **Emanuel Hospital & Health Center** (2801 N Gantenbein Ave, map:FF5) and **Good Samaritan Hospital & Medical Center** (1015 NW 22nd Ave, map:FF6) has one physician referral line, (800)335-3500. The **Multnomah Dental Society** (223-4731) provides emergency and routine referral service at no charge.

NEWSPAPERS AND PERIODICALS

The lone daily in Portland, the *Oregonian* (221-8327), has been published since 1850 and reigns as the king of print journalism in the city. A telephone information service, Inside Line, is available from the newspaper. Call 225-5555 to hear everything from lottery results to movie schedules.

The *Oregonian* is joined on Wednesdays by *Willamette Week* (243-2122), a free, thought-provoking, irreverent, sometimes

controversial newsweekly covering politics, the arts, and civic
matters. Both papers contain substantial and useful entertainment calendars. (The *Oregonian*'s—"A&E"—is published on Fridays.) Relatively new and free also, *Our Town* (224-1774) covers the downtown core, with features on residential interiors, travel, and entertainment. The *Business Journal* (274-8733) and the *Daily Journal of Commerce* (226-1311) cover the city's business beat. *PDXS* (224-7316) is a good free source for local music and slacker news—alternative by most measures. *Just Out* is Portland's free gay and lesbian newsletter, available, like the other free papers, at various locations about town. Finally, parents appreciate the free *Portland Parent Newsmagazine* (638-1049) for its calendar and tot-related news.

PUBLIC OFFICIALS

Mayor **Vera Katz** is enjoying her second term at the helm of the City of Portland (1220 SW Fifth Ave, 823-4120, map:F3) and will keep that position until 2000. City commissioners in 1997 are **Erik Sten** (823-3589), Department of Public Works; **Charlie Hales** (823-4682), Department of Public Safety; **Gretchen Miller Kafoury** (823-4151), Department of Public Affairs; and **Jim Francesconi** (823-3008), Department of Public Utilities. **Barbara Clark** (823-4078) is the city auditor. The commissioners' offices and that of the city auditor are located downtown at 1220 SW Fifth Avenue (map:F3). The Multnomah County commissioners are **Beverly Stein**, chair (248-3308); **Dan Saltzman**, District 1 (248-5220); **Gary Hansen**, District 2 (248-5219); **Tanya Collier**, District 3 (248-5217); and **Sharron Kelley**, District 4 (248-5213). Their offices are in the Multnomah County Courthouse building at 1021 SW Fourth Avenue (map:F3).

▼

Keys to the
City

Senior Services

▲

PUBLIC REST ROOMS

The most centrally located public rest rooms downtown are those in **Pioneer Courthouse Square** (701 SW Sixth Ave, map:H3), near the Tri-Met office. The lobby opens at 8:30am and closes at 5pm weekdays and is open during the afternoon on weekends (hours vary). Farther south, there are public rest rooms in the **Clay Street parking garage** (map:E3) between SW Third and Fourth Avenues.

SENIOR SERVICES

In Multnomah County, the **Aging Services Department** operates a Senior Helpline (248-3646), which assists seniors with information about health services, low-income housing, recreation, transportation, legal services, volunteer programs, and other matters. In Clackamas County, call the **Area Agency on Aging** (655-8640); it has a counterpart in Washington County (640-3489).

SERVICE STATIONS: ALL NIGHT

Jantzen Beach Unocal (12205 N Center Rd, 285-2657, map:CC6) provides 24-hour towing and services. Closer to downtown, **Uptown Chevron** (2230 W Burnside, 224-3859, map:GG6) is open all night, and so is **Burns Brothers**, across the river (621 SE Martin Luther King Jr. Blvd, 238-7347, map:L9).

SHOE REPAIR

The cobblers at **PacWest Center Shoe Repair** (1211 SW Fifth Ave, 225-9414, map:F2), in the PacWest Building, are cheerful and reliable, and are on the job from 8am to 5pm weekdays. **Dr. Sole & Ms. Heel** (429 SW 10th Ave, 222-5456, map:I2) will replace your heel while you wait, and they fix purses and belts, too.

TELEPHONE NUMBERS

(The following phone numbers are in the 503 area code unless otherwise specified.)

Emergency: Police, Fire, Ambulance **911**
Directory Assistance (within Oregon) ....**(503)555-1212**
AIDS Hotline 223-AIDS (2437)
Alcoholics Anonymous 223-8569
Amtrak...273-4865
Animal Control 248-3066
Auto Impound..823-0044
Automobile Association of America (AAA),
    Oregon office..222-6734
Better Business Bureau...226-3981
Birth and Death Records (Oregon Vital Records) 731-4095
Blood Bank 223-4199
Chamber of Commerce 228-9411
Child Abuse Hotline (Multnomah County) 731-3100
City of Portland (general information) 823-4000
Coast Guard................................240-9310 (emergencies: 240-9300)
Drunk Drivers Hotline ....(800)24-DRUNK
Environmental Protection Agency 326-3250
FBI...224-4181
Humane Society (lost pets) 285-0641
Immigration and Naturalization Service
    ("Ask Immigration" Information Hotline) 326-3006
Internal Revenue Service.......................................221-3960
Marriage Licenses (and Passports) 248-3027
Parks and Recreation Information............................823-2223
Passports ....(800)ASK-USPS
Permit Center Information......................................823-7310
Planned Parenthood 775-0861
Poison Control Center 494-8968
Post Office Information..(800)ASK-USPS
Power Outages (24 hours) 464-7777

Recycling Information...234-3000
Red Cross..284-1234
Road Conditions............................(503)976-7277 or (541)889-3999
Ski Information (KINK's "What's Going On" line,
  in season)..226-3102
Sports Organizations:
  Portland Meadows (Horse Racing).............................285-9144
  Portland Power (Women's Basketball)....................236-HOOP
  Portland Pride (Soccer)..684-KICK
  Portland Rockies (Baseball).......................................223-2837
  Trail Blazers (Men's Basketball)..................................234-9291
  Winter Hawks (Hockey)...238-6366
State Patrol (Monday-Friday)...731-3020
Suicide Prevention..215-7082
Time, Temperature, and Weather (KXL).........................243-7575
Tri-Met...238-RIDE (7433)
Visitor Information..222-2223
Voter Information..248-3720
Weather...243-7575
Women's Crisis Line (sexual assault, domestic violence)...235-5333

TELEVISION STUDIO AUDIENCES

KATU (2153 NE Sandy Blvd, 231-4222, map:GG5), Portland's ABC affiliate, airs two shows with studio audiences: **AM Northwest**, the daily interview show (231-4610 for reservations, no tickets required), and **Town Hall**, a weekly, sometimes controversial civic affairs program (231-4620). The show is taped seasonally, and reservations are not available in the summer.

TOWING

Speed's Towing (120 SE Clay St, 238-6211, map:B8) offers 24-hour towing from any of their six Portland-area locations—whether you like it or not.

UNIVERSITIES AND COLLEGES

For a city its size, Portland has many institutions of higher learning. **Portland State University**, the state's urban university, is located at the south end of the South Park Blocks (724 SW Harrison St, 725-3000, map:E1). The **Oregon Health Sciences University**, in southwest Portland, is the only academic institution in the state devoted exclusively to the study of health (3181 SW Sam Jackson Park Rd, 494-8311, map:HH6). In north Portland, the **University of Portland** was founded early in the 20th century by the Catholic archbishop of Oregon (5000 N Willamette Blvd, 283-7911, map:EE8). Another private institution, **Pacific University**, was founded in 1842 in nearby Forest Grove (2043 College Way, 357-6151). Nationally renowned for its academic rigor and free-thinking student body, **Reed College** is located in southeast Portland off Bybee Boulevard (3203 SE

Woodstock Blvd, 771-1112, map:II5). Founded in 1867, **Lewis and Clark College**, a liberal-arts school known for its international programs, is located off Terwilliger Boulevard in southwest Portland (0615 SW Palatine Hill Rd, 768-7000, map:JJ6). Lewis and Clark is also home to the acclaimed **Northwestern School of Law. Marylhurst College**, once a women's college, became coeducational in 1976 (just more than a mile south of Lake Oswego on Hwy 43, 636-8141, map:MM6). **Warner Pacific College** is a liberal-arts school affiliated with the Church of God (2219 SE 68th St, 775-4366, map:HH4). Community colleges are also numerous in the area. **Portland Community College** (244-6111) has three campuses in the metropolitan area: Cascade Campus (705 N Killingsworth St, map:EE5), Rock Creek Campus (17705 NW Springville Rd, map:EE9), and Sylvania Campus (12000 SW 49th Ave, map:JJ7); **Mount Hood Community College** is located in Gresham (26000 SE Stark St, 667-7171), and **Clackamas Community College** is in Oregon City (19600 S Molalla, 657-6958).

VETERINARIANS: EMERGENCY AND WEEKEND SERVICE

Dove Lewis Emergency Animal Hospital (two locations: 1984 NW Pettygrove St, 228-7281, map:FF7; and 18990 SW Shaw St, Aloha, 645-5800) is supported by the Portland Veterinary Medical Association. The northwest Portland branch is open 24 hours and on holidays. Both are open nights and weekends; call for specific hours.

MOVING IN

Contemplating a move to Portland? If a reconnaissance mission is impossible—or to help ease your transition into the city—order the **Portland Chamber of Commerce's relocation packet**. Population, housing, government, taxes, businesses, hospitals, schools, even the weather—the most vital of statistics are compiled here. Send $15 (or $33 for a video, too) and a request to the chamber (221 NW Second Ave, Portland, OR 97209) or call 228-9411.

A strong sense of neighborhood loyalty runs through Portland, and 94 areas have formed **neighborhood associations** to tackle problems and nurture community pride. Activities range from fighting crime through the Neighborhood Watch program to tackling land-use issues and just plain socializing. You can find out more about your neighborhood association by contacting the **Office of Neighborhood Associations** (1220 SW Fifth Ave, Rm 204, 823-4519, map:F3). Finally, there's the **Welcome Wagon** (236-8782), which you can count on for a courteous introduction to the neighborhood.

BUSINESS SERVICES

COMPUTER RENTALS

Bit-By-Bit This well-established, nationwide rental service will rent you an IBM-compatible PC and even deliver and set it up for you anywhere in the Portland metro area. They also lease notebooks, laptops, and Macintoshes, as well as peripheral equipment. Bit-By-Bit offers 24-hour service. ■ *9203 SW Nimbus Ave, Beaverton; 520-0218; map:JJ9.*

COPY SERVICES

Clean Copy For high-quality business copy services, this shop comes highly recommended. It features offset printing, color laser copies, and photocopying, and has desktop publishing services. Free parking and delivery. ■ *1732 SW 6th Ave; 221-1876; map:D1.*

Kinko's The service is usually helpful and friendly—even at 3am (all branches are open 24 hours)—although these shops do high-volume business, and small jobs sometimes don't get the attention they deserve. There are 10 branches in the metro area, and you can rent Macintosh computers or PCs by the hour at any of them. Color laser copiers and fax service are also available. ■ *1503 SW Park Ave (and branches); 223-2056; map:E1.*

Lazerquick Copies With more than 30 locations throughout the Portland metro area, there's no escaping Lazerquick, a home-grown company that began its modest operations in a small Tigard house. Today, in addition to their offset printing and high-speed copying services—and a savings of 3 cents per copy over Kinko's in the do-it-yourself department—Lazerquick provides a host of computer and digital imaging solutions. All stores have scanners and rent Macs and PC-platform workstations. ■ *1134 SW 5th Ave (and branches); 228-6306; map:F3.*

MEETINGS, CONFERENCES, AND RECEPTIONS

Most hotels and many restaurants have private meeting rooms for rent. The following is a list of other rental facilities appropriate for business meetings, private parties, and receptions. Private functions can also be held at the Multnomah County Library (call the branch nearest you to reserve a room), most museums, Portland State University (which has numerous halls, auditoriums, and meeting rooms), and other educational facilities. For a comprehensive guide to a variety of locations at which to exchange wedding vows in the Portland area and environs, check out Bravo's wedding planning guides, found at most major bookstores.

Edgefield The former Multnomah County Poor Farm at Edgefield was acquired by the McMenamin brothers in the early 1990s, and they've turned it into a multiuse theme park offering everything from art to beer to wine to fine dining to cheap movies to blues concerts. There are also overnight accommodations. Twelve rooms are available for private functions, the largest of which seats 176 people (225 standing). Ask for the conference packet when you inquire (and also see review in the Lodgings chapter). ▪ *2126 NE Halsey, Troutdale; take exit 16A from I-84E; 669-8610.*

Jenkins Estate An Arts and Crafts–style house, stable, and gatehouse sit on 68 idyllic acres, 33 of which are landscaped and crisscrossed with trails. The general public is just as welcome as guests are to stroll the grounds, and trail maps are available. The gatehouse is perfect for small business meetings, and the main house can accommodate varying numbers of people, depending on room arrangements. The stable can handle even more guests on its two floors. The old stalls make for great breakout sessions during a meeting or can serve as intimate dining alcoves. Tea and coffee service is available. Make your wedding reservations a year in advance. ▪ *8005 SW Grabhorn Rd, Aloha; 642-3855.*

Menucha Retreat and Conference Center Nonprofit religious, cultural, educational, and governmental groups are welcome at this center, perched high on a bluff overlooking the Columbia River. Part of Portland's First Presbyterian Church, it has a kinder, gentler atmosphere than some of the other conference locales. Trails wind through Menucha's 100 wooded acres, and a swimming pool and other diversions occupy visitors. The home-style cooking is a draw, although no alcohol is allowed in the dining room. ▪ *28711 E Crown Point Hwy, Corbett; 695-2243.*

Montgomery Park Montgomery Park is one of Portland's premier meeting places. There are numerous possibilities here: the Don Campbell Hall can accommodate as many as 300 people for a sit-down dinner, or if that's too grand, choose from four conference and meeting rooms. The (sometimes) sunny atrium is also available and can hold as many as 800 standing guests. Plenty of free parking. ▪ *2701 NW Vaughn St; 228-7275; map:FF6.*

Oregon Convention Center Purposefully recognizable by its twin green towers (glowing when lit from within), this facility just across the river from downtown has 150,000 square feet of open exhibit space with numerous reception, banquet, and meeting rooms. The OCC is spacious—it has contained as many as 40,000 people at one time, although groups of 50 are welcome as well. Outdoor parking accommodates 900 cars, and the facility is wheelchair accessible. A MAX light-rail stop at the front door makes a trip into downtown effortless—or it's a pleasant walk across the Steel Bridge. ▪ *NE Martin Luther King Jr Blvd and Holladay St; 235-7575; map:M9.*

Pittock Mansion This Portland landmark leases space during the evening to recognized organizations, commercial and non-profit alike. The mansion, in its lofty location high above the city, can accommodate 50 for a sit-down dinner or 250 for a standing reception; you'll need to hire the caterer. It's a popular locale— reserve a year in advance for the holiday season. ▪ *3229 NW Pittock Dr; 823-3623; map:GG7.*

Portland Conference Center Conferences, meetings, and receptions are a big business at this full-service facility, whether the party's for 5 or 500. Nineteen rooms include stage areas and tele-conferencing equipment. In-house catering. ▪ *300 NE Multnomah; 239-9921; map:N9.*

Portland International Airport Conference Center Conference rooms are available at the airport by the hour ($15 to $75) or by the day ($7 to $125) for as many as 70 people. ▪*PDX; 460-4050; map:DD3.*

Portland's White House Weddings and private receptions are popular at this elegant bed-and-breakfast inn, the former mansion of local timber baron Robert F. Lytle. The White House features a 1,650-square-foot ballroom, with room for 100 dancers. If you'd like to stay over, the White House has eight lovely sleeping rooms with private baths (see review in the Lodgings chapter). ▪ *1914 NE 22nd Ave; 287-7131; map:FF5.*

Tryon Creek State Park A meeting room for 60 in the Nature Center at picturesque Tryon Creek is available (for a small charge) for retreats and meetings only. No parties, weddings, or receptions. Lovely setting; limited facilities. ▪ *11321 SW Terwilliger Blvd; 636-9886; map:JJ6.*

World Forestry Center Three facilities and a large outdoor plaza are available at the Forestry Center, which welcomes all kinds of parties, from class reunions to academic conferences (no proms, however). There are kitchen facilities and tables and chairs; you arrange for the catering. The largest building can accommodate up to 300 guests. The smallest seats up to 60, classroom-style. This is an exceptionally nice and very popular place. Planning a wedding? Make your reservations at least a year in advance. ▪ *4033 SW Canyon Rd (Washington Park); 228-1367; map:GG7.*

World Trade Center On the mezzanine level are four rooms, the largest of which (the auditorium) seats 220 people. Especially nice is the 10,000-square-foot outdoor plaza, which is entirely covered with glass. The new restaurant, Flags, is available as a banquet hall after hours and on weekends. These spaces are available for business meetings, wedding receptions, and other events. Full catering. ▪ *121 SW Salmon St; 464-8688; map:F5.*

MESSENGER SERVICES

Pronto Messenger Service   It seems that whenever someone wants to send something by messenger in this city, they invoke the verb "Pronto," as in "I'll Pronto it over to you." It's Portland's favorite, especially for crosstown deliveries. ▪ *901 SE Oak St, Suite 202; 239-7666; map:GG5.*

TranServe Systems Inc.   By car, bicycle, or plane—TranServe delivers. They offer overnight or immediate delivery, whether in the city or abroad. ▪ *310 SW 4th Ave, Suite 200; 241-0484; map:I4.*

SECRETARIAL SERVICES

HQ Business Centers   Catering to business travelers, HQ is a national company that offers word processing, phone and beeper service, mail service, binding, fax, and more. It also rents a variety of office spaces and conference space for up to 12 people. ▪ *1001 SW 5th Ave; 220-1600; map:G3.*

Professional Secretarial   This business offers both full-service secretarial and desktop publishing services. They promise to be fast and affordable and have been around since 1984. ▪ *423 SW 4th Ave; 223-1493; map:I5.*

Calendar

JANUARY

Whale Watching [FREE] You can indulge in this classic Oregon pastime any time of year, although the best whale-watching period is through the winter. From mid-December to late January you can sometimes spot 30 gray whales an hour as they swim south along the coast to calve or breed. By mid-March, some grays will already be returning north. (From April through December you may spot "resident" whales that cut short their northern migration to summer along the coast of Oregon, where they remain until they join forces with the next southerly migration.) The Alsea Bay Bridge Interpretive Center is a good place to ask questions. Among the best places to snag a whale-watching cruise are Newport, Depoe Bay, Charleston, Rockaway, and Brookings. See Whale Watch Week in this chapter's December listing for pointers on the best viewing spots from land. ■ *Alsea Bay Bridge Interpretive Center, Waldport; (541)563-2002.*

FEBRUARY

Home and Garden Show This enormous trade show features exhibits for home decorating and remodeling, along with everything you need for the care and feeding of your lawn or garden. ■ *Expo Center; 285-7756; map:CC6.*

Newport Seafood and Wine Festival To find this three-day festival during the last weekend in February, cross the Yaquina Bay Bridge from Newport to South Beach on the Oregon Coast; it all takes place in that community's exhibition hall. More than 100 exhibitors, largely seafood distributors and wineries, display their wares; food and wine are plentiful—for a fee. Adults 21 and over only. ■ *Newport, 114 miles southwest of Portland (take Hwys 99W and 101); (800)262-7844.*

Oregon Shakespeare Festival   The charming southern Oregon college town of Ashland just happens to be home to one of the oldest and largest theater companies in the country. Nearly 350,000 tickets are sold each year (mid-February through October), with audiences filling the festival's three theaters, including the outdoor Elizabethan Theater. Lectures, backstage tours, and Renaissance music and dance are other attractions visitors enjoy. Spring is a good time to go; last-minute tickets are rare in the summer. ▪ *Citywide, Ashland, 300 miles south of Portland (take I-5 and Hwy 99); (541) 482-4331.*

Portland International Film Festival   An event that lives up to its name: 93 films from 30 countries were represented in 1997. Movies are screened at the Northwest Film Center at the Portland Art Museum (and select downtown theaters) during three weeks in February and March. Opening-night parties and closing-night galas are part of the festivities. Tickets are $6.50 per show ($5.50 for museum members) or $100 for a festival pass. ▪ *Northwest Film Center, 1219 SW Park Ave; 221-1156; map:G1.*

RAW: The Reed Arts Weekend   This multiday arts extravaganza features dance, readings, fine-art shows, a film and video component, theater, and music. Whatever the theme, it's a good bet for thought-provoking entertainment. Usually the last weekend in February. ▪ *Reed College; 777-7708; map:II5.*

MARCH

Oregon State Special Olympics   More than 400 disabled athletes compete in ice-skating and skiing—both downhill and cross-country. ▪ *Mt Bachelor, Bend, 163 miles southeast of Portland (take Hwys 26 and 97); (800) 829-2442.*

Portland Saturday Market   [KIDS] [FREE] Select a piece of hand-thrown porcelain or sample a spoonful of jam made at a local berry farm. Billed as the largest open-air crafts market in the country, this beloved Portland institution brings together 274 regional craft artists who display their handmade creations in historic Old Town. Music and lunch, too; every weekend from March through Christmas, 10am–5pm Saturdays, 11am–4:30pm Sundays. ▪ *Under the Burnside Bridge at SW 1st Ave; 222-6072; map:J7.*

Shrine Circus   [KIDS] Grab the kids, they'll love this: it's everything you'd expect from a three-ring circus. (Call to check dates; sometimes the show doesn't hit town until April.) ▪ *Memorial Coliseum; 797-9698; map:O7.*

Hood River Blossom Festival   Before it was a board-sailing mecca, Hood River was known for its orchards, and this festival celebrates that heritage. Tours of wineries and the blossoming fruit orchards are available; the well-marked Blossom Trail is a one-hour driving loop through the most scenic of the scenic. ▪ *Hood River, 60 miles east of Portland (take I-84); (541)386-2000 or (800)366-3530.*

Packy's Birthday Party   [KIDS] Portland's famous elephant is thirtysomething (middle-aged, in elephant years) and hundreds of his admirers flock to the zoo to celebrate with him each year. Everyone is invited to don floppy elephant ears, eat cake, play games, and sign the birthday card. Pay zoo admission and the party is free. ▪ *Washington Park Zoo; 226-ROAR; map:GG7.*

Spring Rhododendron Show   [FREE] Long before the first rosebuds open, Portland's hills and dales are blanketed in blooms – daffodils, ornamental plum and cherry trees, camellias, and, most spectacularly, rhododendrons and azaleas. The city becomes one huge garden, with whole neighborhoods aflame in searing pinks and resounding purples. This rhododendron show is a perfect excuse for visiting the pretty Jenkins Estate. ▪ *Jenkins Estate, 8005 SW Grabhorn Rd, Aloha; 642-3855.*

Trillium Festival   [KIDS] [FREE] Yet another blossom festival, but this one's right in town, in the pristine 645-acre Tryon Creek State Park. During the early spring, when the delicate trilliums bloom, the Friends of Tryon Creek host this weekend celebration featuring a native plant sale, plenty of food, guided walks, and other pleasant diversions. Activities for children, too. ▪ *Tryon Creek State Park; 636-4398; map:KK6.*

MAY

Cinco de Mayo Celebration Portland is home to the nation's largest celebration of Mexico's Independence Day, produced by the Portland/Guadalajara Sister City Association. The event features a marketplace, ethnic food, and stellar entertainment from Mexico, such as Grupo Folklorico, a 39-member ensemble of mariachi singers and dancers. The festivities often begin at the end of April. ▪ *Tom McCall Waterfront Park; 222-9807; map:G6.*

Festival of Flowers [FREE] During one week in spring, usually May, Pioneer Courthouse Square is transformed into living art, rendered in flowers. Past works have ranged from abstract pieces to a stunning patchwork quilt and a miniature Japanese garden.

Some 25,000 potted annuals are arranged in colorful patterns; then, after the show, all are offered to the public at wholesale prices. ■ *Pioneer Courthouse Square; 223-1613; map:H3.*

Indian Art Northwest [FREE] More than 600 Native American artists from all over North America present their contemporary and traditional works for viewing and for sale in Portland's tented Park Blocks each Memorial Day weekend, with a monumental sculpture exhibit in nearby Pioneer Courthouse Square. Lectures, films, and performances before and during the juried art show. ■ *Park Blocks; 230-7005; map:H3.*

Prefontaine Classic Eugene is still one of the best places in the country to rub elbows with world-class runners. This track meet, named for the late Steve Prefontaine, the University of Oregon's 1972 Olympian, draws competitors from around the globe. ■ *Hayward Field, Eugene, 105 miles south of Portland (take I-5); (541) 687-1989.*

US Bank Pole, Pedal, Paddle It's a grueling test of endurance that has become one of central Oregon's most popular events. Some 2,500 people downhill and cross-country ski, canoe or kayak, run and sprint from Mount Bachelor to downtown Bend. Usually the Saturday after Mother's Day. ■ *Mt Bachelor, Bend, 163 miles southeast of Portland (take Hwys 26 and 97); (541) 388-0002.*

JUNE

Britt Festival For more than 35 years, this summer musical extravaganza has been held at the hillside field where the late Peter Britt, a famous local photographer and horticulturist, once had his home. A handsome shell has been constructed, and listeners sit on benches or loll on blankets under the stars. You can sample everything from bluegrass, classical, and jazz to ballet and musical theater. ■ *Jacksonville, 283 miles south of Portland (take I-5); (541) 773-6077 or (800) 88-BRITT.*

Chamber Music Northwest Enjoy a preconcert picnic and "Musical Conversations" before any of 25 performances. This exciting, nationally acclaimed chamber music festival features works from a widely ranging repertoire, performed by some of the nation's top musicians. There's even a Sunday family concert. Mid-June through July. ■ *Reed College and Catlin Gabel School campuses; 223-3202; map:II5 and HH9.*

Oregon Bach Festival Conductor Helmuth Rilling leads this celebrated festival, which features 50 events, including chamber music concerts and recitals from baroque to jazz. You can hear music at Beall Hall on the University of Oregon campus, as well as in downtown Eugene at the impressive Hult Center. Workshops and master classes are also available to the general public (advance registration required). Festival tickets, available through the Hult Center, (541)682-5000, go on sale in March, and many events sell out. ■ *Eugene, 105 miles south of Portland (take I-5); (541)346-5666.*

Pioneer Square Concerts   [FREE] Two notable concert series liven up the already lively Pioneer Courthouse Square from mid-June through August: the mixed-bag Peanut Butter and Jam Sessions are held every Tuesday and Thursday at noon, while Starbucks by Starlight concerts feature jazz on Friday evenings. Throughout the summer there are many special concerts here, too. ■ *Pioneer Courthouse Square; 223-1613; map:H3.*

Portland Rose Festival   [KIDS] [FREE] Would a festival by any other name seem so sweet to Portlanders? Now in its ninth decade, the beloved Rose Festival is a four-week celebration that encompasses many major events: three parades, a world-class rose show, an air show, a hot-air balloon race, and a carnival on the waterfront. It's one of the premier festivals in the nation and an event of which Portlanders are exceedingly proud. ■ *Citywide; 227-2681.*

Rhythm and Zoo Concerts   [KIDS] On Wednesday and Thursday evenings from mid-June to mid-August, thousands of concert-goers flock to the Washington Park Zoo amphitheater to hear a variety of jazz, folk, and ethnic music. Visitors picnic on terraced lawns in the outdoor amphitheater. Pay regular zoo admission; the concerts are free. ■ *Washington Park Zoo; 226-1561; map:GG7.*

Sand Castle Day   [KIDS] Oregon's original and most prestigious sand castle contest is more than a quarter century old. Buckets, shovels, and squirt guns aid the 1,000-plus contestants in producing their transient creations. Categories range from preschool to professional. The event is free to spectators; participants pay an entrance fee. ■ *Cannon Beach, 72 miles west of Portland (take Hwys 26 and 101); (503)436-2623.*

Seattle to Portland Bicycle Ride (STP)   *Bicycling* magazine calls the STP one of the country's top classic century rides. Coming up on its 20th year, this 200-mile ride is sponsored by Seattle's Cascade Bicycle Club, and can be done over a weekend or in a day. Check out the Web site for details: www.cascade.org/stp. ■ *(206)522-BIKE.*

JULY

Arts in the Arboretum   [KIDS] [FREE] For one Sunday in July, the trails at the Hoyt Arboretum come alive with dance, music, mime, puppetry, performance art, and fine art, too. Take a walk and be surprised by the hum of a didgeridoo or a masked dancer slipping behind a cedar tree. ■ *Hoyt Arboretum, 400 SW Fairview Blvd (Washington Park); 823-3654; map:GG7.*

Concours d'Elegance   Those who treasure fine automobiles and love nostalgia will especially enjoy this jewel of an event. More than 350 classic automobiles are on display, and there's live music to set the tone. ▪ *Pacific University, Forest Grove, 23 miles east of Portland (take Hwy 8); 357-2300.*

Fort Vancouver Fourth of July Fireworks   [KIDS] [FREE] The best fireworks to be seen in Oregon are across the Columbia River…in Washington. Portlanders flock to the National Historic Site of Fort Vancouver for a day of activities and stage entertainment climaxing in the largest free aerial display west of the Mississippi. The bombardment lasts a full hour. ▪ *Fort Vancouver, Vancouver, WA; (360) 694-2588; map:BB5.*

International Pinot Noir Celebration   Tickets to this three-day event are harder to find than a '94 bottle of Oregon pinot. Pinot noirs from around the world are showcased; lectures and symposia are given by renowned speakers. The real fun is in the tastings, gourmet meals, and entertainment. ▪ *Linfield College, McMinnville, 39 miles southwest of Portland (take Hwy 99W); (800) 775-4762.*

Music by Blue Lake Concerts   [KIDS] These Thursday evening concerts offer a variety of music by top national and regional artists to appeal to all ages. Reasonable admission for adults; children get in free. ▪ *Blue Lake Park, Troutdale; 797-1850.*

Oregon Coast Music Festival   This two-week musical marathon—always during the last two full weeks of July—includes classical and jazz, and sometimes bluegrass and folk. Concerts are held in Bandon, Charleston, Coos Bay, North Bend, and Reedsport. ▪ *Various coastal cities along Hwy 101; (541) 267-0938.*

Oregon Country Fair   Bacchus smiles on the ex-hippies, still-hippies, and soon-to-be-converted who flock by the thousands to this earthy festival. Offbeat—and often beautiful—arts and crafts, educational exhibits, food, and entertainment abound at the three-day fête, which takes place in a shady, bucolic setting a half hour from Eugene. You can even get a massage. Traffic is also part of the party—consider riding the free bus from downtown. Held the weekend after the Fourth of July. ▪ *Veneta, 125 miles southwest of Portland (take I-5 south to Eugene, then Hwy 126); (800) 992-8499.*

Oregon Microbrewery Festival   [FREE] Organizers dub it the largest beer celebration in the country, and it just keeps getting bigger. In 1997, the festival's 10th anniversary, 72 brewers were invited to bring their wares, and thousands came down to taste. To go with these blue-ribbon suds are food, music, and nonalcoholic drinks. Admission is free, but you'll need to buy the $2 official mug if you want to taste—then buy samples of brew to fill it up. ▪ *Tom McCall Waterfront Park; 778-5917; map:H6.*

Waterfront Blues Festival   Portland gets the blues every Fourth of July weekend. This four-day event is among the bigger blues festivals on the West Coast: more than 40 blues and gospel bands (including a host of big-name performers) play back-to-back on two stages for audiences of some 50,000 fans. Daily festival admission is a donation of $3 and two cans of food for the Oregon Food Bank. ▪ *Tom McCall Waterfront Park; 973-FEST; map:H6.*

World Championship Timber Carnival   This Albany tradition runs the first weekend in July. Champion loggers showcase their talents in a variety of logging-related contests, including tree climbing, log rolling, and ax throwing. ▪ *Albany, 70 miles south of Portland (take I-5); (541)928-2391.*

AUGUST

The Bite: A Taste of Portland   [KIDS] Eat to your heart's content and help the Oregon Special Olympics at the same time. More than 20 restaurants and wineries offer heaps of delectables, while performers at three different venues entertain you. OSO maintains souvenir and information booths; there are also hands-on activities for the kids. Usually the second weekend in August. ▪ *Tom McCall Waterfront Park; 248-0600; map:H6.*

Cascade Festival of Music   Bend's beautiful Drake Park is home to this late August week full of orchestra, family, symphonic pops, and jazz concerts. Murry Sidlin conducts. ▪ *Bend, 163 miles southeast of Portland (take Hwys 26 and 97); (541)382-8381.*

Festa Italiana   Strolling accordion players set the tone at this fest, featuring a food court—courtesy of 10 Italian restaurants—plus a wine garden, art events, and continuous music. Held the last weekend in August. ▪ *Pioneer Courthouse Square; 223-1613; map:H3.*

Hood to Coast Relay   More than 875 12-person teams participate in this 195-mile, around-the-clock relay. Starting times are staggered; runners hit Portland continuously beginning in the evening, then on through the night and into the early morning. It's an event that's fun to watch, although veterans say it's more fun to participate. There's also a Portland to Coast Relay for those who want to skip the trip down the mountain. ▪ *Timberline Lodge, Government Camp, to Seaside; 292-4626.*

Mount Hood Festival of Jazz   It's the premier jazz festival of the Pacific Northwest: three days, three stages, and more than 30 hours of music. This weekend affair has featured such greats as Al Jarreau, Chick Corea, and Ray Charles; about 20 performers or bands participate each year. Sample the offerings of local restaurants in the food fair (no alcohol or glass containers allowed). Tickets range from $29.50 to $45 per day; buy them in advance. ▪ *Mt Hood Community College, Gresham; 231-0161.*

Oregon State Fair [KIDS] The largest agricultural fair still happening on the West Coast is everything a fair should be: food, games, rides, horse shows, and live entertainment. For 12 days, the people of Salem go hog-wild—and carloads of Portlanders join them. Adult admission is $6, children ages 6 to 12 are $3, under 6 are free. Usually the last week of August through Labor Day. ▪ *Fair and Expo Center, Salem, 45 miles south of Portland (take I-5, exit 258); (503)378-3247.*

Scandinavian Festival [KIDS] For four days the Scandinavian population of Junction City celebrates its heritage and honors the ancestry of the area's early European settlers. Crafts, games, dancing, music, and feasting (and feasting and feasting) draw upward of 130,000 visitors. ▪ *Junction City, 90 miles south of Portland (take I-5, Harrisburg exit); (541)998-9372.*

Seaside Beach Volleyball Tournament [FREE] Surf, sand, and 2,000 volleyball enthusiasts combine for this competition, billed as the largest beach volleyball tournament north of California. Spectators have a ball, too. ▪ *Seaside, 70 miles west of Portland (take Hwys 26 and 101); (800)444-6740.*

Senior Prom [FREE] Although this two-hour tea dance is touted as a senior citizens' event, anyone who loves big band music is welcome to sit and listen. More than 2,000 seniors step out under the stars. Door prizes too. ▪ *Pioneer Courthouse Square; 223-1613; map:H3.*

Street of Dreams Each year thousands visit the Street of Dreams, a showcase of 7 to 10 new, custom-built, oh-so-extravagant homes. The first of these elegant enclaves was built in the Portland area in 1975, and there's been a new one every year since. ▪ *Various locations; 684-1880.*

SEPTEMBER

Art in the Pearl [KIDS][FREE] During the Labor Day weekend, this outdoor art show in the Pearl District features some 120 booths with art for sale—by furniture makers, potters, painters, fabric artists, and others. There's also theater—scenes from plays and short plays—staged by the Portland Area Theater Alliance, hands-on art (paper making, for instance), and music, too. The food, much of it ethnic, is better than usual for these kinds of events. A crowd of 25,000 people show up to admire and create art, take in the performances, and munch. ▪ *North Park Blocks; 690-7900; map:J3.*

Cycle Oregon Bike Tour In 1988 the Oregon Department of Tourism introduced Cycle Oregon with a Willamette Valley route; since then the annual tours have showcased much of the rest of the state. About 2,000 cyclists participate in the exceedingly popular weeklong ride. Starts the Sunday after Labor Day. ■ *Route varies; 643-8064 or (800)292-5367.*

Eugene Celebration [KIDS] The Celebration brings five stages of entertainment, food, beverages, a wacky parade, prestigious art shows, and fun for all ages to downtown Eugene. A $5 admission pin, good for all three days, is required for some areas. Kids 12 and under free. ■ *Citywide, Eugene, 105 miles south of Portland (take I-5); (541)682-5215.*

Fall Kite Festival [KIDS][FREE] Lincolnites love to fly kites of all shapes and colors, and so do the more than 20,000 people who attend the festivities (which include a lighted night show, wind permitting). Prizes are awarded for the most innovative tail and most original kite. The dates of this event change depending on the tides, and the event is canceled in bad weather; call to verify. ■ *Lincoln City, 88 miles southwest of Portland (take Hwy 99W); (800)452-2151.*

Mount Angel Oktoberfest [FREE] One of the larger folk festivals in the Northwest begins the second Thursday after Labor Day and runs through Sunday. A traditional harvest festival, the Oktoberfest celebrates the bounty of the earth and the goodness of creation with plenty of live entertainment and plenty to imbibe. Most events are free, and a small cover lets you in the "gartens": the biergarten, weingarten, microgarten, European cabaret, and village bandstand. More than 60 little food chalets offer Bavarian and ethnic foods. ■ *Mount Angel, 26 miles south of Portland (take I-5, Woodburn exit); (503)845-9440.*

North by Northwest Since 1995, this three-day blowout has been giving local music-lovers, as well as scouts seeking new talent, plenty to look forward to. During the day, it's a music industry convention; come nighttime, though, it's a massive music fest, with some 350 bands and solo acts from the United States and abroad performing at two dozen venues all over town. For $20 (in advance) fans can purchase a wristband that will admit them into as many of the shows as they can get to. Call local sponsor *Willamette Week* for information. ■ *Portland; 243-2122.*

Pendleton Round-Up Yeehaw! This four-day rodeo, complete with cowboys, bucking broncos, bulls, and clowns, is one of the biggest in the country—there are more than 600 contestants and 50,000 spectators in attendance. Admission ranges from $8 to $17.50. A downtown carnival keeps things hopping while the rodeo riders recover. Come see the Happy Canyon Pageant and Dance in the evening. Held the second week in September. ■ *Pendleton, 210 miles east of Portland (take I-84); (800)457-6336.*

OCTOBER

Friends of the Library Book Sale [FREE] The Friends of the Multnomah County Library stage the state's largest book sale: thousands of books, CDs, tapes, videos, and sheet music. Admission is free on Saturday and Sunday; the members-only "presale" is held Friday evening (memberships are available at the door). Call for this year's location. ▪ *Portland; 248-5439.*

Greek Festival [FREE] For three days, the Portland Greek community celebrates with traditional foods, music, dancing, and various festivities. There are demonstrations of cooking, iconography, and church tours. ▪ *Holy Trinity Greek Orthodox Church, 3131 NE Glisan St; 234-0468; map:FF5.*

Salmon Festival [KIDS] This weekend festival features interactive activities that are designed to help people of all ages understand and appreciate endangered salmon and their habitat. Guides lead visitors on walks to see the spawning fish, and there are environmental displays and arts and crafts. Great food, too. ▪ *Oxbow Park, Gresham; 797-1850.*

ZooBoo [KIDS] If the haunted train ride doesn't scare you away, the throngs of thrill seekers at this popular event just might. Show up early to walk through a maze or play games in the activity plaza. Though older kids love ZooBoo, it might be too spooky for the littlest pumpkins. ▪ *Washington Park Zoo; 226-1561; map:GG7.*

NOVEMBER

Catlin Gabel Rummage Sale One of the world's largest rummage sales recently celebrated its 50th anniversary. Even those who don't generally devote their Saturday mornings to garage sales come by sometime during this four-day event to browse. All proceeds benefit the private school's financial aid program. ▪ *Expo Center; 297-1894; map:CC6.*

Meier & Frank Holiday Parade [KIDS][FREE] This annual parade through the heart of Portland provides the first jolt of holiday spirit. Held the day after Thanksgiving. ▪ *Downtown; 241-5328.*

Northwest Film and Video Festival The Northwest Film Center hosts the premiere of this 10-day festival, a showcase of outstanding work from regional artists. Approximately 40 films are included, usually dramatic shorts, documentaries, animation, and experimental works. The festival then goes on to tour the Northwest. ▪ *Northwest Film Center, 1219 Park Ave; 221-1156; map:G1.*

Pioneer Courthouse Square Holiday Happenings [KIDS][FREE] Generally, the festivities begin the day after Thanksgiving with the lighting of the Christmas tree in the square. Another big—

and truly delightful—event: a rousing carol sing-along. Some years a caroling contest called The Great Figgy Pudding is held, and every year a tuba concert features some 200 tubas. Come sing for fun and prizes. ▪ *Pioneer Courthouse Square; 223-1613; map:H3.*

Portland Lo/Op   Oregon Rowing Unlimited presents the Portland Loop Regatta during the first Saturday in November. The 4½-mile race attracts some of rowing's hottest crews: Harvard, Cornell, Stanford, University of Washington, and UC Berkeley race alongside locals from the University of Oregon, Oregon State, and Lewis and Clark. ▪ *Willamette River; 635-3408.*

DECEMBER

Christmas Ships   [KIDS] [FREE] Every year, local boating enthusiasts bedeck their vessels with lights and parade the Columbia and Willamette for several weeks in December. Call for the schedule. ▪ *Columbia and Willamette Rivers; 223-2223.*

Festival of the Trees   [KIDS] Fifty-five 8-foot trees are thematically decorated, and there are gingerbread displays, wreaths, Christmas stockings, crafts demonstrations, and holiday entertainment. An auction is held on opening night; bids for trees and displays start at $500. Admission is $4 for adults; kids are free. Usually held the first week in December. Sponsored by the Providence Medical Foundation, this event benefits needy hospital patients. ▪ *Oregon Convention Center; 215-6070; map:M9.*

The Nutcracker   [KIDS] This merry production by the Oregon Ballet Theater puts even the most adamant Scrooge into the holiday spirit. It generally runs for two weeks before Christmas. ▪ *Civic Auditorium, 222 SW Clay St; 2-BALLET; map:E3.*

Singing Christmas Tree   In early December, 400 volunteers join forces for this lavish production, which, over the past 30-odd years, has become a Portland holiday tradition. Artful lighting enhances the group's formation—in the shape of a Christmas tree. The nine performances are usually sold out, so buy tickets early. ▪ *Civic Auditorium, 222 SW Clay St; 557-TREE; map:E3.*

Timberline New Year's Eve   Ski in the New Year as Timberline extends its skiing operations for New Year's Eve festivities and midnight fireworks. ▪ *Timberline Lodge, Government Camp, 66 miles east of Portland on Mt Hood (take Hwy 26); 272-3311.*

Whale Watch Week   [FREE] During the week between Christmas and New Year's Day, volunteers from the Marine Science Center in Newport assist visitors in sighting gray whales from 24 stations along the coast. The Yaquina Bay Lighthouse, Cape Perpetua, and Depoe Bay are among the best places for viewing; volunteers are available from 10am to 1pm (morning light is best). It all happens again at spring break—although by then the grays are heading north. (See also Whale Watching in this chapter's January listing.) ▪ *Newport, 114 miles southwest of Portland (take Hwys 99W and 101); (541)867-0100.*

Zoo Lights Festival [KIDS] For the whole month of December, the zoo is ablaze with lights. Stroll the grounds, or hop on the decorated zoo train for a ride. Evenings feature live holiday music by local choirs, elves bearing treats, costumed characters, and puppet shows. ▪ *Washington Park Zoo; 226-1561; map:GG7.*

Index

We Stand By Our Reviews

Sasquatch Books is proud of *Portland Best Places*. Our editors and contributors go to great lengths and expense to see that all of the restaurant and lodging reviews are as accurate, up-to-date, and honest as possible. If we have disappointed you, please accept our apologies; however, if a recommendation in this 4th edition of *Portland Best Places* has seriously misled you, Sasquatch Books would like to refund your purchase price. To receive your refund:

1) Tell us where you purchased your book and return the book and the book-purchase receipt to the address below.

2) Enclose the original lodging or restaurant receipt from the establishment in question, including date of visit.

3) Write a full explanation of your stay or meal and how *Portland Best Places* specifically misled you.

4) Include your name, address, and phone number.

Refund is valid only while the 4th edition of *Portland Best Places* is in print. If the ownership, management, or chef has changed since publication, Sasquatch Books cannot be held responsible. Postage and tax on the returned book is your responsibility. Please allow six to eight weeks for processing.

Please address to Satisfaction Guaranteed, *Portland Best Places*, and send to:

SASQUATCH BOOKS
615 Second Avenue, Suite 260
Seattle, WA 98104

Portland Best Places
REPORT FORM

Based on my personal experience, I wish to nominate the following restaurant, place of lodging, shop, nightclub, sight, or other as a "Best Place," or confirm/correct/disagree with the current review.

_____

_____

_____

_____

(Please include address and telephone number of establishment, if convenient.)

REPORT:

Please describe food, service, style, comfort, value, date of visit, and other aspects of your experience; continue on the other side if necessary.

_____

_____

_____

_____

_____

_____

_____

_____

I am not concerned, directly or indirectly, with the management or ownership of this establishment.

_____
SIGNED

_____
ADDRESS

_____
PHONE   DATE

Please address to Portland Best Places *and send to:*

SASQUATCH BOOKS
615 Second Avenue, Suite 260
Seattle, WA 98104

Feel free to email feedback as well: books@sasquatchbooks.com

Portland Best Places

REPORT FORM

Based on my personal experience, I wish to nominate the following restaurant, place of lodging, shop, nightclub, sight, or other as a "Best Place," or confirm/correct/disagree with the current review.

_____

_____

_____

_____

(Please include address and telephone number of establishment, if convenient.)

REPORT:

Please describe food, service, style, comfort, value, date of visit, and other aspects of your experience; continue on the other side if necessary.

_____

_____

_____

_____

_____

_____

_____

_____

I am not concerned, directly or indirectly, with the management or ownership of this establishment.

_____
SIGNED

_____
ADDRESS

_____

_____/_____
PHONE   DATE

Please address to Portland Best Places *and send to:*

SASQUATCH BOOKS
615 Second Avenue, Suite 260
Seattle, WA 98104

Feel free to email feedback as well: books@sasquatchbooks.com

Did you enjoy this book?

Sasquatch Books publishes high-quality books and guides related to Alaska, the Pacific Northwest, and California. Our books are available at bookstores and other retail outlets throughout the region. Here is a partial list of our current titles:

GUIDEBOOKS

Alaska Best Places®
Restaurants, Lodging, and Adventure
Edited by Nan Elliot

Seattle Best Places®
Restaurants, Shops, Hotels, Nightlife, Arts, Sights, and Outings
Edited by Nancy Leson

Vancouver Best Places®
Restaurants, Shops, Hotels, Nightlife, Arts, Sights, and Outings
Edited by Kasey Wilson

Northwest Best Places®
Restaurants, Lodgings, and Touring in Oregon, Washington, and British Columbia
Edited by Stephanie Irving

Northwest Budget Traveler
Cheap Eats, Cheap Sleeps, Affordable Adventure
Edited by Nancy Leson

Northern California Best Places®
Restaurants, Lodgings, and Touring
Edited by Rebecca Poole Forée

RECREATION GUIDES

Inside Out: Oregon
A Best Places® Guide to the Outdoors
Terry Richard

Inside Out: Washington
A Best Places® Guide to the Outdoors
Ron C. Judd

Inside Out: British Columbia
A Best Places® Guide to the Outdoors
Jack Christie

Inside Out: Northern Rockies
A Best Places® Guide to the Outdoors
Susan English and Kathy Witkowsky

FIELD GUIDES

Field Guide to the American Bison
Field Guide to the Bald Eagle
Field Guide to the Geoduck
Field Guide to the Gray Whale
Field Guide to the Grizzly Bear
Field Guide to the Humpback Whale
Field Guide to the Orca
Field Guide to the Pacific Salmon
Field Guide to the Sasquatch
Field Guide to the Slug

REGIONAL COOKBOOKS

The Northwest Best Places® Cookbook
Recipes from the Outstanding Restaurants and Inns of Washington, Oregon, and British Columbia
Cynthia Nims and Lori McKean

Breakfast in Bed Cookbook
B&B Recipes from Northern California to British Columbia

Northwest Berry Cookbook
Finding, Growing, and Cooking with Berries Year-Round
Kathleen Desmond Stang

Artisan Bread Cookbook
Cooking with the New Breads
Gwenyth Bassetti and Jean Galton

In Season
Culinary Adventures of a San Juan Island Chef
Greg Atkinson

For a complete catalogue of Sasquatch Books titles, or to inquire about ordering our books, please contact us at the address below.

SASQUATCH BOOKS
615 Second Avenue, Suite 260   Seattle, WA 98104
(206) 467-4300 or (800) 775-0817
email: books@sasquatchbooks.com / www.sasquatchbooks.com